A
BIOGRAPHICAL HISTORY
OF
GREENE COUNTY,
PENNSYLVANIA

By

Samuel P. Bates

CLEARFIELD

Excerpted from
History of Greene County, Pennsylvania
By Samuel P. Bates
Chicago, 1888

Re-titled and Reprinted
Genealogical Publishing Co., Inc.
Baltimore, 1975

Reprinted for
Clearfield Company by
Genealogical Publishing Co.
Baltimore, Maryland
1993, 2000, 2007

Library of Congress Catalogue Card Number 75-7875
ISBN-13: 978-0-8063-0676-6
ISBN-10: 0-8063-0676-9

Made in the United States of America

PUBLISHER'S NOTE

As the Table of Contents corresponds to the pagination of the parent work, the original page numbers of the excerpted section, i.e. pp. [561]-898, have been retained.

Made in the United States of America

iii

CONTENTS.

BIOGRAPHICAL SKETCHES.

v

CONTENTS.

CONTENTS

CONTENTS.

BIOGRAPHICAL SKETCHES.

ALEPPO TOWNSHIP.

ASBURY ANTILL, farmer and stock-grower, son of John and Isabella (Chenith) Antill, was born in this county March 24, 1836. His mother was born in Ohio. His father, who was a farmer and miller, was born and died in Greene County, Penn. The subject of this sketch was the fourth in a family of nine children, all of whom grew to be men and women. He was reared on the farm and has been an industrious farmer all his life. He is the owner of 243 acres of well-improved land where he resides in Aleppo Township. In 1857 Mr. Antill married Sarah, daughter of Moses and Hannah (Whipkey) King. Mrs. Antill is of Dutch extraction, and a member of the Methodist Episcopal Church. Their children are—William, Harvey, Maggie, wife of Benjamin Chambers, Jr., Louis, John and Asbury K. Mr. Antill is a Democrat in politics.

BENJAMIN CHAMBERS, farmer and stock-grower, was born in Marshall County, West Virginia, October 13, 1840, is the son of J. A. and Susan (Kerr) Chambers, natives of West Virginia, and of German ancestry. His father, who spent all his life as a farmer in his native State, reared a family of seven children, of whom the subject of this sketch is the oldest son. He was reared on the home farm, attended the district school and has made farming and stock-growing his chief pursuit. He came to this county in 1865 and settled on his present farm in Aleppo Township, consisting of 324 acres of well improved land. In 1866 Mr. Chambers was united in marriage with M. J., daughter of A. J. and Lucinda (Ayers) Hinerman. Her parents were of German origin. Mr. and Mrs. Chambers' children are C. T., G. A., Ward, Lucinda, John A., Olive Dillie, Leota, Elizabeth and Pearl. Mr. Chambers is a Republican. Mrs. Chambers is a member of the Christian Church.

W. W. CLENDENNING, farmer and stock-grower, was born in Marshall County, West Virginia, October 28, 1838. He is a son of Archibald and Jane (Cooper) Clendenning, who were natives of Ireland. They came to America and settled in Greene County, where

Mr. Clendenning was a farmer for many years and died in 1877. Of a family of four children, the subject of this sketch is the youngest. He was reared on the farm and received a common school education. He has made farming his main occupation, and is the owner of 133 acres of land, all of which he has accumulated through his own efforts. Mr. Clendenning was united in marriage August 26, 1862, with Miss Sarah, daughter of James and Jane (McCaslin) Kincaid, and sister of Colonel Maxwell McCaslin. Mr. and Mrs. Clendenning have eight children, viz.: Robert Maxwell, William N., Milton L., Anna F., John, Mary, Nellie Grant and Jessie K. Mr. Clendenning and wife are members of the Church of God.

J. T. ELBIN, Associate Judge of Greene County, and one of the earliest settlers of Aleppo Township, now living, was born in Allegheny County, Maryland, March 18, 1824. He was left an orphan when a small child and was reared by his grandfather, John Elbin, who was a prominent farmer of Greene County, and died intestate in 1845. Judge Elbin was thrown out in the world without a dollar, but was ambitious to be independent and worked as a farm hand by the day and month until he succeeded in accumulating enough to invest in land. He has been engaged in farming and stock-growing in this county since 1848, and has been very successful in all his business ventures. In 1847 he was united in marriage with Hannah, daughter of John and Hannah (Sidwell) McVay, and they are the parents of six children, viz.: Lucinda, wife of L. Sammons; Rachel, wife of George Grim; Henry, who is an undertaker; John W., a farmer; Belle, wife of George Ullom, and Mary Ann, deceased. Mrs. Elbin belongs to the Cumberland Presbyterian Church, and the Judge is a member of the Church of God, in which he takes an active interest, and has served as superintendent of the Sabbath-school. He is a Democrat, and was elected Associate Judge in 1884. He is a member of the I. O. O. F., and has served as Justice of the Peace for a period of twenty years; elected in 1860, and held the office until 1880.

AZARIAH EVANS, farmer and stock-grower, was born in Washington County, Penn., August 29, 1828, and is a son of Caleb and Anna (Smalley) Evans. His father was a native of Fayette County, and his mother was born in Washington County. They were of Welsh extraction. His father, a farmer by occupation, came to Greene County in 1839, and in 1841 he settled in Aleppo Township, where he died in 1860. He reared a family of fourteen children, twelve of whom grew to be men and women, and eight of the family are still alive and in active life. The subject of this sketch is next to the oldest of those now living and was reared on the home farm, receiving a common school education. Mr. Evans has spent his life as a farmer, having lived in Greene County since he was thirteen years of age. He has been very successful, and owns at present a fine farm of 274 acres. He was united in marriage September 3, 1848, with Miss Mary, daughter of William and Elizabeth (Courtwright) Griffith, who were of Irish origin. Mr. and Mrs. Evans have two children living—Elizabeth A., wife of William B. King, and Samuel L., a farmer and stock-grower, who married Lucinda, daughter of James and Julianna (Chess) Parson. Mr. and Mrs. Evans have met with well deserved success. Both have been very hard workers and noted for their liberality. Mr. Evans' name often appears on the church subscription papers, and he has given liberally to both the church and the Sabbath school. Though not a member of any church, he is ever anxious for the success of any church or moral enterprise. His wife is a member of the Church of God. Mr. Evans is a Republican. In 1862 he enlisted in Company A, Eighteenth Pennsylvania Cavalry, and served until the close of the war, being discharged by general order. Among the engagements in which he took part was the famous battle of Gettysburg. He was at one time an active member of the Patrons of Husbandry.

CHRISTIAN GRIM, farmer and stock-grower, son of Jacob and Keziah (Courtwright) Grim, was born in Greene County, Penn., April 12, 1859. His parents were also natives of this county, and of German origin. His father was a farmer during his lifetime. Christian Grim is the eldest of three children, and was reared on the home farm, receiving his education in the common schools. He is a successful farmer, and has the management of his own and Mrs. Grim's farm, amounting in all to 250 acres. His wife was the widow of the late Madison, son of Peter Ullom, a native of Aleppo Township. Mr. and Mrs. Ullom were the parents of five children, viz.—Eliza, wife of Isaac McCracken; Isaac B., a student of Delaware College, Ohio; Clara, Lantz H. and Thomas H. Mrs. Grim's maiden name was Melissa Hupp. She is a daughter of Isaac Hupp, and of German and English lineage. Mr. and Mrs. Grim were married September 7, 1881. They are members of the Church of God. They have three children—Flora, John C. and Ella. Mr. Grim is a deacon in the church. In politics he is a Democrat.

JOHN HENRY, farmer and stock-grower, was born in Somerset County, Penn., July 25, 1827. He is a son of John and Elizabeth (Imell) Henry, who were, respectively, natives of Pennsylvania and Maryland, and of German origin. His father was a farmer all his life. He also learned the blacksmith's trade, and was well known in Somerset County for many years as a hotel-keeper. Of his ten children the subject of this sketch is the ninth. He was reared on the farm in Turkey Foot Township, where he attended the district school. Mr. Henry has been a successful farmer, and

29

owns 165 acres of well improved land. He was married in Somerset County, February 11, 1847, to Hannah (Garey) Miller, daughter of Peter Garey and widow of Michael Miller. Mrs. Henry is of Dutch descent. Their children are—Amanda, wife of Samuel Pletcher; Mary, wife of J. Matheny; Rebecca, wife of H. Jacobs; Christiana, wife of W. Showalter; William H., Elizabeth, wife of J. McCracken; Peter, Susannah, wife of N. Miller, and Nancy, wife of J. Elbin. Mr. and Mrs. Henry are members of the German Baptist church. Mr. Henry is a Republican. In 1862 he enlisted in the One Hundred and Fortieth Pennsylvania Volunteer Infantry. He was in several engagements, and was wounded at the battle of Spottsylvania. On account of this wound he is now receiving a small pension. Mr. Henry's grandfather was in the Revolutionary war, and his uncle, Peter Henry, was in the war of 1812 under General Harrison.

ANDERSON HINERMAN, farmer and stock-grower, was born May 10, 1832, in Aleppo Township, this county, on the farm where Christian Grim now resides. He is a son of Jesse and Sarah (Shutterly) Hinerman. His mother was born in the State of Delaware, and his father in Millsboro, Washington County, Penn. Both his grandfathers came from Germany, and his grandmothers were of American origin. Mr. Hinerman, the third in a family of ten children, received his early education in the subscription school. Having been reared as a farmer, he has made this occupation his life work, and has met with success, being the owner of a fine farm of 170 acres well stocked and improved. On November 4, 1856, Mr. Hinerman was united in marriage with a daughter of Silas and Jane (Rickey) Ayers, who were of American ancestry. Mr. and Mrs. Hinerman's children are Solomon, Stanton, Tillie M., Clara Dell, Blanche A., Walter F., Rosa Balton and Sarah J. (deceased). Mr. Hinerman is a Republican and a member of the I. O. O. F. He and wife are members of the Church of God, in which Mr. Hinerman is superintendent of the Sabbath-school and has been elder for eighteen years.

J. S. HINERMAN, farmer and stock-grower, was born in Aleppo Township, October 21, 1845. His parents were Jesse and Sarah (Shutterly) Hinerman, the former born in Washington County, Penn., and the latter in Wilmington, Del. They were of German origin, Mr. Hinerman's father, who was a farmer through life, died April 3, 1877. His family consisted of ten children, of whom the subject of our sketch is the youngest. He was reared on the home farm and acquired a common school education. From his youth he has been engaged in agricultural pursuits and has been quite successful. He is the owner of a fine residence and eighty-seven acres of well cultivated land. Mr. Hinerman was married in 1866 to Rebecca, daughter of Leonard Straight. Her parents were natives of Pennsylvania, and of Dutch extraction. Mr. and Mrs. Hinerman are the parents of the following named children—Ida, Alta, Sarah E., Luther W., Mary J., Curtis, Clida, Charles B. and John. Mr. Hinerman, who is a Republican, was elected justice of the peace in 1880 and re-elected in 1885. He and his wife are members of the Church of God.

LINDSEY HINERMAN, farmer and stock-grower, was born June 16, 1828, on the farm he now owns in Aleppo Township, Greene County, Penn. He is a son of George and Mary (McConnell) Hinerman, who were of German and Irish ancestry. His grandfather, George Hinerman, was a British soldier, but remained in this country. He was, like many other members of the family, a farmer. Mr. Hinerman's father came from Millsborough, Washington County, Penn., to Greene County in 1823, where he spent his life as a farmer and died in 1876. Lindsey is the fifth in a family of eight children. He was reared on the farm and attended the subscription schools. He has made farming his main pursuit and owns 467 acres of valuable land, well stocked and improved. Our subject was employed on the Baltimore & Ohio Railroad from 1848 to 1853. In May, 1853, Mr. Hinerman married Miss Elizabeth, daughter of Jacob and Mary (Whipkey) Slonaker. Their children are M. S., Martha J., wife of John Tasker; Sarah, wife of H. Wise; Emeline, wife of Sherman W. S. McCracken; David, Mary, J. W. H. and Ellsworth. Mr. Hinerman is a Republican.

WILLIAM HOUSTON, deceased, who was a farmer and stock-grower by occupation, was born in Ireland in 1791. When twelve years of age he came to America and settled in Washington County, Penn., where he learned the shoemaker's trade and followed it as a business until he came to Greene County in 1836, and bought the farm in Aleppo Township which is still in possession of the family. Here he died in 1854. In 1820 Mr. Houston married Esther, daughter of Captain James Dickey, of Washington County, Penn. Their family consisted of seven children, three of whom are living. They are W. D., a carpenter and contractor; Samuel, a carpenter and farmer; and Joseph. The last two mentioned were soldiers of the late war, in Company H, Fifteenth Pennsylvania Volunteer Cavalry. The family are highly respected in the community in which they live.

HIRAM P. MOSS, farmer and stock-grower, son of Jacob and Eleanor (Winnett) Moss, was born in Richhill Township, this county, March 22, 1844. His parents were of English and Irish lineage. His mother was a native of Washington County, Penn. His father, who was a cabinet-maker and carpenter during his lifetime, was born in Fayette County, and died in 1878 in Greene County. His

family numbered eight children, Hiram Porter being the youngest.
In 1868 the subject of our sketch was united in marriage with Miss
Emma Jane Courtwright. Their children are Maggie, Clara, Mettie,
May, Mary Addie, Arthur and Emmett Earl. Mr. Moss learned
cabinet-making and the carpenter's trade with his father, but has
devoted his time chiefly to farming and the raising of stock, and is
the owner of ninety-three acres of valuable land. He and his wife
are members of the Presbyterian Church.

REV. JACOB M. MURRAY, minister and school teacher, was
born in Fayette County, Penn., May 25, 1857. He is a son of
James A. and Mary (Miller) Murray, who were natives of Fayette
County and of German and Irish lineage. His father, who is a
minister in The Brethren Church, also engages in farming to some
extent and now resides in Aleppo Township, where he settled in
1860. Of his family of nine children six are still living. The
subject of this sketch is the eighth in the family and was reared on
his father's farm in Aleppo Township. He acquired his education
in common and select schools and in Monongahela College at Jefferson, Penn. He began teaching when only seventeen years of age
and is now considered one of the most prominent educators in
Greene County. At the age of twenty he united with the Church
of The Brethren, and was ordained as a minister of that denomination when he was twenty-six. Since 1887 he has had charge of a
congregation at Aleppo, Penn. Mr. Murray is a frequent contribu-
tor to the religious journals. He is held in high esteem by all who
know him. He was united in marriage, March 17, 1877, with Miss
Julia A., daughter of Henry and Elizabeth (Evans) Riggle, who
were of German origin. Mr. and Mrs. Murray have four children,
three of whom are living—Harry Y., Oscar C. and Vernie. Mr.
Murray is a Democrat. His wife is a member of The Brethren
Church and is held in the highest esteem by all who know her.

JOSEPH McCRACKEN, P. O. Cameron, Marshall County, West
Va., was born in Washington County, Penn., February 13, 1827. He is
a son of Daniel and Mary (Crall) McCracken, natives of Pennsylvania, and of Irish and Dutch descent. His father, who died in
West Virginia, was a farmer all his life. His family consisted of
eight children, of whom the subject of this sketch is the oldest. He
was reared on the farm and received his education in the common
school. He has been a very successful farmer and stock-grower,
having at one time owned over six hundred acres of land. On February 20, 1853, Mr. McCracken married Miss Mary E., daughter of
Jennings J. Moss, and they have nine children, viz.: Joseph, a
farmer; J. C., a physician; George and J. M. B., farmers; Mary, wife
of H. T. Winnett; S. W. S. and Samuel E. Two of the children are

deceased. Mr. McCracken is a Republican. He and his wife and children are members of the Methodist Episcopal Church.

S. W. S. McCRACKEN, farmer, son of Joseph and Elizabeth (Moss) McCracken, was born in this county, where he was reared on a farm and attended the district school. He is one of the industrious and successful young farmers of his township. In 1888 Mr. Mc-Cracken was united in marriage with Miss Emma, daughter of Lindsey Hinerman, one of the wealthy and influential citizens of the county. Mr. McCracken is a Republican.

JAMES McVAY, farmer and wool-grower, and breeder of short-horn cattle, is among the most prominent, influential and successful farmers of Greene County. He was born in Morris Township, this county, March 21, 1824, and is a son of John and Hannah (Sidwell) McVay, and are natives of Pennsylvania, and of German and Irish descent. His father was a farmer all his life and died in Greene County. His family consisted of ten children, eight of whom grew to maturity. The subject of this sketch is the second and was reared on the farm, attending the subscription schools. Mr. McVay started in the world with little else than a determination to succeed. He commenced to buy stock when he was still a young man, buying for other parties a short time, but soon engaging in the business for himself. He has succeeded in accumulating a handsome fortune. In 1865 Mr. McVay bought 244,000 pounds of wool. His land in Greene County amounts to 540 acres, in a high state of cultivation. In 1840 Mr. McVay married Susan, daughter of Henry and Mary (Williams) Neel, and they are the parents of the following children: Mary M., wife of H. H. Parry; Warren, R. M., William I. and Hannah M., wife of H. C. Snyder; D. L. is deceased. Mr. McVay is a Democrat. His wife is a member of the Cumberland Presbyterian Church.

GEORGE McVAY, farmer and stock-grower, was born in Aleppo Township, Greene County, Penn., August 11, 1832. He is a son of John and Hannah (Sidwell) McVay, natives of Washington and Greene counties, respectively. Mr. McVay is a member of a family of twelve children. He is the sixth, and was reared in his native township, where he attended the common schools. He has made farming and stock-dealing his business through life and has been greatly prospered, being at present the owner of 300 acres of valuable land in this county. In 1852 Mr. McVay was united in marriage with Miss Maria Smith, now deceased. They were the parents of four children, viz.: Elizabeth, Anthony, Sarah and Hannah. Mr. McVay's present wife was Miss Elizabeth Long. They have two children—Samuel Patrick and Clara. Mr. McVay is a Democrat. He has served five years as constable and one term as director of the poor in Greene County.

LEWIS PARRY, farmer and stock-grower, was born in South Wales, Great Britain, February 11, 1838, and is a son of Roger L. and Elizabeth (Pugh) Parry, natives of Wales. They came to America in 1842, first settling in Pittsburgh. They subsequently moved to Washington County, Penn., and settled in Aleppo Township, Greene County, in 1858. Mr. Parry's father was a farmer and blacksmith. Six members of his family grew to maturity, Lewis being the oldest. He was reared in Washington County, where he also received his education. Mr. Parry began life as a poor boy, working by the day or month, but by industry and economy he has made himself a nice and comfortable home. He now owns 116 acres of good land in Greene County. In November, 1859, Mr. Parry married Mary C., daughter of John and Sarah (Hunt) Wood. Her parents, who were of Dutch and Irish descent, were natives of Greene County. Mr. and Mrs. Parry's children are—Sarah, wife of Morgan B. Lewis; John R., William W., Lou, Emma and Mertie. Mr. Parry is a Cumberland Presbyterian, and his wife is a member of the Disciple Church. In 1862 he enlisted in Company A, Eighteenth Pennsylvania Cavalry, and was a non-commissioned officer. He was taken prisoner in Adams County, Penn., June 30, 1863. He subsequently joined the regiment in Virginia, serving in all two years and ten months, and was honorably discharged July 12, 1865. Mr. Parry is a Republican, and a prominent member of the I. O. O. F.

WILLIAM M. PARRY, physician and surgeon, was born in Westmoreland County, Penn., May 12, 1843, and is a son of Roger L. and Elizabeth (Pugh) Parry, natives of Wales. His father was a blacksmith by trade, but engaged in farming after coming to America. The subject of this sketch is the third in a family of six children. He was reared on a farm, received a common-school education, and subsequently took a course in the Academy at West Liberty, Ohio County, W. Va., where he remained for several years and studied medicine with Dr. Cooper of that place. Dr. Parry began the practice of his profession at Jacksonville, Penn., remaining there for a period of two years. In 1870 he located in Aleppo, where he has since been in active practice. Dr. Parry has been very successful. He owns 200 acres of valuable land where he resides, and has a lucrative practice. He was united in marriage, September 13, 1871, with Mary A., daughter of Rev. Lewis Sammons. Mrs. Parry is of Welsh and German extraction. Their children are Edith, Jessie, Jane, Roger and Burdette. Dr. Parry is a Presbyterian, and his wife is a member of the Baptist Church. She is also an ardent prohibitionist and a strong advocate of woman's suffrage. He is a Republican, and takes great interest in educational matters, having for eight years served as school director. He is a member of the Greene County Medical Society. August 12, 1862, Dr. Parry enlisted in Co. D, Twelfth

West Virginia Volunteer Infantry, and served till the close of the war. He is a member of the I. O. O. F., and is Past Master of the Masonic fraternity.

B. F. PHILLIPS, farmer and stock-grower, was born in Washington County, Penn., July 10, 1833, and is a son of Levi and Sarah (McCracken) Phillips, natives of Pennsylvania, and of Irish origin. His father was a farmer all his life. The subject of our sketch, the youngest of eight children, was reared on the farm, where he received a common-school education. Mr. Phillips has made farming and stock-growing his employment through life, and owns 340 acres of land, which he has procured entirely by his own exertions. He was united in marriage, in 1871, with Miss Sarah, daughter of Matthias and Sarah (McClain) Roseberry, natives of Greene County. Mr. and Mrs. Phillips are the parents of four children—Joseph M., Arthur Lee, Maggie R. and Levi N. Mr. Phillips is a Republican in politics.

REV. LEWIS SAMMONS, deceased, a minister of the Baptist Church, was born January 22, 1815, and was a son of John and Mary (Jones) Sammons. His parents were of Welsh and Irish descent. His father was a ship captain, and in early life ran on the Ohio and Mississippi rivers. After leaving the river he followed the carpenter trade and auctioneering. Rev. Mr. Sammons was an only child. He was born in Monongahela Township, this county, but was reared in Fayette County, Penn. He received his education in the common schools, and early in life learned the cooper's trade, at which he worked until 1836. It was in that year he accepted his first charge as a minister, and he engaged in ministerial work during the remainder of his life. He was united in marriage, November 18, 1841, with Miss Elizabeth, daughter of Jacob and Susannah (Gans) Rumble, who were of German ancestry. To Mr. and Mrs. Sammons were born six children, viz: Lebbeus, who is a farmer; Mary, wife of Dr. Parry; Rossell, a prominent farmer; James J., a surveyor and teacher, who has taught for many terms in Ohio, West Virginia, Pennsylvania and Nebraska; J. L., a physician of West Virginia, and Sarah E., a teacher of music. Mrs. Sammons is still living, and is a member of the Baptist Church. Rev. Sammons was the minister in charge at Enon Baptist Church in 1851, and was ordained in 1853. He came to Greene County in 1857, settling in Aleppo Township nine years later. He was ever an active temperance worker and Republican. He was successful in all his business pursuits, owning at the time of his death a well-improved farm where his family reside in Aleppo Township. The family are Republicans, and highly educated, four of them having taught ten terms of school.

ROSSELL SAMMONS, farmer and stock-grower, was born in Fayette County, Penn., July 12, 1852. His father was Rev. Lewis

Sammons, a well-known Baptist minister and active temperance advocate, who died in this county in 1879. He has written many articles against intemperance, and always preached against the great evil. Of his family of six children, Rossell is the third. He lived in Center Township until he was thirteen years old, when he came to Aleppo Township. His means for an education were limited to the common schools. In 1872, in company with his brother, Mr. Sammons established a saw-mill in Greene County, where they were very successful. Mr. Sammons bought a small farm and has since added to it other purchases until at present he owns 360 acres of fine land, well stocked and improved. In 1881 he was united in marriage with Miss Sarah, daughter of Joseph and Eliza (Lemmons) Evans. Mr. and Mrs. Sammons' children are Lewis E., Joseph Wiley, Olive G. and Osceola. Mr. Sammons is a Republican in politics.

LUTHER A. SMITH, farmer and stock-grower, was born in Richhill Township, Greene County, November 21, 1852. His parents were Andrew and Ellen (Little) Smith. His father was born in Scotland, and came to America when a young man. He settled in Greene County, where he died in 1880. His mother was a native of Washington County. Of a family of six children, Luther Smith is the fifth who grew to maturity. He was brought up on his father's farm and received a common-school education. He has been a successful farmer, and owns 103 acres of excellent land where he resides in Aleppo Township. Mr. Smith has been twice married, his first wife being Mary, daughter of John and Ellen (Cox) Edgar, whom he married in 1871. They were the parents of three children—Alonzo D., William B. and Harry. Mrs. Smith died in this county. Mr. Smith's present wife is Hannah, daughter of Lewis and Jane Pettit. They were married in 1885, and have one child—John C. Mr. Smith is a member of the I. O. O. F.

WILLIAM TEDROW, farmer and stock-grower, was born in Somerset County, Penn., June 17, 1823, and is a son of Henry and Elizabeth (Johnson) Tedrow, who were of German and English origin. His father, who was a farmer, died in Aleppo Township in 1876. Of his family of nine children, the subject of this sketch is the second. He was reared on the home farm and received a limited education in the old log school-house of the district. He has made a success of his farming and stock-growing, and now owns 326 acres of well improved land. Mr. Tedrow was married in Somerset County, November 17, 1844, to Sarah A., daughter of Leonard and Elizabeth (Whipkey) Straight, who were of German and English extraction. Mrs. Tedrow died January 29, 1888. Their children are Josiah, William H., Mariah, Mary E., wife of E. B. Moos; Catharine A., wife of James Whipkey; Minerva J., wife of M. Bayles.

Mr. Tedrow is a Democrat. He belongs to the Church of God, of which his deceased wife was also a member.

DAVID ULLOM, farmer and stock-grower and dealer in wool, was born in Aleppo Township, this county, December 11, 1845, and is a son of Peter and Matilda (Kinney) Ullom, natives of Pennsylvania. His father has spent a long life as a farmer, being now eighty years of age. Mr. David Ullom is the youngest in a family of six children and was reared on the farm with his parents, receiving a common school education. He has spent his life as a farmer and has given a good deal of attention to the raising of fine stock. He has engaged in wool buying extensively and has been very successful. Mr. Ullom owns a fine farm of 200 acres, and is one of Aleppo's most prominent citizens. On October 14, 1869, he married Marry Ellen, daughter of Jacob and Catharine (Huffman) King. Her parents were of English and German origin. Mr. King is a farmer by occupation. Mr. and Mrs. Ullom have one child—Frankie D. The family are members of the Church of God. Mr. Ullom is a trustee in the church and secretary and treasurer of the Sabbath-school. In politics he is a Democrat.

J. M. WHITE, farmer and stock-grower, who was born in Somerset County, Penn., July 14, 1826, is a son of Edward and Nancy (Rush) White. His parents were natives of Somerset County, and of English lineage. His father, who came to Aleppo Township in 1828, was a farmer. He died December 13, 1853. His mother lived until 1872. The subject of this sketch is the second in a family of six children, and was reared on the farm, receiving his education in the common schools. He chose farming as his occupation, has made his own way in the world, and is the owner of a well improved farm where he resides in Aleppo Township. Mr. White was united in marriage, February 13, 1848, with Rebecca, daughter of Henry and Elizabeth (Simons) Hemett, and they are parents of three children, viz—Perry J., Stephen and Sarah Esther (deceased). Mrs. White is a member of the Friends' Church. Mr. White is a Democrat, has been for seventeen years justice of the peace, and has served as school director in his township. He is a prominent member of the I. O. O. F.

JOSHUA WOOD, farmer and stock-grower, was born in Tyler County, W. Va., October 8, 1842. He is a son of John and Sarah (Hunt) Wood, who were, respectively, of Scotch and German and English origin. His father was born in Greene County, where he spent all his life as a farmer and died in 1868. His family numbered ten children, of whom Joshua Wood is the ninth. He was reared in Richhill Township, and attended the common schools. Early in life he learned the carpenter's trade, at which he worked till 1878, when he began farming. He is the owner of a well

stocked and improved farm of 180 acres. In 1861 Mr. Wood enlisted in Company H, Twentieth Volunteer Infantry, where he
served three months, then re-enlisted in Company B, Seventh West
Virginia Volunteer Infantry and served till 1862, when he was discharged for disability, having had two of his fingers shot off. He
subsequently spent some time in Great Salt Lake City. In 1874
Mr. Wood married a widow lady of Parkersburg, W. Va. Her first
husband was John Milton Parker, a railroad engineer on the Baltimore & Ohio Roilroad, who was killed in 1871 by the explosion of
his engine. Mr. and Mrs. Parker were the parents of two children
Mertie and Kate Parker. Mrs. Wood's maiden name was Emma
A. Barrett, a daughter of Caleb and Jemima (Goucher) Barrett, who
were of German origin. Mr. and Mrs. Wood have three children—
Earl, Herald and Iona. Mr. Wood is a Democrat. He and wife
are members of the Christian Church.

GEORGE WOODRUFF, farmer and stock-grower, who was
born in Jefferson Township, September 18, 1832, is a son of Benjamin and Sarah (Tuttle) Woodruff, who were of Dutch and Irish
descent. Mr. Benjamin Woodruff was a farmer and stock dealer
through life. The subject of this sketch is an only child. He was
reared as a farmer and has made a success of his business. In 1880
he settled in Aleppo Township where he still resides. Mr. Woodruff learned the blacksmith's trade, but has devoted all his time to
agricultural pursuits, and owns a good farm of 200 acres. He was
married in 1851, to Elizabeth, daughter of James and Rhoda (Lewis)
Nuss. Their children are Susan, wife of W. Balden; Alice, wife of
F. Drake; Benjamin, George, Andrew, David, William, James and
Elizabeth. The deceased is John Y. Mr. and Mrs. Woodruff are
industrious and economical, and have acquired their present possessions entirely by their own efforts.

CENTER TOWNSHIP.

S. H. ADAMSON, retired farmer, Rogersville, Penn.—The sub-
ject of this sketch is one of the pioneers of Greene County, Penn.
He was born in Morgan Township, May 2, 1822, and is a son of
Charles and Sarah (Hatfield) Adamson, natives of Pennsylvania.
They were the parents of nine children, of whom only four are liv-
ing. Charles and Sarah Adamson departed this life in Greene
County. S. H. Adamson was twice married; first, September 17,
1843, with Lucy Knight, who was born in this county March 7,

1825. Mrs. Adamson was a daughter of James and Cassandra Knight, who were natives of Greene County, where they remained through life. By this marriage Mr. Adamson is the father of six children, of whom only two are living—James K. and Charles. Mrs. Adamson departed this life November 17, 1868. Mr. Adamson was united in marriage the second time, with Mary (Hipert) Crouse, February 7, 1869. She is a daughter of Peter Hipert, and was born in Richland County, Ohio, June 26, 1837. Mr. Adamson was reared on a farm and has been engaged in farming almost all his life. He was in the mercantile business at Rogersville for a period of two years, and in 1849 was elected auditor of the county and served three years. In 1859 he was elected county treasurer and served in that position two years. He was elected county commissioner in 1881 and filled that office three years. Mr. Adamson owns about 450 acres of land. He is one of the enthusiastic Democrats of the county.

GEORGE A. BAYARD, merchant, Rogersville, Penn., was born in this county, April 11, 1832. He is a son of Samuel P. and Hannah Bayard (*nee* Mitchell) who were natives of Greene County, where they resided until Mr. Bayard's death, which occurred July 17,.1885. His widow survives him. George was united in marriage, October 6, 1859, with Martha Morris, who was born in this county, August 19, 1837. She is a daughter of Ephraim and Martha Morris, deceased. At a very early age Mr. Bayard learned the trade of a tanner, which he followed until he was twenty-five years old. He then engaged in farming until 1878, when he began merchandising in Rogersville, where he owns a general store. He received the appointment of postmaster at Rogersville in 1880, and has been filling that position ever since.

HENRY BOWLER, retired farmer, Rogersville, Penn.—The gentleman whose name heads this sketch is well known in Center Township, having lived on his present farm since the date of his birth, May 27, 1818. His parents were John and Mary Bowler, the former a native of Maryland and the latter of Greene County, Penn., where they resided until their death. Mrs. Bowler died in 1819, and her husband in 1845. On June 5, 1849, Henry Bowler married Penelope Stewart, who was born in this county in 1815. Her parents were William and Naoma Stewart, natives of Pennsylvania, who departed this life in Monroe County, Ohio. To Mr. and Mrs. Bowler were born two children—Elizabeth S., wife of Stephen Knight; and William, who married Ruth Seckman. Mrs. Bowler departed this life December 31, 1880. Mr. Bowler was reared on a farm and engaged very successfully in farming during the more active part of his life. He is the owner of about 237 acres of land in Center Township. In politics he is a Republican.

THOMAS T. BURROUGHS, farmer, P. O. Rutan, was born in Washington County, Penn., September 20, 1827. His parents were Samuel and Temperance (Reeves) Burroughs, also natives of Washington County. They lived in Greene County for a short time after their marriage, then moved to Washington County, Iowa, and remained until their death. Thomas was united in marriage January 1, 1852, with Eliza J. Scott. She was born March 3, 1829, on the farm where she lives in Center Township. Mrs. Burroughs is a daughter of John and Susannah Scott (nee Nicehonger), who were natives of Greene County, where they were married and remained through life. Mr. and Mrs. Burroughs have a family of nine children—Hamilton S., Arabella, wife of P. F. Headley; Charlotte A., wife of Leroy Marsh; Elmira, wife of T. N. Millikin; John M., James H., William E., Bertha V. and Thomas B. Mr. Burroughs has spent his whole life as a farmer, and owns 165 acres of land, constituting his home farm.

H. S. BURROUGHS, physician, Rutan, Penn., was born in Center Township, this county, December 28, 1852.* His parents, Thomas T. and Eliza J. Burroughs (nee Scott), are natives of Greene County and residents in Center Township. The Doctor was united in marriage June 28, 1882, with Maggie A. Hopkins, born October 1, 1859. Her parents are Samuel and Martha Hopkins (nee Millikin), who are natives of this county and reside in Morris Township. Dr. Burroughs began reading medicine May 1, 1875, with Dr. John T. Iams, of Waynesburg, Penn. He graduated from the Jefferson Medical College of Philadelphia, Penn., March 12, 1879, and in the following April commenced the practice of his profession at Rutan, Penn., where he still resides with his family. The Doctor is well qualified for the duties of his profession and has a good practice. He is a Baptist, and his wife is a member of the Methodist Church.

JAMES CALL, retired farmer, P. O. Rogersville, was born in Center Township, Greene County, Penn., September 17, 1825. His father and mother, James and Sarah (Hoge) Call, were natives of Greene County, where they were married and spent the remainder of their lives. They departed this life at the home of their son James Mrs. Call March 7, 1862, and her husband June 13, 1868. In October 22,.1849, James Call married Martha Vanwey, who was born in Perry County, Ohio, December 31, 1833. Her parents, John and Anna (Mains) Vanwey, were natives of New Jersey, and after marriage resided in Perry County, Ohio, until their death. To Mr. and Mrs. Call have been born seven children, of whom six are living Harvey L., Robert H., Zadok G., Mary E., wife of Asa W. Morris; Ida M., wife of Thomas R. Knight and Martha A. William is deceased. Mr. Call was reared on a farm, and has engaged in farming as a business through life. He owns about 140 acres of land, where he and family reside. He engaged in merchandising in Oak Forest about nine years. In 1860 he was elected justice of the peace of Center Township, and served ten years. He and family are representative citizens of Center Township, Greene County, Penn.

THOMAS J. CARPENTER, farmer, P. O. Rutan, was born in Gilmore Township, this county, January 1, 1858. He is a son of Joseph and Elizabeth Carpenter (*nee* Stewart). His father was born in New York and his mother in Greene County, Penn., where they were married and have since made their home. Thomas J. Carpenter was twice married; first, January 11, 1879, to Belle Grove, who was born in Center Township, June 14, 1860, and is a daughter of William and Rebecca (Shaw) Grove. By this marriage Mr. Carpenter is the father of one child—W. E. Carpenter. Mrs. Carpenter departed this life October 7, 1883. Mr. Carpenter's second wife was Jessie L. Supler, whom he married September 23, 1885. She was born September 16, 1865, and is a daughter of Martin and Lizzie R. (Goodwin) Supler, who reside in Richhill Township. Mr. and Mrs. Carpenter have one child—Floyd M. Mr. Carpenter was engaged in merchandising until twenty two years of age, at which time he began farming, in which he has engaged as a business ever since. He owns 112 acres of land, where he lives with his family. He and wife are members of the Methodist Episcopal Church. His deceased wife was a member of the Christian Church.

R. B. CHURCH, farmer, Holbrook, Penn., was born in Center Township, Greene County, Penn., June 17, 1842. His parents are Elijah and Anna Church (*nee* Moore), who are natives of Greene County, where they now reside. The subject of this sketch was united in marriage July 13, 1867, with Sarah Thomas, who was born in Center Township April 18, 1851. She is a daughter of John and Mary Thomas (*nee* Wood), the former deceased. Mr. and Mrs. Church are the parents of four children, two of whom are living—George W. and Hamilton. The deceased are Fannie and Asa C. Mr. Church has followed the occupation of farming through life, and owns 166 acres of land where he and family live. During the late Rebellion he entered the service of his country in Company F, Eighty-fifth Volunteers, serving four years and four months. He was in a number of serious engagements, in one of which, in 1863, he was severely wounded. Mr. and Mrs. Church are consistent members of the Christian church, and are among the leading families of Center Township.

G. M. CHURCH, cabinet-maker, Rogersville, Penn., was born in Greene County, Penn., February 13, 1845, and is a son of Elijah and Anna Church, who were natives of this county, where they now reside. Mr. Church was united in the holy bonds of matrimony July 31, 1870, with Nancy L., daughter of William and Sarah

Sharpnack. Mrs. Church was born at Rice's Landing, Penn., October 11, 1845. She and her husband have a family of three children, two of whom are living, viz., William E. and Anna S. Mr. Church is a cabinet-maker by trade, which he followed the most of his life. He owns a nice furniture store and good property in Rogersville, where he and family reside. When the war broke out he enlisted in the service of his country in Company F, Eighty-fifth Pennsylvania Volunteers, and served two years, during which time he passed through a number of serious engagements. In politics Mr. Church is a Republican. He and family are among the leading citizens in the village where they reside.

CEPHAS CLUTTER, a retired farmer of Hunter's Cave, Penn., was born in Washington County, Penn., January 6, 1804, and is a son of William and Sarah Clutter (*nee* Rutan). His parents, who were natives of New Jersey, were married in Washington County, Penn., and remained there until their death. The subject of our sketch was united in the holy bonds of matrimony August 25, 1827, with Laura Day, who was born in Greene County July 25, 1809. Mrs. Clutter is a daughter of William and Mary Day (*nee* Sutton), who were also natives of New Jersey, and after marriage settled in Greene County, Penn., where they remained until their death. To Mr. and Mrs. Clutter were born seven children, five now living, viz.—William, Zebulon, John M., Mary J., wife of Lewis Baltzell; and Spencer B. The deceased are Franklin and Robinson. Mr. Clutter has always lived on a farm, and has been engaged in farming and stock-raising all his life. He owned at one time over 640 acres of land in this county. About 400 acres of this he has given to his children, and owns 240 acres where he resides. Mrs. Clutter, who was a devoted member of the Methodist Episcopal Church, died July 19, 1885. She and her husband made their home in Center Township for nearly half a century.

J. M. CLUTTER, farmer, Harvey's, Penn., was born in Greene County, Penn., February 29, 1832. His father and mother are Cephas and Laura (Day) Clutter, natives of Washington and Greene Counties, respectively. They were united in marriage August 25, 1827, and settled in Greene County, where they have since resided. Mrs. Clutter departed this life July 19, 1885. Her husband is still living, having reached the advanced age of eighty-four years. The subject of our sketch was united in marriage January 1, 1856, with Elizabeth Ullom, who was born in this county November 14, 1834. Mrs. Clutter is a daughter of Daniel T. and Anna (Johnson) Ullom, who were residents of this county until Mr. Ullom's death. His widow is still living at the old homestead. Mr. Clutter was reared on a farm, and has been a successful farmer through life. He owns 146 acres of good land, where he and family reside. He is considered one of the most substantial farmers and among the leading citizens of Center Township.

W. H. COOK, retired farmer, Harvey's, Penn., was born in Norwich, Connecticut, May 7, 1817. He is a son of William and Margaret (Harvey) Cook, the former a native of Scotland and the latter of England. They were married in New York City, where they remained sometime, then moved to Connecticut, and in 1818 moved to Greene County. Penn. Soon after their arrival in the county, Mr. Cook took a trip on a keal boat down the Ohio River, and was never heard of after he left Wheeling, W. Va. His widow remained in Greene County until her death, which occurred in 1875. W. H. Cook was their only child, and was united in marriage, November 2, 1847, with Elizabeth Rinehart, who was born in Waynesburg in 1825. Mrs. Cook is a daughter of Jesse and Lucy (Workman) Rinehart, natives of Greene County, where they remained until their death. Mr. and Mrs. Cook are the parents of seven children, viz.: Jesse R., Margaret, wife of Jacob Braddock; Maria H., wife of Abner Phillips; Samuel H., Lora, Francis L., wife of Hiram Smith; and Thomas H. Mr. Cook is a house-joiner by trade, which he has followed almost all his life. In later years he engaged extensively in farming, and owns 350 acres of land in this county. Mr. Cook has served as school director, and belongs to the Methodist Episcopal Church, of which his wife, who died May 16, 1885, was also a faithful member.

LAYTON CROUSE, farmer, Rogersville, Penn.—The gentleman whose name heads this sketch is one of the prosperous farmers of Center Township, where he was born August 23, 1827. He is a son of Samuel and Rebecca Crouse, also natives of this county and residents therein until their death. They were the parents of nine children, five living. Layton was united in marriage, January 5, 1861, with Catharine M. Thomas. Mrs. Crouse was born in Greene County, June 28, 1839, and is a daughter of Eli and Sarah Thomas (*nee* Knight), also natives of this county. Mr. and Mrs. Crouse are the parents of ten children, five of whom are living, viz.: Mary B., Janette, Elizabeth, Campbell and Sherman. The deceased are Lucy, Sarah J., Franklin, Eli and Walter S. Mr. Couse was raised on a farm and has been engaged in farming all his life. He owns 140 acres of land where he and his family live. In politics he is a Republican.

S. B. EAGON, farmer, Rogersville, Penn., was born in Center Township November 25, 1831. His father and mother, Uriah and Cassandra (Adamson) Eagon, were natives of Pennsylvania. The former was born August 21, 1802, and the latter March 21, 1804. They were married October 10, 1822, and were the parents of nine children, of whom six are living. The subject of our sketch was united in marriage, September 8, 1853, with Sarah A. Thomas, who

was born in Center Township January 23, 1832. Her parents were
Eli and Sarah Thomas, natives of Pennsylvania, who departed this
life in Center Township. To Mr. and Mrs. Eagon have been born
three children, of whom two are living—Jesse R. and Sarah J.,—
Uriah is deceased. Mr. Eagon has been engaged in farming the
greater part of his life, and owns about 156 acres of land where he
and his family reside. During the rebellion he entered the service
of his country, enlisting in Company A., Eighteenth Pennsyluania
Cavalry, and served two years and ten months. In politics he is a
Republican and. is a member of the G. A. R.

A. G. FORDYCE, retired farmer, White Cottage, Penn.—The
subject of this sketch is one of the pioneer citizens of Greene County.
He was born December 4, 1807. His father and mother were Jacob
and Elizabeth Fordyce, the former a native of New Jersey and the
latter of Fayette County, Pennsylvania. They settled in Greene
County and remained until their death. A. G. Fordyce was united
in marriage the first time, March 11, 1827, with Nancy Leonard, who
was born in this county March 2, 1809. Her parents were William
and Elizabeth Leonard, both now deceased. By this marriage Mr.
Fordyce is the father of twelve children, of whom eight are living,
viz.: Jacob, Elizabeth, wife of LaFayette Eagon; Maria, wife of
Jesse Wood; Sarah, wife of Edward Wood; William, Silas, Barnet,
and Clarinda, wife of A. R. White. Mrs. Fordyce departed this life
October 22, 1855. On October 30, 1856, Mr. Fordyce was again
united in marriage with Elizabeth Simmons, who was born in Washington County, Penn., May 28, 1823. Mr. Fordyce's parents were
Spencer and Mary Simmons, who settled in Greene County and remained until their death. By the second marriage Mr. and Mrs.
Fordyce have three children, only one of whom is living—AlbertG.
Mr Fordyce was reared on a farm, has been engaged in farming all
his life, and owns a farm of 280 acres. In politics he is a Republican. Mr. and Mrs. Fordyce are faithful members of the Christian
Church, of which his deceased wife was also a devoted member. Mr.
Fordyce has fifty-three grand-children, twenty-eight great-grandchildren and some of them are married.

SILAS FORDYCE, a farmer of Holbrook, Penn., was born June
20, 1842, on the old Fordyce homestead in Center Township, Greene
County, Penn. His parents were Archibald G. and Nancy Fordyce
(nee Leonard), who were born in this county—Mr.Fordyce Dec. 4,
1807, and his wife March 2, 1809. They were married March 11,
1827 and remained in the county until Mrs. Fordyce's death, which
occurred October 22, 1855. After her death Mr. Fordyce was united
in marriage with Elizabeth Simmons, a native of Washington County,
Penn. On January 23, 1862, Silas Fordyce married Mary J. Orndurf,
who was born in Whiteley Township, October 1, 1842. She is a

daughter of Jesse and Isabella Orndurf, the latter deceased. Mr. Fordyce and wife are the parents of ten children, of whom nine are living—Nancy B., William L., Jesse, Louella E., Susan, Archibald, Nevada, Garfield, Frank,—and Lillie (deceased). The subject of this sketch was raised on a farm, and has been engaged in farming and stock-raising almost all his life. He owns 300 acres of land where he resides with his family. In politics Mr. Fordyce is a Republican. When the war broke out he enlisted in the Eighteenth Pennsylvania Cavalry and served his country one year and eight months, during which time he was in a number of serious engagements. He and his wife are consistent members of the Christian Church.

JESSE FORDYCE, deceased, was a resident of Center Township, Greene County, Penn., where he was born May 28, 1831. He was a son of Jacob and Martha Fordyce, natives of Greene County, now deceased. Jesse was united in marriage, November 10, 1859, with Rachel Orndoff. Mrs. Fordyce was born in Center Township, this county, September 19, 1829, and is a daughter of William and Salome Orndoff (nee Wisecarver). Mr. and Mrs. Fordyce are the parents of one child—Ardella, born April 5, 1861. Mr. Fordyce was reared on a farm and engaged in farming through life. At the time of his death he was the owner of ninety-six acres of land, where his widow and daughter now reside. He belonged to the Methodist Protestant Church, of which Mrs. Fordyce is also a devoted member. In politics Mr. Fordyce was a Republican. He departed this life April 14, 1885, and by his death the township lost a good citizen, and his family a kind father and husband.

S. R. FORDYCE, farmer, Rogersville, Penn., was born in Center Township August 7, 1841- He is a son of Jacob and Martha Fordyce, who were natives of Greene County and now deceased. On June 22, 1867, S. R. Fordyce married Elizabeth Ornduff, who was born in Greene County March 13, 1850. She is a daughter of Jesse and Susan Orndurf (nee Wear). Mr. Orndurf was born in Franklin Township May 20,1816, and Mrs. Orndurf in West Virginia November 21, 1826, and they reside in Center Township. Mr. and Mrs. Fordyce are the parents of two children—Archibald and Edison. Mr. Fordyce was born and reared on his present farm, and has been engaged in farming the most of his life. He owns about 111 acres of land where he and family reside. In politics he is a Republican. During the late rebellion he enlisted in the service of his country in Company I, Eighth P. R. V. C., and was in the service almost three years, passing through many serious engagements. Mr. and Mrs. Fordyce are faithful members of the M. P. Church.

D. W. FRY, Waynesburg, Penn., was born in Wayne Township, Greene County, Penn., February 26, 1838, and is a son of George and Elizabeth Fry. His parents were born in Greene County—his father in 1813, and his mother in 1818. She died November 16, 1883. They were the parents of seven children, five of whom are living. The subject of this sketch was united in marriage, March 10, 1859, with Sarah, daughter of John Simington. She departed this life April 18, 1860. Mr. Fry was a second time married, July 14, 1861, with Mary M. Eagon, a native of Greene County, where she was born May 13, 1843. Her parents, Uriah and Cassandra Eagon, are both deceased. Mr. and Mrs. Fry are the parents of three children—Elizabeth S., wife of Joseph Huffman; George W. and Louie. Mr. Fry was reared on a farm and has devoted all his time to farming. He owns 230 acres of land, on which are substantial buildings. He also engaged in the mercantile business at Rogersville for a period of eighteen months. In politics Mr. Fry is a Republican, and he and his wife are prominent members of the Christian Church.

W. C. FRY, farmer, Waynesburg, Greene County, Penn.—The subject of this sketch was born in June, 1847, on the farm where he resides in Center Township, Greene County, Penn. He is a son of William and Susannah (Strosnider) Fry, pioneers of the county. William Fry, Sr., was born June 9, 1808, and his wife in 1812. They were united in marriage in 1832 and have resided in this county all their lives. They are the parents of eleven children, nine of whom are living. W. C. is the sixth. He was united in marriage in April, 1878, with Lizzie R., daughter of Abnor M. Bailey. She was a native of Greene County, born in 1857. To Mr. and Mrs. Fry were born two children—Alonzo B. and Lida B. Mrs. Fry, who was a kind and affectionate wife and mother, departed this life August 1, 1884. Mr. Fry was reared on a farm, and owns 120 acres of land in Center Township. In politics he is a Democrat, and belongs to the Christian Church.

JOHN S. FUNK, farmer, Rutan, Penn., was born in Jefferson Township, this county, November 7, 1827. His parents, Henry and Levina (Smith) Funk, who were natives of Pennsylvania, were united in marriage in Greene County, where they resided until their death. The subject of this sketch was united in the holy bonds of matrimony, June 4, 1854, with Margaret Craft, who was born in Fayette County November 6, 1832. Mrs. Funk is a daughter of Benjamin and Mary Craft, who were natives of Fayette County, and after marriage moved to Greene County, and remained until Mr. Craft's death. His widow is still living. Mr. Funk and wife are the parents of four children—George, Elizabeth, James and Wellington. Mr. Funk taught school for fifteen years in the earlier part of his life, and has since devoted his time exclusively to farming. He still takes an active interest in the educational affairs of his township, and

HISTORY OF GREENE COUNTY. 581

has served as school director. He is the owner of a good farm of 105 acres, where he and family reside.

EAGON GOODEN, a retired farmer of Rutan, Penn., was born in Wayne Township, this county, February 22, 1823. He is a son of William F. and Mary (Shields) Gooden, who were natives of Greene County, where they were married. Mrs. Gooden is deceased. Her husband is now a resident of Guernsey County, Ohio. The subject of this sketch was united in marriage September 19, 1850, with Elizabeth Wells. Mrs. Gooden was born in Greene County August 20, 1829, and is a daughter of James and Rhoda (Orndoff) Wells, also natives of this county, where they were married and remained until the death of Mrs. Wells. Mr. Wells is still living and resides in Center Township. Mr. Gooden and wife are the parents of eleven children, of whom ten are living—William T., Margaret J., wife of Reasin Davis; Mary, wife of James Morris; James B., John J., Rhoda, wife of Henry Luellen; Eliza A., wife of Thomas L. McKerrian; Sarah A., wife of Charles N. Marsh; Harriet F., Flora B., and Jesse (deceased). In early life Mr. Gooden taught school for about nineteen years; he would teach in the winter and work as a farm hand through the summer. His first purchase of land was in Wayne Township. It consisted of eighty-two acres which he sold, and in 1869 bought his present farm of 162 acres. In politics Mr. Gooden is a Democrat. He has served as judge and inspector of elections, and has been school director of his township.

SETH GOODWIN, farmer, Rutan, Penn., was born in Washington County, Penn., February 6, 1828, and is a son of John and Sarah A. (Gardner) Goodwin, natives of Pennsylvania. His parents were married in Washington County and remained there until about the year 1832, at which time they moved to Greene County and spent the remainder of their days. The subject of our sketch was united in marriage April 4, 1854, with Mary Hill, who was born in Greene County March 16, 1832. Her parents were Dan and Matilda Hill (nee Penn), who were also natives of Pennsylvania, and after their marriage settled in this county and remained until 1854. They then moved West and remained for twenty-eight years, returning in 1882 to their native county in Pennsylvania, where Mr. Hill departed this life. His widow survives him. Mr. and Mrs. Goodwin are the parents of twelve children, the following are living—John W., Daniel H., Sarah M., wife of J. L. Hays; Thomas C., Mary F., Harry B. S., Elizabeth, Nan, and Nettie. Mr. Goodwin has been a tiller of the soil most of his life, and owns 200 acres of valuable land where he and family live. He and wife are prominent members of the Baptist Church.

JOHN T. GOODWIN, farmer, Rutan, Penn., is one of the prosperous citizens of Center Township. He was born in Greene

County, July 31, 1840. His parents were John and Sarah A. Goodwin (*nee* Gardner). They were natives of Pennsylvania, where they were married in Washington County, and about the year 1832 moved to Greene County and remained until their death. John T. was united in marriage, August 18, 1861, with Margaret A. Smith. Mrs. Goodwin was born in Center Township, February, 1842, and is a daughter of Edmund and Elizabeth (Adamson) Smith, who were natives of Greene County, where they were married and resided until Mr. Smith's death in 1887. His widow is still living. To Mr. and Mrs. Goodwin have been born four children—Edmund S., Thomas R., Emma J. and Flossie E. Mr. Goodwin makes quite a success of his farming, and owns about 186 acres of excellent land, where he and family reside. Mr. and Mrs. Goodwin are leading members of the South Ten-Mile Baptist Church.

SAMUEL J. GRAHAM, farmer, Waynesburg, Penn., was born in Center Township, this county, November 22, 1837. His parents, George and Sarah B. (Mason) Graham, were natives of Greene County and residents therein until their death. Samuel was united in marriage, October 5, 1861, with Lizzie E. Boyd. She was born in Washington Township, this county, October 6, 1842, and is a daughter of James and Martha Boyd. Her parents are also natives of this county; her father is now deceased. By this marriage Mr. Graham is the father of three children, two of whom are living—Sarah A. and James B.—and Florence E. is deceased. Mrs. Graham, who was a faithful Christian wife and mother, departed this life April 12, 1871. After her death, November 1, 1875, Mr. Graham was united in marriage a second time, with Sarah A. Price, who was born in Marion County, West Virginia, May 21, 1851. Her parents are Eli T. and Amanda Price (*nee* Troy), natives of West Virginia, where they were married and spent their lives. Mrs. Price is now deceased. By the last marriage Mr. Graham is the father of two children—Charles W. and George E. P. Mr. Graham was reared on a farm and devotes his time wholly to agricultural pursuits. He is the owner of about 163 acres of valuable land. He and wife are prominent members of the M. E. Church.

JAMES HOGE, miller, Oak Forest, Penn., a descendant of one of the pioneer families of the county, was born in Center Township, September 23, 1834. His father and mother were George and Sarah Hoge, who died in this county. James was united in the holy bonds of matrimony, December 23, 1855, with Margaret Kent, a native of Greene County, born September 2, 1835. Mrs. Hoge is a daughter of John and Keziah Kent, who reside in Wayne Township, this county. Mr. Hoge and wife are the parents of eight children, of whom five are living, viz: Elizabeth, Maryetta, Lucy B., Jesse B. and Flora M. The deceased are Albert W., Rinehart K. and Margaretta.

Mr. Hoge is a carpenter by trade, which he followed for many years. He engaged in farming for some time, but for the last fifteen years has been operating a grist-mill. He owns land in the county, a number of houses and lots, one-half interest in mill property at Oak Forest, also one-half interest in the Hoge & Hoge Clothing Store at Waynesburg, Penn. Mr. Hoge has filled the office of justice of the peace for ten years, and is one of the most enterprising and industrious men of the county, and has carried on the undertaking business for thirty years and is still in the same business. He is also in the wagon-making and repairing business.

WILLIAM HOGE, farmer, Rogersville, Penn., was born in Greene County, Penn., December 31, 1830. His father and mother were Morgan and Elizabeth Hoge (*nee* Lippencott), who were natives of this county, where they made their home through life. William Hoge was twice united in marriage, the first time February 20, 1867, with Eliza A. McQuay. By this marriage Mr. Hoge is the father of four children—Samuel M., William McKinley, Elizabeth N. and David J. Mrs. Hoge died August 17, 1875. November 10, 1878, Mr. Hoge married for his second wife Esther M. Carter, born in Greene County in 1859. Her father and mother were James and Martha Carter, the latter deceased. Mr. and Mrs. Hoge are the parents of five children, viz: Mary J., Cinderella, Levi L., Martha and Jesse. Mr. Hoge is a successful farmer, and owns 250 acres of land—his home farm. He and wife are zealous members of the Baptist Church.

LEVI HOGE, farmer, Holbrook, Penn., was born June 24, 1833. His parents were Morgan and Elizabeth Hoge, who were born in Greene County, Penn., and resided there through life. Levi, the subject of our sketch, was united in the holy bonds of matrimony, October 12, 1868, with Susannah Orndoff. Mrs. Hoge was born in Center Township, April 22, 1840, and is a daughter of William and Salome Orndoff, who, like Mr. Hoge's people, were natives of Greene County, where they remained until their death. Mr. and Mrs. Hoge are the parents of one child—Mary J. Mr. Hoge was raised on a farm, and following out the careful instructions there received, he has, by his industry and economy, proven himself one of the most substantial farmers in his township. He owns a nice farm of 236 acres in Center Township, where he and family live. Mr. Hoge and family are prominent members in the Christian Church.

JOSEPH HOGE, retired farmer, P.O. Oak Forest, Penn., is one of the pioneers of the county, and was born in Franklin Township, November 16, 1806. His parents, Solomon and Mary Hoge, were natives of Virginia, and when first married moved to Greene County, Penn., and remained until their death. Joseph was three times married, first December 4, 1828, to Mary Coen, a native of Greene

County. By this marriage Mr. Hoge is the father of ten children, five of· whom are living. Mrs. Hoge, who was a faithful Christian wife and mother, died in 1842. In 1843 Mr. Hoge married for his second wife Miss Jane Blair, who was born in this county February 17, 1817. By this marriage there were seven children, four now living. Mrs. Jane Hoge departed this life August 22, 1856. Mr. Hoge subsequently married Mrs. Jane M. (Wood) Watson, June 22, 1857. She was born in Washington County, Penn., November 16, 1812. Mr. and Mrs. Hoge have one child. Mr. Hoge was reared on a farm, and has been engaged in farming all his life. He has resided on his present farm about sixty-four years. In politics he is a Republican. He and wife are members of the Baptist Church, in which he has been deacon for nearly fifty years.

WILLIAM HOGE, farmer, P. O. Holbrook, Penn., was born in Center Township, December 15, 1830. He is a son of Joseph and Mary (Coen) Hoge, who are natives of Greene County. Mrs. Hoge is deceased. October 4, 1855, William Hoge was united in marriage with Mary A. Graham, who was born in Franklin Township, Greene County, December 30, 1824. Her parents were William and Margaret (Muckle) Graham, the former a native of this county, and the latter of New Jersey. They were married in Greene County, Penn., where they settled and remained until their death. To Mr. and Mrs. Hoge have been born three children, of whom two are living—William G., and Margaret M., who is the wife of John M. Scott. The deceased is Henry H. William G. was born July 28, 1855, and was married July 20, 1878, to Mary A. Moore. Mrs. Mary ·A. Hoge, wife of William G., died August 24, 1883. He was married again June 11, 1885, to Miss Alice M. Orndoff. Margaret M. was born July 5, 1859, and married January 29, 1885, to John M. Scott. Mr. Hoge has been engaged in farming the most of his life, and owns 241 acres of land in Center Township. He and Mrs. Hoge are zealous members of the Baptist Church, and are among the leading families of the township.

T. J. HUFFMAN, farmer, Oak Forest, Penn.—The subject of this sketch was born in Center Township, Greene County, Penn., August 30, 1829. He is a son of Joseph and Sarah (Hunt) Huffman. On December 27, 1855, Mr. Huffman was united in marriage with Caroline Hathaway, who was born in Washington County, Penn., and is a daughter of Jacob and Jane Hathaway, residents of Washington County, Penn. Mr. and Mrs. Huffman have a family of nine children, eight of whom are living, viz: Joseph, Jacob, Robert, Daniel, Charlie W., Lizzie, Belle and Dora, and Jennie (deceased.) Mr. Huffman was reared on a farm, and has been engaged in farming throughout his life. He owns about 240 acres of land in Greene County.

Mr. and Mrs. Huffman are prominent members of the Christian Church, and highly respected by all who know them.

REASIN HUFFMAN, farmer, Waynesburg, Penn., is one of the industrious farmers of Center Township, Greene County, Penn., where he was born June 24, 1831. His parents were Joseph and Sarah Huffman (*nee* Hunt), who were natives and residents of this county until their death. On October 15, 1859, Mr. Huffman was united in the holy bonds of matrimony with Sidney Stewart (*nee* Thomas). Her father was a native of Ohio, and her mother of Greene County, Penn. They now reside in Monroe County, Ohio. To Mr. Huffman, and wife have been born nine children, eight of whom are living—Joseph L., William R., Albert L., Emma F., Biddie E., Alexander C. J., John F., Isa O., and Nancy (deceased). The subject, like his brothers, was reared on a farm and has devoted his life principally to agriculture pursuits. He owns about 200 acres of land. In politics Mr. Huffman is a Democrat, has filled the office of school director in his township, and he and wife are devoted members of the Christian Church.

S. B. HUFFMAN, farmer, Waynesburg. Penn., was born on the Huffman homestead in Center Township, this county, September 26, 1847. He is a son of Joseph and Sarah (Hunt) Huffman, who were natives of Pennsylvania, residing in Greene County until their death. Mr. Huffman was united in marriage, May 11, 1872, with Ella Neel, a native of Greene County, born March 21, 1853. She is a daughter of Remembrance and Nellie Neel (*nee* Thomas), natives of Pennsylvania, the latter deceased. Mr. Huffman and wife are the parents of six children, five of whom are living—Harry, Charlie, Josie, Ray and Roy. Remembrance (deceased). Mr. Huffman has been engaged in farming all his life, and owns 160 acres of land where he and family reside. In politics Mr. Huffman is a Democrat, and is school director in his township. He and wife are active members of the Christian Church.

SAMUEL IAMS, retired farmer, Harvey's, Penn., was born in Washington County, Penn., April 8, 1817. His parents, John and Anna (Coulson) Iams, were natives of Washington County, where they were married and remained through life. Mr. Iams died in December, 1866, and Mrs. Iams in November, 1886. They were the parents of five children, of whom three are living. Samuel was united in marriage, October 29, 1840, with Nancy Grimes, who was born in Greene County, August 15, 1817. Her parents were Peter and Mary (Sherwin) Grimes, deceased. The former was a native of this county, and the latter of Baltimore, Maryland. Mr. and Mrs. Samuel Iams are the parents of seven children, of whom five are living—Dr. John T., of Waynesburg, Penn.; G. P.; Ida, wife of Byron Braddock; Carrie, wife of James B. Throckmorton; and Samuel S. The deceased are

Mary A. and Cordelia. Mr. Iams is a mill-wright by trade, which he followed for many years. He subsequently engaged in farming and stock raising, and owns about 420 acres of land in Greene County. Mrs. Iams and family are members of the Methodist Episcopal Church.

F. G. JACOBS, farmer, P. O., Rutan, was born in Greene County, Penn., November 25, 1832. His father, Daniel Jacobs, was born in New Jersey. His mother, whose maiden name was Hannah Rayle, is a native of Maryland. They were married in Greene County, Penn., where they still reside. The subject of this sketch was united in marriage, June 24, 1858, with Catharine Nelson, who was born in this county February 14, 1832. She is a daughter of Samuel and Barbara (Ranner) Nelson. The former was born in Virginia and the latter in Greene County, Penn., where they were married and spent the remainder of their lives. Mr. and Mrs. Jacobs have seven children —Daniel, Hannah, wife of Melvin Headley; William R., Barbara E., Mary B., Henry and Delia M. In early life Mr. Jacobs taught school for a few years, but subsequently devoted his time to farming. He owns about 225 acres of land where he and family live. Mr. and Mrs Jacobs are zealous members of the Methodist Protestant Church.

A. J. JOHNSTON, farmer, Hunter's Cave, Penn., was born in Washington County, Penn., January 18, 1816. His parents were Andrew and Climena (Conklin) Johnston the former a native of New Jersey, and the latter of Pennsylvania. After marriage they settled in Washington County, and in 1820 moved to Greene County and remained until their death. The subject of our sketch was united in holy bonds of matrimony, December 9, 1847, with Phoebe McCullough, who was born in Washington County, April 3, 1817. Mrs. Johnston is a daughter of Thomas and Sarah (Dunn) McCullough. They were also natives of Washington County, where they remained two years after their marriage, then moved to Greene County and spent the remainder of their lives. Mr. and Mrs. Johnston have four children: Sarah A., wife of William Heaton; George W., Andrew J., and Eliza A. Mr. Johnston has been engaged in farming and stock raising all his life, and owns about 400 acres of land—his home farm. Mrs. Johnston and the children are members of the Methodist Episcopal Church.

COLUMBUS JOHNSTON, farmer, P. O. Rogersville, was born in Center Township, Greene County Penn., June 4, 1831. He is a son of Andrew and Climena (Conklin) Johnston who were natives of Washington County, but after marriage resided in Center Township, Greene County, until their death. Columbus was united in marriage March 5, 1855, with Emeline Bane, who was born in Washington County, June 17, 1838. Mrs. Johnston is a daughter of Nathan and Hannah Bane (*nee* Carter), who were also natives of Washington

County, and moved to Greene County about 1844, remaining until Mr. Bane's death. His widow is still living and resides in West Virginia. Mr. Johnston and wife are the parents of four children— Nathan B., Lizzie A., Dora M., and Lewis B. (deceased). Mr. Johnston was reared on a farm and has made farming his business through life, and by strict honesty and industry has procured a nice home, consisting of 108 acres of land, where he and family reside. He and Mrs. Johnston are active members of the South Ten Mile Baptist Church. In politics he is a Republican.

DAVID KNIGHT, retired farmer, P. O. Oak Forest, Penn., was born in Greene County, Penn., October 24, 1818. His parents, James and Cassandra Knight, were natives of Greene County, where they were married and remained until their death. David was united in marriage June 6, 1839, with Mary A. Fry. Mrs. Knight was born in this county February 26, 1819, and is a daughter of John and Mary Fry. They were also natives of Greene County, but moved to West Virginia and resided until their death. To Mr. Knight and wife have been born nine children, seven of whom are living—Mary, Joshua, Cassie J., Thomas J., Lucy A., Jemima and Harriet. The deceased are Catharine and Eli. Mr. Knight has been successfully engaged in farming all his life, and owns about 134 acres of land. In politics he is a Democrat. The Knight family are pioneers of the county, and among its most highly respected citizens.

THOMAS KNIGHT, farmer, P. O. Rogersville, Penn., was born in Franklin Township, Greene County, Penn., November 27, 1820. His father and mother, James and Cassandra Knight, were natives of this county, where they resided until their death. Thomas Knight was united in marriage November 18, 1841, with Nancy Wood, who was born in Jackson Township, October 13, 1822. Mrs. Knight was a daughter of Micajah and Jane Wood, the former a native of Pennsylvania, and the latter of Ireland. Both died in Greene County. Mr. Knight by this marriage is the father of eight children, of whom five are living. Mrs. Knight died March 3, 1863. On December 24, 1863, Mr. Knight married for his second wife Miss Edna Sellers, who was born in Center Township, October 30, 1829. Her parents were Christopher and Nancy (Johnson) Sellers, both natives of Pennsylvania, who departed this life in Greene County. Mr. Knight and wife have two children, one living. Mr. Knight is a cabinet-maker by trade, but has been engaged in farming for many years. He owns 212 acres of good land.

LEVI H. MARTIN, P. O. Rogersville, Penn., is one of the substantial farmers of Center Township, this county, where he was born March 1, 1843. His parents, Daniel and Rachel (Rush) Martin, were natives of Greene County, where they were married and remained until Mr. Martin's death, April 6, 1879. His widow is still living. Levi was united in marriage, December 24, 1867, with Rachel Eddy, who was born July 24, 1842, in this county, and is a daughter of John and Elizabeth (Kughn) Eddy. Her parents are natives of Greene County and reside in Wayne Township. Mr. and Mrs. Martin have a family of three children, two of whom are living—Belle and Levi E. Mr. Martin was reared on a farm, and has engaged in farming as his occupation through life. He is the owner of 150 acres of good land in Greene County. He and Mrs. Martin are active members of the Christian Church, and the family are highly respected in the community.

A. B. McCLELLAND, merchant, Oak Forest, Penn.—The subject of this sketch is one of the leading merchants of Center Township. He was born in Waynesburg, Penn., February 25, 1840. His parents were Dawson and Sarah (Hughes) McClelland, who were natives and residents of this county through life. Asa B. was united in marriage March 10, 1861, with Nancy Donahoe. She was born in Greene County, November 30, 1841, and is a daughter of William and Nancy Donahoe, both deceased. Mr. McClelland is a blacksmith by trade, which he followed about twenty-five years, then engaged in farming and merchandising. He owns a general store at Oak Forest, Penn. In politics he is a Republican, and served as postmaster for five years at Oak Forest under the Republican administration. He and wife are faithful members of the Baptist Church.

J. P. McGLUMPHY, farmer, P. O. Rutan, was born in Center Township, Greene County, Pennsylvania, July 16, 1822. He is a son of Edward and Magaret (Haines) McGlumphy. His father was a native of Ireland, and his mother of Maryland. They were the parents of seven children, of whom four are living. Mr. McGlumphy was united in marriage February 11, 1847, with Lida A. Thomas. Mrs. McGlumphy was born in this county March 12, 1831, and is a daughter of James and Elizabeth Thomas. Mr. and Mrs. McGlumphy are the parents of four children—Maria S., wife of Henry Scott; Hiram R.; Elizabeth M., wife of F. M. Carpenter, and Lucy J., wife of W. H. Throckmorton. Mr. McGlumphy has been a farmer all his life, and owns a nice home where he and family reside. He and wife are prominent members of the Cumberland Presbyterian Church, and are highly respected by all who know them.

JESSE McNEELY, farmer, P. O. Rutan, Penn., was born in Wayne Township, Greene County, Pennsylvania, April 11, 1851. He is a son of John and Elizabeth McNeely, who were natives of Pennsylvania and settled after marriage in Greene County, where Mrs. McNeely departed this life in Wayne Township. Mr. Mc-

Neely afterward married a Mrs. Coen, whose maiden name was Stockdale. They moved to Center Township and remained until Mr. McNeely's death. His widow came to her death June 13, 1888, by the falling of a porch roof. She was standing on the porch when the roof fell in and killed her instantly. Jesse was united in marriage November 6, 1875, with Melissa VanCleve, who was born in Center Township, August 7, 1852.. Her parents were John and Ursula (Throckmorton) VanCleve, also natives of this county and and residents of Center Township. Mr. and Mrs. McNeely have two children—James A. and John H. In connection with his farming Mr. McNeeley has been engaged extensively in the lumber business. He is the owner of seventy-six acres of land, where he and family reside. He has served as school director of his township and was elected justice of the peace February, 1888, for a term of five years. Mrs. McNeely is a devoted member of the Methodist Episcopal Church.

JOHN MEEK, a successful farmer, P. O. Rutan, Penn., was born in Washington Township, this county, May 29, 1833. His parents, John and Elizabeth (Boyd) Meek, were also natives of this county, where they remained until their death. On October 15, 1859, John Meek was united in marriage with Jane Simpson. Mrs. Meek was born in Greene County, February 7, 1840, and is a daughter of John and Mary (Auld) Simpson, Her father was born in Greene County, Penn., and her mother was a native of Ireland. Both died in this county. Mr. and Mrs. Meek have three children—Miles, John W. and Ottowa A. Mr. Meek has been engaged in farming all his life, and owns 224 of land where he and family reside. Mr. and Mrs. Meek are leading members in the Methodist Protestant Church.

WILLIAM MILLIKIN, farmer, P. O. Rutan, was born in Morris Township, this county, April 3, 1832. His parents, David and Lida (Rogers) Millikin, were natives of Greene County, the former of Irish and the latter of English descent. They were united in marriage in Greene County, where they remained through life. William was united in marriage, September 1, 1852, with Rebecca Simpson, who is a native of this county, born March 9, 1835. Her parents were John and Mary Simpson, the former a native of Pennsylvania, and the latter of Ireland. They were residents of Greene County, Penn., for the greater part of their lives. To Mr. and Mrs. Millikin have been born eight children, of whom six are living— John W., Robert I., Thomas N., Harry B., Maggie J. and Sadie M. The deceased are Lida A. and Cora V. Mr. Millikin is one of the substantial farmers of Center Township, and by his industry and good management has made a comfortable home for himself and family. His farm consists of about 300 acres of land, on which are good buildings. Mr. and Mrs. Millikin are consistent members of the Methodist Protestant Church.

JOHN MORRIS, farmer, Rogersville, Penn., was born in Center Township, this county, March 28, 1832. His parents, Ephraim and Martha (Roseberry) Morris, were natives of Greene County, where they were married and spent all their lives. John Morris was twice united in marriage, first November 11, 1854, with Sarah Church, a native of Center Township, and daughter of Elijah and Anna Church (nee Moore). Her parents are natives and residents of this county. By this marriage Mr. Morris is the father of six children, viz: Martha A., wife of Harvey Call; James M., Asa W., John J., Arta M., wife of Goodwin Hunt, and Elijah. Mrs. Morris departed this life March 10, 1878. November 30, 1879, Mr. Morris married for his second wife Elizabeth Phillips, a native of Marshall County, W. Va. Her parents were Joseph and Anna (Inghram) Phillips, natives of West Virginia, both now deceased. Mr. and Mrs. Morris are the parents of two children—Joseph G. and Sarah A. Mr. Morris is quite a genius, and has learned several different trades. He is a carpenter, stone-mason and blacksmith, and succeeds in almost any kind of work. He has been engaged in farming for several years, and owns about 300 acres of land where he and family reside. During the Rebellion he entered the service of his country in Company F, Eighty-fifth Pennsylvania Volunteers, and served over a year, receiving a wound at Williamsburg from a piece of a shell. Mr. Morris was elected commissioner of Greene County and served three years, being one of the few Republicans who ever held that office in the county.

ELI ORNDURF, farmer, P. O., Rogersville, Penn., one of the substantial citizens of Center Township, was born in Greene County, Penn., February 25, 1828. He is a son of William and Salome (Wisecarver) Orndurf, the former a native of Virginia, and the latter of Pennsylvania. They departed this life in Greene County, in 1885. They were the parents of twelve children, of whom eleven are living. Eli Orndurf was united in the holy bonds of matrimony, March 23, 1854, with Martha A. Wyly, who was born in Greene County, September 6, 1834. Mrs. Orndurf is a daughter of James and Mary Wyly (nee Neel), natives of this county. Mrs. Wyly died February 14, 1876. Mr. Wyly is still living. To Mr. Orndurf and wife have been born seven children—William H., Mary S., wife of Edmund Scott; James L., Susan, Joseph S., Barney and Mattie I. Mr. Orndurf has been a farmer all his life, and owns 365 acres of land where he and family reside. In politics he is a Republican.

W. B. ORNDOFF, farmer and stock-raiser, Oak Forest, Penn., one of the substantial and industrious farmers of Center Township, was born in this county, January 15, 1837. He is a son of William and Salome (Wisecarver) Orndoff, who departed this life in 1885. William B. was united in marriage, September 12, 1868, with Mary E. Scott, who was born in Greene County, September 22, 1844. She is a daughter of John and Charlotte Scott (nee Mason), both natives of this county and residents of Jackson Township. Mr. and Mrs. Orndoff are the parents of five children—Bertha, Orvil D., Judson H., John D. and Hersey. Mr. Orndoff has been engaged in farming for many years, and owns 338 acres of land in Center Township. In politics he is a Republican, and has served on the school board in his township.

ISAAC ORNDOFF, farmer, Rogersville, Penn., is a descendant of the old pioneer family of Orndoffs. He was born in Center Township, April 4, 1846, and is a son of William and Salome (Wisecarver) Orndoff, the former a native of Virginia, and the latter of Pennsylvania. They were married in Greene County, and remained there through life. Isaac Orndoff was twice married, the first time April 4, 1869, to Margaret R. Seckman, who was born in Rogersville, May 18, 1848. Mrs. Orndoff was a daughter of John W. and Lila Seckman, the former deceased. By this marriage Mr. Orndoff is the father of three children—Emma E., John S. and Lora M. Mrs. Orndoff departed this life October 25, 1874. Mr. Orndoff's second wife, whom he married in 1877, was Harriet Headley, who was born in Gilmore Township, this county, May 3, 1848. She is a daughter of John and Eliza Headley. Mr. and Mrs. Orndoff are the parents of six children—Jesse F., Eddie G., Sweet, Isaac B., Charlie W. and Georgie A. Mr. Orndoff has been a farmer all his life, and owns eighty-five acres of land where he and family reside in Center Township, Greene County, Penn.

D. S. ORNDOFF, farmer, Oak Forest, Penn., was born in Virginia, March 29, 1854. His father and mother are William and Margaret Orndoff, natives of Virginia, where they still reside. On November 20, 1875, D. S. Orndoff married Mary S. Orndoff, who was born in Greene County, Penn., March 25, 1851. Mrs. Orndoff is a daughter of William and Salome Orndoff (nee Wisecarver). The former was born in Virginia, and the latter in Pennsylvania. They settled in Greene County and remained until their death. To Mr. and Mrs. Orndoff have been born four children—Maggie B., Lizzie M., Edsa S. and Effa A. Mr. Orndoff came from Virginia in 1875, and has remained in Greene County ever since. He is engaged in farming, and owns 220 acres of land in Center Township. He and wife are consistent members of the Christian Church, and are highly respected throughout the community.

JESSE ORNDURF, retired farmer, White Cottage, Penn., was born in Franklin Township, this county, May 20, 1816. His father and mother were Jesse and Catharine Orndurf, who were natives of

Virginia, but came to Greene County, Penn., and spent their later life. Mr. Orndurf departed this life in 1816, and after his death Mrs. Orndurf was united in marriage with John Gordon. Both are now deceased. Jesse Orndurf was united in marriage the first time with Isabella Mooney, who was a daughter of Thomas and Cassandra Mooney, the former a native of Ireland, and the latter of Pennsylvania. By this marriage Mr. Orndurf is the father of four children, only one of whom is living—Mary J., wife of Silas Fordyce. Mrs. Orndurf departed this life in 1851. In 1853 Mr. Orndurf married for his second wife Susan Wear, born in West Virginia, November 21, 1826. Mrs. Orndurf is a daughter of William and Sarah Wear. Her father died in Portsmouth, Ohio, and her mother in West Virginia. By the second marriage Mr. and Mrs. Orndurf have six children—Elizabeth, wife of S. R. Fordyce; William, who married Eliza Mitchell; Inghram, the husband of Sidney White; Jesse B., who married Mollie L. Hughes; Sarah A , wife of C. V. Smith, and Sidney, wife of Thomas Stewart. Mr. Orndurf has been engaged in farming all his life, and has given his children a great deal of property. He owns at present 400 acres of land in Greene County. He and wife are zealous members of the Methodist Protestant Church. In politics he is a Democrat.

S. B. OWEN, physician, Oak Forest, Penn.—Among the successful young physicians of Greene County, Pennsylvania, we take pleasure in mentioning the name of Dr. S. B. Owen, who was born in Greene County, January 4, 1857. He is a son of Isaac N. and Anna Owen (nee Rush), who are natives of this county, where they have spent most of their lives. Doctor Owen was united in marriage August 28, 1879, with Laura K. Donley, who was born at Mt. Morris, Penn., August 28, 1862. She is a daughter of David L. and Louisa Donley (nee Evans). Her father is a native of this county, and her mother of West Virginia. They have resided in this county since their marriage. To Dr. S. B. Owen and wife have been born two children—Mabel D. and Edward L. The Doctor commenced reading medicine with his father in 1879, and graduated from the Starling Medical College of Columbus, Ohio, March 6, 1884. He began the practice of his profession at Oak Forest, Penn., the same year, where he receives a large patronage and meets with good success.

JOHN PATTERSON, farmer, P. O., Hunter's Cave, Penn., was born in Washington County, Penn., August 18, 1819, and is a son of John and Mary (Enlow) Patterson. His father is a native of Adams County. Mrs. Patterson was born in Washington County, Penn., where they were married and remained until their death. On September 15, 1846, John married Mahala Patterson, a native of Morris Township, Greene County, Penn., born January 15, 1828. Her parents, John and Elizabeth (Shriver) Patterson, were natives of Greene County and resided therein through life. Mr. and Mrs. Patterson are the parents of six children, three of whom are living— James E., Samantha, wife of Jacob Schrode; and Ida B. The deceased are Nancy E., Mahalia S. and John W. Mr. Patterson was raised on a farm and has made farming the occupation of his life. He is the owner of 220 acres of good land where he and his family reside. Mr. and Mrs. Patterson are leading members of the Methodist Episcopal Church.

JESSE C. PATTERSON, farmer, Waynesburg, Penn., is one of the industrious young farmers of Center Township, where he was born September 22, 1854. He is a son of James and Mary J. (Parshall) Patterson, natives of Washington and Fayette counties, respectively They were married in Greene County and remained there until their death. Mrs. Patterson departed this life March 7, 1884, and her husband July 16, 1885. Jesse C. was united in marriage January 18, 1883, with Rebecca Wade, who was born in this county December 4, 1862. Her father and mother are Greenberry and Mary (McCormick) Wade, natives of West Virginia, where they lived for many years. They subsequently moved to Greene County, Penn., and reside in Mt. Morris. Mr. and Mrs. Patterson are the parents of two children, one living, James E., and Wade (deceased). Mr. Patterson has been engaged in farming through life, and owns 102 acres of land which constitutes his home farm. In politics he is a Democrat; he has held the office of school director in his township, and he and Mrs. Patterson are consistent members of the Baptist Church.

O. S. PHILLIPS, farmer, P. O. Hunter's Cave, was born in Washington County, Penn., August 21, 1829. He is a son of John and Lida (Rutan) Phillips, the former a native of Greene and the latter of Washington County, where they were married and remained until about the year 1844. They then moved to Greene County and remained until Mr. Phillips death, which occurred at Fairfax Court House during the rebellion. After his death his widow lived with her son O. S., with whom she made her home until her death. Mr. O. S. Phillips was united in marriage, August 1, 1850, with Charity Graham, who was born on the farm where she resides, August 16, 1833. Her parents were George and Sarah B. (Mason) Graham, natives of this county and residents of Center Township until their death. To Mr. and Mrs. Phillips have been born the following named children—George W., Margaret J., wife of Simon Moore; Samuel O., Belle L., wife of W. McCullough; Benjamin F., Sadie L., Dora M., Birdie W., Olive C. and Guy C. The deceased are Rhoda A. and Willis B. Mr. Phillips was raised on a farm and has been engaged in farming and stock-growing all his life. He owns about

440 acres of land in Greene County.   In politics he is a Democrat, has filled the office of school director in his township, and he and his wife are active members in the Methodist Episcopal Church.

LEVI PORTER, Harvey's, Penn., was born in Franklin Township this county, June 5, 1845.   His parents, John and Hannah (Rinehart) Porter, were natives of Greene County, where they were married and remained until their death.   Levi was united in marriage September 3, 1873, with Lizzie, daughter of David and Elizabeth Kent. Her father was a native of Pennsylvania, and her mother of New Jersey. Both are now deceased.   Mrs. Porter was born in Franklin Township.   She and Mr. Porter had a family of four children—Linnie L., Mattie M., Alma E. and Florence A.   Their mother died October 3, 1883.   Mr. Porter was afterwards united in marriage, March 30, 1885, with Linnie Bradford, who was also a native of Franklin Township, born October 20, 1856.   She is a daughter of Robert and Sarah J. Bradford (nee Kent), also natives of Pennsylvania and residents of Greene County until Mrs. Bradford's death.   Mr. Bradford is still living. By his last marriage Mr. Porter is the father of two children—Goldie M. and Viola E.   Mr. Porter has been engaged in different lines of business during his life, but at present devotes his time principally to farming, and owns one-hundred and thirty-eight acres of land where he and his family reside.   Mr. and Mrs. Porter belong to the Methodist Episcopal Church, of which his deceased wife was also a devoted member.

W. P. REESE, miller, Rogersville, Penn.—Among the stirring business men of Rogersville we take pleasure in mentioning the name of William P. Reese, who is a native of Greene County and was born November 28, 1884.   He is a son of John D. and Catharine Reese, who were pioneers of Greene County, and remained in it until their death.   William was united in marriage September 11, 1869, with Maria Fry, who was born in this county, March 21, 1847.   Mrs. Reese is a daughter of George and Elizabeth Fry, who were born in Greene County. Mr. Fry in 1813, and his wife in 1818. Mr. Fry is still living.   Mr. Reese and wife are the parents of seven children—John L., Cora B., George C., Catharine E., William A., Alice M. and Allen T.   Mr. Reese is a miller by occupation, owns a grist and planing-mill in Rogersville, also 225 acres of land in Greene County.   He is a member of the Masonic Order and his political views are Democratic.   He has been a citizen of Rogersville for nine years.

PHILLIP RUSH, farmer, Rogersville, Penn., was born in Morris Township, Greene County, Pennsylvania, October 17, 1834. He is a son of Abraham and Lida Rush (nee Bottomfield), the former a native of New Jersey, and the latter of Pennsylvania. They were married in Greene County and resided there until their death.   In

1857 Phillip Rush married Catharine M. Huffman, who was born in Center Township, this county, in 1837. Her parents, Joseph and Sarah (Hunt) Huffman, were natives of Pennsylvania, and resided in Greene County until their death. To Mr. and Mrs. Rush have been born eleven children, ten of whom are living—Stephen B., Joseph L., Francis M., Nancy E., Clarinda, Timothy R., John, Vada, Lucy, May and Ora. Thomas J. is deceased. Mr. Rush has been a farmer all his life, and owns 123 acres of valuable land where he and his family reside. Mrs. Rush is a devoted member of the Baptist Church.

C. W. SCOTT, farmer, Rutan, Penn., was born December 16, 1837, on the farm where he and family reside in Center Township. He is a son of John and Mary A. Scott (nee Teagarden), who were natives of Pennsylvania and residents of Greene County until their death. Mrs. Scott departed this life in 1856, and her husband lost his life in a collision on the Baltimore & Ohio Railroad, near Columbus, Ohio, October 6, 1860. They were the parents of four children. On October 6, 1859, C. W. Scott was united in marriage with Rachel Webster, who was born in this county November 30, 1839. Her parents were John and Elizabeth (Cowell) Webster, also natives of this county. Mr. Webster died in 1871 and Mrs. Webster in 1874. To Mr. and Mrs. Scott have been born five children, four living—William H., George M., John, Flora, and Mary E. (deceased). Mr. Scott was raised on a farm, has spent his life in farming, and is the owner of 124 acres of land. He has served as director of the poor in Greene County for three years. Mrs. Scott is a faithful member of the Baptist Church.

THOMAS SCOTT, farmer, P. O. Rutan, Penn., was born in Center Township, Greene County, December 24, 1834. His parents, Elias and Harriet (Kent) Scott, were natives of this county, where they were married and remained through life. Mr. Scott died August 20, 1884, and his wife June 14, of the same year. On September 13, 1855, Thomas Scott married Elizabeth A. Turner. Mrs. Scott was born in Greene County, June 12, 1838, and is a daughter of Rev. James L. and Nancy (Patterson) Turner. Her father was a native of New York and her mother of Greene County, Penn. Both are now deceased. By this marriage Mr. Scott is the father of eight children—Wesley S., Walter P., Elias, Harriet N., Ida L., Albert F., Carrie E. and James E. Mrs. Scott died July 16, 1876. Mr. Scott was subsequently united in marriage December 20, 1879, with Anna B. Drake, who was born in Greene County, October 5, 1849. Her parents, Francis and Eliza Drake, were natives of this county. Mr. Drake is deceased. By the second marriage Mr. Scott is the father of three children—Harry R., Leah N. and William. Mr. Scott has been a farmer all his life, and owns 133 acres

31

of land where he and family live, besides property in West Virginia. He has been a member of the school board of his township. He and Mrs. Scott belong to the Methodist Protestant Church, of which his deceased wife was also a devout member.

GEORGE W. SCOTT, farmer, Rutan, Penn., was born in Center Township, this county, April 30, 1837. His parents are James and Charlotte (Strawn) Scott, natives of Greene County, where they were married and remained until Mr. Scott's death in 1884. His widow is still living. George W. was united in marriage July 4, 1864, with Amanda J. Woods, who was born in Waynesburg, Penn., October 25, 1843, and is a daughter of Samuel and Leah Woods (nee Divers). Mrs. Scott's mother was born in Baltimore, Md., and her father was a native of Washington County, Penn., where they were married. They settled in Waynesburg and remained until their death—Mrs. Woods dying June 6, 1885, and her husband June 21, 1886. To Mr. and Mrs. Scott have been born six children, viz.—Emma L., wife of George B. McNeely, M. D.; Mary C., Cora, Nellie L., Reynolds and Claude. Mr. Scott has devoted his life chiefly to farming, and owns 131 acres of land where he and family reside. When the war broke out Mr. Scott entered the service of his country in Company I, Eighth Pennsylvania Reserves, and served three years. He passed through many serious engagements, and was wounded three times. He has filled the office of auditor of his township. Mrs. Scott is a consistent member of the Methodist Episcopal Church.

HENRY A. SCOTT, farmer, P. O. Rutan, was born in Greene County, Penn., April 11, 1842. He is a son of James and Charlotte (Strawn) Scott, who were natives of Greene County, where they resided until Mr. Scott's death, which occurred April 9, 1884. His widow is still living. Henry was united in marriage January 28, 1864, with Catharine Morris. Mrs. Scott was born in this county July 7, 1848, and is a daughter of Ephraim and Martha (Roseberry) Morris. Her parents were also natives of Greene County, and residents therein through life. To Mr. and Mrs. Scott have been born six children, of whom four are living—James F., Lucy J., Asa and Sarah. Mr. Scott has been engaged in farming through life, and owns 184 acres of land where he and family live. Mrs. Scott is a devoted member of the Methodist Episcopal Church.

JOSHUA SCOTT, farmer, P. O. Rutan, is one of the pioneers of Greene County, Penn. He was born December 20, 1824, and is a son of James and Mary Scott (nee Sellers). His parents were natives of Greene County, where they resided until their death. On October 10, 1843, Joshua Scott married Nancy J. Rinehart. She was born in this county in 1826, and is a daughter of Samuel and Mary Rinehart, both deceased. To Mr. Joshua Scott and wife were born four children, of whom three are living—Mary E., Christopher and Samuel. James is the deceased. Mr. Scott has engaged in farming throughout his life, and owns 160 acres of land where he and family reside. He belongs to the Methodist Protestant church, of which his wife, who died January 1, 1866, was also a faithful member. By her death the family were bereft of a faithful and devoted wife and mother.

ASA M. SELLERS, farmer, Rogersville, Penn.—The gentleman whose name heads this sketch is a descendant of one of the pioneer families of Greene County, Penn., where he was born July 8, 1828. His father and mother were David and Elizabeth Sellers, who were also natives of this county, and remained here until their death. Asa Sellers was united in marriage March 31, 1855, with Jane Orndoff. Mrs. Sellers was born in Center Township March 23, 1832. Her parents were William and Salome Orndoff (*nee* Wisecarver). To Mr. and Mrs. Sellers have been born six children, of whom four are living—Elizabeth S., wife of Carey Grimes; William L., Atkinson H. and David R. The deceased are Mary A. and Adda M. Mr. Sellers has been engaged in farming and raising stock all his life, and owns about 200 acres of land where he and family reside. In politics he is a Republican.

THOMAS SMITH, farmer, Rutan, Penn., was born in Center Township January 6, 1836. He is a son of Edmund and Elizabeth (Adamson) Smith, who were natives of Greene County, where they were married and remained until Mr. Smith's death, February 11, 1887. Mrs. Smith is still living. Thomas is their oldest child, and was united in marriage April 19, 1855, with Susannah Scott, who was born in Center Township, September 24, 1836. Her parents, Elias and Harriet (Kent) Scott, were natives of Greene County and residents there until their death. Mr. and Mrs. Smith are the parents of eight children, seven living—James L., Hiram R., Laura A., wife of Lindsey D. Grove; William L., Emerson B., Fannie A., Elzie and Harriet E. (deceased). Mr. Smith's life has been devoted to farming and the raising of stock. His farm in Center Township consists of 289 acres of land, on which are fine substantial buildings. Mr. Smith has filled the office of director of the poor, and has been a member of the school board. He and wife are members of the Baptist Church.

JOB C. SMITH, farmer, Rutan, Penn., was born in Center Township December 1, 1848. He is a son of Edmund and Elizabeth Smith (*nee* Adamson), natives of Greene County, Penn., where they resided until Mr. Smith's death in 1887. His widow is still living. Job C. was united in the holy bonds of matrimony August 1, 1875, with Christie A. Slusher, who was born in Washington County, Penn., November 11, 1846, and is a daughter of David and

Elizabeth Slusher (*nee* Moore). Her parents are also natives of Washington County, and moved to Greene County in 1872. In 1880 they went to Iowa, where they still reside. Mr. and Mrs. Smith have six children—Bessie E., Hattie E., Guy B., Clyde D., Loyd L. and Goldie Z. Mr. Smith is an industrious farmer, and is the owner of 106 acres of land where he and family live. He and wife are zealous members of the Baptist Church.

J. C. SMITH, retired farmer, Rutan, Penn., was born in Morgan Township, Greene County, Penn., May 11, 1814. His parents, Job and Mary (Cravan) Smith, were natives of Pennsylvania, settled after marriage in Morgan Township, and remained during life. They were the parents of three children. J. C. is their only child living, and was united in marriage July 4, 1839, with Elizabeth Scott. She was born in Center Township March 20, 1821, and is a daughter of John and Susannah Scott (*nee* Niceswunger). Her parents, who were natives of Greene County, are both deceased. Mr. and Mrs. Smith are the parents of eleven children, of whom ten are living— William, Sarah A., wife of William Cowen; John, Maria J., wife of James Wells; Mary, Thomas J., Hiram S., Samuel H., Lydia, wife of George Grimes; and Emma A., wife of Samuel Showalter. The deceased is Job, who died in the Andersonville prison. Mr. Smith has been a farmer all his life, and owns a nice home where he and family reside. He and wife are active members of the Methodist Protestant Church.

STEPHEN STRAWN a retired farmer residing near Waynesburg, Penn., was born in Franklin Township September 5, 1817. He is a son of Abner and Juda (Grant) Strawn, who were natives of Pennsylvania and died in Washington County. Stephen was united in the holy bonds of matrimony July 15, 1841, with Margaret J. Jewell. Mrs. Strawn was also a native of Franklin Township, born November 3, 1823, and is a daughter of Samuel and Margaret (Mason) Jewell, the former a native of New Jersey and the latter of Ireland. They are now deceased. To Mr. and Mrs. Strawn have been born eight children, seven of whom are living—John, Eliza, wife of Jacob Wilson; Samuel, William, Abner, Mason and Morton T. The deceased is Elizabeth, who was the wife of J. B. Smith. Mr. Strawn has been a farmer all his life, and is the owner of ninety-seven acres of land where he and family reside. He has served as school director and inspector of elections in his township.

SAMUEL THOMPSON, P. O. Rogersville, Penn., was born in Center Township, Greene County, Pennsylvania, January 1, 1839. He is a son of Joseph and Margaret (Bowler) Thompson. The former is a native of West Virginia, and the latter of Greene County, Penn., where they were married and made their home until Mr. Thompson's death, which occurred July 7, 1867. Mrs. Thompson is still living. She resides with her son Samuel, who was united in marriage March 4, 1865, with Sarah E. Call. Mrs. Thompson was born in Center Township in 1840, and is a daughter of James and Sarah E. Call who were natives of Pennsylvania, and departed this life in Greene County. Mr. and Mrs. Thompson are the parents of nine children, of whom eight are living—Thomas, Harry, Mary B., Maggie, James, Lindsey, Essa and Coral. Henry is deceased. Mr. Thompson was reared on a farm and has devoted almost all his life to farming. He owns about 320 acres of land. When needed in the surface of his country he enlisted in Company F, Eighty-fifth Pennsylvania Volunteers, served for three years, and was in a number of serious engagements. He and wife are faithful members of the Christian Church.

JAMES THROCKMORTON, retired farmer, P. O. Harvey's, Penn., is one of the pioneer farmers of Center Township. He was born in Franklin Township, this county, February 22, 1816. His father and mother were Joseph and Catharine (Hulsart) Throckmorton, natives of Monmouth County, New Jersey, where they were united in marriage in 1809. Soon after marriage they moved to Franklin Township, Greene County, Penn., and remained until Mrs. Throckmorton's death in March, 1853. After her death Mr. Throckmorton was united in marriage the second time in Morrow County, Ohio, with Laura Gilbert, and remained in that county until her death. He then returned to Greene County, Penn., and made his home with his children until his death, September 15, 1881. James, the subject of our sketch, was united in marriage January 9, 1840, with Mary M., daughter of William S. and Jane (Gettys) Harvey. Mrs. Throckmorton was born in Center Township, May 3, 1821. Her father was a native of Philadelphia, Penn., and represented Greene County in the State Legislature. Her mother was born in Fayette County, Penn. After marriage they settled and remained in Center Township until their death. To Mr. and Mrs. Throckmorton have been born nine children, of whom eight are living— Joseph G., Catharine C., wife of Daniel Hopkins; Mary E., wife of Andrew Frantz; William H.; Maggie C., wife of Robert Dinsmore; Sadie A.; Carrie L., wife of George C. Davis, and Emma F., wife of John M. Burroughs. Mr. Throckmorton is a millwright by trade, which he followed for fifteen years. He has since engaged in farming, and owns 120 acres of land where he and family live. Mr. and Mrs. Throckmorton are active members of the Methodist Episcopal Church, and the entire family are highly respected by all who know them.

SAMUEL THROCKMORTON, deceased, who was a farmer of Rogersville, Penn., was born in Franklin Township, May 21, 1818. He was a son of Morford and Margaret (Hill) Throckmorton. His father came from New Jersey, and his mother was a native of Greene County, Penn., where they were married and spent all their lives. Samuel was united in marriage July 24, 1844, with Nancy Reese, who was born near Waynesburg, Penn., January 31, 1825. Mrs. Throckmorton is the only daughter of John and Elizabeth (Drips) Reese, also natives of Greene County, where they remained until their death. To Mr. and Mrs. Throckmorton were born eight children, of whom seven are living, viz., Elizabeth M., wife of James B. Smith; William S., John R., James B., Thomas M., Albert B. and Charlie. The deceased is Margaret, who was the wife of Morgan Ross, and departed this life February 6, 1883. Mr. Throckmorton was a farmer and wool-grower in his life-time. At the time of his death he owned about 980 acres of land, and his wife about 200 acres. He was a member of the M. E. Church, and during the last half of his life he held at various times the position of trustee and leader in his chosen denomination. Mrs. Throckmorton is a faithful member of the Presbyterian Church. Mr. Throckmorton was killed by lightning, July 28, 1881, while at work in the field with four of his sons. By his death the county lost a good citizen and his family a kind husband and father.

JESSE ULLOM, merchant, Rogersville, Penn. — Among the substantial business men of Rogersville, we take pleasure in mentioning Jesse Ullom, who was born in Greene County June 20, 1836. He is a son of Daniel T. and Anna (Johnson) Ullom, who were natives of Greene County, where they resided until Mr. Ullom's death, in October, 1881. His widow survives him. This union was blessed with twelve children, nine of whom are living— three sons and six daughters. On March 29, 1861, Jesse was united in marriage with Phœbe Morris, who was born in this county November 11, 1843. She is a daughter of Ephraim and Martha Morris, both deceased. Mr. and Mrs. Morris were the parents of ten children, of whom eight are living. Mr. and Mrs. Ullom have a family of seven children, four living, viz., Thomas M., Mattie A., John T. and Jesse F. The deceased are Fannie L. and two infants. Mr. Ullom has been engaged in farming and merchandising all his life. He owns forty-seven acres of land, nice property in Rogersville, also a general country store. In 1881 he was elected to the office of justice of the peace in Center Township, and has been serving in that capacity ever since. He and wife are active members of the Methodist Protestant Church.

ROBERT WATSON, farmer and stock-dealer, Holbrook, Penn., was born in West Bethlehem Township, Washington County, April 12, 1847. He is a son of John and Anna Watson. His father was a native of Ireland, and came with his parents to America when ten years of age. His mother is a native of Pennsylvania, where she and Mr. Watson were married in Washington County, and remained there until their death. Mr. John Watson departed this life in 1856, and Mrs. Watson in 1869. They are buried on the farm at the head of Castile, where the family settled when they first came to this country. In 1870 Robert Watson married Kate Anderson, who was a native of Amwell Township, Washington County, and born in 1848. Her parents were John and Anna (Howshow) Anderson, natives of Pennsylvania and residents in Greene County through life. Mr. and Mrs. Watson have seven children—Samuel, John I., Smith, Anna F., George W., Maggie and Lizzie. Mr. Watson was reared on a farm and has made farming and stock-dealing his business through life. He owns about 112 acres of land where he resides with his family. During the late Rebellion he went into the service of his country in Company D, Sixth Pennsylvania Cavalry, and served until the close of the war. He and wife are consistent members of the Christian Church, and are highly respected by all who know them.

SAMUEL WEBSTER, a successful farmer and stock-dealer, Rutan, Penn., was born in Jefferson Township, this county, November 23, 1833. He is a son of John and Elizabeth (Cowell) Webster. The former was a native of New Jersey, and the latter of Greene County, Penn., where they were married and remained until about the year 1868, at which time they moved to Iowa, where Mr. Webster departed this life, November 9, 1871. His widow then returned to Greene County, and died May 11, 1874. They were the parents of twelve children, eleven of whom are living. In September, 1856, Samuel Webster married Lucinda Goodwin, a native of Center Township, and daughter of John Goodwin, now deceased. By this marriage Mr. Webster is the father of two children, one living, Mary E., wife of Andrew Johnson, and John, deceased. Mrs. Webster departed this life in 1860. Mr. Webster was afterwards married, September 29, 1863, to Nancy Higinbotham, who was born in West Virginia, October 7, 1834. Her parents were Thomas and Lucretia Higinbotham, who departed this life in West Virginia. Mr. and Mrs. Webster are the parents of eight children—Lucinda J., wife of Daniel W. Jacobs; William W., Anna M., Samuel H., Bertha B., Maggie A., John I. and Adolphus S. Having been reared on a farm, Mr. Webster has devoted his whole attention to farming and stock-dealing, and owns about 425 acres of land in Greene County, besides hotel property at Ryerson's Station, Penn. He is one of the enterprising and industrious business men of Center Township. Mr. and Mrs. Webster are leading members in the Baptist Church.

BENJAMIN L. WOODRUFF, physician, Holbrook, Penn., was born in Washington County, Penn., August 3, 1822, and is a son of Jesse and Rebecca (Wilson) Woodruff. His father was born in Elizabeth, N. J., June 15, 1784. His mother was born August 27, 1788, in Washington County, Penn., where they made their home for a number of years. Jesse Woodruff departed this life March 3, 1862, and his wife April 8, 1870. The Doctor was united in marriage the first time March 31, 1847, with Martha, daughter of Samuel Barnett. Mrs. Woodruff was a native of Washington County, Penn. By this marriage Dr. Woodruff is the father of three children—William B., Emily, and Dr. Samuel W. (deceased). Mrs. Woodruff departed this life January 25, 1854. The Doctor was afterwards united in marriage, September 13, 1855, with Acinda Lough, who was born in West Virginia, April 10, 1836. Her parents, John and Sarah (Basnett) Lough, were natives of West Virginia, and remained there until their death. By his second marriage Dr. Woodruff is the father of seven children, six living—Newton C. (late editor Waynesburg *Messenger*), Dora, Lillie, Bessie, Acinda, Benjamin L., and Flora (deceased). Dr. Woodruff began reading medicine about 1844, with Dr. W. G. Barnett, and graduated in 1848. He first engaged in the practice of his profession in Rogersville, Penn., and from there went to West Virginia and remained until 1861. He then moved to his present location, and has been in active practice ever since. He owns 420 acres of land where he and family reside. He and wife are members of the Christian Church.

E. W. WOOD, farmer, Oak Forest, Penn., is among the representative farmers and wool dealers of Greene County. He was born in Franklin Township, October 28, 1837. His parents were John D. and Nancy (Crichfield) Wood, also natives of this county, where they were married and remained until their death. Mr. Wood departed this life September 26, 1876, and his wife October 12, 1849. They had a family of seven children, of whom five are now living. E. W. Wood was united in marriage, October 17, 1867, with Mary J. Patterson, who was born in Whiteley Township, this county, September 11, 1844. She was a daughter of William and Rhoda Patterson, also natives of Greene County, and residents therein through life. To Mr. and Mrs. Wood were born five children, of whom four are living, viz: C. Endsley, Norman, Edward, Mary, and Charles B. (deceased). Mr. Wood is a tanner by trade, in which he engaged until twenty-five years of age. He then enlisted in Company K, Fifteenth Pennsylvania Cavalry, and served his country three years. He is a member of McCullough Post, No. 367, G. A. R. When the war was over he engaged in the wool and stock business, and also farmed extensively. He is the owner of 160 acres of land where he and family live. Mr. Wood is a member of the M. E. Church, of which his deceased wife was also a devoted member. She departed this life January 30, 1881, and by her death the family was bereft of a kind and affectionate wife and mother.

CARMICHAELS BOROUGH AND CUMBERLAND TOWNSHIP.

WILLIAM A. AILES, farmer and stock-grower, P. O. Carmichaels, was born in Washington County, December 25, 1835. He is a son of James and Elizabeth (Nixon) Ailes, who were also natives of Washington County, Penn., and were of English and Irish descent. His grandfather was Amos Ailes, also a native of Washington County. William is the youngest of a family of seven children. He has remained on the farm with his parents, where he received his education, and wisely chose farming as his business. His farm consists of 300 acres of land, well stocked and improved. Mr. Ailes was united in marriage, March 1, 1858, with Miss Lucinda, daughter of Thomas and Dorcas (Bell) Patterson. Mrs. Ailes' parents were of Irish descent. Mr. and Mrs. Ailes' only child, Mary Bell, was born in 1880, and died in 1886. In politics Mr. Ailes is a Republican; in religion they are both Cumberland Presbyterians.

WILLIAM ARMSTRONG, deceased, who was a farmer and stock-grower, was a son of Abraham and Ruth (Conwell) Armstrong, and was born in Greene County in October, 1805. His parents were natives of Pennsylvania, and of English descent. His father was a farmer by occupation, and among the early settlers of the county. William was the oldest of a large family, and was reared on the farm in Cumberland Township, where he attended the subscription schools. He was united in marriage with Miss Mary Williams, of English descent. She was born in 1807. They were the parents of nine children—Maggie, wife of Archibald Grooms; George W., a farmer; Emma, wife of William M. Murdock; Elizabeth, wife of Josiah L. Minor; Sarah, wife of Oliver Griffeth; Alice, wife of James K. Gregg; Cinthy, wife of Richard Gwynn; Lyda, wife of N. H. Biddle, and James, a farmer. Mr. Armstrong made farming the business of his life, met with great success, and at the time of his death was the owner of a well-improved farm in Cumberland Township, where he died in 1849. In politics he was a Democrat; in religion a Cumberland Presbyterian, of which church his widow is also a faithful member.

ALFRED T. ARMSTRONG, deceased, who was a farmer and stock-grower, was born in Greene County, Penn., February 1, 1807. He was a son of William and Elizabeth (Russell) Armstrong. His mother's parents were of Scotch-Irish origin. Alfred was the oldest in a family of seven children; he was reared in this county and attended the subscription schools. He engaged in farming as a business, and met with more than ordinary success. He was united in marriage, February 22, 1837, with Miss Helen M., daughter of Jeremiah and Anna (Alexander) Davidson. Mrs. Armstrong's father was a native of this county, and her mother of Mercer County, Penn. They were of English descent. Mr. and Mrs. Armstrong had a family of ten children, of whom six are living—Russell, Barclay, Elizabeth, wife of Jesse Benner; John, Neri, and Maggie, wife of William Elliott. Mr. Armstrong was a Democrat, and a devoted Presbyterian, of which church his widow is also a zealous member. He died in 1878.

JOSEPH H. ARMSTRONG, deceased, was a farmer and stock-grower. He was born in Cumberland Township, Greene County, Penn., July 25, 1819, and died July 4, 1887, in his sixty-seventh year. His father, William Armstrong, also his grandfather were among the earliest Scotch-Irish settlers of this county. They were all farmers. Joseph was the sixth in the family, and was reared on the farm where he died. His education was obtained in the township and the old Greene Academy at Carmichaels. He was industrious, frugal and a good financier, owning at the time of his death 225 acres of well improved land. He was united in marriage November 23, 1843, with Mary A., daughter of James and Mary (McClelland) Flenniken. Her ancestors were also farmers, and among the earliest settlers of the county. They were of Scotch-Irish descent. Mr. and Mrs. Armstrong were the parents of three children—Lizzie, wife of Daniel Thompson, of Uniontown, Penn.; Mary Louisa, wife of Robert Denham, and William W., who is a farmer and has charge of the home place. In politics Mr. Armstrong was a Democrat.

NERI ARMSTRONG, merchant, Carmichaels, Penn., was born in Cumberland Township, December 27, 1855. He is a son of Alfred and Helen M. (Davidson) Armstrong, natives of Fayette and Greene counties respectively, and of Irish descent. Mr. Armstrong's father was a farmer, and reared a family of ten children, of whom Neri is the ninth. He received a common-school education, remaining on the farm with his parents until 1884, when he went to Carmichaels to engage in business for himself. He there opened a grocery and drug store which he still retains. He is a man of good business qualifications, industrious, prompt and obliging, has a great many friends and a fair patronage. In 1876 Mr. Armstrong married Frances, daughter of I. L. Craft. Mrs. Armstrong is a native of Greene County, and of German descent. They have two children—Myrtle and Alfred. Mr. Armstrong is a Democrat and a member of the town council. He and Mrs. Armstrong are prominent members of the Presbyterian Church.

J. K. BAILEY, farmer and stock-grower, was born in Cumberland Township, Greene County, Penn., August 30, 1814. He is a son of William and Zillah (Johnson) Bailey, the oldest in their family of seven children. His parents were natives of Pennsylvania, were members of the Society of Friends, and of English origin. His father was twice married, his first wife being Miss Sarah Miers. By this marriage he was the father of one child, a daughter, who is now the wife of Miller Haines, and resides in Columbiana County, Ohio. J. K. Bailey's sisters and brothers were: Amanda, wife of James Murdock; Rev. E. E., now a missionary to the Indians; Ruth Ann, wife of Samuel Rea; William, Zillah, the widow of R. Richardson, and L. M. (deceased). Mr. Bailey was reared in Cumberland Township, and has made farming his business, in which he has met with great success. In 1835 he was married to Miss Delilah, daughter of John and Phœbe (Hibbs) Craft, who were natives of Pennsylvania, and of English ancestry. Mrs. Bailey was born in Cumberland Township, August 10, 1812. Her mother was a member of the Society of Friends. Mr. and Mrs. Bailey's children are —Zillah, wife of N. H. Biddle; John Milton; Phœbe, wife of R. S. Long; W. Calvin; Clarinda, wife of Joseph Hawkins, Lydia B., wife of Corbly Fordyce; Almira is the wife of John Rinehart, and J. K. Jr. The family are all members of the Cumberland Presbyterian Church, in which Mr. Bailey has served for many years as elder and Sabbath-school superintendent. In politics Mr. Bailey is a Republican, and has served for twenty-five years as justice of the peace, in which office both his father and grandfather preceded him.

REV. E. E. BAILEY, missionary, was born in Greene County, Penn., August 6, 1817, a son of William and Zillah (Johnson) Bailey, also natives of this State. His parents were of Quaker origin and of English ancestry. His father came to Greene County when he was about nine years old with his parents, Eli and Ruth Bailey, from Chester County, Penn.; he died at the advanced age of eighty-two years. He was twice married, and the Rev. E. E. is a child of his second wife, and grew up on the farm with his parents, receiving his early education in a log cabin school-house, afterwards attended school at Greene Academy and at Waynesburg, Penn. At the age of sixteen he joined the Cumberland Presbyterian Church in Greene County. He was licensed to preach and ordained by the Union Presbytery of the Cumberland Presbyterian Church. He labored some in West Virginia, six miles west of Morgantown, but mostly in Fayette County, Penn., where he was engaged in the ministry for a term of years. Having had a desire for missionary work he then went West, where he engaged in missionary work among the Indians, and met with good success. In 1887 he was sent to his present position among the Cherokee Indians by the board of missions of the Cumberland Presbyterian Church. In 1839 Mr. Bailey was united in marriage with Miss Mary, daughter of John and Margaret (Dowlin) Rea. Mrs. Bailey is of Irish descent. They have five children—Harvey M., John F., Hannah J., Margaret E. and William R. Mr. Bailey is a Prohibitionist.

JOSEPH TAYLOR BAILEY, farmer and stock-grower, Carmichaels, Penn., was born in Dunkard Township, Greene County, June 10, 1820, and is a son of Joseph and Hannah (Johnson) Bailey, natives of Pennsylvania. His father, who was a farmer and miller, came when a young man to this county, where he was married and reared a family of six children. Of these Joseph Taylor is the youngest, and was reared in Greene and Fayette counties. Early in life he learned the miller's trade with his father, and followed it for forty years. He erected and operated a grist-mill for nearly twenty-eight years. He is a successful farmer and at the present time the owner 320 acres of valuable land in Cumberland Township. He was married in Fayette County, Penn., November 16, 1854, to Miss Martha Jane, daughter of Francis and Martha (Morehouse) Lee. Mrs. Bailey is of English descent. Her father was a blacksmith and farmer. Mr. and Mrs. Bailey have two children—Eli and Frances. In politics Mr. Bailey has ever been a strong Democrat. He and his wife are prominent members of the M. E. Church.

ELLIS B. BAILEY, farmer and stock-grower, was born in Greene County, Penn., November 21, 1824, and is a son of Eli and Peria (Gregg) Bailey. His parents were natives of Chester County, Penn., were members of the Society of Friends, and of English descent. His father was a farmer. Mr. Bailey's ancestors were among the earliest settlers in Greene County, and often had to flee to the forts for protection. His father died in 1854, in Fayette County, where he had resided since 1837. His family consisted of ten children, eight of whom grew to maturity. Of these Ellis B. was the sixth. He was reared in Fayette County, attended Madison College and had entered the senior year, when he left school and commenced farming and stock-growing. He has made his own way in the world, and is among the wealthiest men of Greene County, owning over 1,000 acres of well improved land. He is a man possessed of more than ordinary energy, his success in life having been due largely to his strong determination to succeed, coupled with a willing disposition to work. His business life has not, however, all been sunshine. He lost $23,000 by the failure of the Exchange Bank of Waynesburg, and $2,000 by the destruction of his wool in a big fire at Boston. But every reverse in business seemed only to make him more determined, and to add new strength to his ambition. He has devoted his time to farming, stock-dealing and buying land, and he has dealt considerably in wool. He was never given much to speculating; but gave his business close attention and careful oversight, and has succeeded in accumulating a handsome fortune. He was married in Fayette County, Penn., March 7, 1850, to Harriet, daughter of John and Sarah (Barton) Gaddis. Her parents were Quakers, and of English descent. Mr. and Mrs. Bailey have six sons and two daughters—William H., John E., Joseph E., George E., Eli F., Richard L., Sarah F., wife of Thomas H. Hawkins, and Anna R., wife of George F. Luse. The two daughters and three sons are married; all are intelligent business men and good citizens. In politics Mr. Bailey has been a Whig and a Republican. He has served nine years as school director in Cumberland Township. All the family are members of the Presbyterian Church, in which Mr. Bailey has been elder and superintendent of the Sabbath-school.

J. E. BAILEY, farmer and stock-grower, was born in Cumberland Township, Greene County, May 22, 1858. He is a son of Ellis B. Bailey, whose biography appears in this volume. He is the fourth in a family of eight children. He received a common-school education, and also attended Greene Academy at Carmichaels, Pennsylvania. Mr. Bailey married Miss Ella, daughter of J. M. and Charlotte (Rinehart) Morris. They have one child, Earl, an interseting little fellow of four years. Mrs. Bailey's father, Morris Morris, is a prominent farmer and stock-grower of Greene Township, and one of its most influential citizens. He is an ardent Democrat and has taken an active part in the politics of the county. Mr. Bailey is a representative young man of his township, is a Republican in politics, and a member of the Presbyterian Church.

GEORGE E. BAILEY, farmer and stock-grower, son of Ellis B. and Harriet (Gaddis) Bailey, was born in Cumberland Township, Greene County, Penn., December 8, 1860. His father is a prominent farmer, and resides in this township. George E. is the fifth in a family of eight children. After attending the district school, he entered Greene Academy at Carmichaels, and subsequently attended Monongahela College at Jefferson, Pennsylvania. He is an industrious, energetic young man, and has made farming and the raising of fine stock a decided success. He spent the summer of 1883 in the South and West, as the general agent of a large book publishing establishment of Philadelphia. In politics Mr. Bailey is a Republican; and he is a zealous, active member of the Presbyterian Church.

W. H. BARCLAY, farmer and stock-grower, Khedive, Penn., was born March 6, 1836, where he now resides on a farm of one hundred and seventy-eight acres. He is a son of Hugh and Phœbe (Craft) Barclay, the oldest of their five children. His grandfather, Hon. Hugh Barclay, was of Scotch-Irish descent. He was a representative of the Pennsylvania State Legislature, and during his term introduced the bill establishing the Greene Academy at Carmichaels, Penn. W. H. Barclay's father was a farmer all his life. His family consisted of five children, all of whom are married. Mr. Barclay was reared on the farm, received his education in Greene Academy, and has made farming the business of his life. In 1856 he was married to Sarah E., daughter of John P. Minor. She died in 1862. In 1866 Mr. Barclay was again united in marriage with Martha J., daughter of Henry and Mary (McCann) Arford. Mr. and Mrs. Barclay are the parents of seven children—Sarah Ellen, George P., W. H., Myrtle V., Phœbe E., Norval L. and Harry S. Mr. Barclay is a Republican, and he and his wife are members of the Cumberland Presbyterian Church, in which he is a trustee.

G. A. BARCLAY, merchant-miller, was born in Cumberland Township, this county, February 25, 1850. He is a son of Hugh and Phœbe (Craft) Barclay, and grandson of Hon. Hugh Barclay. His father and grandfather were prominent among the early farmers of the county. Mr. Barclay is the youngest of a family of six children. He was reared on the farm, receiving his education in the common school and in Waynesburg College. Early in life he learned the miller's trade and operated a mill for a period of four years. In 1882 he engaged in the same business at Carmichaels where he has met with good success. In 1870 Mr. Barclay was united in marriage with Rhoda, daughter of Samuel Kendall, deceased. Mrs. Barclay is a native of this county. Her father was a Baptist minister. To Mr. and Mrs. Barclay have been born six children—Ida L., Stephen H., John F., Ettie, Gertrude and Clarence. Their mother is a devoted member of the Baptist Church. Mr. Barclay is a Republican in politics. He is a school director and member of the town council of Carmichaels Borough.

JAMES BARNS, the subject of this sketch, was born June 24, 1790, and died March 12, 1883. He was the youngest son of Thomas and Sarah Barns, who were among the pioneer settlers of West Virginia. They settled in the woods near where the thriving town of Fairmont now stands. His parents were among the first Methodists in West Virginia, his father being a class leader many years, and his father's house a preaching place for a long time. At the age of fifteen, Mr. Barns left his home to learn the trade of a millwright, and served an apprenticeship of five years. In 1811 he had an attack of fever, the only sickness that ever caused him to lie in bed one day, during a period of nearly ninety-three years. He was badly injured in 1870, by the running away of a team of horses, from the effect of which he was confined to his room for six weeks. On December 10, 1812, he was united in marriage with Miss Rhoda Davidson, of Fayette County, Penn.—a worthy companion of a worthy man. Their union was blessed with nine children, five of whom were living, also present when he died. This worthy couple were converted at a camp-meeting held in 1819, near Brownsville, Penn., and their habitation became emphatically a house of prayer as long as they lived. In 1824 he became dissatisfied with the government of the Methodist Episcopal Church, of which he and his companion were devoted members. He took a deep interest in the controversy that agitated the church, and culminated in the organization of the Methodist Protestant Church, and identified himself with the new organization in 1830. He was elected as a lay representative from the Pittsburgh Annual Conference to the first General Conference of the Methodist Protestant Church, which held its session in Georgetown, D. C., in May, 1834. He was also a member of the General Conference of 1838, which held its session in Pittsburgh, Penn. In February, 1868, God took his beloved companion from him. Her loss was painfully felt by him and his children, though assured of her future and eternal happiness in heaven. On March 1, 1870, he married Mrs. Mary Lantz, with whom he lived in the enjoyment of great domestic happiness until February 12, 1880—the date of her death. Two years later, he sold his farm and the old homestead, in which he had lived sixty-seven years, to his son-in-law, Isaac B. Patterson, who married his youngest daughter, Mary Ellen. This was very agreeable to all his children, as it keeps in possession of the family the dear old homestead where they were born and raised. Mr. Barns had a good constitution, and he took good care of it. His habits were exemplary; he was strictly temperate and regular in his manner of life. He always cultivated a cheerful disposition; lived in communion and fellowship with God; was always usefully and honorably employed, and to these things owed his long life, at the close of which he makes this note: "Have had great enjoyment all through life, and also health. Have not laid in bed one day from sickness since 1811." Thus after a sojourn longer than that usually allotted to man, James Barns peacefully passed away; the last of as good a family as Virginia ever produced, consisting of four brothers—William Barns, M. D.; John S. Barns, Esq.; Thomas Barns and James Barns. There were three sisters— Sarah Willie, Phœbe Shinn and Mary A. Thrapp. These all lived and died in the faith, and left behind them families that revere their memories and imitate their virtues. "Children of parents passed into the skies."

ISAAC T. BIDDLE, deceased, who was a farmer and stock-grower, was born in New Jersey, in the year 1799. He was a son of Timothy and Mary (Taylor) Biddle, natives of New Jersey and of English and German origin. His father, who was a shoemaker in early life, came to Washington County, Penn., in 1802, and carried on farming for twenty-eight years. In 1840 I. T. Biddle came to Greene County and bought a farm in Cumberland Township, and one year later his father, Timothy Biddle, came to the same farm. I. T. took charge of the farm and continued his father's business of farming and stock-growing, devoting his time principally to the raising of fine sheep.   He succeeded in accumulating a handsome fortune, but in later years met with serious reverses by the failure of three banks in which he lost about $40,000.   This proved a serious disarrangement in his financial affairs, but he was a good business man and died in fair circumstances after reaching a good old age. His widow, whom he married in Washington County, still survives him. Her maiden name was Jane Kerney, daughter of William and Elizabeth (Montgomery) Kerney. Mrs. Biddle was born in Washington County, September 16, 1804, and is of Irish lineage.   Mr. and Mrs. Biddle had a family of eleven children, Seven now living—Eliza, wife of Edward Carson; Mary, wife of Lewis Jennings; Morgan, who married Eunice Patterson; Nathan H., married Zillah Bailey and lives on the old homestead; John, married Mary Barclay; Amanda, wife of Dis South; and Edith F., wife of Walter Richey. Mr. and Mrs. Biddle have been faithful members of the Cumberland Presby- terian Church, in which he served as elder for many years. Mrs. Biddle has property in Carmichaels, where she still resides, an active and remarkably well preserved woman for her age, and loved and respected by all who know her.

N. H. BIDDLE, farmer and stock-dealer, P. O. Carmichaels, was born in Washington County, Penn., August 25, 1829. His father was Isaac T. Biddle, now deceased. His mother's maiden name was Jane Kerney; she was born in 1804 and is still living. Harvey came with his parents from Washington County to Cumber- land Township in 1840, and has made it his home till the present time. He is the fourth in a family of eleven children, seven of whom are living. He was reared on a farm and has been engaged in farm- ing and stock-dealing all his life, owning at present over seven hundred acres of valuable land in Greene County.   Mr. Biddle was united in marriage, December 25, 1856, with Zillah, daughter of J. K. Bailey.   Their family consists of four sons and two daughters— Newton M., Flora, wife of Thomas Patterson; William C., Richard L., Jesse T. and Virtue C·   Mr. and Mrs. Biddle are zealous members of the Cumberland Presbyterian Church at Carmichaels, Penn., in which he is one of the elders.   Mr. Biddle takes an active interest in the educational affairs of the county, served as school director for twelve years, and has been a member of the board of trustees of Waynesburg College for a number of years and is still a member.

SAMUEL BUNTING.—Among the representative men of Cum- berland Township we mention Samuel Bunting, a farmer and stock- grower, who was born in Fayette County, Penn., April 28, 1836. He is a son of Samuel and Nancy (Butler) Bunting, natives of Penn- sylvania, and of German and English origin. Mr. Bunting's father, who has made milling the business of his life, has now reached the advanced age of eighty-four years. Samuel was the fourth in his family of eleven children, and was brought up in Fayette and Greene counties, having lived in the latter since he was eight years old. Early in life he learned the miller's trade with his father, continued in the business until 1885, and has since been engaged in farming where he now resides near Carmichaels, Penn. He was united in marriage February 22, 1859, with Agnes, oldest daughter of Samuel and Mary (Cree) Horner. Mrs. Bunting is of English descent. Her father was a wealthy miller, and also engaged somewhat extensively in farming. In politics Mr. Bunting is a Prohibitionist. He and his wife are zealous and active members of the Presbyterian Church, in which he is an elder, and is also serving as assistant superintendent of the Sabbath-school.

S. S. BAYARD, farmer and stock-grower, was born near Waynesburg, Penn., December 27, 1839, and is a son of Perry A. and Nancy (Sayers) Bayard. His parents were natives of Greene County, descendants of the early pioneers, and of French and English origin. Mr. Bayard's father was a farmer and mechanic; in early life he was a stone-mason in Whiteley Township. S. S. is the fifth in a family of seven children; he was reared in Greene County, attended the schools in Whiteley Township, and afterwards entered Waynesburg College. He is a farmer by occupation, and owns 200 acres of well improved land where he resides in Cumberland Township. He has about twenty acres of his farm in choice fruit trees. In 1866 he married Miss Jane, daughter of W. T. E. Webb, Esq., of Waynesburg. Her mother's maiden name was Mary Stull; she was of French origin and a native of Kentucky. Her father was born in Virginia and was of English descent. Mr. and Mrs. Bayard are the parents of four children, two of whom are living. In politics Mr. Bayard is a Republican. In 1862 he enlisted in Company K, Fifteenth Pennsylvania Volunteer Cavalry, and was Sergeant of the company. He was in several prominent engagements of the late war—among others the battles of Antietam and Stone River, and was discharged for disability in 1863. Both his grandfathers were in the Revolutionary war. Mr. and Mrs. Bayard are active members of the Cumberland Presbyterian Church, and both are prominent teachers in the Sabbath-school.

JEREMIAH CLOUD, retired miller and distiller, Carmichaels, Penn., was born in Cumberland Township, Greene County, September 3, 1797. He is a son of Joel and Susannah (Carrington) Cloud, being the oldest in a family of twelve children. His father was of English-German descent, a native of Chester County, Penn., and was both a farmer and a cooper. His mother was of Welsh origin. He received a common school education, and at an early age learned the hatter's trade, which he followed until he attained his majority. He

32

was married by Rev. William Barley October 3, 1822, to Jane, daughter of John and Sarah (Wright) Morgan, who were of English descent. Three of his seven children are now living—Thomas, a farmer; Marion, a millwright; and Sarah Ellen, wife of Joseph Everly. At the age of twenty-one Mr. Cloud engaged with his father in the distillery business, in which he continued for a period of twenty years. By reason of the meagre facilities of that early day, the distilling art being then in its most primitive state, they could make but slow progress, one barrel a day being considered a big day's work. A grist-mill was erected by him in 1846, which for many years was a great convenience and benefit to the people of his neighborhood. He retired from the cares of an active business life at an advanced age. Mr. Cloud is the owner of 203 acres of valuable farming land in Cumberland Township, He is a self-made man, his success in life being due largely to his strong will and remarkable energy. He has been an enthusiastic Republican ever since the party was organized; and so steadfast was he in the support of Republican principles that he was never prevailed upon but once to vote for a Democrat. He was an active politician, but neither desired nor held an office. His thorough knowledge of politics, however, made him a very popular leader of his party. Mr. Cloud was reared a Quaker, and although he never joined any religious denomination, his sympathies were with the Society of Friends, of whose doctrines he has ever been an earnest advocate. Mrs. Cloud, deceased, was a zealous member of the Baptist Church.

CAPTAIN HIRAM H. CREE, farmer and stock-grower, was born May 21, 1819, where he now resides on the farm of 160 acres, which has been in the possession of the family since 1785. He is a son of Hamilton and Agnes (Hughes) Cree, natives of Pennsylvania, which has been the home of the Crees for many generations. The Captain's father was a farmer, who, in 1848, died at the age of seventy-eight, on the farm where Hiram H. now resides. His family consisted of ten children. Hiram, one of the youngest, was reared on the farm, and attended the common school in Cumberland Township. He engaged in farming until 1847, when he went to Cincinnati, Ohio, and was employed as salesman in a large wholesale dry-goods house. After five months spent in that business, he resumed his farming until 1862, when he went into the army, enlisting in Company A, One Hundred and Sixty-eighth Pennsylvania Infantry. When the company was organized he was unanimously elected its Captain, in which capacity he served most faithfully throughout his term. He was ever a gallant soldier, highly esteemed by all his company. In 1864 he married Miss Elizabeth, daughter of James S. Kerr, and they are the parents of two children—Ellen Agnes and Rose Allena. In politics the Captain is a Republican, in religion a Methodist, and his wife is a member of the Cumberland Presbyterian Church.

JOHN CRAGO, a retired farmer of Cumberland Township, was born February 15, 1814, and is a descendant of one of the pioneer families of Greene County. He is a son of John Crago. He owns 330 acres of well improved land, where his great-grandfather settled and was afterwards killed by the Indians. The Cragos all came of industrious and energetic ancestors, and are noted for their morality and patriotism; they were represented in the Revolutionary war. John Crago, of whom we now write, received his education in the subscription schools of his township, where he was married in 1840 to Eleanor, daughter of John and Mary Flenniken, both natives of Greene County, and of Irish and English descent. They have two children—Caroline, wife of M. L. McMeans; and William H., a farmer, who was born in Cumberland Township April 5, 1843. He grew up on the farm, attended the district school, and has made farming his chosen occupation. In 1862 Mr. Crago enlisted in a cavalry company, which was afterwards consolidated and became Company D, Twenty-second Pennsylvania Cavalry. He was discharged for disability March 22, 1864. Mr. Crago has been blind for a number of years; but is possessed of such a wonderful memory that he can go all over his farm and attend to almost any kind of work. He transacts his own business affairs, in which he has been greatly prospered, having at present a competence sufficient to keep him in comfort the rest of his days.

J. N. CRAGO, teacher and carriage manufacturer, Carmichaels, Penn., was born in Cumberland Township October 10, 1832. He is a son of Thomas and Cassandra Crago. His ancestors, who were of English descent, were among the early pioneers of this county. His father, who died in 1884, spent his life in farming. Mr. Crago is the oldest of five children, all of whom were born and reared in Cumberland township. He attended the common schools and Greene Academy. He learned the cabinet-maker's trade, serving the regular apprenticeship. Early in life he began to teach school, and has been identified with the teachers of Greene County for thirty years. About the close of the war he began the manufacture of carriages at Carmichaels, and has devoted much of the time since to that business, in which he has made a reputation for good style and fine workmanship. In 1861 he married Permelia, daughter of William Spencer. Mrs. Crago is of English descent. They have a family of five children—Richard, Thomas, Samuel, Bertie and Mary. Mr. and Mrs. Crago are zealous members of the Carmichaels Cumberland Presbyterian Church. Mr. Crago is trustee of the church, and served for many years as superintendent of the Sabbath-school.   He is a Republican and is a member of the I. O. O. F.

T. J. CRAGO, surveyor and school teacher, was born near Carmichaels, this county, July 16, 1843.   His ancestors were among the pioneer farmers of the county.   His parents, Thomas and Cassandra (Hughes) Crago, were of Irish and English descent.   His father, who was a farmer and teacher, died in 1884.   Mr. Crago is the fourth in a family of five children.   He was reared in this county, attended Greene Academy, and became a teacher early in life.   In 1862 he enlisted in Company C, in what was known as the Ringold Cavalry, which was consolidated with the Twenty-second Pennsylvania Cavalry in 1864, his company then being Company D.   He was in many engagements—among others the battles of Winchester and Lynchburg.   He was discharged May 28, 1865, at the close of the war, and has since taught school in Greene County, with the exception of two winters.   He has also engaged to some extent in farming and surveying.   Mr. Crago was united in marriage June 23, 1868, with Fannie J., daughter of James Wright, and is the father of three children—Mary, Albert and James.   Mrs. Crago's parents were natives of Westmoreland County, and of Irish and Dutch descent.   She died March 26, 1887, a faithful member of the Cumberland Presbyterian Church.   Mr. Crago is also one of the leading members of that denomination.   In politics he is a Republican; he is a member of the G. A. R., and commander of Post 265 of Cumberland Township.

THOMAS J. CRAGO, boat builder, was born in Cumberland Township, Greene County, Penn., June 30, 1847.   He is a son of Joseph and Maria L. (Thomas) Crago, and grandson of Thomas and Priscilla (Thurman) Crago, who were of English descent.   His grandfather was a farmer, and one of the early settlers of the county.   He was the father of fifteen children, of whom Thomas Crago's father, Joseph, was the youngest.   Joseph was born in Cumberland Township, August 7, 1811.   He had two older brothers in the war of 1812, and his grandfather, Archibald Crago, was killed in this township by the Indians.   Thomas, the oldest in a family of seven children, received a common-school education, and early in life engaged in the saw-mill business.   He has also paid considerable attention to boat-building, having built a number of boats and started them out from his place of business.   In addition to his saw-mill, he owns a nice little farm of thirty-eight acres, which he has secured through his own industry and a strong determination to succeed.   In 1866 he was united in marriage with Mary E., daughter of John Ridge.   They have eight children—Amos A., W. L., Lorenzo, Susannah, Louella, Bertha, Grover Cleveland and Tina M.   In politics

Mr. Crago is a Democrat, and he and wife are members of the M. E. Church, in which he is a trustee.

GEORGE G. CROW, dentist, Carmichaels, Penn., was born in Fayette County, Penn., January 1, 1837. He is a son of Michael and Sarah (Gant) Crow, also natives of Fayette County, and of German origin. His father was a miller and farmer. Dr. Crow is the third in a family of thirteen children, five of whom reached maturity. He was reared on the farm and attended the common schools of Fayette County. Early in life he began the study of dentistry at Smithfield, Penn. In 1859 he came to Greene County and located at Carmichaels, where he has practiced ever since. He has made a thorough study of his profession, and bears the well-deserved reputation of being a first-class dentist. He has many friends in Greene County, and has had several students in dentistry who have since become successful practitioners. Dr. Crow was the first dentist to locate in Greene County. May 1, 1861, he married Sarah, daughter of Daniel Darling. Mrs. Crow is of English descent. They have three children—G. W., Ella and Frank. At the breaking out of the Rebellion the Doctor promptly enlisted in the Eighth Pennsylvania Volunteers, and was afterwards a member of Company I, Thirty-seventh Regiment of U. S. Infantry. This company was made up of men from Waynesburg and Carmichaels. Dr. Crow was Third Sergeant, and was in eleven general engagements, among others the battles of Malvern Hill, Harrison's Landing, second Bull Run, Antietam, Fredericksburg, the Wilderness and Spottsylvania. At the close of his term he returned to Carmichaels, and continued his practice in dentistry. He was instrumental in organizing the Dental Society of Greene County, and served five years as its president. The Doctor's family are members of the M. E. Church, in which he takes an active interest, being a trustee and superintendent of the Sabbath-school. In politics he is a Republican.

JERRY DAVIDSON, owner and proprietor of the Davidson Hotel, Carmichaels, Penn., was born in Cumberland Township, May 26, 1834. His parents, Alexander and Elizabeth (Gallaher) Davidson, were natives of Fayette County, Penn., and of Irish descent. His father was a farmer, and reared a family of eight children, of whom Jerry is the fifth. He was reared on the farm and received a common-school education. He followed farming as a business until 1875, when he engaged in the hotel business in Carmichaels. Mr. Davidson keeps an excellent table, and always has first-class horses and carriages for the accommodation of commercial travelers and the traveling public. Mr. Davidson has been twice married, first in 1856 to Miss Selanta Flenniken. Of their three children two are living—J. Calvin, a blacksmith, and Frank F., a tinner. They are both married and doing well in their business at Carmichaels, where they reside. Their mother died in 1872. Mr. Davidson's present wife's maiden name was Harriet Stone. She was the widow of Ira J. Hatfield. They have two children—Henry Alexander and George S. Mr. Davidson is a member of the I. O. O. F. In politics he is a Democrat, in religion a Presbyterian. Mrs. Davidson is a member of the Cumberland Presbyterian Church.

JOHN M. DOWLIN, farmer and stock-grower, was born in Jefferson Township, Greene County, Penn., October 16, 1855, and is a son of John and Elma (Bell) Dowlin. His father, who is a native of Cumberland Township, is also a farmer and stock-dealer, and resides in Jefferson Township. He is a Democrat, and was United States Revenue Collector for a number of years. John M. Dowlin's grandfather was Paul Dowlin, a farmer of English descent. Mr. Dowlin is the only son in a family of six children. He was reared on the farm and attended the common school. He makes a business of farming and raising fine cattle and sheep, and superintends the home farm, consisting of 400 acres of most valuable land. He was married in Washington County, Penn., February 1, 1875, to Miss Rebecca J., daughter of Simon and Mary (Reynolds) Moredock. Their children are—Dessie L., Albert L. (deceased), John, Gertrude, Simon E. and Charles B. In politics Mr. Dowlin is a Democrat. He and Mrs. Dowlin are prominent members of the Cumberland Presbyterian Church.

J. F. EICHER, who was born in Fayette County, Penn., February 23, 1820, is a foundryman and manufacturer and dealer in farming implements. His parents, Abraham and Mary (Freeman) Eicher, were natives of Pennsylvania, and of Irish and English descent. His father's family consisted of twelve children, of whom Mr. Eicher was the ninth. When eighteen years of age he went to Pittsburgh to school. He learned the moulder's trade at Connellsville, Penn., serving an apprenticeship of three years. He then lived for seven years at Uniontown, Fayette County, and in 1850 came to Carmichaels, where he has since been engaged in his present business, and has met with unusual success. Mr. Eicher was married at Connellsville, February 14, 1842, to Miss Rosa A., daughter of William Glendenning. They are the parents of ten children, six of whom are living, viz: George, Emma, Wallace B., Robert, Sarepta and Anna M. Mr. Eicher has been an ardent Republican ever since the organization of the party. Mr. and Mrs. Eicher are faithful members of the M. E. Church.

WILLIAM C. ELLIOTT, blacksmith, was born in Washington County, Penn., April 26, 1848, and is a son of Samuel and Susannah (Bane) Elliott. His mother was born in Virginia, and his father, who was a veterinary surgeon, was a native of Washington County, Penn. William C. is the seventh of a family of nine children. He was reared in his native county, where he owns a fine farm. He attended the graded schools, and early in life learned the blacksmith trade, which he has followed ever since. In 1882 he married Miss Margaret Armstrong, and they have one child—Anna Mary. Mr. Elliott came to Greene County in 1883. In politics he is a Democrat, and he is a member of the I. O. O. F. Mr. and Mrs. Elliott are leading members of the Presbyterian Church.

WILLIAM FLENNIKEN, farmer and stock grower, was born March 25, 1808, on the farm where he now resides in Cumberland Township. He is a son of John, and grandson of James Flenniken, who came from east of the mountains to Greene County, and engaged in farming in Cumberland Township. William's mother's maiden name was Mary McClelland; her parents were of the Scotch-Irish descent. His father was born in Cumberland Township in 1774, and died in 1855. Of his nine children William is the fourth, and was reared on the farm with his parents. He attended subscription school taught in one of the old log school houses of that day, and afterwards engaged in farming as his life work. He has met with unusual success, and now owns the fine farm of 140 acres where he resides. His wife was Miss Isabella, daughter of George C. and Isabella (McClelland) Seaton, natives of Virginia. Mr. and Mrs. Flenniken have four children—George C., a farmer in the West; Mary A., William F., who is at present on the home farm; and Laura J., wife of Oscar Hartley. In politics Mr. Flenniken is a· Republican; his wife is a faithful member of the Presbyterian Church.

WILLIAM FLENNIKEN, meat merchant, who was born in Cumberland Township, July 30, 1838, is a son of John W. and Hettie (Wright) Flenniken. His mother was born in Bucks County, Penn., and his father was a native of Greene County. They were of Scotch-Irish descent. Mr. Flenniken's ancestors were among the early settlers of Pennsylvania, coming to Greene County as early as 1767. His father was a farmer; his family consisted of seven children—four sons and three daughters. William was fifth in the family, and was reared on the farm in Greene County, where he remained until 1886. He then came to Carmichaels, where he has since resided. In 1863 he married Eliza A., daughter of William and Achsah (Smith) Hartman. Mr. and Mrs. Flenniken are prominent members of the Presbyterian Church, in which. Mr. Flenniken has served as trustee.

ALFRED FROST, deceased, was among the most prominent merchants of Greene County, and was born in Pennsylvania, April 5, 1802. He was a son of William and Mary (Murphey) Frost, natives of Washington County. Mr. Frost was reared on the farm and attended the common schools. He chose farming as his vocation; but after his father's death he was obliged to work as a hired farm hand until he accumulated enough to begin business for himself. By dint of industry and economy he succeeded in acquiring a very fair share of this world's goods. In early manhood he engaged in the mercantile business, and for years owned a store in Carmichaels. He was united in marriage, January 23, 1830, with Mary, daughter of Henry and Elizabeth (Stairs) Sharpnack, of German origin. Mr. and Mrs. Frost were the parents of three children—Mary E., now living in Carmichael's at the old home; William H. (deceased), late of Kansas City, Missouri, who married Caroline Fair, of Leavenworth City Kansas; Elizabeth, who is the wife of George D. D. Mustard, and the mother of the following children—John, Mary S., Charles, William D., James A. and George D. Mr. and Mrs. Frost were prominent members of the Methodist Episcopal Church.

GEORGE T. GREGG, farmer and stock grower, was born in Cumberland Township, Greene County, July 12, 1852. He is a son of Joseph and Rebecca (Minor) Gregg, natives of this county, where they were married in 1844. Mr. Gregg's grandfather, Joseph Gregg, was born in Delaware, and was one of the early settlers of Greene County, Penn. He was a farmer and miller by trade. Mrs. Gregg's ancestors were of English descent, and also among the early settlers of the county. George T. Gregg's father, also of English descent, was born in Greene Township, and was a farmer and stock dealer until the time of his death. George's grandfather, John P. Minor, was a soldier in the war of 1812. Mr. Gregg is the third in a family of six children, three of whom are now living. He was reared in this county, attending the common schools and Greene Academy at Carmichaels, Penn. He was united in marriage, September 30, 1870, to Miss Pratt, daughter of James and Milly (Mt. Joy) Pratt, who were natives of Fayette County, Penn., and of English descent. Mr. and Mrs. Gregg have four children—Flora B., Joseph Charles, Myrta Rebecca and Orpha Ethel. Their mother is a faithful member of the Baptist Church. In politics Mr. Gregg is a Republican. Financially, he has been very successful, having 300 acres of land under his present control, and owing a fine farm of 114 acres where he now resides.

GENEALOGY OF THE MINOR FAMILY IN AMERICA.— The following genealogical record will be of interest to all the Minor family: The first member of the family who came to America was Thomas Minor, who was born in England in 1608, and came to this country in 1630. In 1634, he married Frances Palmer. Clement, son of Thomas and Frances Minor, married Frances Wiley in 1662. Their son William, who represents the third generation of the Minor family in America, married Anna Lyle in 1691. Stephen, son of William and Anna Minor, who married Ohalia Updike, was born in 1705, and was the eight son of the fourth generation. Samuel Minor was the fonrth son in the fifth generation. He was married, and his oldest son was Abia Minor. Abia was the father of John P. Minor, who married Huldah McClelland. Rebecca is the fourth of nine children and is the fourth of the eight generation. She is the wife of Joseph Gregg, of Greene County, Pennsylvania, who is the father of the subject of the preceeding sketch.

WILLIAM GROOMS, retired blacksmith, was born in Carmichaels, Penn., August 14, 1828. His parents were Benjamin and Isabella (Kerr) Grooms, natives of Maryland and Pennsylvania respectively, and of English and Scotch descent. His grandfather, William Grooms, was one of the early settlers of Greene County. His father was a farmer and carpenter, and had a family of six children, of whom William is the second of the three living. He was reared in Carmichaels, attended the common schools and Greene Academy, and in early life learned the blacksmith trade, in which he engaged for a number of years. In 1846 Mr. Grooms married Malinda, daughter of Moses and Susan (Vankirk) McIlvaine. They have six children—Susan, wife of James Lincoln; Elizabeth, wife of George Demain; Arabella, wife of Levi Taylor; William and B. F., blacksmiths; and Eliza Jane, a teacher. In politics Mr. Grooms is a Republican. In 1861 he enlisted in Company I, Eight Pennsylvania Volunteers and served three years. He re-enlisted in Company B, Fifty-seventh Volunteer Infantry and served till the close of the war. He has been road commissioner, and was postmaster at Carmichaels for a number of years. Mr. and Mrs. Grooms are members of the Methodist Episcopal Church, and he is a member of the G. A. R. Post.

JOSIAH GWYNN, farmer and stock-grower, who was born near where he resides, October 20, 1812, is a son of Joseph and Martha (Dowlin) Gwynn. His grandparents on the maternal side were natives of Montgomery County, Penn., and were of Welsh origin. Mr. Gwynn's grandfather, Joseph Gwynn, came from London, England, to what is now Greene County, and was among the early settlers in this part of Pennsylvania. His grandfather Gwynn came to this county before the Revolutionary war, and settled on the farm which Josiah now occupies. This was then an Indian settlement— or rather, an Indian neighborhood, and he took what was then called " tomahawk claim." He left this country with the intention of returning to London, but got no farther than the Island of Cuba, and there he engaged in a sugar plantation, and on his return he found other parties had settled on two of his claims. He served as county commissioner in what is now Washington and Greene counties. Josiah Gwynn's father farmed on the home place throughout his life. He was drafted in the war of 1812, and died in 1864, at the age of seventy-five. Josiah is the oldest of a family of eight children. He attended school on his own farm, in the old-fashioned log school-house, which he has since seen replaced by one of hewn logs, that by a frame building, and the frame ready to be superseded by a substantial brick. Mr. Gwynn has made farming the business of his life, and owns 200 acres of the original entry made by his grandfather. He was married March 28, 1841, to Lydia, daughter of George W. and Susannah (Myers) Phillips. Mrs. Gwynn was born in Chester County, Penn., in 1824. Her father was a farmer and butcher, of English descent. Mr. and Mrs. Gwynn have eight children, six living—Martha L., wife of Wilson Huston; Joseph C., George W., E. E., wife of Lacy Craft; John R. and J. F. All are members of the Cumberland Presbyterian Church, in which Mr. Gwynn is elder and superintendent of the Sabbath-school. He has always been a liberal high-minded gentleman, and highly respected in the community.

J. F. GWYNN, merchant, who was born in Cumberland Township, September 2, 1842, is a son of John Gwynn. His great-grandfather, Joseph Gwynn, Sr., came from London, England, settled in Greene County, and served in the Revolutionary war. Mr. Gwynn's father was born December 25, 1818, on the farm taken up by Joseph Gwynn, Sr., when he first came to this county. He was married in the fall of 1840 to Elizabeth, daughter of Jesse and Mary (Wright) Rea, who were of English descent. J. F. Gwynn is the elder of two children. He received his education in Greene Academy and Waynesburg College. In 1862 he enlisted in Company F, Fifteenth Pennsylvania Cavalry, but was transferred to the U. S. Signal Corps, where he served till the close of the war. He was in many engagements, among others, Stone River, Chickamauga, Mission Ridge and around Atlanta, etc. At the close of the war he returned to his native town and engaged in the mercantile business in which he has met with success. Mr. Gwynn was united in marriage January 24, 1868, with Elizabeth, daughter of William Hartman. They have three children—William, John and Anna. Mr. Gwynn is a Republican. He has served as school director, is a member of the G. A. R., and is adjutant of Carmichaels Post 265. He and his wife are zealous members of the Cumberland Presbyterian Church.

WILLIAM HARTMAN, born in Jefferson, Greene County, Penn., February 14, 1817, is a son of Adam and Elizabeth (Stickels) Hartman. His parents were of German descent, his mother being a native of Pennsylvania and his father of Ohio. His father's family consisted of eight children, of whom William is the fifth. He attended the schools of Greene County and learned the cabinet-maker's trade, in connection with which he has devoted considerable time to contracting and building. He was united in marriage November 8, 1838, with Acsah, daughter of Daniel Smith. Their children are— Ann, wife of William F. Flenniken; and Elizabeth, wife of J. F.

Gwynn. Mr. Hartman is a Republican, and was elected justice of the peace in 1858. He has also been a member of the town council and burgess of Carmichaels. Mr. and Mrs. Hartman are members of the Cumberland Presbyterian Church, in which he has been superintendent of the Sabbath-school and served as elder for many years.

J. W. HATHAWAY, deceased, who was a merchant in Carmichaels for many years, was born in Jefferson Township, this county, May 19, 1821, and was a son of Samuel and Elizabeth (Estel) Hathaway. His mother was born in New Jersey and his father in Pennsylvania, and they were of English and Dutch descent. When Mr. Hathaway was only one year old his father died, and he was reared by his grandfather, Matthias Estel, who sent him to school and induced him to learn a trade. He chose the chair-maker's trade, served a regular apprenticeship, and worked at the business for a time at Newtown. There he began business as a clerk in a store at the age of sixteen. At nineteen years of age he went to Carmichaels as clerk. He was for many years junior member in the firm of Carson & Hathaway, merchants; afterwards buying his partner's interest he became sole owner of the large merchandising establishment there. He was an energetic, careful and thrifty manager of business, always exercising the keenest tact in his ventures and investments, yet conducting the same with a motive of honesty and fair dealing toward all, bearing the respect of everybody. Years ago when Carmichaels was the business center of Greene County Mr. Hathaway—added to a continued large retail trade—did considerable business at wholesale. He also dealt quite extensively in stock and real estate, and at the time of his death was the owner of 550 acres of valuable land. He was united in marriage January 1, 1846, with Miss Ary, daughter of William and Keziah (Wiley) Anderson, who were of Scotch-Irish descent. Her father was a millwright, and she had two brothers in the war of 1812. To Mr. and Mrs. Hathaway a family of ten children were born, six of whom, together with Mrs. Hathaway, survive the deceased. The children are— Charles, Samuel, William, Jacob and Lawrence, of Carmichaels; and Mrs. Mary McGinnis, of Lincoln, Ill. Mr. Hathaway was well known and was regarded as a man of great business ability, sound judgment and sterling integrity. He had been a member of the Cumberland Presbyterian Church for over forty-five years, and was a ruling elder in that church for thirty-two years. He was without question a true Christian.

JOSEPH HAMILTON, deceased, was a farmer and stock-grower and a successful business man. He was a self-made man, and by reason of his industry, economy and business ability, succeeded in accumulating a goodly share of this world's possessions.

He died in 1871, leaving to his wife and children over 400 acres of valuable farming land near Carmichaels, Penn. Mr. Hamilton was born in the State of Pennsylvania in 1808, was a son of Joseph Hamilton, and was of Scotch-Irish origin. His father was a manufacturer of boots and shoes. Mr. Hamilton received a common school education; he came to Greene County in 1859 and settled in Cumberland Township. His wife, whom he married in Fayette County, Penn., was Miss Catharine Coursin. Of their eight children, seven are now living—William, Elizabeth, wife of Richard Moffett; Mary, Sarah, Catharine Noah and Nancy J. Mr. Hamilton was known throughout his life as a staunch Democrat and a strict adherent of the Presbyterian Church.

I. R. JACKSON, retired carpenter and contractor, was born in Cumberland Township, Greene County, Penn., April 19, 1824. He is a son of Stephen and Hannah (Miller) Jackson, natives of this county. His grandfather, a pioneer farmer, was born in Maryland. Mr. Jackson, whose father was a millwright and carpenter, was the third in a family of five children. He learned the carpenter trade, in which he engaged in Cumberland Township for a period of thirty-five years. He was united in marriage April 12, 1846, with Mary A., daughter of B. M. and Martha (Murdock) Horner. Mrs. Jackson's parents were among the early settlers of the county. Of the seven children born to Mr. and Mrs. Jackson, only one survives— Emma C. The deceased are: James J., Mary Ann, Louisa J., Alice L., Stephen T. and Margaret A., who was the wife of William Grooms and mother of two children, one of which, James A. Grooms, is still living. Mr. Jackson is a Democrat, and has served as burgess of Carmichaels Borough. He and his wife are devoted members of the Methodist Episcopal Church.

WILLIAM KERR, manufacturer of saddle-trees, was born in Washington County, Penn., September 12, 1803, and is a son of James and Elizabeth (Boke) Kerr, also natives of Washington County, and of Irish descent. His father was a blacksmith, and reared a family of eight children. William was the third and received a common school education. He learned the saddle-tree trade, and has made it the business of his life, most of which he has spent in Cumberland Township, where he was married in January, 1824. His wife was Elizabeth, daughter of James Curl. Mr. and Mrs. Kerr are the parents of ten children, eight of whom are living. They are: Mary A., wife of Elias Flenniken, of Greensboro, Penn.; Rachel, wife of James Flenniken; John C., of Carmichaels; Lettie J., wife of Thomas Lucas; Elizabeth M., wife of William H. Sharpnack; Sarah E., wife of Thomas Nutt; Hiram A. and William W. Mrs. Kerr died August 29, 1874, a consistent member of the

Methodist Episcopal Church, to which Mr. Kerr also belongs, and has been steward and class-leader. In politics he is a Democrat.

JAMES KERR, farmer and stock-grower, Carmichaels, Penn., was born in Washington, Washington County, Penn., March 31, 1808, and is a son of Archibald and Mary (Huston) Kerr, who were of Irish and English descent. His mother was a native of Washington County, and departed this life in Greene County, Penn., in her eighty-seventh year, and his father, a farmer and hotel-keeper, was born in Ireland and died in Virginia in his eighty-fourth year. He had a family of eight children, of whom James was the fourth, and was reared on the farm in Cumberland Township. He attended the common school and chose farming as a business, working by the day and month to get his start in life. He drove hogs from Greene County to Baltimore for twenty-five cents and two meals a day. He has ever practiced the most careful economy and strict integrity in all his dealings, and is now the owner of a valuable farm of 375 acres. Mr. Kerr was united in marriage August 29, 1833, with Miss Ellen, daughter of George and Betsey (Lowery) Davis. Mrs. Kerr was born in Greene County, April 1, 1813. Her parents were natives of Pennsylvania and of German descent. Mr. and Mrs. Kerr have eight children, five living—David, Elizabeth, wife of Captain H. H. Cree; Alexander, Huston and Archibald. The deceased are George, James and Willie. In politics Mr. Kerr is a Democrat. He has served as school director in the township. They are prominent members of the Presbyterian Church.

JOHN C. KERR, manufacturer of saddle-trees, was born in Carmichaels, Penn., December 28, 1832. He is a son of William and Elizabeth (Curl) Kerr, being the third in their family of eight children. He was reared in Greene County, and early in life learned his trade with his father, who still resides near Carmichaels, where John C. has worked for many years. In 1859 Mr. Kerr married Caroline, daughter of Amos Horner. They were the parents of two children—Mary Ellen, wife of John Bell, and Margaret, wife of John Mossburg. Their mother died in 1865. Mr. Kerr was a second time united in marriage, February 9, 1869, with Elizabeth, daughter of Henry and Elizabeth (Rice) Sharpnack. Her parents were of Welsh and English descent. Mr. and Mrs. Kerr have four children, all boys—William Henry, George S., Robert O. and Jesse F. Mr. and Mrs. Kerr are devoted members of the Cumberland Presbyterian Church. In politics Mr. Kerr is a Republican, and has been a member of the town council of Carmichaels, where he has resided for over twenty-five years.

ARCHIBALD KERR, of the firm of Kerr Brothers, furniture dealers and funeral directors, Carmichaels, Penn., was born in Cumberland Township, September 22, 1851. He is a son of James and

Eleanor (Davis) Kerr, natives of Greene County, and of Irish descent. His father is one of the prominent farmers of Cumberland Township. Archibald is the seventh in a family of eight children. He received a common-school education, and early in life learned the cabinet-maker's trade. He worked by the day and job for eight years in Virginia and Pennsylvania, and in 1876 engaged in his present business at Garard's Fort, Penn., where he remained for two years. He then came to Carmichaels, where he has always had the reputation of doing first-class work. In 1873 Mr. Kerr married Frances, daughter of James Clawson. Mrs. Kerr is of English descent. They have a family of five children—Charles Edward, Lida E., Jesse, Alexander and Harry. Mr. Kerr is a leading member of the M. E. Church, and his wife is a Cumberland Presbyterian. In politics Mr. Kerr is a Democrat. He is a member of the town council, and belongs to the I. O. O. F. Lodge at Carmichaels, Penn.

NORVAL LAIDLEY was born in Cumberland Township, this county, May 4, 1829. He is a son of T. H. and Sarah (Barclay) Laidley, being the oldest in their family of twelve children. He was reared in Carmichaels, receiving his education in the old Greene Academy. Early in life he learned the saddler's trade, serving an apprenticeship at Carmichaels, where he soon engaged in the business for himself and continued therein for twelve years. He afterwards started a general store in company with his younger brother, A. D. Laidley, to whom he sold his interest in 1876 and left him sole proprietor of their merchandising establishment.

J. B. LAIDLEY, physician and surgeon, Carmichaels, Penn.— Among the best known physicians in Greene County is the gentleman whose name heads this sketch. He is a son of Dr. Thomas H. and Sarah (Barclay) Laidley, and was born in Carmichaels, August 21, 1830. The Doctor's father was also a prominent physician, and practiced in Carmichaels and vicinity for over half a century. His grandfather, Thomas Laidley, was a soldier in the Revolutionary war, and his maternal grandfather, Hon. Hugh Barclay, was a member of the Pennsylvania State Legislature in 1804. The Doctor is the second in a family of twelve children, ten of whom are now living. He received his education at Greene Academy, and subsequently studied medicine at the medical department of the University of Wooster, at Cleveland, Ohio, where he graduated March 1, 1856. He then returned to Carmichaels, where he has practiced continuously except during a part of the years 1861–'62, when he served as Surgeon of the Eighty-fifth Regiment Pennsylvania Volunteers. In 1859 he was united in marriage with Mary E., daughter of William Galbraith, who was for many years a prominent physician of Jefferson, in this county, where Mrs. Laidley was born. They have three living children—William Galbraith, Edmund Wirt and John Collier.

Dr. and Mrs. Laidley are members of the M. E. Church, in which he has been an official member since he united with the church. He has been school director for thirty years, and has been known as a friend of education. He is a member of the G. A. R., Post No. 265, of Carmichaels, Penn.

HON. T. H. LAIDLEY was born in Carmichaels, Penn. He is a son of Dr. T. H. Laidley, who was among the most prominent physicians of Greene County. Mr. Laidley was the seventh in a family of eleven children. He was reared in Carmichaels, attending the Greene Academy. He learned the trade of a tinner and followed it as an occupation for eight years. He subsequently clerked on a boat on the Monongahela River for a period of eight years. He married Sarah W., daughter of John W. Flenniken. Her father was a descendant of the early pioneers of this county. Mr. Laidley is the father of three children—Hettie, Thomas H., Jr., and Albert. Mr. Laidley is a Democrat, and has taken considerable interest in the politics of his county. He served as county auditor for several terms. He also represented his county in the State Legislature two terms, at the close of which he engaged in the mercantile business. He is a Presbyterian, of which church his deceased wife was also a member. She died in 1885.

R. S. LONG, stock dealer, farmer and stock grower.—The subject of this sketch was born in Greene County, Penn., October 24, 1835. He is a son of Jerry and Lucretia (Stephens) Long, who were natives of this county and of English origin. His father was reared on a farm where he spent the early part of his life. He afterwards made a specialty of stock-growing, in which he dealt quite extensively in the West, and succeeded in accumulating a handsome fortune, being at the time of his death, in 1863, the owner of 1,300 acres of well-improved land in Greene County, and extensive stock interests in the West. He was married in his native county, and all of his six children were born in Cumberland Township. They are as follows: Milton, Elizabeth, wife of Corbly Garard; Mary, R. S., W. S., Sarah A., wife of James Stephens, and Nancy V., wife of Wallace Eicher. Richard was reared on the farm and attended the common school. In business he has very closely followed the example of his father, and has met with about the same success. At the age of twenty-two he went west and engaged in buying stock, of which he made heavy shipments from Iowa to Chicago. He deals principally in sheep and cattle, and of the latter owns at present 900 head, in company with others in the West. His home farm consists of 261 acres of land, well stocked and improved. He was married, December 4, 1861, to Miss Phœbe C., daughter of J. K. Bailey, and they are the parents of three children—J. C., D. Annie Laurie and Lucretia V. Nellie. In politics Mr. Long is a Republican, and he and wife are members of the Cumberland Presbyterian Church, in which he is one of the leading officers.

MILTON LONG, farmer and stock-grower, P. O. Khedive, was born in Cumberland Township, January 29, 1838.   He is a son of Jerry and Lucretia (Stephens) Long, also natives of this county.   He comes of a long line of farmers, of whom his father was one of the most prominent, and also eminently successful as a cattle-dealer in the West.   Mr. Long is the third in a family of six children; he attended the common school of his district, remaining on the farm until 1861, when he enlisted in Company F, First Pennsylvania Cavalry and served his country three years.   He passed through the engagements of Gettysburg and Fredericksburg, and was also in the battle of the Wilderness.   When he came home from the army he went to Page County, Iowa, and engaged in buying and shipping stock to Chicago, Illinois.   After remaining there for a period of eight years, he returned to Cumberland Township, where he has since been engaged in his present occupation, and owns 330 acres of well improved land. In 1872 he married Mary E., daughter of Robert McClelland, who died in 1859.   Her mother's maiden name was Elizabeth Weaver; she was of German and English descent.   Mr. and Mrs. Long have one child—Mabel.   In politics Mr. Long is a Republican, he is a member of the G. A. R., and he and his wife are members of the Cumberland Presbyterian Church.

JAMES MURDOCK, retired tailor, was born in Cumberland Township, this county, August 3, 1811, and is a son of Charles and Ann (Campbell) Murdock.   Mr. Murdock's grandfather was one of the earliest settlers of Greene County, coming here among the Indians.   His mother was born in Ireland.   His father, who was of Scotch origin, was born in Greene County, Penn., in 1789.   His family consisted of eight children—six sons and two daughters, of whom James was the oldest.   He was united in marriage in 1838 with Amanda, daughter of William Bailey.   Mrs. Murdock was born in this county in 1816, and is of English descent.   To Mr. and Mrs. Murdock were born six children—Zillah, Anna E., William M., Mary (deceased), Ellis B. and Ellen.   Mr. Murdock is a Republican. He has been school director, was for two years burgess of Carmichaels, and served as justice of the peace for a period of ten years. Both are faithful members of the Cumberland Presbyterian Church. They are among the oldest and most highly respected citizens of Carmichaels.

WILLIAM M. MURDOCK, merchant-tailor, was born in Carmichaels, August 28, 1844, and is a son of James and Amanda (Bailey) Murdock, natives of Greene County.   Mr. Murdock is the third of a family of six children.   He was reared in Carmichaels and learned the tailor's trade with his father.   His first work was for the

Government. In 1862, when eighteen years of age, he enlisted as a soldier in Company K, Fifteenth Pennsylvania Volunteer Cavalry, and served until 1865. He was at the battle of Stone River and in several other engagements and skirmishes. At the close of the war he came home and worked at his trade with his father. In 1870 he engaged with his brother in the merchant tailoring business, in which they have continued quite successfully ever since. In 1866 he married Emma, daughter of William and Mary (Williams) Armstrong. They have four children—Augustus L., Mary, wife of F. Davidson; Louise and Lottie. Mr. Murdock is a member of the G. A. R. Post; and both are leading members in the Cumberland Presbyterian Church.

SIMON MOREDOCK, retired farmer and stock-grower, born in Jefferson Township, Greene County, Penn., is a son of George and Priscilla (Anderson) Moredock. His grandfather, James Anderson, was of Irish descent. Mr. Moredock's father, who was a farmer, had a family of twelve children, ten of whom grew to maturity. Simon is the fourth child, was reared in Jefferson Township, and received his education in the old stone school-house of the district. Early in life he engaged in the distillery business which he followed for ten years. He then bought a farm and has since devoted himself wholly to agricultural pursuits. In 1848 he was united in marriage with Mary J., daughter of John and Jane (Kincaid) Reynolds, who were of Welsh and Dutch descent. Mr. and Mrs. Moredock have six children—Sarah, wife of B. Sharpnack; George W., M. A., Rebecca J., Daniel and Minerva. Mr. Moredock is a Democrat; and both are members of the Cumberland Presbyterian Church, in which he has served as elder.

REV. JOHN McCLINTOCK, pastor of the New Providence Presbyterian Church, in Cumberland Township, Greene County, Penn., was born in Washington, Penn., November 10, 1808, and is a son of William and Mary (McGowan) McClintock. His mother was a native of Pennsylvania and of Scotch-Irish descent. His father was born in County Donegal, Ireland; but when quite a young man, came with his two brothers, to America and settled in Washington, Penn., where they spent the rest of their lives, all dying within nine months. Mr. McClintock is one of five children. He received his early education in the subscription school; then learned the weaver's trade, serving a regular apprenticeship of five years. When he reached his majority he entered Washington College, Penn., and graduated in the regular classical course with the class of 1836, Having chosen the ministry as his profession, he subsequently entered the Western Theological Seminary, at Allegheny, Penn., and was licensed to preach in April, 1837. He seized every opportunity of preparing himself for the high calling which he had chosen, and

33

accepted as his first work the cause of missions, the field being Smyrna, in Asia. In July, 1839, he came to Greene County and accepted his present charge, in which capacity he still continues, having outlived all but three members of his original congregation. By reason of his most earnest, efficient work, Rev. McClintock's is among the largest congregations in Greene County. He has also been instrumental in doing great good outside of his own church, having baptized 261 persons and performed 207 marriage ceremonies. He was married, in Washington, Penn., April 17, 1834, to Miss Mary, daughter of James and Margaret (Hawkins) Orr. Mrs. McClintock was also a native of Washington, Penn., born December 11, 1803, and of Scotch-Irish descent. Her grandparents came from Ireland; her father was a magistrate for many years, and among the prominent men of Washington County, where he settled in 1800. Mrs. McClintock is a lady of great piety and motherly kindness, and is most highly respected by those who know her best. Few have as many friends as this aged couple who have worked side by side in the vineyard of the Lord for more than fifty years. Their union has been blessed with six children—Margaret E., Mary, John C., a minister; and Ann, living; and James and William, deceased. Their family is highly respected, and they have a prosperous, happy home near Carmichaels, Penn., where they now reside.

REV. DR. JOHN McMILLAN was born at Fagg's Manor, Chester County, Penn., November 11, 1752. His parents, William and Margaret (Rea) McMillan, emigrated to America in 1742. They were Scotch-Irish, and devout Presbyterians. They had eighteen children. Their three sons who attained maturity were Thomas, William, and John, the youngest, whose name heads this sketch. It was his father's wish that John should be a minister of the gospel. He received a classical education at Princeton College, was first licensed to preach October 26, 1774, and was among the pioneer preachers of Washington and Greene counties. He was a strong man, and engaged in physical as well as mental labor. Early in life he formed the habit of writing and committing all his sermons. He was always greatly interested in his work, and has given account of revival meetings in which he frequently labored through a whole night. Soon after the Revolutionary war, about the year 1778, he removed with his family to Washington County, Penn., where he was the founder of Jefferson College, now known as Washington and Jefferson College, and was president of the institution at the time of his death. He was married by the Rev. Mr. Carmichaels, August 6, 1777, to Miss Catharine, daughter of William Brown. Seven children were born to them, viz: William, John, Samuel, Jane, Margaret, Mary and Catharine. Jane, the oldest daughter, was twice married, her first husband being the Rev. Mr. Morehead. She was afterwards united in marriage with Samuel Harper, a merchant and farmer, who was born and raised near Philadelphia. He spent most of his business life in Greene County, Penn., and was one of its most prominent citizens. He was an elder in the Presbyterian Church for many years, and served one term as sheriff of the county. Samuel Harper was twice married and had ten children, the youngest of whom is H. Harper, now a prominent citizen of Carmichaels, Penn. He was born in Cumberland Township, this county, September 29, 1819, was reared on the farm and attended school at Greene Academy, but devoted himself principally to farming, and met with great success. In 1862 Mr. Harper married Rebecca M., daughter of William and Rebecca (Norris) Johnson. Her parents were natives of Chester County, Penn., and of English descent. They were members of the Society of Friends. Mr. Harper is Republican in politics. He and Mrs. Harper are prominent members of the M. E. Church. Having retired from the more active duties of life, they now reside in Carmichaels, where they have a neat, substantial residence. Mr. Harper's brother, John McMillan Harper, was born in 1812, in Greene County, where he grew to manhood. He was educated at Greene Academy. His vocation was that of farming, for which he seemed especially adapted, being a powerful man, six feet and two inches in height, always strong and robust and in the enjoyment of excellent health. He was married in Jefferson Township, this county, to Miss Isabella Hughes, and they had one child, Margaret Jane, who is the wife of E. C. Stone, of Brownsville, Penn. During the late war Mrs. Stone's father, John Harper, raised a company of cavalry, of which he was soon elected Major, but by some means was defrauded out of his command. While at home, buying horses for the regiment, at which time he succeeded in getting 600, another was installed Major in his place. He then resigned and returned home, spending the remainder of his life on the farm, where he died in 1878, honored and respected by all who knew him.

PROF. W. M. NICKESON, principal of the Carmichaels High School, was born in Washington, Washington County, Penn., August 28, 1839. His parents, Solomon and Phœbe (Watson) Nickeson, were also natives of Washington County, and of Scotch and German origin. His father, who is a farmer and stock-grower, worked at the cooper's trade in early life. The Professor is a member of a family of thirteen children—five girls and eight boys. He was with his parents on the farm until eighteen years of age, and attended the public schools of Washington County. He subsequently entered Waynesburg College, where he completed the regular course of study and afterwards received the degree of Master of Arts. After teaching in Greene and Washington counties for ten years, he returned to Washington, studied law, and was admitted to practice in

1867. He resumed his teaching, however, and had been engaged therein for twenty-four years, when he was elected superintendent of schools in Greene County in 1881, and served a term of three years. Since then he has been principal of the schools of Carmichaels, making in all thirty-one years that he has been connected with the schools of this and Washington counties. In 1866 Mr. Nickeson married Anna S., daughter of William Gass, who is of Irish and German descent, and a resident of Clarksville, Penn. Mr. and Mrs. Nickeson have two children—Frances M. and William Edmon. Mr. Nickeson has served as burgess of Carmichaels, also as justice of the peace for one term. He is a prominent member of the I. O. O. F., and he and wife are active members of the Methodist Episcopal Church, in which he is trustee, and superintendent of the Sabbath-school.

I. B. PATTERSON, farmer and stock-grower, P. O. Carmichaels, Penn., was born on Ruff's Creek, in Greene County, September 28, 1834. His parents, Thomas and Dorcas (Bell) Patterson, were natives of Pennsylvania. His father was a farmer and drover, and often sold stock in the Baltimore market on commission for the citizens of Greene County. He was the father of eight children, of whom I. B. is next to the youngest. He was educated in the common schools of the county, chose farming and stock-growing for his business, and owns 355 acres of valuable land in the county. In 1858 he married Mary E., daughter of James Barns, whose portrait appears in this volume. It is said that Mr. Barns brought the first steam engine into Greene County, and was also founder of its first woolen-mill. He departed this life in 1883, at the advanced age of ninety-three years. Mr. and Mrs. Patterson are the parents of seven children—William B., Thomas, James L., Isaac N., John L., Minnie and Franklin M. Mr. Patterson is a Democrat. Mr. and Mrs. Patterson are prominent members of the Carmichaels Cumberland Presbyterian Church, in which they have ever been faithful, earnest workers.

J. G. PATTERSON was born in Franklin Township, Fayette County, Penn., August 23, 1830. He is a son of James and Jane (Smith) Patterson, who were born near Philadelphia, and of Scotch-Irish descent. Mr. Patterson's father was a farmer, his family consisting of nine children, of whom J. G. is the seventh. He was reared in Fayette County, Penn., attending Madison College at Uniontown, and Greene Academy at Carmichaels, Penn. He studied medicine with Dr. W. L. Lafferty, of Brownsville, Penn., and practiced one year at Havana, Mason County, Illinois. He then engaged in the drug business in Pittsburgh, Penn., for a period of eleven years. In 1854 he married Miss Nancy J., daughter of John McAllister, and they are the parents of two children—Julian S., who is a physician at Carlisle, Penn., and Anna, wife of George L. Denney, of Fayette County, Penn. In 1862 Mr. Patterson enlisted in the One Hundred and Sixty-eighth Pennsylvania Volunteer Infantry. When the company was organized he was elected First Lieutenant. In 1863 he resigned on account of ill-health, returned to Greene County and engaged in the oil business, and subsequently in mechanical pursuits. In politics Mr. Patterson is a Democrat, in religion a Presbyterian. His wife is a devoted member of the M. E. Church.

J. H. REA, farmer and stock-grower, P. O. Carmichaels, was born in Cumberland Township, August 26, 1831, and is a son of John and Margaret (Dowlin) Rea, who were of Scotch-Irish descent. His mother was a native of Pennsylvania, and his father, who was a blacksmith, was born in New Jersey and came to Greene County in 1803, and died November 25, 1847. Of their ten children, nine grew to maturity, the youngest of whom is the subject of this sketch. He has lived all his life on a farm, with the exception of two years spent in the army. He owns the farm of 106 acres where he now resides. He was united in marriage, August 26, 1852, with Miss Orpha, daughter of Benjamin and Mary (Long) Worthington. Mrs. Rea is of English origin. Their family consists of seven children— Calvin B., Margaret Alice, wife of James Craig; Frank L., a stock-dealer in the West; Mary M., Walter G., Anna V. and John Linn. They are all members of the Presbyterian Church, in which Mr. Rea has been elder, trustee, and superintendent of the Sabbath-school. Mr. Rea takes a great interest in educational matters, has served as school director, and filled most of the important offices of his township. In 1861 he enlisted as a private in Company F, First Pennsylvania Cavalry. At the regular organization of this company at Harrisburgh, August 17, 1861, he was elected Captain, and was promoted to the office of Major, November 14, of the same year. He was discharged for disability, January 12, 1863, and was carried home on a stretcher, in what was then thought to be a dying condition. He is a member of the G. A. R. Post.

SAMUEL W. REA, farmer and stock-grower, Carmichaels, Penn., was born in the township where he resides, February 2, 1829. He is a son of Jesse and Mary (Wright) Rea, natives of Montgomery County, Penn. His parents were of Scotch-Irish origin, and came to Greene County in May, 1828, where Mr. Rea, who was a farmer all his life, died in 1870. Samuel W. was the only son in a family of four children. He was with his parents on the farm until he attained his majority, and attended the district school in the township and Greene Academy at Carmichaels. He has devoted his time to farming and the growing of fine stock, and has met with more than average success. He owns a fine farm of 360 acres in Cumberland Township. Mr. Rea was united in marriage, in 1848, to Miss

Ruth Ann, daughter of William and Zillah (Johnson) Bailey. Their children are—Jesse L., Amanda Jane, wife of H. Kerr, has one daughter, Ruth E. Kerr; L. M., who married Josephine Hewitt, and is the father of one child, Anna Mary; John M., M. Zillah, E. F., C. Albert and Calvin W. William B., Hannah Frances, James W. and Nettie are deceased. In politics Mr. Rea is a Republican. He has been school director in his township, and filled important offices in Carmichael's Cumberland Presbyterian Church, of which his family are all members.

JOSEPH REEVES, farmer and stock-grower, was born in Cumberland Township, Greene County, Penn., November 23, 1816, and is a son of John B. and Sarah (Luse) Reeves, natives of Pennsylvania. His father was a farmer, and lived to be eighty-five years of age. His family consisted of twelve children—six sons and six daughters. Joseph was the sixth in the family, received his education in the common schools, and chose farming as his business, which he has followed all his life. He started out in the world with nothing but a willing mind and strong muscle, first working by the day and month. He has met with marked success, and is now the owner of 550 acres of well improved land where he resides. In 1840 he married Miss Rebecca, daughter of Phineas and Hannah (Ross) Clawson, who were of English descent. Mr. and Mrs. Reeves were the parents of six children, five living—Hannah J., wife of Wesley Evans; Sarah Ellen, wife of J. B. Sharp; Eliza M., wife of James Chafen; Phineas C. and John L. Their mother was a faithful member of the Baptist Church. Mr. Reeves' first son, Phineas C., is a farmer and at present resides with his parents. He was born in Greene Township, January 9, 1850, and received a common school education. In 1875 he was united in marriage with Miss Anna Davis. They have five children—Charles R., Rosa Pearl, Ernest J., Joseph B. and F. A. In politics their father is a Republican, and is a leading member in the Methodist Episcopal Church.

DANIEL RICH, farmer and stock-grower, Khedive, Penn., was born in Cumberland Township, Greene County, April 25, 1830, and is a son of David and Margaret (Morrison) Rich. His parents were also natives of Greene County, and of German and English ancestry. His father and grandfather were both farmers and among the early settlers of the county. Daniel is the ninth in a family of thirteen children, twelve of whom grew to maturity. He was reared on the farm, attending school in the township, and also graded school in Virginia. He chose farming as his occupation and is now the owner of 360 acres of valuable land in Cumberland Township, where he resides and is regarded as one of the leading men of Greene County. He lived four years in Monroe County, Ohio, where he was united in marriage, October 8, 1858, with Miss Lany, daughter of Levi

Stephens, a native of Greene County, Penn., and of German origin. They have two children—A. L., born in Monroe County, Ohio, August 13, 1859, and Phœbe C., who is the wife of Columbus Scott Their son, A. L., was reared on their present farm, in Cumberland. Township, to which his parents returned soon after his birth. He was married, October 8, 1882, to Miss Kate, daughter of C. C. Harry; and they have one child—Stephen Harry, an interesting boy of five years. In politics Mr. Daniel Rich is a Republican, and was elected justice of the peace in 1880, also in 1885. He is energetic and successful in his business, and has always held the confidence of his neighbors. He has settled up fifteen estates for heirs in the neighborhood, to the entire satisfaction of the parties concerned. His family are all members of the Cumberland Presbyterian Church, in which he has served as trustee and superintendent of the Sabbath-school.

ALBERT M. RICHEY, now a resident of Iowa, was born in Fayette County, Penn., February 10, 1810. His parents were Samuel and Elizabeth (Humbert) Richey, natives of Pennsylvania and of German and English ancestry. His father was a soldier in the war of 1812. Leaving his native county at the age of twenty-one, Albert came to Greene County, after having learned cabinet-making, in Fayette County, Penn., and carried on business until 1878. At that time he went West and engaged in the same business at Indianola, Iowa, where he still resides. His family consists of seven children. His oldest and only child in Greene County is Miss Emeline Richey, of Carmichaels, Penn., where she is owner and proprietor of a large dry-goods and dress emporium. Miss Richey is deserving of special mention, her life having been so much out of the range of most of her sex. She was reared in Carmichaels and attended Greene Academy until 1854, when she was employed by J. W. Hathaway, as clerk in his store. Here she displayed such excellent taste and good judgment in the selection and purchase of goods, and such business ability, that Mr. Hathaway soon trusted her to do all the buying in the East, and gave her complete control of the store during the last few years she remained with him. In the fifteen years she was with him Mr. Hathaway's business was far more prosperous than ever before. Miss Richey has met with the same success in her own store, which she opened in 1869. She has a good trade in dry-goods and millinery, and also makes a specialty of fine dress-making, receiving the patronage of many prominent ladies for miles around Carmichaels. She is always prompt and obliging, conducts her business in a business-like way and has met with marked success in all her undertakings.

THOMAS RINEHART, retired farmer and stock-grower, Ceylon, Penn., was born in Greene County, February 14, 1802. His parents, John and Peggy (Inghram) Rinehart, were of Irish and German descent. His ancestors were among the earliest settlers of the county, in which many descendants of both families now reside, some of them having held prominent positions therein. The present President Judge of Greene County is a nephew of Thomas Rinehart, the the subject of our sketch. Mr. Rinehart's father was a farmer all his life. Thomas was his second son and was reared in Greene County, attending the subscription schools. He manifested excellent business proclivities early in life, and was untiring in his zeal to make the best of every opportunity, as a result of which he now owns a fine farm of 200 acres, where he lives in Cumberland Township. Here he was married and is the father of two children—Thomas Franklin and Margaret Ann. Mr. Rinehart is a Democrat, and he and his wife are consistent members of church.

THOMAS W. ROGERS, photographer, who was born in Beallsville, Washington County, Penn., July 17, 1846, is a son of James R. and Sarah (McLean) Rogers, also natives of Washington County. Mrs. Sarah Rogers died in 1854. Mr. Rogers, who is a carpenter and contractor, now resides in the State of Indiana. His family consists of seven children now living—five sons and two daughters (five dead). Thomas, who is the third son, was reared in Washington County on the farm, and attended school at Beallsville. In 1861 he learned photography, at which he worked for over three years before he opened his establishment in Carmichaels, where he has been a very popular and successful photographer. In 1869 Mr. Rogers married Miss Belle, daughter of Joseph Daugherty. They are the parents of five children, viz.—Olly, Velma, Wilber, Ina and Fred. Mr. Rogers is modest and unassuming but industrious and energetic in his business, and has always had the respect and confidence of the community, from which he has received a liberal patronage. In politics he is a Republican; and he and Mrs. Rogers are among the most faithful and prominent members of the Methodist Episcopal Church.

A. J. SHARPNACK, farmer and stock-grower, of Cumberland Township, Greene County, Penn., was born August 25, 1847, on the farm where he now resides. He is a son of Henry and Elizabeth (Rice) Sharpnack. Mr. Sharpnack's father, who died in 1879, made farming the business of his life. Mr. Sharpnack is the youngest of nine children, five of whom are living. He was reared in Cumberland Township on the farm with his parents, where he attended the district school. He wisely chose his father's occupation—that of stock-growing and farming. He owns an improved and well stocked farm. In 1868 he married Caroline M. Rinehart. They have two sons—Levi and Henry. Their mother died and Mr. Sharpnack was again united in marriage with Martha, daughter of David Bowser.

Their children are—Lora, Malinda, Chester A. Arthur, Elizabeth Ann, Lilian Dell, and James G. Blaine.   Mrs. Sharpnack is a devoted member of the Baptist Church.

LEVI A. SHARPNACK, farmer and stock-raiser, Carmichaels, Penn., was born in Cumberland Township, Greene County, December 24, 1850.   He is a son of John and Sarah (Antram) Sharpnack, who were natives of Pennsylvania, and of German and English origin.   His father was an industrious and energetic farmer and stock-raiser until his death, April 8, 1858.   His family consisted of eleven children, seven living, of whom Levi is the youngest and the only son.   He was reared on the farm and received a common school education; has made choice of farming as his occupation through life, and meets with great success.   He owns ninety-two acres of valuable land where he now resides.   In 1874 he married Elizabeth, daughter of William and Susan (Curl) Armstrong.   Mr. Sharpnack is of Irish descent.   Their children are: Linton, Chauncey, Ora, Charles and Launa.   Mr. Sharpnack is a strong Democrat, and one of the most influential citizens of his township.

THOMAS L. STEWART, deceased, was born in Dunkard Township, Greene County, in the year 1813.   His parents, Leonard and Elizabeth (Ferrell) Stewart, were of English descent, and among the early settlers of the county.   His father was a farmer.   Thomas L. was reared in Dunkard Township, and followed farming as his occupation.   In 1842 he married Miss Eliza, daughter of John and Elizabeth (Hopton) Johnson.   They are the parents of three children: Joseph, Mary E. and Johnson, who married Sarah Durr, and is the father of two children—Charles and G. Pearl.   Joseph, their oldest son, was born in Cumberland Township, Greene County, October 24, 1844, and received a common school education.   In 1882 he married Miss Amanda, daughter of E. Y. Cowell.   Mrs. Joseph Stewart was a member of the Baptist Church.   She died in 1884, leaving one child, Mary.   Mr. Stewart and his sons are strict adherents to the Republican party.

ELIAS STONE, deceased, who was a farmer and stock grower, was born in Greensboro, Greene County, Penn., September 22, 1808. He was a son of James and Nancy (Sedgewick) Stone, who were natives of Greene County, and descended from its earliest settlers. The history of the family on both sides shows them to have been farmers usually, and of Irish descent.   Mr. Stone was the second in a family of eight children.   He was reared in Monongahela Township, this county, where he attended the subscription schools.   He devoted his business life to farming and the growing of fine stock.   In 1833 he married Mary, daughter of Samuel and Nancy (Lackey) Huston. Her parents were natives of Pennsylvania and of Irish descent.   Mr. and Mrs. Stone were the parents of three children.   Lizzie, Nan and

Fannie. Their mother died in 1843. Mr. Stone was Republican in politics, and a member of the Methodist Episcopal Church. He was twice married, and his widow and two children, Frank and Amanda, survive him. He died in 1872.

D. C. STEPHENSON, farmer and stock grower, was born in Greene Township, Greene County, Penn., June 5, 1826. His parents, Alexander and Rachel (Jones) Stephenson, were natives of this county, and of Welsh and Scotch-Irish descent. His grandfather and great-grandfather were Hugh and Daniel Stephenson, who were farmers and soldiers in the Revolutionary war; they came to Greene County soon after its close. His father served as justice of the peace in Greene County for a period of fifteen years. The history of the Stephenson family gives farming as their usual occupation. Mr. Stephenson's grandfather was born in Greene County, where he spent all his life. He died in 1857 in his eighty-second year. Mr. Stephenson is the oldest in a family of four children—two sons and two daughters. He was reared on the farm in this county, where he attended the district school. In 1861 he came to Cumberland Township and engaged in farming until 1869, when he came to Ceylon and kept store for a period of sixteen years. He was united in marriage, in Henry County, Iowa, with Miss Martha, daughter of Isaac and Mary (Barclay) Johnson. Mrs. Stephenson is a great grand daughter of the Hon. Hugh Barclay. Her grandfather was also Hugh Barclay, and her grandfather Johnson's name was William. Mr. and Mrs. Stephenson have eight children—Mary E., wife of Noah M. Hartley; Alexander M., a farmer; Fannie, Hugh C., of Iowa; J. W., a teacher, Anna M., Flora M. and I. T. (deceased). In politics Mr. Stephenson is a Democrat, and has served as postmaster in Greene County for fifteen years. He has made his own way in the world, and by means of his energy and untiring zeal in his business has become one of the most prosperous farmers in the county and highly respected by all who know him.

JOHNSON TOPPIN, retired farmer, Carmichaels, Penn., was born in Maryland February 25, 1808, and is a son of John and Rebecca (Johnson) Toppin. They were members of the Society of Friends, and of English descent. His father was a farmer and carpenter through life. Johnson was one of three sons and three daughters, and spent most of his life in Greene County, Penn., where he also attended school. He learned the gunsmith trade, in which he engaged for a time, then followed ship carpentering as a business. He also ran on the river as captain on a keel boat for nineteen years. He afterwards bought a farm in Cumberland Township, where he lived until 1885—the date of his retirement. In 1833 he was united in marriage with Miss Harriet, daughter of John and Jane Dalby. Mrs. Toppin was born in 1813 and is also a native of

Pennsylvania. Of their five children, three are living—two in Iowa. They are all married: Matilda, wife of William Gass; Rebecca Ann, wife of J. K. Parshall, and Almira, wife of Thomas W. Linch. Mr. Toppin is a Democrat; and his wife is a faithful member of the Methodist Church.

T. P. WARNE, farmer and stock-grower, Carmichaels, Penn., was born in Carroll Township, Washington County, Penn., January 26, 1847. He is a son of Joseph and Elizabeth (Irwin) Warne. His father and mother were natives of Washington and Chester counties respectively, and were of English and Irish descent. His father, who has met with marked success as a farmer, still resides on the old home farm in Carroll Township, Washington County, and also owns a fine farm of 250 acres in Cumberland Township, Greene County. Mr. T. P. Warne, who is the second in a family of seven children, attended school at Monongahela City, where he started in business as a coal merchant and remained there for a period of nine years. In 1882 he sold out his coal interests, and came to this county in 1885 and has since been engaged in farming in Cumberland Township. Mr. Warne was united in marriage, April 21, 1887, with Anna E. Long. Her parents were James and Mary (McClelland) Long, of English and Irish ancestry. Mrs. Warne is third in their family of six children; and is a faithful member of the Presbyterian Church. Mr. Warne is a Democrat, and one of the leading citizens of his community.

LEM H. WILEY, musician, Peoria Ill., was born in Greene County, Penn., April 17, 1844. He acquired a common school education, and worked at the blacksmiths trade with his father. In 1862 he went to Peoria County, Ill., and in the fall he enlisted in the Seventy-seventh Regiment Illinois Volunteers, as chief musician, being then only eighteen years of age. This position he filled faithfully until the regiment was mustered out of service at the close of the war. Upon returning home, Mr. Wiley became a member of the celebrated Light Guards Band of Peoria, with which he remained nine years, during which time he also opened a music business. In 1872 he was one of the twenty-four cornetists at P. S. Gilmore's World's Peace Jubilee at Boston; and has been a member and leader of a number of the noted bands in the United States. He was married, August 17, 1872, to Miss Alta, daughter of Levi Wilson, of Peoria, Ill. In 1880 he became a leader in Haverly's Original Mastodon Minstrels, organized in Chicago, and remained with them five years, during which time he played in all the large cities in the United States and most of the principal cities in the old world. In January, 1885, he became manager of the new Grand Opera House in Peoria, Ill., a position he still holds. Mr. Wiley is considered by the world a thorough musician and remarkable cornetist.

A. J. YOUNG, farmer and stock grower, Rice's Landing, Penn., was born in Washington County, February 7, 1831, and is a son of Abraham and Hannah (Rose) Young. His parents were natives of Washington and Greene counties, respectively, and of German and English ancestry. Mr. Young is the seventh in a family of ten children. He was reared in West Bethlehem Township, Washington County, and acquired his education from the common schools of his neighborhood. He chose farming as his occupation, and owns 165 acres of well improved land in Cumberland Township, Greene County, where he took up his abode in 1854. In the same year he was united in marriage with Miss Rachel, daughter of Joseph and Sarah (Swan) Ailes. The former was a native of Washington County, and the latter of Greene County, and a descendant of one of its earliests settlers. Mrs. Young's great-grandfather, John Swan, settled on the farm now owned by A. J. Young, in 1767, and had to build a fort to protect himself from the Indians. Mr. and Mrs. Young are devoted members of the Cumberland Presbyterian Church, the former ruling elder of the church. Mr. and Mrs. Young are the parents of two children— Amy H., who died when four years old; and William A., a carpenter and farmer, residing on the home farm. He was united in marriage in 1884 with Miss Maggie M., daughter of Jacob and Rachel Braden, and they have one child, Walter B.

MORGAN YOUNG, farmer and stock grower, Rice's Landing, Penn., was born in Washington County, February 8, 1829, and is a son of Abraham and Hannah (Rose) Young. His parents were of Scotch-Irish and Dutch descent. His mother was a native of Greene County and his father, who was a farmer and stock raiser during his life-time, was born in Washington County, Penn. Both died on the same day in January, 1853, his wife surviving him just four hours. They had a family of ten children. Morgan, who was the sixth, was reared on the farm, attended the common school, and has made farming the business of his life. He is the owner of a well improved farm consisting of two hundred and seventeen acres well stocked and kept in good condition. Mr. Young has been twice married; first, in 1850, to Harriet, daughter of Thomas M. and Maria (Phillips) Norris. Mrs. Young was of Dutch descent. They had four children—A. L., a teacher and farmer in Ohio; Amy M., wife of T. O. Bradbury; Mary Ellen and James E. Their mother died in June, 1876. Mr. Young's second wife was Miss Emma, daughter of Aaron and Sarah (McCullough) Bradbury, who were of English descent. Mrs. Young's father, now a farmer of this county, was for many years a farmer and tanner of Washington County, Penn. Mr. and Mrs. Young have one child, Harry H. B. In politics Mr. Young was a Democrat until 1884, since which time he has been a strong Prohibitionist, and has filled various important offices in his township.

He was justice of the peace for a period of ten years. They were both members of the Shepherds Methodist Episcopal Church, in which both were stewards, and Mr. Young has been trustee, superintendent of the Sabbath-school, and class leader for thirty years, until two years ago, when they united with the Methodist Episcopal Church at Rice's Landing.

DUNKARD TOWNSHIP.

EMANUEL BEALL, overseer of the poor of Greene County, Penn., was born in Monongahela Township, this county, December 31, 1819, and is a son of Thomas and Marian (Engales) Beall. His father was a native of Loudoun County, Va., and his mother was born in Greene County, Penn. They were of English and German extraction. Emanuel's grandfather, William Beall, was a pioneer settler of Greene County, and his maternal grandfather was a soldier in the Revolutionary war. The subject of this sketch is next to the oldest in a family of eleven children. He remained on the farm with his parents until he was near twenty-four years of age, then located in Monongalia County, W. Va., where he engaged in farming and stock-raising. Mr. Beall has made his own way in the world, and at present is the owner of 500 acres of land. He owned at one time over 900 acres. Mr. Beall is a Democrat in politics, and at present is overseer of the poor of this county. He takes an active interest in the public schools, and has served a number of years as school director. In 1869 he returned to his native county and settled in Dunkard Township, where he still resides. He has made the raising of fine sheep a specialty, and has met with great success in his business. Mr. Beall has been three times married, and is the father of eleven children, viz: John T., Bertha J., wife of Daniel Morris; William J., Charlotte, Martha, Barnet, Nancy, George W., Andrew J., Miriam and Columbus. Mr. Beall is a faithful member of the Baptist Church, of which he is clerk.

THORNTON COALBANK, a farmer and stock-grower, born in West Virginia in 1821, is a son of Samuel and Elizabeth (Everly) Coalbank, who were also natives of West Virginia, and of Welsh and English extraction. His father was a farmer all his life. Thornton, the fifth in a family of eleven children, remained on the farm with his parents until he reached his majority. He received his education in the district schools of West Virginia, and Greene County,

Penn., where he has resided since 1842. Early in life he learned the shoemaker's trade, which, in connection with farming, he has followed through life, and has met with financial success, being at present the owner of a valuable farm lying along the Monongahela River. Mr. Coalbank has been twice married, first in Greene County in 1846, to Miss Sarah Hartly, who died in 1875. By this marriage Mr. Coalbank was the father of eleven children, most of whom grew to maturity. Ten years later he married Miss Agnes, daughter of John and Susannah (Bright) Davis. Mr. and Mrs. Coalbank are leading members in the Baptist Church.

AMBROSE DILLINER, retired farmer and stock-grower, was born in Dunkard Township, Greene County, Penn., September 14, 1815. He is a son of George and Sarah (Ramsey) Dilliner, who were natives of this county, and of Irish and German origin. His grandfather, Augustine Dilliner, came to Greene County more than a hundred years ago, and settled above the mouth of Dunkard Creek, in Dunkard Township, where he spent the remaining portion of his life. George Dilliner died in 1824, leaving a family of twelve children, of whom Ambrose is the youngest son. He was reared on his father's farm and received a common-school education. Mr. Dilliner learned the millwright business in early life, and engaged therein for ten years. He owned and operated a saw-mill in this township from 1867 till 1881. He has been quite an extensive lumber dealer, but has made farming his chief occupation, and owns a farm of 130 acres lying along the Monongahela River. Mr. Dilliner was united in marriage, March 23, 1857, with Miss Elizabeth, daughter of William and Sarah (McKee) Griffin. Her parents were natives of Delaware, but have resided in Dunkard Township, this county, for about three-quarters of a century. To Mr. and Mrs. Dilliner have been born seven children, only three of whom are living—Sarah, wife of Jacob Kemp; Lydia F., wife of J. E. Sturgis, and W. L. The deceased are Caroline, Elizabeth, George S. and Walter. W. L., the youngest child living, has charge of the home farm, where he was born April 27, 1850. In 1877 he married Miss M., daughter of David and Jemima (Evans) Rich, and they have three children—Emma, Mamie and Walter S. Mr. and Mrs. Dilliner are members of the Methodist Episcopal Church, in which he has been an official member for forty-six years, and has served as Sabbath-school superintendent. Mr. Dilliner is a Republican, and a member of the Masonic fraternity.

IRA D. KNOTTS, physician and surgeon, was born in Dunkard Township, this county, March 9, 1857. He is a son of William and Ruth (South) Knotts, who were also natives of this county, and of German and Scotch descent. His father is a farmer and stock-grower by occupation, and resides in Dunkard Township, where the Doctor is in successful practice. The Doctor is a grandson of Jonathan

Knotts, who was born in this county in 1797, and was a soldier in the war of 1812. He died in Fayette County, Penn., having lived to the advanced age of ninety years. Dr. Knotts is the fourth in a family of seven children. He was reared on a farm in Perry Township, and his early education was obtained in the district school and Monongahela College at Jefferson, Penn. He subsequently went to Mount Union College, Ohio, and took the regular course up to the senior year, when he left for the purpose of studying medicine. He took the regular medical course in the University of Philadelphia, graduating with high honors in 1887. The Doctor was a diligent student, ambitious to acquire all possible knowledge in his profession. He pursued his studies with unabated zeal, and was awarded the $75 prize offered to his class for the best examination in hygiene. This trophy of honor is a fine microscope, which he finds of great value in his practice. He is a man of more than ordinary energy, and his professional skill and gentlemanly demeanor have won for him a liberal patronage where he is located, in Dunkard, Greene County, Penn. The Doctor, September 15, 1884, in a competitive examination in Latin Physics and English Composition, passed the best examination, and obtained as his reward for the same a scholarship for three years in the University of Philadelphia, Penn.

JOHN B. MASON, farmer and stock-grower, who was born in Perry Township, Greene County, Penn., July 22, 1816, is a son of Peter and Naomi (Jones) Mason. His father, who was born in Cumberland County in 1793, was the son of John E. Mason, one of the first shoemakers in Dunkard Township. Peter Mason was a farmer by occupation, and died January 1, 1888, leaving a family of eleven children. Mrs. Naomi Mason was a confirmed invalid for twenty-one years, and died August 28, 1870. John B., the second son, was reared in Whiteley Township, where he attended the district schools. He has spent a long life in his chosen occupation, and is one of the most successful and best known citizens in his township. He is the owner of a well-improved farm where he resides, near Davistown, Penn. After his mother's death Mr. Mason took care of his aged father until his death. In 1840 John B. Mason married Miss Hannah, daughter of John and Margaret (Wilson) Phillips. They are faithful members of the Methodist Episcopal Church, in which Mr. Mason has served as class-leader for over forty years. He is also actively interested in the Sabbath-school, and has been superintendent for many years.

GEORGE G. MILLER, farmer and and stock-grower, was born in Dunkard Township, this county, December 30, 1836, and is a son of Daniel and Rebecca (Garrison) Miller, who were natives of Pennsylvania, and of German and Irish extraction. Mr. Miller's father and Jonathan Miller, his grandfather, were farmers and millers by occupation. The farm where the subject of this sketch now resides is a part of a 700-acre tract of land purchased by his grandfather in 1808. Mr. Miller's grandfather died in 1849, and his father in 1887, in his seventy-seventh year. George G. was an only child. He was reared on the home farm and received a common-school education. He also attended Greene Academy and Allegheny and Waynesburg Colleges, and subsequently taught school for several years. On September 22, 1862, Mr. Miller enlisted in Company E, Fourteenth Pennsylvania Volunteer Cavalry. He was orderly sergeant of the company, and passed through many severe battles. .He was with General Averill on his famous raids to White Sulphur Springs, Lewisburg, and Salem. The U. S. Government showed its appreciation of the services rendered by the latter expedition by issuing to every man who returned from Salem a complete outfit of clothing free of cost. Returning home at the close of the war, he again engaged in teaching for a time, and always took an active interest in the teachers' institute of the county. For the past few years Mr. Miller has devoted his time and talent wholly to farming and stock-growing, and his farm consists of 230 acres of well improved land. Mr. Miller has been twice married: First, in Washington County, to Miss Margery, daughter of John and Jane (Gregg) Hopkins. She was of Irish lineage, and died in 1874. Their children were—Laura, Ellen (deceased), Estelle and Charles. In 1877 Mr. Miller married Miss Elizabeth McCormick, daughter of Joseph and Mary (Watson) McCormick, of Dunkard Township, and they are the parents of four children, viz., Wayne, Warren D., Peri and James Clifton. Mrs. Miller is a member of the Methodist Protestant Church. Mr. Miller is a Republican, and a prominent member of the G. A. R.

ASA MILLER, retired miller, farmer and wool-carder, was born in Dunkard Township, this county, May 24, 1812. His parents were of German ancestry and natives of Frederick County, Maryland. His father, Jonathan Miller, was born February 10, 1774, and his mother, Susannah (Tombs) Miller, was born January 7, 1773. They were united in marriage August 8, 1799, and came to Greene County, Penn., in 1802, where he bought a large tract of land and water-mill on Crooks Run. He immediately put in steam power, by bringing the first engine into the county. The old mill burned in 1856, and was rebuilt by our subject in 1858, and he is now using the engine he first purchased for the old mill. Jonathan and wife were the parents of eight children, five sons and three daughters, and their home was a welcome to the poor and needy. Both were members of the Dunkard Church. He died in December, 1849, and she in August, 1852. The Millers are remarkable for longevity, sagacity and uprightness of character. Of the eight children the youngest was seventy-one before any died. Jacob, the oldest, died in 1885, aged eighty-five years. Asa Miller, our subject, received a good education, attended Washington and Jefferson Colleges in Washington, Penn. He spent his early life as miller, a business he has been connected with through life. He has had success as a farmer and general business man, and owns a mill and over 200 acres of land within one mile of his birth-place in Dunkard Township. He was united in marriage in Monongalia County, West Virginia, September 21, 1837, with Mary, daughter of Owen and Elizabeth (McVicker) John. The former was of English and the latter of German descent. Mr. and Mrs. Miller are the parents of the following children —Susan E., wife of E. McElroy; William L., Jesse F., Amanda K., wife of John Keener; Henry J., an eminent surgeon and physician of Tennessee. The deceased are: J. Q. and Mary V. Mrs. Miller is a devoted member of the Dunkard Church.

I. A. MORRIS, retired farmer and stock-grower, was born September 22, 1811, on a farm near Uniontown, Fayette County, Penn., and is a son of Griffith and Hannah (Springer) Morris. His parents were natives of Pennsylvania, and of Welsh and Irish origin. His father came to Greene County in 1824, locating in Dunkard Township, where he spent the remaining portion of his life. His family consisted of eight children, of whom the subject of this sketch is the second. He was reared on the farm and received his early education in the district schools. He very naturally chose farming as an occupation, and engaged therein successfully until he retired from the cares of his more active life. His farm is well improved and consists of 200 acres, where he resides in Dunkard Township. Mr. Morris was united in marriage May 4, 1837, with Miss Nancy, daughter of Samuel and Retilda (Bright) Everly. Her father was born in Virginia, and her mother was a native of Delaware. They were of Irish lineage. Mr. and Mrs. Morris have a family of eight children—Martha J., wife of Josiah Hall; Clarinda, wife of William Hord; Clark, a stonemason; George W., a farmer; Loranda, wife of Isaac Courtwright; Samuel, a merchant at Uniontown, Penn.; Delia, wife of James Sargent, and Single. Mr. and Mrs. Morris are members of the Methodist Episcopal Church, in which he has been a class-leader and superintendent of the Sabbath-school.

JAMES McCLURE, deceased, was born in Perry Township, Greene County, Pennsylvania, February 24, 1816, and was the son of William and Jane (King) McClure. His father was born in Ireland, and his mother in Perry Township, this county. James McClure was a farmer and stock-grower during his lifetime and at the time of his death, in 1886, was the owner of 400 acres of valuable land in Greene County. He was a self-made man, having no educational advantages except such as were afforded by the subscription schools. His success in life was due largely to his great industry and unfailing determination to succeed. In politics Mr. McClure was a Demo-

34

crat, and served as assessor and school director in his township.   He was united in the holy bonds of matrimony, February 22, 1838, with Miss Susan, daughter of Reuben and Rebecca (Johns) Brown.   Her father was of Irish and English origin.   Her mother was of Welsh extraction.   To Mr. and Mrs. McClure were born twelve children, eleven of whom are living, viz: Owen, a farmer; Mary J., wife of William Hatfield, of Morgan Township; William L., a gold miner in California; Reuben M., a farmer in Iowa; Anna, Emma, Isabella, wife of Charles Haver; Miranda, Minerva, Josephine, James M., and Rebecca (deceased), who was the wife of Alfred Jamison.   Their mother is a faithful member of the Goshen Baptist Church.

THOMAS B. ROBERTS, a farmer and stock-grower, who was born in Dunkard Township, this county, July 9, 1840, is a son of David and Mary (Jamison) Roberts.   His parents were also natives of this township, and of Irish and English extraction.   His father was a farmer, drover and stock-grower, and spent his life in Dunkard Township.   Thomas B. is the youngest of a family of four children, and attended the district schools of the neighborhood.   He has diligently followed his occupation of farming and stock-growing, and owns sixty acres of good land where he resides, near Davistown, Penn.   Mr. Roberts was united in marriage in this county, November 17, 1863, with Miss Lucretia, daughter of Hiram and Elizabeth (Hunt) Stephens, and they have a family of seven children, viz: Louisa, wife of M. Donley; Mary A., Lucretia B., William Albert, Jesse Jamison, Pleasant E. and John M.   Mr. Roberts is a Republican, and has served as school director of his township.   He and Mrs. Roberts are prominent members of the Methodist Episcopal Church.

DAVID STEELE.—Among the representative farmers of Dunkard Township we mention David Steele, who was born October 16, 1838.   His parents, Jesse and Rachel (Zook) Steele, were natives of Greene County, and of Dutch and Irish extraction.   They were descendants of the earliest settlers of the county.   David's father was a farmer in Dunkard Township, and for many years resided on the farm which David now owns.   He reared a family of eight children, of whom David is the fourth.   He was reared on the farm with his parents, and attended the district schools.   He wisely chose his father's occupation, and has met with moderate success.   In 1870 David Steele married Melissa, daughter of George Stoops.   Their children are: George Lee, Edward W., Dora E., Alfred Moss and Jesse.   Mr. Steele is a Democrat in politics, and one of the most highly respected citizens in the township.

THOMAS B. STEELE, of Dunkard Township, Greene County, Penn., was born March 1, 1841, on the farm where he now resides. He is the son of John and Nancy (Bowen) Steele, who were natives of Pennsylvania, and of Irish and English ancestry.   His grandfather, John Steele, who was a farmer and drover, died in 1862, having reached the advanced age of ninety-four years. Thomas Steele's father was born in 1797 and lived to be eighty-two years of age. He was a farmer and stock-grower, and spent most of his life in Dunkard Township. His family consisted of eleven children, who all grew to maturity. Thomas, the tenth child, was reared on the home farm, attended the district school and has been an industrious farmer all his ife. He was united in marriage, January 13, 1864, with Miss Rebecca, daughter of John Stevenson. Mrs. Steele is a native of Greene County, and of English and German descent. They are the parents of five children, viz.: John M., Artie B., Sadie L., R. B. and Nannie. In politics Mr. Steele is a Democrat. He and wife are leading members of the Baptist Church.

ABRAHAM STERLING, farmer and stock-grower, P. O. Greensboro, Penn., was born in Fayette County, Penn., March 12, 1837. His parents, Andrew and Julia Ann (Mosier) Sterling, were also natives of Fayette County, and of German ancestry. His father spent his life as a farmer and stock-grower in Fayette County, and reared a family of six children. Abraham is the second in the family. He chose farming as his occupation and has engaged therein all his life, with the exception of the time spent in building roads and bridges. Mr. Sterling is a natural mechanic. He has taken several contracts for building roads and bridges, and has always completed his work satisfactorily. Mr. Sterling was united in marriage in Greene County with Miss Jemima, daughter of Asa Miller, and they had one son—Asa. Mrs. Sterling died in 1869. In politics Mr. Sterling is a Democrat. He and his brother own a fine farm of 280 acres situated in Dunkard Township.

JOSEPH SOUTH, farmer and stock-grower, who was born September 5, 1822, is a son of Elijah and Nancy (Johnson) South, who were natives of Greene County, and descendants of its early settlers. Joseph South's grandfather, Elijah South, Sr., came from New Jersey to Greene County, Penn., in the spring of 1796. He took up a tract of several hundred acres of land, a part of which is the farm now owned by the subject of this sketch. It contains 108 acres of valuable land. The Souths have usually been farmers. In 1852 Mr. South married Miss Melissa, daughter of Amos Wright, who was of English lineage. Mr. and Mrs. South have three children, viz.: John C., principal of Schools at Wichita, Kan.; Rachel M. and Dora Alice. The family are all members of the Baptist Church, in which Mr. South takes an active interest, and has served as deacon and superintendent of the Sabbath-school.

REV. FRANK SOUTH, Wiley, Penn., was born in Dunkard Township, Greene County, Penn., August 22, 1858. He is a son of Nicholas and Margaret (Lucas) South, who were also natives of this county. His ancestors were among the earliest English and Dutch settlers in this part of the State, and the history of the family shows them to have been farmers, usually, and enterprising people. The subject of this sketch was reared on the farm in Dunkard Township, and received his early education in the district schools. In 1877 he united with the Methodist Episcopal Church, and was licensed to preach in 1884. He now has charge of the Methodist Episcopal Churches at Davistown and New Geneva, Penn. Mr. South was on the farm with his parents until he reached his majority, and has since been in the employ of an oil company in Dunkard Township, and has proven himself faithful to the duties he has assumed. In 1886 Mr. South was united in the holy bonds of matrimony with Miss Ellen, daughter of Lewis Dowlin, who was born in Cumberland Township, this county, December 1, 1818. He was the son of John and Elizabeth (Gwynn) Dowlin, who came from Bucks County, and were of Scotch and English ancestry. Ellen was the tenth in their family, and is a devoted member of the Baptist Church.

L. G. VANVOORHIS, a farmer and stock-grower, born in Washington County, Penn., June 2, 1810, is a son of Daniel and Mary (Fry) Vanvoorhis. They were born and reared in Washington County, and were of German origin. His father, who was a contractor and builder, also dealt largely in live stock, and was at one time owner of a grist-mill, oil-mill and saw-mill. He died in Washington County, Penn., leaving a family of eleven children, of whom ten are living. The subject of this sketch is the second child, and was reared on the home farm, where he attended the common schools. He has been a farmer most of his life, and has resided in Greene County since 1838. Mr. Vanvoorhis has met with marked success in his business. His present farm consists of 170 acres of good land, and he has given 400 acres to his children. He was united in marriage in Washington County, November 15, 1832, with Essie, daughter of Luke and Mary (West) Fry. Her parents were natives of Washington County, and of Dutch extraction. Mr. and Mrs. Vanvoorhis are the parents of eight children: Jane, wife of Joseph Ross; Isaac, a wealthy farmer and drover of this county; Mary, wife of E. S. Taylor; Minerva C., widow of John Long; G. Jerome, Daniel F., Laura, and Dora, wife of Joseph Call. Mr. and Mrs. Vanvoorhis are members of the Baptist Church, in which he has served as deacon for a number of years. He has taken an active interest in the educational affairs of his township, and has been a member of the school board.

ISAAC VANVOORHIS, a farmer and stock-grower of Dunkard township, was born in Washington country, Pennsylvania, January 15, 1836. He is the oldest son of L. G. and Essie (Fry) Vanvoorhis who were also natives of Washington County, and of German extraction. His father, who for many years has been a prominent farmer, is now a resident of Greene County. Isaac Vanvoorhis was reared on the farm in Dunkard Township, where he attended the district school. During his early life he remained with his parents on the farm, where he commenced dealing in stock and has since spent most of his time in that business. He buys large lots of cattle in the Chicago markets, ships them to Greene County for pasture and sells numbers of them to the citizens of the county. Mr. Vanvoorhis has met with great financial success in the stock business, and also owns one of the most valuable farms in Greene County. It consists of about 500 acres of land, on which are good buildings and improvements. In 1858 Mr. Vanvoorhis married Miss Ross, a daughter of Bowen and Ann (Gantz) Ross. Mrs. Vanvoorhis is a native of this county, and is of German and Irish origin. Their children are—Anna, wife of E. J. Moore; Martin, Cora, Charles R. and A. L. (deceased). Mrs. Vanvoorhis is a faithful member of the Baptist Church. Her husband is a Republican in politics, and has served on the school board of his township.

FRANKLIN TOWNSHIP AND WAYNES-BURG BOROUGH

THOMAS ADAMSON, retired farmer and stock-grower, was born in Morgan Township, Greene County, Penn., November 9, 1819. His parents were Charles and Sarah (Hatfield) Adamson, natives of this county, and of Irish and English extraction. The Adamson family came to America many years ago, and four brothers settled in Bucks County, Penn., where they engaged in farming. They were all members of the Society of Friends. One of these brothers was the grandfather of Thomas Adamson, also named Thomas, who came to Greene County among the early settlers. He died on the farm where Charles Adamson, who died in 1868, was born and raised. Thomas is one of a family of eight children, only four of whom are now living. Early in life he learned the carpenter's trade, which he followed for six years, then engaged in farming. In 1845 Mr. Adamson had saved enough money, through industry and economy, to enable him to buy the farm of 120 acres where he and family reside. He has at different times added to that purchase until he now owns 220 acres of well-improved land. He was united in marriage, in 1843, with Sarah, daughter of John Hoge, and they are the parents of four children—Caroline, wife of Freeman Smith; Mary, wife of B. F. Bell; Stephen C. and John H. Mrs. Adamson died in 1874. The following year Mr. Adamson married Elizabeth Hoge, a cousin of his first wife. In politics Mr. Adamson is a Democrat.

CYRUS ADAMSON, farmer and stock-grower, who was born in Greene County, Penn., April 19, 1826, is a son of James and Margaret (Smith) Adamson. His parents were natives of this county, and of English lineage. His father was an industrious and successful farmer through life. Of his ten children, Cyrus is the eighth. Having been reared on the farm, he naturally took to the occupation of farming, in which he has met with success. His farm near Waynesburg, Penn., contains 224 acres of valuable land. Mr. Adamson was united in the holy bonds of matrimony, in February of 1851, with Esther, daughter of John Hoge. Her ancestors were among the earliest settlers of the county. To Mr. and Mrs. Adamson have been born four children—Margaret M., John F., James M. and Albert T. John F., the oldest son, married Margaret, daughter of Neal Zollars, and they have two children—Harry N. and Howard C. Cyrus Adamson is a Democrat. His wife is a zealous member of the Baptist Church.

J. P. ALLUM, proprietor of the Allum House, Waynesburg, Penn., was born in Richhill Township, this county, February 2, 1842, and is a son of James and Eveline (Gregory) Allum. His father, who was a farmer, was killed by a threshing machine, February 14, 1850. Of a family of ten children, Mr. J. P. Allum was the fifth. He was reared on the farm in Richhill Township, where he attended the common schools. In 1861 he enlisted in Company B, First West Virginia Cavalry, as a private. He was promoted to Second Lieutenant and served during the whole of the war, being enlisted a part of the time under the famous Gen. Custer. Mr. Allum was present at the surrender of Gen. Lee to Gen. Grant, April 9, 1865. In 1877 he came to Waynesburg, where he opened a hotel. He is a man well qualified for the business he has chosen. He was married in 1866 to Miss Jennie R., daughter of William Carroll. Mrs. Allum is a native of Greene County, and of German extraction. They have but one child living—Anna. Mr. and Mrs. Allum are members of the Disciple Church. Mr. Allum, who is a Democrat, served as jury commissioner from 1886 to 1888, and served in the council of Waynesburg one term. He is a member of the I. O. O. F.

A. I. ANKROM, farmer and stock-grower, Waynesburg, Penn., was born on the farm where he resides, April 21, 1833, and is a son of Joseph and Charlotte (Rinehart) Ankrom. His father was born in this county in 1807, and is now a resident of Franklin Township.

The subject of this sketch is the oldest of a family of four children. He received a good English education in his native township, and was a successful teacher for a number of years. In later life Mr. Ankrom devoted his time wholly to farming and stock-growing, and is one of the prosperous citizens of his township. In 1856 he married Miss Margaret, daughter of Abner and Eliza (Murdock) Fordyce, who is a devoted member of the Methodist Protestant Church. Her parents were natives of Greene County, and of Scotch-Irish extraction. To Mr. and Mrs. Ankrom have been born four daughters, viz: R. Anna, Charlotte E., Emma L. and Jennie Leona. In politics Mr. Ankrom is a Republican, and has served one term as United States Store-keeper. In early life he was an active member of the I. O. O. F.

H. B. AXTELL, attorney at law, Waynesburg, Penn., was born in Morris Township, Washington County, May 28, 1844. His parents, Zenas and Asenath (Patterson) Axtell, were also natives of Washington County, where they were married. On April 1, 1852, they moved to Morris Township, Greene County, where Mr. Axtell, who was born May 25, 1812, departed this life May 25, 1844. Mrs. Axtell, who was born June 4, 1818, resides on the old homestead in Morris Township. They were the parents of six children, five of whom are living, and all reside in this county. H. B. Axtell, Esq., the second in the family, was united in marriage, April 2, 1879, with Miss Maggie Worley, who was born in Wayne Township, this county. Her parents were David A. and Minerva (Inghram) Worley, both deceased. H. B. Axtell acquired his education in the common schools and Waynesburg College. He remained on the farm with his parents until twenty-one years of age, then engaged in teaching for a period of ten years. In 1874 he began the study of law with Messrs. Donley and Inghram, and was admitted to the bar in October, 1876. He commenced the practice of his chosen profession at Waynesburg in 1877, and since 1878 has been in partnership with J. W. Ray, Esq. In politics he is a Republican.

WILLIAM H. BARB, attorney at law, was born in Monongalia County, W. Va., September 28, 1850, and is a son of Gideon and Sarah (Webb) Barb. His parents were natives of Virginia, and of German and English extraction. His father was a farmer all his life, and died February 5, 1885. Of his family of nine children, W. H. Barb is the sixth. He was reared on the farm, where he attended the district school. In 1866 his parents moved to Greene County, and Mr. Barb entered Waynesburg College. At the age of eighteen he began teaching, and thus was enabled to pay his own expenses through school. He began the study of law with Messrs. Wyly and Buchanan, and completed his studies in the office of Messrs. Donley and Inghram. Mr. Barb was admitted to the bar October 1,

1877, and has since devoted his entire time to the practice of his profession. He is a Democrat in politics, and was elected District Attorney in 1881, holding the office for a period of three years. He has also been for several years an efficient member of the school board of Waynesburg. On May 9, 1877, Mr. Barb married Miss Buena Vista, daughter of P. A. Myers, Esq., of Greene Township, this county. where Mrs. Barb was born. They have two children—James A. and Frank.

JASON M. BELL, farmer and stock-grower, Waynesburg, Penn., was born in Morris Township, Greene County, Pennsylvania, May 21, 1807. He is a son of Jason and Sallie (Noel) Bell, who were natives of Winchester, Virginia, and of English descent. His father, who was a farmer, came to Greene County in 1795 and settled in Franklin Township. He reared a family of eight children—four sons and four daughters. Jason was reared on the home farm in Morris Township. He has successfully followed the occupation of farming through life. Mr. Bell was united in marriage, in 1833, with Cassandra, daughter of William Inghram, and they are the parents of five children—Thomas, Eliza, Maria, Alice and Harriet. In politics Mr. Bell is a Republican. He is one of the oldest and most highly respected citizens of this township.

DR. STEPHEN L. BLACHLY, so remarkable for his medical qualifications, was born in Sparta, Washington County, Penn., December 11, 1815, and has spent all his professional life in the locality where his father so long wore the wreath of medical honor. Having completed his preparatory education in Washington College, in his native county, he read medicine under the direction of his father, and afterwards entered Jefferson Medical College, at Philadelphia, from which he received his degree. He was associated with his father in the practice of his profession until the death of the latter, in 1849, practiced alone until 1877, and since that time has associated with him his son, Dr. Oliver L. Blachly. Dr. S. L. Blachly is one of the oldest practitioners in the county, and one of the oldest members of the Washington County Medical Society, of which he has been President at various times. He is a member of the State Medical Society of Pennsylvania, of which he was elected first Vice-President in 1873, and by which he was appointed Censor for the eighth district in 1874, which position he has held by annual appointment ever since. His intelligent discharge of his professional duties has secured for him the confidence of his neighbors and good will of his professional brethren. He has been a member of the Upper Ten Mile Presbyterian Church for over forty years, and has been an elder for twenty-five years. Dr. Blachly was married, January 9, 1840, to Sarah, daughter of Benjamin Lindley, a descendant of Francis Lindley who came with his Puritan brethren from Holland in the Mayflower. By this marriage there were five children, two of whom died in infancy. Those living are—Mary Minerva, wife of Stephen Day, a merchant in Sparta, Penn.; Dr. Oliver L. and Henry Spencer, a druggist of Waynesburg, who was born in Washington County, Penn., July 7, 1850. There he was reared and attended school, and subsequently attended Waynesburg College. When in the senior year of his college studies he abandoned his study and embarked in the drug business, in 1870, in Waynesburg, where he is one of the leading business men. He was united in marriage, in 1885, with Helena, daughter of Samuel Melvin (deceased), and they have one child, Stephen S. Blachly.

HON. C. A. BLACK, attorney and counsellor at law, was born in Greene County, Penn., February 6, 1808. His parents, Jacob and Margaret (Grinstaff) Black, were natives of Virginia, of English and German ancestry, and among the first settlers of Greene County, Penn. They reared a family of twelve children. The subject of our sketch was reared on a farm and acquired his education in the common schools of the county. Very early in life he commenced reading law in the office of Enos Hook, and completed his study in the office of Samuel Cleavenger, after which he engaged in the practice of his chosen profession. In 1842 he was elected State senator and served six years. He filled the office of secretary of the commonwealth under Governor Bigler, and served as the first State superintendent of public schools of Pennsylvania. Mr. Black has been a successful practitioner and has enjoyed an extensive practice. In 1872 he was elected a member of the constitutional convention at Philadelphia, Penn. In 1844, Mr. Black married Miss Maria, daughter of William Allison. Their union was blessed with two children—Mary, wife of Hon. James Inghram, and Albert of Washington, D. C. Mrs. Black departed this life in 1871. She was the idol of her family, and a general favorite among a large circle of acquaintances. She was a Christian of deep and earnest religious convictions, and a member of the Cumberland Presbyterian Church.

WILLIAM BLAIR, county commissioner of Greene County, Penn., was born in Franklin Township, March 7, 1839. He is a son of John and Margaret (Orndoff) Blair, who were natives of this county, and of English descent. The Blairs, who were among the earliest settlers of the county, came from New Jersey and settled in Franklin Township. William Blair's father engaged in the business of stone-masonry for many years. His grandfather, W. J. Orndoff, was a soldier in the revolutionary war. The farm of 125 acres, where William resides, has been in the possession of the family for more than a quarter of a century. In 1861 Mr. Blair married Catharine, daughter of John T. Hook, and sister of W. A. Hook, an attorney at Waynesburg. Mr. and Mrs. Blair are the parents of seven children—F. L., Jesse, Agnes, Lizzie, John C., Maggie and Ida H. Three of their children belong to the Disciple Church, of which Mr. and Mrs. Blair are prominent members. He has served as deacon for fifteen years and as Sabbath-school superintendent for twenty years. Mr. Blair is a Democrat and a member of the I. O. O. F. He takes an active interest in the education of his children, and has served two terms as school director.

JAMES BOYD, farmer and stock-grower, Waynesburg, Penn., was born on Ruff's Creek, March 12, 1850. His parents, James and Martha (Camp) Boyd, were natives of this county, and of German origin. James is the fifth in a family of nine children, eight of whom grew to maturity. He was reared on the home farm, attending the district school, and has engaged in farming as his chief occupation. He is the owner of a fine farm of 120 acres where he resides in Franklin Township. In 1874 Mr. Boyd was united in marriage with Miss Anna, daughter of Abraham and Harriet (Watson) Arnold, and they have an interesting family of five children—Gertrude, Wilbert, Seymour, Emery and Martha. Mr. and Mrs. Boyd are prominent members of the Baptist Church.

R. E. BROCK, M. D., read medicine with his cousins, Drs. Hugh W. and Luther S. Brock, at Morgantown, W. Va. Graduated at Jefferson Medical College, Philadelphia, March 3, '79. Has been engaged in continuous practice at Waynesburg, Penn., since that time.

C. E. BOWER, superintendent of the W. & W. Railroad, was born at Fredericktown, Washington County, Penn., April 11, 1849. He is a son of Charles W. and Charlotte (Hook) Bower, natives of Pennsylvania, and of German descent. His father was a steam engineer, and died in Waynesburg in 1885. The subject of our sketch was reared in Waynesburg, where he attended the college. During the war he and his father were engineers on a United States steamer in the Government service on the Tennessee River. At the close of the war C. E. went into the oil business in Dunkard Township. He subsequently engaged in the iron business at Waynesburg, where he still owns one-half interest in the foundry. In 1872 Mr. Bower was united in marriage with Miss Josephine, daughter of Godfrey Gordon, and they are the parents of two childern—Gerome and Oliver. He has been superintendent of the W. & W. R. R. since 1881.

JAMES A. J. BUCHANAN, attorney at law, was born in Greene County, Penn., February 8, 1824, and is a son of Andrew and Rhoda (Stephenson) Buchanan. His mother was born in New Jersey and his father in Chester County, Penn. They were of Scotch-Irish extraction. His father, who was a prominent attorney, came to

Waynesburg in 1803, where he practiced law until his death in 1848. In 1832 and '33 he was a member of the State Legislature; and from 1836 to 1839 he served as a member of Congress. He served as county commissioner of Greene County when he received fifteen dollars for his services. The subject of this sketch was next to the youngest in a family of eleven children. He was educated in the Greene Academy at Carmichaels and at Washington College. At the age of twenty he commenced the study of law in his father's office, and in 1845 was admitted to the Greene County bar. In 1855 he was admitted to practice in the Supreme Courts of Pennsylvania. Mr. Buchanan, who is a Democrat, is a member of the I. O. O. F., and a Sir Knight Templar in the Masonic fraternity. He was married in this county to Miss Mary A., daughter of Daniel Boner. Mrs. Buchanan is of Scotch origin. Of their six children only two are living—Harriet, wife of William T. Lantz, cashier of the Farmers' and Drovers' Bank of Waynesburg; and Mary A., wife of Daniel S. Walton, Esq., attorney at law of Waynesburg.

HARVEY CALL, merchant, Waynesburg, Penn., was born in Oak Forest, Center Township, and is the son of James and Martha Call. His mother was born in Ohio and his father in Pennsylvania. They were of German and Irish descent. His father was a farmer and merchant in early life, and kept a general store at Oak Forest. Mr. Call is the oldest in a family of six children. He was reared on the farm, attended the district schools, and farmed until he was twenty-one years old. In 1872 he began clerking in a store, and in 1873 went to Fairbury, Ill., where he was employed as a salesman until 1875. He then returned to his native county and was again employed as a clerk in Waynesburg for a short time, and then engaged in the mercantile business for himself in the year 1876, and has since been very successful. In 1875 Mr. Call married Martha A., daughter of Captain John Morris, of Rogersville, Penn. They have one child—Clyde Morris Call. Mr. Call is a Republican. His wife is a member of the Disciple Church.

JOHN CALL, agent for mill works, was born in Oak Forest, Greene County, Penn., September 21, 1833. He is a son of James and Sarah (Hoge) Call, also natives of this county, and of Scotch lineage. His father was a farmer and miller. He owned and operated a mill at Oak Forest for over forty years. He died in 1872. His family consisted of eight children, of whom the subject of our sketch is next to the youngest. He was reared at Oak Forest, attended the common school, and early in life learned the miller's trade with his father; in 1851 commenced working at millwrighting; in 1875 commenced contracting and building in Waynesburg, followed that business for eight years, during which time built the jail and sheriff's house. He afterwards learned the new milling process,

and contracts for and builds roller mills. He also takes contracts
for other buildings. Since 1884 he has been engaged with the Roller
Mill Company of Waynesburg. In 1855 Mr. Call married Miss
Elizabeth, daughter of William Fry. Mrs. Call was born in Center
Township, this county, and is of German origin. They have four
children, viz: William W., Mattie E. (deceased), Emma S. and La-
fayette G. Mr. and Mrs. Call are members of the Baptist Church.
He moved to Waynesburg in the year 1871.

G. W. CHAPMAN, of the firm of Lemley & Chapman, livery-
men, Waynesburg, Penn., was born in Greene County, Penn., July
15, 1851, and is a son of John and Sarah (Lemley) Chapman. His
parents were also natives of this county, and of English lineage.
His father was a farmer and engineer by occupation. The subject
of our sketch is the oldest in a family of four children. He was
reared in his native county and received his education in the district
schools. He started out in life working by the month as a farm
hand, and subsequently worked at the blacksmith's trade in Waynesburg for a time. Mr. Chapman then bought a team and engaged in
hauling and farming until 1887, when he began the livery business
in partnership with his uncle. He was united in marriage in 1880
with Lucinda, daughter of James Bradford. Mrs. Chapman is a
native of Greene County and of English extraction. Their children
are—Hattie E. and Emma L. Mr. Chapman is a Democrat. He
and wife are members of the Methodist Episcopal Church.

A. I. COOKE, agent for the Adams Express Company, was born
in Waynesburg May 7, 1853. He is a son of Joseph and Sarah
(Bowman) Cooke, the former a native of New Jersey and the latter
of Pennsylvania. His father, a journalist by profession, was engaged
in the newspaper business in New Jersey, and after coming to
Pennsylvania was an editor until the breaking out of the war. He
was the owner of the *Commonwealth*, a paper published at Washington, Penn. In 1853 he came to Waynesburg, where he edited and
published the *Eagle*, which paper subsequently merged into the
Republican. At the breaking out of the Rebellion Mr. Cooke
promptly enlisted in Company A, Eighteenth Pennsylvania Cavalry,
and was elected Commissary Sergeant of his company. He was
wounded three times, was taken prisoner, and suffered all the horrors
of Andersonville and Libby prisons. At the close of the war he
was discharged and returned to Waynesburg, where he was appointed
postmaster, and held the position for twenty years. He is now living a retired life in Waynesburg. His family consists of six children, four of whom are now living. They are George A. B., an
editor at Three Rivers, Mich.; Mary A., widow of Charles B. Bradley; Henry, a soldier killed in the battle of Winchester; Winfield
Scott, Leslie (deceased), and A. I. All the sons, except A. I. and

Leslie, served as privates in the Union army. The subject of this sketch, Mr. A. I. Cooke, was assistant postmaster in Waynesburg for twenty-one years. Since 1874 he has been express agent, and is now running a freight and omnibus line at Waynesburg. He was married in 1875 to Arabella Blackmore Adams, a daughter of Major Dawson Adams. Mrs. Cooke was born in Waynesburg. Her father was a tanner by trade, and was of English extraction. Mr. and Mrs. Cooke's children are Sallie A., Robert A. and Jessie B. Mr. Cooke Cooke is a Republican, and is a prominent member of the I. O. O. F., in which order he has taken many degrees. He is also a member of Encampment No. 119.

JACOB COLE, ex-county commissioner, farmer and stock-grower, was born in Morris Township, Greene County, Penn., October 28, 1823. He is a son of John T. and Mary (Crodinger) Cole, who were of English and Dutch extraction. They came to Greene County and settled in Morris Township in 1815, on a farm near Nineveh, resided there until 1835, then removed to Wayne Township, and spent the balance of their lives. Five of their eight children grew to maturity, and all reside in this county. Jacob, the fourth member of the family, was from his youth engaged in agricultural pursuits. He attended the common school, and subsequently bought a farm in Wayne Township and engaged in farming and stock-raising. His farm in Franklin Township contains 100 acres. In 1879 Mr. Cole retired from the active work of the farm, and has since resided in Waynesburg. The same year he was elected county commissioner and served one term. In 1845 he was united in marriage with Frances, daughter of Abraham and Mary (Hamilton) Tustin. The marriage of Mr. and Mrs. Cole has been blessed with eight children, seven of whom grew to maturity—Mary J., deceased, who was the wife of Israel Shriver; Isaac S., a farmer; Elizabeth, wife of Jesse Knight; Caroline, wife of Miner Carpenter; J. T., Abijah and William. In politics Mr. Cole is a Democrat. He is ever interested in school affairs, and has been school director in his township. He took an active interest in the Granger movement, and served as treasurer of the society for several years in Wayne Township.

DAVID CRAWFORD, deceased, was one of the prominent attorneys of Waynesburg, where he practiced his chosen profession for many years. He was born in Greensboro, Greene County, Penn., June 18, 1825, and was a son of David Crawford, one of the early settlers of the county. Mr. Crawford was the only son in a large family, and at the time of his death, which occurred in March, 1886, he had but three sisters living, viz., Mrs. Margaret Hager, of Rockford, Illinois; Mrs. Mary Barrickman, of Virginia; and Mrs. Dr. James Way, of Waynesburg. Mr. Crawford's earlier education was acquired in the rude log school-houses of Greene County. When twelve years of age he was employed to carry the Waynesburg *Messenger*, and in 1841 he walked to Wheeling, W. Va. After arriving in that city he worked in a chair factory for some time, then returned to Waynesburg and went to work in a saddle and harness shop kept by Amos Cleavenger. He improved all his leisure hours in study and his industry attracted the attention of Hon. Jesse Lazear, who was one of the prominent men of Waynesburg and cashier of the Farmers' and Drovers' Bank. Mr. Lazear gave him a position as clerk in the bank, and as all his time was not taken up with his duties there, he was enabled to attend Waynesburg College at the same time. He took an active interest in the literary society of which he was a member, and was debater for the Union society in its first contest with the Philomathean, in 1852. His opponent in this contest was Lorenzo Danford, who was afterwards elected member of Congress from Ohio. After Mr. Crawford had finished his education he read law in the office of John C. Flenniken, and was admitted to practice in 1853. He practiced law until he received the appointment of chief clerk of the Indian Bureau at Washington, D. C., which office he held during the administration of Pierce and Buchanan. He was a member of the Board of Commission and was sent to conclude a treaty with the Chippewas. He succeeded in settling without war, and so attracted the fancy of an Indian chief that he presented him with a saddle and bridle handsomely ornamented with beads and trinkets. After the expiration of his term of office, Mr. Crawford resumed his law practice and succeeded in accumulating a fair share of this world's goods. He served as cashier of the Farmers' and Drovers' Bank for a period of twelve years. Mr. Crawford took an active interest in the Democratic party in Pennsylvania and other States. He was a useful member in the Cumberland Presbyterian Church, and a strong advocate of temperance. He was united in marriage, February 5, 1857, with Miss Elizabeth, daughter of Major Remembrance H. Lindsey.

A. G. CROSS, physician and surgeon, was born at Waynesburg, Greene County, Penn., July 23, 1823. He is a son of Robert and Mary (Syphers) Cross, natives of this State. His father was among the early settlers of this county. Dr. Cross was the youngest in a family of thirteen children. He was reared on the farm near Waynesburg and received his literary education in Waynesburg College. He studied medicine under Dr. Inghram of Waynesburg, and began the practice of his profession in 1857. The Doctor has had quite an extensive practice and is one of the oldest physicians in Waynesburg. He has also written considerably for the press. His writings, which have been mostly on theological subjects and open letters to Robert G. Ingersoll, have been widely read and extensively copied.   In 1848 Dr. Cross married Miss Harriet, daughter of Jesse Rinehart, and they have a family of five children—Wilber F., Robert I., Jesse R., Marietta and Walter L.   The Doctor and wife are members of the Methodist Episcopal Church, in which he has served as local preacher, class leader, steward, trustee and superintendant of the Sabbath school.   He is a Democrat, and served one term as county treasurer.   He is a Sir Knight Templar in the Masonic Fraternity.

WILLIAM G. W. DAY was born in Waynesburg, this county, the 28th day of January, 1828, in a log house that stood on the lot adjoining the ground on which the Cumberland Presbyterian Church now stands.   His father was Aaron D. Day, once well known in the county.   He was a brick-maker by trade, carried on the business for many years, and many buildings, public and private, stand as monuments to his skill and industry.   He was born in New Jersey and came to Pennsylvania, with his father, when a small boy and settled wiih the family in Morris Township, Washington County, and died in Waynesburg in June, 1863, aged seventy-five years.   The paternal grandfather of the subject of this sketch, whose name was Moses Day, was born in Wales, and was a soldier in the Revolutionary war, serving seven years, lacking three months, when at home on a furlough on account of a wound received at the battle of Bunker Hill. The subject of this notice spent his early life in the country home, where he attended the subscription school three months in the year, and later on was a student at Waynesburg College a part of two sessions; but bad health compelled him to abandon study and gave up his purpose of a college course and pursue a different life for the time.   His first active business in life was in riding as constable for over two years, being re-elected to the office.   He was among the first officers appointed under the Internal Revenue law, holding the position of storekeeper and gauger for about three years, having received his appointment in the winter of 1866.   After this he was twice elected a member of the Town Council of the borough of Waynesburg, and for a number of years was a member of the board of trustees of Waynesburg College and one of the building committee of the new building.   In 1870 he purchased the Waynesburg Republican newspaper, organ of the Republican party of Greene County, and was editor and proprietor of the same for fifteen successive years thereafter, making a success in his new venture, and publishing, as admitted by all parties, the best newspaper ever before edited in the county.   It was his paper that introduced the propriety and said the first word in favor of building a narrow-gauge railroad to Waynesburg; and alone, without encouragement and through much ridicule, he persisted for months in writing up the enterprise, and in personal efforts, until finally friends enlisted in the cause and

the road was built. Mr. Day married Jane M., daughter of L. L.
Miner, Esq., once one of the leading attorneys at the Waynesburg
bar, and three children was the result of this union—a daughter,
Marguerite, and two sons, Lawrence Minor and Lewis Edwin
Mr. Day is a member of the Cumberland Presbyterian Church,
and a trustee of the church property at Waynesburg.

HARVEY DAY, a farmer and stock-grower of Franklin Township, was born in Greene County, Penn., June 17, 1831. He is a
son of Benjamin and Sarah (Tharp) Day, who were natives of New
Jersey, and of German origin. His father, who was a successful
farmer, came among the early settlers to this county, where he spent
the remaining portion of his life. He died in 1861. Harvey is the
sixth in a family of eight children. Having been reared on a farm,
he naturally engaged in farming as his life work, and is now the
owner of a well improved farm of 275 acres. Mr. Day is a self-
made man, having started out in life with very little means. He at
one time met with a heavy loss by fire, in which his house and other
buildings were completely destroyed. He did not yield to this dis-
couragement, however, but soon replaced them with neat substantial
buildings. In 1852 Mr. Day married Miss Louise, daughter of
Nathan and Hannah (Carter) Bane, who were natives of Washington
County, Penn. Mr. and Mrs. Day's children are: Sarah E., wife of
J. A. Maple; Hannah J., wife of E. C. Kelsey; Nancy A., wife of
Elias Piatt; May E. and Charles Benton. Their parents are members of the Baptist Church at Ruff's Creek, Penn. Mr. Day is a
Democrat, and has served as county auditor and school director of his
township. He takes a great interest in thoroughbred stock and has done
much to improve the stock in Greene County. He is a man of strong
will power and unusual energy, to which his success in life may be
largely attributed.

B. B. W. DENNY, hardware merchant, was born four miles
west of Waynesburg, October 29, 1852. He is a son of M. W. and
Jane (Luse) Denny, natives of Pennsylvania, and of English extraction. His grandparents came from England to Ohio, then moved to
Pennsylvania and were among the early settlers of Greene County.
Mr. Denny's father, who died in 1875, was the owner of 800 acres
of land, and was an extensive dealer in stock. His family consisted
of four children, B. B. W. being the second. He was reared on a
farm in Center and Jefferson townships, and received his education
in Waynesburg College. He has been engaged in farming and
stock-growing, and, in partnership with his brother, owns a hardware
store in Waynesburg. He was united in marriage January 3, 1882,
with Miss Alice, daughter of Samuel Melvin.

HON. J. B. DONLEY, an attorney of Waynesburg, Penn., was
born at Mount Morris, this county, October 10, 1838. He is a son

of Hon. Patrick and Margaret (Morris) Donley also natives of this county. His ancestors were among the earliest settlers of Greene County, and have usually been farmers. Mr. Donley's great-grand-father was a captain in the Revolutionary war, and his grandfather Morris was a soldier in the war of 1812. His father was a farmer and merchant, and was a member of the State Legislature in 1861 and 1862, serving two terms. At the age of eighty-four years he still resides at Mount Morris, where he has spent many years of his life. Of his family of eight children Hon. J. B. Donley is the fourth. He graduated at Waynesburg College in 1859, when he went West and located in Abingdon, Illinois, having obtained a position as principal of schools. In 1860 he became professor in Abingdon College. When the war broke out Prof. Donley promptly enlisted under the first call of President Lincoln, but on account of the large number offering the company was not received into the service and disbanded, and Prof. Donley continued teaching until the summer of 1862, when he again enlisted and helped raise Company I of the Eighty-third Volunteer Infantry. When the company was organized he was elected captain, being the youngest captain in the regiment. It was the Eighty-third Illinois Infantry that fought the rebels alone at the second battle of Fort Donnelson. This regiment was distinguished for the great number of large men within its ranks, and was among the best regiments organized in the State. Captain Donley was discharged in July, 1865, when he returned to his native county, and went to Albany, New York, and in 1866 graduated from the law department of the Albany University. In 1867 he was admitted to practice at the Waynesbuag bar, and was appointed register in bankruptcy during the same year, holding the position until 1869, when he became a member of the Forty-first Congress, having been elected thereto in 1868. He votes the Re-publican ticket, casting his first vote for President for Abraham Lincoln in 1860. He is president of the board of trustees of the Methodist Episcopal Church, of which he is a member. He is also assistant superintendent in the Sabbath-school. Captain Donley is president of the Waynesburg Park Company. He is a prominent member of the Knights of Honor, and a Master Mason in the Masonic fraternity. He also belongs to the G. A. R. Post of Waynesburg. Captain Donley was married in this county, in 1871, to Miss Ellen W., daughter of Col. John H. Wells, a retired attorney of Waynesburg. They have three children—Nellie W., Grace E. and Patrick. The family are members of the Methodist Episcopal Church.

THOMAS E. DOUGAL, farmer, stock-grower and speculator, Waynesburg, Penn., was born in Washington County, Penn., May 23, 1845, and is a son of David and Elizabeth (Porter) Dougal. His

35

mother was a native of Pennsylvania. His father, who was born in England, was a teacher by profession, to which he devoted most of his life, engaging a short time in farming and merchandising. Thomas was the oldest son in a family of eleven children, and enjoyed the advantages of a good education. He attended the schools in his native county, also the high school at Uniontown, Penn. He very naturally took up his father's profession, and engaged in teaching for ten years. He then engaged in farming and stock dealing; has made a success of the business and owns 178 acres of land. Mr. Dougal has been a resident of Greene County since 1865—the year he was married. His wife's maiden name was Clarissa Wanee. Her parents were Thomas and Elizabeth Wanee, natives of Pennsylvania. Mr. and Mrs. Dougal were the parents of ten children—Elizabeth E., Isabella I., Thomas A., John S., David W., Anna L., Dora B., Archibald and Mary, twins, and Viola. Mr. Dougal is a Republican in politics, in religion a Presbyterian. Mrs. Dougal is a zealous member of the Methodist Church.

R. F. DOWNEY, attorney and counsellor at law, was born in Waynesburg, Penn., May 18, 1849. He is a son of Robinson and Catharine (Inghram) Downey, who were of Scotch-Irish descent. His father came to Waynesburg in 1837 and studied law. He was admitted to the bar in 1839, and was a successful practitioner and business man. He dealt largely in real estate, having erected many of the best buildings in Waynesburg. He died in 1874. Mr. Downey was a member of the Baptist Church, of which he was a liberal supporter. For many years he edited a paper in Waynesburg. He was one of the earliest and strongest friends of Waynesburg College, never neglecting an opportunity to further the interests of that institution. His children were all students in the college and, with one exception, are graduates of the school. Mr. Downey was one of the most respected and best beloved of Greene County's citizens. His children are R. F., John J., who died in the army, Emma (deceased), F. W. and Kate. R. F. Downey, the subject of this sketch, was reared in Waynesburg and educated in the college, where he graduated in 1867. He then studied law with his father, and was admitted to the bar in 1871. He has been a successful practitioner, devoting his entire time to his profession.

J. W. ELY, physician, Waynesburg, Penn., was born in Whiteley Township, this county, September 24, 1855. He is a son of George and Mary (Warrick) Ely, who were natives of Washington County and moved to Greene County in 1840. Mrs. Ely departed this life December 30, 1887. Dr. Ely remained on the farm with his parents until he was eighteen years of age, at which time he began teaching school through the winter, and going to school during the summer months. He acquired his education in the select schools and

Waynesburg College. The Doctor was married, June 23, 1878, to Lucy, daughter of Godfrey Gordon, of Waynesburg. Mrs. Ely was born August 9, 1857. They have one child, Mary R., born August 11, 1880. In August, 1878, Dr. Ely opened a store at Garard's Fort, and in April of the next year he moved his store to Newtown, Penn., where he received a large patronage. On June 22, 1879, his store and entire property was destroyed by fire; but not being easily discouraged, he began the study of medicine with Dr. Sherbino, of Waynesburg, and graduated at the Medical College of Cincinnati, Ohio, in 1882 with high honors. He then returned to Waynesburg, and took Dr. Sherbino's place in the practice and has secured a liberal patronage in the county, being its only homeopathic physician. He is a Republican, and a member of the Methodist Episcopal Church.

JONAS ELY, farmer and stock-grower, Waynesburg, Penn., was born in Washington County, Penn., August 28, 1823. He is a son of Jonas and Euphen (Wilson) Ely, who were of German and Scotch extraction. His mother was also a native of Washington County. His father, who was a farmer and stock-grower, was born in Berks County, Penn., and came to Greene County in 1843. He settled near Waynesburg on the farm now owned by J. A. J. Buchanan, Esq. Mr. Ely reared a family seven children, of whom Jonas is the sixth. He received a common school education in Washington County, where he remained on the farm with his parents until their death. His father died in 1863 and his mother in 1860. Mr. Ely has been successful as a farmer, and is the owner of 384 acres of land. In 1870 he bought his present farm, to which he moved in 1875. The following year he erected one of the finest houses in Franklin Township, where he now resides. Mr. Ely was united in marriage in Greene County, in 1845, with Miss Elizabeth, daughter of William and Margaret (Milligan) Hill, who were of English and Irish origin. Mrs. Ely's father was born in Franklin Township in 1798. To Mr. and Mrs. Ely have been born three children—William and Jonas, farmers; and Belle, who is the wife of Jonathan Funk, Esq., of Waynesburg, Penn. Their mother is a consistent member of the Cumberland Presbyterian Church. Mr. Ely takes great interest in the schools of the county, and has served seventeen years as school director. He has also been for several years secretary of the Green County Agricultural Society. In politics he is a Republican. Jonas, his second son, was born October 15, 1848, and is a successful farmer. In 1878 he married Miss Alice, daughter of Madison Saunders, of Waynesburg, Penn.

W. W. EVANS, of the firm of Ragan & Evans, editors and proprietors of the *Waynesburg Independent*, was born in Marshall

County, W. Va., February 8, 1851. His parents were Walter and Sarah (Roberts) Evans. His father was of Welsh extraction and born in Baltimore, Maryland. Mr. and Mrs. Evans were married in Marshall County, where they remained a short time and then moved to Iowa. Here Mrs. Evans' health began to fail and they returned to Virginia, where she died in 1854. When an infant Mr. Evans was carried on horseback by his parents from Baltimore to Marshall County, W. Va. Mr. Evans' second wife was Susannah Hutchinson (*nee* Francis). She is still living. Mr. Evans died January 3, 1882. He was the father of fourteen children, twelve of whom are living. W. W. Evans, the subject of our sketch, was united in marriage, April 29, 1874, with Miss Mary, daughter of W. T. E. and Mary (Stull) Webb. Her father was a native of Wheeling, W. Va., and her mother of Louisville, Ky. To Mr. and Mrs. Evans have been born three children—Wilbert W., Erma, and Jesse (deceased). Mr. Evans remained on a farm until twelve years of age, when he went with his parents to Moundsville, W. Va., his father having been elected to the office of recorder of Marshall County. At the age of fifteen he began learning the printer's trade and has since been engaged in that business. In 1872 he purchased the *Moundsville Reporter*, which he owned for a period of seven years. He came to Waynesburg in 1880, and purchased a half interest in the newspaper of which he is now associate editor and proprietor. Mr. Evans is a member of the Knights of Honor and the Royal Arcanum. When sixteen years of age he united with the M. E. Church, of which his wife is also a member.

J. M. FUNK, lumber dealer, Waynesburg, Penn., was born in Richhill Township, this county, February 5, 1846. He is a son of Jacob and Mary (McGlumphy) Funk, of German and Irish descent, the former a native of Maryland and the latter of Greene County, Penn. His father was a farmer, and died in Waynesburg in 1884. J. M. Funk is one of a family of three children—all boys. He grew to manhood in Waynesburg, and chose farming as his chief pursuit. When twenty years of age, however, he learned the carpenter's trade, serving the regular apprenticeship of three years. In 1872 he established himself in business in Waynesburg and, although he met with a serious loss by fire, May 25, 1881, which amounted to some ten thousand dollars, he immediately rebuilt and is now owner and proprietor of a planing-mill, in which a large number of men are employed the year round. He does contracting and building, and has a number of substantial residences in Waynesburg. In 1878 Mr. Funk married Miss Belle, daughter of Jonas Ely, a prominent farmer of Franklin Township. Mr. and Mrs. Funk are members of the Cumberland Presbyterian Church. He is a Democrat, and has served as a member of the town council and of the school board in the borough. He is also a member of the I. O. O. F.

J. C. GARARD, Esq., prothonotary, Waynesburg, Penn., was born in Greene County. He is a son of Justus and Emeline (Mestrezat) Garard, also natives of this county, and of French and English descent. The family were among the earliest settlers of the county, Mr. Garard's great-grandfather being the Rev. John Corbly, one of the pioneer Baptist ministers. His grandfather Garard was a farmer, and Justus Garard, his father, was a cabinet-maker and engaged in that business for years at Mapletown, Penn. The subject of our sketch was reared in Monongahela Township, where he received his early education in the common schools. He afterwards spent some time in the State Normal School at California, Penn., and Wayesburg College. After leaving college he taught school until 1878, when he was elected clerk of the courts of Greene County and served six years. Mr. Garard was elected prothonotary in 1884 and re-elected in 1887, and has filled that office very acceptably. In politics he is a Democrat. He was married in Fayette County, Penn., in 1879, to Miss A. B. Schroyer, at Masontown, Penn.

CAPTAIN JOHN ADAM GORDON, farmer and stock grower, Waynesburg, Penn., was born in Whiteley Township, Greene County, June 16, 1816. His parents were Mark and Susan (Shriver) Gordon, who were of Irish and German extraction. His father, who was a farmer all his life, was a native of West Virginia, came to Greene County, Penn., in 1796 and settled in Whiteley Township. His family consisted of ten children. John Adam was reared on the home farm where he received his early education, and subsequently attended Greene Academy at Carmichaels, Penn. He devoted four years of his life exclusively to teaching and also taught about twenty winter terms, spending the summer months in farming, which he has made his chief pursuit. In 1880 he bought his present farm and moved to Franklin Township, where he built a neat and substantial residence in 1887. Mr. Gordon has been twice married; first, in 1842, to Miss Rebecca, daughter of John Crawford, of Carmichaels, Greene County. Mrs. Gordon died in 1853. Of their five children only two are living—Rebecca, and Rev. M. L. Gordon, D. D., now a missionary in Japan. The deceased are B. Jennings, who died when a child; John Crawford, who was a prominent physician at Waynesburg; and William Lynn, a teacher, who died in Michigan in 1886, he taught in Pennsylvania and Wisconsin and Charleston, S. C., and was principal of a college in Austin, Texas at his death. Mr. Gordon's second wife was Miss Margaret, daughter of Ephraim Crawford, of Fayette County, Penn. They are the parents of five sons: Thomas J., a farmer; Solomon, Robert who died in childhood; Edgar C. and James R. Mr. Gordon has the distinction of being the first superintendent of public schools in Greene County, to which position he was elected in 1856, and was re-elected in 1860. When the war of the Rebellion broke out he resigned and assisted in raising a company, which formed part of the Eighty-fifth Regiment Pennsylvania Volunteers (Col. Howell's). It was Company G, of that organization. Mr. Gordon was elected First Lieutenant of said company, and served in that capacity until Capt. I. M. Abraham was promoted to Major of the regiment; was then commissioned Captain by Gov. A. I. Curtin, of Pennsylvania, serving in all three.

SOLOMON GORDON, a retired farmer and-stock grower who was born in Whiteley Township, April 2, 1801, is a son of John A. and Cassandra (Holland) Gordon. The former was a native of Maryland and the latter of West Virginia, where they were married. They were the parents of seven children, the youngest of whom is Solomon. His father, who was a farmer, came to Greene County in 1795 and located in Whiteley Township, where Solomon grew to manhood. The subject of this sketch has been for many years a successful farmer in Franklin Township. He was united in marriage the first time, in 1824, with Sarah Inghram, who was a descendent of one of the pioneer families in this county, and died in 1858. They were the parents of five children—Elizabeth, wife of R. Huss; William I., a farmer who owns two hundred acres of land; Adam, superintendent of the poor farm; James, and John who was a soldier in the war of 1861 and died in the army. Mr. Gordon married for his second wife the widow of George B. Willison. Her maiden name was Sarah Manuell. In politics Mr. Gordon is a Democrat.

HON. BASIL GORDON, Associate Judge of Greene County, Penn., was born in Whiteley Township, this county, December 27, 1822. He is a son of Mark and Susan (Shriver) Gordon. His mother was born in Greene County and his father in Virginia. Both were of German extraction. His father came to Greene County when a child, and was a farmer by occupation. Basil was the fourth in a family of ten children. He was reared on a farm in this county, and educated in Greene Academy at Carmichaels, Penn. Mr. Gordon has made farming his occupation and has been very successful. He was united in the holy bonds of matrimony, May 20, 1847, with Mariar, daughter of Arthur Inghram, and they are the parents of five children, viz., John A., a farmer; Susan, Virginia, wife of Thomas Montgomery; Josiah and Alice. The Judge is trustee in the M. P. Church. He has served as township auditor, superintendent of the poor and school director.

HON. JOHN B. GORDON, deceased, was born in Whiteley Township, Greene County, Penn., December 4, 1798. He was a son of John A. and Cassandra (Holland) Gordon, natives of Virginia, where their marriage ceremony was performed. They moved to Greene County, Penn., about 1795, and remained until their demise. Mrs. Gordon departed this life in 1805 and her husband in 1816. John B. Gordon, the subject of this sketch, was the fifth of a family of seven children, of whom only one, Solomon, survives. July 12, 1847, Mr. Gordon was united in marriage with Miss Delilah Inghram, a native of Franklin Township, this county, where she was born April 23, 1821. Mrs. Gordon is a daughter of William and Elizabeth (Rinehart) Inghram, who were also natives of this county. Mr. Inghram died in 1845 and Mrs. Inghram in 1864. To Mr. and Mrs. Gordon were born five children, four of whom are living, viz., Lizzie I., George W., Lucy E. and John B. The deceased is Carrie L. George W. was united in marriage with Helen Scott, and they are the parents of two children—Lucy D. and Carrie L. Hon. John B. Gordon was reared on a farm and received instructions from his father in the art of husbandry, which honorable occupation—in connection with raising stock for the markets—he followed until his death. At that time he owned one thousand acres of land in Greene County. He, in common with many of the inhabitants of middle and western Pennsylvania, had a passion for military life. He was elected Major of the Forty-sixth Regiment of militia, held the office for seven years and took much pride in discharging its duties. Mr. Gordon served his fellow citizens in civil as well as in a military capacity. Having been elected to the office of county commissioner in 1825, he served two terms; and was a member of the House of Representatives in 1847 and 1848. Mr. Gordon departed this life December 28, 1876, and by his death the county lost a good citizen, and his family a kind father and husband.

THOMAS GOODWIN, ex-treasurer of Greene County, is at present a farmer, and was born in Franklin Township, this county, September 25, 1807. He is a son of Moses and Elizabeth (Hagan) Goodwin, natives of Maryland. His father, who lived to an old age, was born in 1790 and spent most of his life on a farm in Greene County. Of their eight children, only two are living. Thomas was the fourth in the family. He was reared on the home farm, attended the subscription schools, and has made farming his main occupation. He started out in the world with but little means, but by his great energy and patient endeavor was enabled to purchase his present farm in 1877. Mr. Goodwin is a Democrat in politics. He was elected treasurer of the county in 1873, and served one term. In 1832 he married Miss Catharine, daughter of Jesse Orndoff. Her mother's maiden name was Catharine Strosnider. Her father was a soldier in the war of 1812.

H. M. GRIMES.—Among the descendants of the pioneers of Greene County we mention H. M. Grimes, an enterprising farmer of

Franklin Township, who now owns and resides on the farm where he was born, January 26, 1837. His mother's maiden name was Margaret Muckle. She was a native of this county. His father, William Grimes, was born in New Jersey. Of his six children, the subject of this sketch is the youngest. He was reared in Franklin Township, where he received his education in the district schools. Mr. Grimes has been very successful in his chosen pursuit, and is the owner of 338 acres of land. In 1861 he married Harriet, daughter of Arthur Rinehart. Their children are—William A., J. W., Lucy, Mary E., Albert R. and H. C. Mrs. Grimes is a zealous member of the Methodist Episcopal Church. In politics Mr. Grimes is a Democrat.

D. H. HAINER, freight and ticket agent for the Waynesburg and Washington Railroad, at Waynesburg, Penn., was born in Washington County, Penn., October 9, 1845, and is a son of Henry and Elizabeth (Riggle) Hainer. His father, who has all his life been a farmer, was born in Germany, and came to Washington County, Penn., in 1832, where he lived until he moved to Richland County, Ohio, where he now resides. Mr. Hainer is the oldest in a family of eight children. He was reared on the farm, attended the common schools, and was later a student in the Academy at Savannah, Ohio, and Lexington, Ohio, Male and Female Seminary. Early in life he taught school for a time. He was then employed as a salesman in Lexington, Ohio, for five years, when he was accepted as a full partner with his former employer. He continued in the mercantile trade with him for five years, when he sold out and returned to Washington County, and engaged in farming from 1875 until 1879. He then came to Waynesburg, where he engaged in business with his uncle until 1883, when he was appointed to his present position. Mr. Hainer was married in Washington County in 1873, to Alice, daughter of David S. Walker, and they have one child, a daughter—Adda E. The entire family are members of the Presbyterian Church, in which he is an elder and also superintendent of the Sabbath-school.

SAMUEL HARVEY was born in Center Township, Greene County, March 2, 1820, and is a son of Thomas and Anna (Higinbotham) Harvey. His mother was born in Fayette County, and his father in Philadelphia. They were of English and French descent. His father, a farmer by occupation, came to this county in 1807, and settled on a tract of land eleven miles west of Waynesburg, known as the "Old Harvey Farm," and resided there until his death in 1876, in the eighty-seventh year of his age. Of his three sons, Samuel is the oldest, and was reared on said farm in Center Township, where he received an education of the rural district, and chose farming as his occupation, at the same time dealing in wool, live-stock and real estate. Mr. Harvey has been a successful business man, and is one of Greene County's self-made men, his success being entirely due to his own efforts and business ability. In 1881 he moved to Waynesburg, and is still engaged in the wool trade. In 1846 Mr. Harvey married Sarah I. Throckmorton. Their children are—William C., who enlisted, at the age of seventeen years, in Company I, One Hundred and Sixteenth Pennsylvania Volunteers, and took part, under Gen. Hancock, in the famous "Battle of the Wilderness," and died of typhoid fever in 1864; Anna M., wife of the late Dr. J. S. Barmore, of Chicago; Kate E., wife of Dr. J. T. Iams, of Waynesburg; Alice I., and Charles T., a farmer and stock-dealer, who still resides on the old Harvey farm in Center Township. Mr. and Mrs. Harvey are members of the South Ten-Mile Baptist Church, where he has served as deacon and trustee for many years.

WILLIAM THOMPSON HAYS—Among the early settlers of Waynesburg as the county seat of Greene, was William Thompson Hays, who was born in Adams County, Penn., April 8, 1775, and who died in Waynesburg, June 29, 1846. He was married in Newville, Cumberland County, Penn., to Mary McKibben, and in 1804 removed to Waynesburg, embarking in the mercantile business on Main street, on the corner now known as the "Fisher Building," opposite the present F. & D. National Bank. Afterwards, losing his wife by death, he married Sarah Wilson, daughter of James Wilson, Esq., the first post-master of Waynesburg, who lived and kept the post-office opposite the court-house on the site occupied by the Messenger building. Mr. Hays was one of the early representatives of his adopted county in the State Legislature, he and his brother, Adam Hays, who was a bachelor and came with him and made his home in Waynesburg, both having served the people of Greene in that capacity. Adam Hays was also at one time sheriff of the county, and died February 28, 1848, aged about sixty-six. W. T. Hays was also, for a period of about twenty years, phrothonotary of Greene County, he being successor of John Boreman, Esq., who was the first protho-notary of the county. In 1813, while in the mercantile business, Mr. Hays brought on to Waynesburg, and was instrumental in establishing the *Messenger* newspaper, with John Baker as editor and publisher. The paper was first printed about where the tele-graph office now is, just west of the Walton House, Mr. Hays own-ing the premises and living in the house adjoining, occupying the present site of the Walton House. He had four children who lived to reach maturity—two by each wife. By the first, George W., who was educated at Cannonsburg College, Penn., studied medicine with Dr. Hays, of Sharpsburg, Md., and died with the cholera while in the practice of his profession, at that place, in 1834. Maria C., the daughter, was married to Laurence L. Minor, a prominent attorney of Waynesburg, who died in that place in 1883, she still surviving.

By his second wife were born James W. and Henrietta. She was married to William Campbell, son of Benjamin Campbell, one of the early and prominent merchants of Waynesburg, and both her husband and herself, with a large family of children, still live in that place. James Wilson Hays was born in Waynesburg, on December 21, 1817, and received such education as was attainable in his youth in the subscription schools of the town. The first business engaged in on his own account was as editor and proprietor of the Waynesburg *Messenger* in about 1842, as successor to Hon. C. A Black. His editorial career at this time included the presidential canvas of Polk against Clay, and that of Francis R. Shunk for Governor. At a later period Mr. Hays was associated with Col. James S. Jennings as co-editor of the *Messenger*, including the presidential canvas of 1860, in which Lincoln was elected President. In 1853, during the presidency of Pierce, Mr. Hays received an appointment as clerk in the post-office department at Washington City. This position he occupied some three years, resigning on account of failing health. He held a position, in 1849–50, on the Pennsylvania Canal at Pittsburg, under appointment by canal commissioners of the State. Mr. Hays was married in 1842 to Hannah Minor, daughter of Abia Minor, Esq., and grand-daughter of Hon. John Minor, who was one of the original, or first associate judges of Greene County at its formation. Mrs. Hays died in 1862. Seven children were born to them, who lived to reach maturity, viz.—William Thompson, married to Jennie Jewell; Sarah Sophia, to Ira L. Nickeson; James W., to Emma Smith; Frances Henrietta, to James M. Ferrell; Abia Minor, to Nannie Huston; Hannah Maria, to James L. Smith, and Jesse Lazear, to Sadie Goodwin—all living at this date (1888) except Mrs. Nickeson, who died May 4, 1888. In 1867 Mr. Hays removed from Waynesburg, where he had been connected with his brother-in-law, Hon. William Cotterel, in the tanning and leather business, to Graysville, Richhill Township, and engaged in merchandising, from which place his children were all married, and where he continued to reside until October, 1887, when he returned to his native town, Waynesburg. In 1875 he was elected, on the Democratic ticket, to the senate of Pennsylvania, for the fortieth district, embracing the counties of Greene and Fayette, and re-elected to a second term on the expiration of the first.

JOSEPH S. HERTIG, dentist, was born in Fayette County, Penn., November 28, 1834, and is a son of John G. and Elizabeth (Showalter) Hertig. His mother, who was of German extraction, was born in Fayette County. His father was a native of France, and a farmer and school teacher by occupation. Dr. Hertig, the oldest of eleven children, was reared on his father's farm, attending the district school. He spent his early life as a teacher, having taught five terms in Fayette County, Ohio, and subsequently in this county. In 1858 he commenced the study of dentistry at Smithfield, Penn., and began practicing in 1868 in New Holland, Ohio. He subsequently located at Delphos, Allen County, Ohio. Returning to Fayette County in 1862, he remained for four years, then came to Waynesburg, where his skill and gentlemanly demeanor soon won for him a large and lucrative practice among the influential families of the town and vicinity. The Doctor is thoroughly posted in all the details of his profession, and devotes his time diligently to study. He was married in Fayette County, in 1864, to Miss Nancy, daughter of William Scott. Their children are—Horace and Owen, the latter a graduate of Waynesburg College, and at present a student in the Dental College at Philadelphia, Penn. Dr. Hertig is a prominent member of the Odontological Society of Western Pennsylvania.

MAJOR B. F. HERRINGTON, a farmer and stock-grower, of Franklin Township, was born in Greene County, Penn., November 18, 1843, and is a son of Thomas and Caroline (Kramer) Herrington. His father was a manufacturer of boots and shoes and carried on his business for many years in the southern part of Greene County. His family consisted of ten children, of whom B. F. is the sixth. He received his early education in the common schools of his native county, and subsequently attended Duff's Commercial College at Pittsburg, Penn. Mr. Herrington was employed as a clerk in a store for a number years, and engaged in the mercantile trade at Morrisville, Penn., in 1861. The year following he enlisted, as a private, in Company A, Eighteenth Pennsylvania Cavalry. When the regiment was organized, he was elected Second Lieutenant of Company G., and was subsequently promoted to the position of First Lieutenant and then Captain. He was taken captive and suffered the horror of prison life for sixteen months in Libby, Macon, Ga. and Columbia, S. C. Major Herrington was one of the six hundred officers who were placed under the fire of the Union gun when the Union men bombarded Charlestown, S. C. Soon after his return home he was commissioned Major of the eighth division of the National Guards of Pennsylvania and served five years, was commissioned again with same rank and assigned to duty on the staff of Gen. Gallagher as commissary of division. He again engaged in the mercantile business in Waynesburg, where he had a good trade and liberal patronage. The Major was united in marriage, in 1860, with Miss Maggie Johns. She died in 1877, leaving a family of three children—Ella, Herman and Daisy. In 1887 he began farming, and was united in marriage, the same year, with Nannie (Wisecarver) Worley. Major Herrington is a Republican, and a member of the I. O. O. F. He was the first Commander of the McCullough G. A. R. Post, No. 367.

JESSE HILL, retired farmer and stock-grower, Waynesburg, Penn., was born November 23, 1814, on the farm he now owns. His parents, Samuel and Elizabeth (Cather) Hill, were natives of Greene County, and of Irish and English extraction. His father was a farmer all his life; his family consisted of eleven children. Jesse is the youngest son. He was reared on his father's farm, educated in the old-fashioned log school-house and has made farming the business of his life. He owns 150 acres of good farming land, and valuable town property in the borough of Waynesburg. In 1841 Mr. Hill married Maria, daughter of Thomas Hoskinson. Of their six children five are living—Carrie, wife of Dr. W. S. Throckmorton, of Nineveh, Penn.; Thomas B., a physician at Ruff's Creek, Penn.; Elizabeth, wife of J. D Nulton; Willie E. and Jesse F., who was born March 11, 1853, and has charge of the home farm. He was married in 1881, to Philena, daughter of Thomas Ross, and they have two children—Frank and Willie R. Mr. and Mrs. Jesse Hill, Sr., are members of the Baptist Church. Mr. Hill was for fifteen years clerk of the county commissioners.

NORVAL HOGE, by occupation an organ builder, was born in Waynesburg, March 8, 1835. He is a son of John and Rebecca (Oakes) Hoge, natives of Pennsylvania, and of Scotch-Irish descent. His grandfather was a carpenter and came from Winchester, Va. The history of the family shows them to have been farmers and mechanics, and many of the family have succeeded in accumulating a fair share of this world's goods. Mr. Hoge, unlike his ancestors, has turned his attention to study rather than to making money. He has given most of his time to organ building, and has also engaged in repairing all kinds of machinery, making sun dials, building flying shuttle looms, etc. Mr. Hoge has made twelve organs, and his knowledge of almost any kind of complicated machinery gives evidence of unusual mechanical genius. The greater part of his life has been spent in Waynesburg. He attended the common-school and college, and early in life began to develop a taste for mechanics, being able to repair clocks and watches when a mere boy. For several years he was engaged with a Pittsburgh firm, in tuning pianos and organs, and from some of the most celebrated musicians of the United States his work has received the highest endorsements, among which is the following:

"MR. NORVAL HOGE—My Dear Sir: "Allow me to compliment you upon the magnificent manner in which you tuned the piano for our use. I have never, outside of Boston and New York, met with an instrument that stood so splendidly to pitch throughout our entire programme. It certainly shows the work of an artist. Accept my own and company's thanks for your care. Yours,

"LEM H. WILEY, WALTER EMERSON."

Mr. Hoge also repairs and runs steam engines, and since 1886 has run the engine at the roller mills at Waynesburg. In 1856 he married Catharine M., daughter of Reasin Huffman, and they have four children, viz.: Mary Elizabeth, Almira Jane, Minnie May and Thomas J. The family are members of the Waynesburg Baptist Church.

ASA B. HOGE, commercial traveler, was born in Morgan Township, Greene County, Penn., September 23, 1841, and is a son of Solomon and Rachel (Huss) Hoge, natives of this State. His father, who was a miller and grain speculator, was born in this county in 1803, and died in Waynesburg in 1878. Mr. Hoge's grandparents, who were natives of Virginia, and of Scotch-Irish extraction, were members of the Society of Friends. His father's family consisted of eight children, of whom Asa B. is the fifth. He was reared in his native county and received his education in the old Greene Academy at Carmichaels, Penn. Mr. Hoge remained with his parents until eighteen years of age, when he went to Baltimore, Md., and was for two years employed as a clerk in a store. He then went to Pittsburgh, Penn., and was salesman in a large jobbing house for a period of twelve years. In 1876 he went to Philadelphia and accepted his present position as traveling salesman, visiting the larger towns and cities throughout Pennsylvania and Virginia. Mr. Hoge has made his own way in the world. He meets with success in his business, and is the owner of valuable property on Main street in Waynesburg. He was united in marriage in 1877 with Miss Mary, daughter of John and Jane (Walker) Phelan, and sister to Richard Phelan, a prominent attorney of the Waynesburg bar. Mr. and Mrs. Hoge have a bright and interesting family of two little daughters—Jane P. and Mary Frances.

JAMES M. HOGE, attorney at law, was born in this county June 16, 1853. He is a son of Solomon and Sarah (Overturff) Hoge, natives of Pennsylvania, and of Scotch-Irish extraction. His father was a farmer and also justice of the peace for many years, and died December 6, 1874. James M. is the second son in a family of twelve children, all but one of whom grew to maturity. His paternal ancestors were Quakers and among the pioneer settlers of this county. Mr. Hoge received his education in Waynesburg College. He made a special study of surveying, and has devoted much of his time to that business. He studied law with Hon. C. A. Black, at Waynesburg, and was admitted to the bar in 1882. In 1883 he clerked in the prothonary's office, and on the death of prothonotary, was appointed by Governor Pattison to fill unexpired term, and in 1885 was appointed notary public, at the same time engaging in the practice of law. He was married in 1878 to Martha M., daughter of John McNeely. Mrs. Hoge is of Irish descent.

They have one child—Owen Solomon. Mr. and Mrs. Hoge are members of the Baptist Church. He is a Democrat, and has passed all the degrees in subordinate Lodge of I. O. O. F.

ISAAC HOOPER, tobacconist, Waynesburg, Penn., was born in Washington County, Penn., March 19, 1819, is a son of Isaac and Mary (Steen) Hooper, natives of Pennsylvania, and of Scotch extraction. His father was a farmer of Washington County. His family consisted of six children, of whom Isaac is the youngest. He was reared in the borough of Washington, where he attended school and early in life learned the cigar maker's trade. In 1842 he came to Waynesburg, where he has since engaged in his present business, selling most of his cigars in Greene County. Mr. Hooper was married in 1842 to Miss Rebecca, daughter of Samuel Prigg. She was born in Washington County, and is of German origin. They have six children, viz.: Melvina, wife of A. J. Sowers, a prominent merchant of Waynesburg; Saumuel P., a tobacconist; Mary (deceased), Virginia, wife of John Campbell; Margaret, wife of Robert Adams; and Dora. Mr. and Mrs. Hooper are members of the Baptist Church, in which he is deacon. He is a Republican, and a member of the I. O. O. F.

W. A. HOOK, Esq., Waynesburg, Penn., was born October 13, 1838, and is a son of John T. and Eliza (Inghram) Hook. His parents were descendants of the earliest settlers of Greene County, and of Scotch-Irish origin. Mr. Hook's father was a saddler by trade, and died November 3, 1883, at Waynesburg, where he had spent his life. William A., the oldest son, was reared and educated in Waynesburg. He reached his senior year in college, when on account of sickness he was compelled to give up school. He chose the law as his profession, and studied in the office of Wyly & Buchanan, in Waynesburg. Mr. Hook was admitted to the bar of this county in 1871, and in 1872 was elected district attorney, in which capacity he served for six years. He is an active member of the Democratic party, and a successful lawyer.

THOMAS HOOK, farmer, was born in Waynesburg, Penn., on the 27th day of September, 1840. He is a son of John T. and Eliza (Inghram) Hook, also natives of this county. His ancestors were among the early settlers of the county. His father, who was a soldier in the war of 1812, was a harness-maker for many years, and in later life engaged in farming. Thomas was reared in Waynesburg where he remained until twelve years of age, then moved with his parents to a farm in Franklin Township where he still resides. He attended the common school, and early in life chose farming as his chief occupation. Mr. Hook has been twice united in marriage—first, in 1863, with Miss Sarah, daughter of William Patterson, a prominent farmer of Whiteley Township. Their children are—Ida, wife of William Ely, and Lucy, a student in Waynesburg College. Mrs. Hook died in 1887. Her husband afterwards married, in 1885, Miss Susan, daughter of Uriah Inghram. She is a member of the M. E. Church. Mr. Hook is a Democrat, and has been school director in his district.

THOMAS HOSKINSON, who was born in Waynesburg, Penn., July 9, 1834, is a son of George and Sophia (Adams) Hoskinson, who were natives of Pennsylvania and of English origin. His father, who was a farmer and merchant, died in 1884. His family consisted of eight children, of whom Thomas is the oldest. He was reared in Waynesburg, and obtained his education in the graded scnools and Waynesburg College. When he was twelve years old his father moved on a farm, where Thomas remained with his parents until he was twenty years of age. He then came to Waynesburg and clerked in a general store. The main part of his business career has been spent in the mercantile trade. He was engaged in business in Waynesburg from 1864 to 1878, when he closed out his business and has since met with success as a salesman. Mr. Hoskinson was married in Waynesburg, in 1860, to Sarah A., daughter of George F. Wolfe. Mrs. Hoskinson is also a native of this county, and of German descent, and a graduate of Waynesburg College. Their children are—George Ellsworth, a printer by trade in Pittsburgh, Penn.; Lida, a teacher in Topeka, Kansas; Louise T., Franklin, and Charles W., who died at the age of four in 1877. Mr. and Mrs. Hoskinson are prominent members of the Cumberland Presbyterian Church. He is a leading member in the organization of Odd Fellows and Knights of Honor.

WILLIAM R. HUGHES, farmer and stock-raiser, was born August 18, 1851, on the farm where he resides near Waynesburg, Penn. He is a son of Hiram and Sarah A. (Burks) Hughes, who were of English extraction. His mother was a native of Virginia. His father, who was a farmer all his life, was born in Greene County, and had a family of four children, two of whom are living. He died in 1854. His oldest daughter was the wife of A. J. Lippencott, a son of William Lippencott, who is a prominent farmer in Franklin Township. William R. was reared on the farm and attended the district schools and the College at Waynesburg. He taught school for a number of years, but has made farming his chief occupation. His home farm contains 106 acres of valuable land. Mr. Hughes was united in marriage April 23, 1878, with Miss Anna, daughter of Caleb and Sarah (Greene) Rigdon. Her parents were English and natives of Maryland. Mr. and Mrs. Hughes are the parents of three children—Bertha, Clarence L. and Arthur E. Their mother is a devoted member of the Methodist Episcopal Church.   In politics Mr. Hughes is a Democrat.

JOHN T. IAMS, M. D., of the firm of Iams & Ullom, physicians and surgeons, Waynesburg, Penn., was born at Mt. Morris, this county, March 25, 1846.   He is a son of Samuel and Nancy (Grimes) Iams. His parents are natives of Pennsylvania, and of English extraction. His father was a millwright in early life and afterward a farmer. He now resides in Center Township, and is over seventyyears of age Dr. Iams is the second in a family of seven children.   He lived with his parents on the farm until he reached his eighteenth year, when he entered Waynesburg College, remaining two years.   He then taught for three years.   In 1868 he began the study of medicine in the office of Dr. Gray, of Jacksonville, remaining with him for one year.   He then entered Bellvue Medical College at New York, where he took the regular course and graduated in 1871.   He practiced at Jacksonville until 1879, when he moved to Waynesburg, where he has since resided.   Dr. Iams is a member of the State and county medical societies, and was elected a member of the American Medical Association which met in Chicago in 1886.   He was United States examining surgeon for pensions from 1880 to 1885.   He was commissioned first assistant surgeon to the Tenth Regiment, N. G. P., May, 1888.   Dr. Iams was married May 16, 1874, to Kate E., daughter of Samuel Harvey, of Waynesburg.   Their children are Annette and Samuel Harvey.

FREDERICK ILLIG, farmer and general dealer, Waynesburg, Penn., was born in Germany November 7, 1835.   His father, Charles Illig, was a brewer, and of his five children Fred is the oldest.   He was the first member of the family to come to America. In 1854 he crossed the ocean and settled in Pittsburgh, Penn., where he obtained a position as clerk in a store.   He has since made four trips across the water.   Some years later he settled in Washington, Washington County, Penn., where he soon became an active dealer in grain and cattle.   In 1879 he located at Waynesburg, where he has since carried on a large business, a principal feature of which is his creamery.   Mr. Illig succeeded in accumulating a handsome competence for himself and family.   He owns valuable town property in Waynesburg and a good farm adjoining the borough.   He also has two farms in Washington County, containing 260 acres. Mr. Illig received a liberal education in Germany.   His success in this country has been due mainly to his own industry and untiring energy.   He is a Republican in politics.   He was united in marriage in Germany, in 1854, with Miss Caroline Claser, also a native of Germany.   Their children are—Charles, Lucy, George, Carrie and William.

WILLIAM INGHRAM, a retired farmer and stock-grower, was born in Franklin Township, Greene County, Penn., July 31, 1822. He is a son of William and Elizabeth (Rinehart) Inghram, natives of this county, and of Irish and Dutch extraction. His father, who was a.farmer, had a family of seven children, four daughters and three sons, of whom William is the youngest. He was reared in his native township, received his education in the old log school-house, and has been a successful farmer all his life. He owns a fine farm of 400 acres. In 1851 Mr. Inghram married Martha, daughter of Solomon Hoge, and they were the parents of the following children— Frank, Alice, James, a farmer; Elizabeth, wife of John Murdock; Emma, Maggie, Jessie and Olive. Their mother died in 1885, a faithful member of the Methodist Church. Frank, the oldest of the family, was born June 14, 1853. He was reared in Franklin Township, and received his education in Waynesburg College. He started in life as a school teacher, but subsequently began farming and dealing in cattle, and has been successful in that business. In 1876 he married Rebecca, daughter of Uriah Inghram, and they have two interesting children—Mark and Alice.

JAMES INGHRAM, President Judge of the Fourteenth Judicial District, was born in Waynesburg, Greene County, Penn., September 12, 1842. He is a son of Arthur and Elizabeth (Cather) Inghram, who were natives of this State and of English ancestry. His father read medicine and graduated at Jefferson Medical College, after which he practiced in Greene County for many years. Dr. Arthur Inghram and wife were the parents of five children, of whom the subject of this sketch is the fourth, and was reared in Waynesburg. He acquired his education in the common schools and Waynesburg College, graduating in the classical course in 1859. He then commenced the study of law in the office of Lindsey & Buchanan, was admitted to the bar in 1863, and continued in active practice until 1883, when he was elected president judge. Judge Inghram was united in marriage in 1871 with Miss Mary, daughter of the Hon. C. A. Black, a prominent attorney of Waynesburg. The Judge is a member of the Masonic fraternity and I. O. O. F: Mrs. Inghram is a consistent member of the Presbyterian Church.

COL. JAMES S. JENNINGS was born in Waynesburg, Greene County, Penn., August 22, 1829. His father, Benjamin Jennings, was a native of New Jersey, born in 1779; in his youth removed and located near Carmichaels, Greene County, Penn.; in the year 1800 removed to and settled in Waynesburg, where he remained until his death, which occurred in the year 1861. Benjamin Jennings was a carpenter by trade, and many of the early erected buildings in Waynesburg and near by were the results of his industry and skill. He was for many years a justice of the peace in

36

Waynesburg, and served one term as county commissioner. He was twice married, his last wife being Elizabeth Stockdale, mother to the subject of this notice. Col. Jennings received his education in his native place at the public schools and Waynesburg College. He learned the printing business in the Waynesburg *Messenger* office, and was subsequently for many years co-editor and proprietor of that paper. In 1858 he was married to Laura E. Weethee, of Athens County, Ohio, a native of that State and a graduate of Waynesburg College. They have three children—William C., now a citizen of Kansas; Charles B., a printer by trade, but at present deputy postmaster at Waynesburg; and Mary L., who is also an assistant in Waynesburg postoffice. In 1863, while connected with the *Messenger* office, Colonel J. was elected to, and served one term as treasurer of Greene County. During the Gubernatorial term of Governor Pollock, of Pennsylvania, Colonel J. was honored by appointment of aid on the Governor's staff as Colonel, and the same honor conferred on him by Governor Packer. In 1867 Colonel Jennings removed to a farm in Athens County, Ohio, where he remained for about twelve years. He was there for a time engaged in the land and mineral business, with a view to develop the mineral resources of his neighborhood, and was, with this view, connected with the construction of the Ohio Central Railroad. But the panic of 1873 coming on, the enterprise that had been so promising failed to materialize in time, and his pecuniary interests, as well as those of all concerned, severely suffered. While in Ohio his Democratic friends nominated him as their candidate for the State Legislature, but being in a district hopelessly Republican, without success. He was urged by his Democratic friends in his Congressional District, and by the Democratic newspapers therein, to allow his name to be used as the Democratic candidate for Congress, but the Colonel persistently declined the nomination. His name was also prominent before the State Convention in Ohio as candidate for Governor at the time Bishop was nominated and elected. In the year 1879 Colonel J. removed from Ohio to the State of Kansas to take a fresh start and recover from the money losses sustained in his Ohio mineral enterprises. But his love for his native county had such hold on him that he concluded to return to Waynesburg, and in January, 1883, he again took charge of the *Messenger* on a lease. On the election of Cleveland to the Presidency, in 1886, he was by him appointed postmaster of Waynesburg, which position he holds at the present time, with his family around him as assistants, except the son, who is "growing up with the West."

WILLIAM R. JOHNSON, contractor and builder, was born in Cumberland Township, this county, November 30, 1834, and is a son of Richard and Mary (Smith) Johnson. His parents were natives of this State. Jonathan Johnson, his grandfather, was born in Chester County, Penn., in 1796, and came with his parents to Greene County when Richard Johnson was but a small boy. Richard was a brick-layer, and worked at his trade until his death in 1885. His family consisted of nine children, of whom six are living. William R. is the fifth, and was reared in Cumberland Township, on the farm with his parents. At the age of fifteen he learned the brick-layer's trade with his father, and has done considerable business as a contractor and builder, having erected most of the fine buildings in Waynesburg. Mr. Johnson was united in marriage, in 1855, with Miss Minerva, daughter of Reuben and Susan (Hayes) Fleming. Her parents were natives of Virginia, and of Irish descent. Their children are—Ida, widow of E. P. Lantz (deceased), and Emma, wife of J. A. F. Randolph, Esq. Mr. Johnson is a member of the Masonic fraternity.

REV. C. P. JORDAN, retired minister of the Methodist Protestant Church, was born in Greene County, Penn., January 22, 1827, and is a son of John and Rebecca (West) Jordan. His parents were natives of eastern Pennsylvania, and of English and German lineage. His father was a mill-wright by occupation. He was among the early settlers of this county, and died in 1834. His family consisted of nine children, of whom five grew to be men and women. Rev. C. P. Jordan is the only surviving member of the family. He was reared in Jefferson Township, and in Waynesburg, where he attended school. Early in life he learned the boot and shoemakers trade, which he followed as a business for five years. He then learned the carpenter's trade, at which he worked until he was licensed to preach and admitted to the Pittsburgh Conference. In 1856 he accepted his first charge, and for years has devoted his time to the ministry in Pennsylvania, West Virginia and Ohio. The greater part of his ministerial work has been in Pennsylvania, and largely in his own county. He has been an active member of the order of Odd Fellows, and was a charter member of the Sons of Temperance society in this county. He has been actively engaged in the mission work of the church, and has organized fifteen Methodist Protestant churches during his ministry. He was a revivalist in the true sense of the word. In 1861 Rev. Jordan married Mrs. Maria Cunningham. His first wife, whom he married in 1850, was Mary, daughter of Nicholas Johnson. She and her two children died in 1854, all within four days.

HIRAM KENT, of the firm of Kent & Driscoll, carriage manufacturers, Waynesburg, Penn., was born in Center Township, this county, July 27, 1847, and is a son of John and Keziah (Shields) Kent. His ancestors were among the early settlers of Greene County. His father, a farmer, had a family of thirteen children, of whom Hiram is the eighth, and was reared in his native township. He attended the common schools, and in early life learned the wagon-maker's trade, at which he worked until 1880, when he began his present business. In 1871 Mr. Kent married Miss Lucy A., daugh-ter of Dawson McClelland, and they have three children—Minnie R., Nancy Maria and Z. Wilber. Mr. Kent is a Democrat, and a prominent member of the I. O. O. F. He is now Noble Grand of the Lodge, No. 469, in Waynesburg.

COL. JOHN M. KENT, born in Waynesburg, Penn., February 29, 1836, is a son of Peter M. and Mary (Hook) Kent, who were of English and Irish origin. His father, who was a native of Ohio, came to Greene County, Penn., when he was a young man, taught school for a number of years, and later in life worked at the stone-mason's trade. He died in 1852. Col. Kent, the third in a family of eight children, was reared in Greene County, and received his early education in the common schools. He was a plasterer by trade, also engaged in contracting and building until the war broke out. He enlisted in Company I, Eighth Pennsylvania Reserves, was elected First Lieutenant and served in that capacity one year. He was then elected Captain for the remainder of his term of service. He returned home and raised a company, and was elected Captain of the Fifth Pennsylvania Heavy Artillery, in Company K, in which position he served until the close of the war. Col. Kent was twice wounded, first at the battle of Fredericksburg, Va., in December, 1862, when he was reported as among the killed, having been pro-nounced by the physician mortally wounded. The second time he was wounded at Spottsylvania. He participated in many skirmishes and ten regular battles, among which were the Seven Days' battle in front of Richmond, Bull Run, South Mountain and Antietam, in 1862, and the Wilderness and Spottsylvania battles in 1864. At the close of the war Col. Kent returned to Waynesburg, where for five years he engaged in his former business of contracting and building. In 1869 he was appointed United States Store-keeper and Gauger, which position he held for sixteen years. In 1874 he enlisted in the Pennsylvania National Guards, in Company K of the Tenth Regi-ment; was elected Captain, and soon after elected Major. He was subsequently elected to the position of Lieutenant-Colonel, in which capacity he served until he resigned in 1887. In 1886 he took charge of the Hotel Walton, of which he was proprietor for nearly two years, when he removed with his family to Pittsburgh, Penn. The Colonel was married September 21, 1871, to Nanna A. Wallace, a native of Pittsburgh, Penn., and of Scotch-Irish descent. They are the parents of two children—William H. and James W. Mrs. Kent is a member of the Presbyterian Church. The Colonel is a Republican in politics. He has served as a member of the town council, and as Quartermaster of the G. A. R. Post at Waynesburg. He was always noted for his energy and zeal in organizing and conducting military and civic parades and demonstrations in his native town.

CAPT. W. C. KIMBER, fire insurance agent, was born in Fayette County, Penn., April 11, 1821. He is a son of Benedict and Mary S. (Vernon) Kimber, natives of Pennsylvania, and of English descent. His father was a glass-blower in early life, but later was engaged in boat-making. He owned and operated a number of boats, and was for many years Captain of a steamboat. The subject of our sketch was the oldest of a family of six children, and was reared in Brownsville, Penn., where he attended school. When quite a young man he went on the river with his father. He subsequently became Captain of the steamboat "Empire," one of his father's boats running on the Ohio and Mississippi rivers. Capt. Kimber was on the river from 1838 to 1885, with the exception of fifteen years. A part of that time he was engaged in transporting freight across the plains, and part of the time in the milling business. In 1859 he was elected to the Legislature of Kansas from Doniphan County, serving the first term after the organization of the State. He was married at Brownsville, Penn., in 1846, to Miss Dorotha Ann, daughter of Dr. Henry W. Stoy. They were the parents of three children, viz: Lewis E., book-keeper for the National Transit Company at Oil City, Penn.; Charles E., a miner in Colorado, and Laura D., who died in Waynesburg in 1878. Mrs. Kimber died at Oil City in 1883.

I. H. KNOX, editor of the Waynesburg *Republican*, was born at East Finley, Washington County, Penn., April 23, 1862. He is a son of John S. Knox, who has been a merchant and postmaster at East Finley for thirty-five years. His parents were of English and Scotch descent. Mr. Knox is one of a family of eight children, four of whom are now living. He was reared in Washington County, and attended Waynesburg College. When he left Waynesburg College he was a member of the senior class. During a period of three years he was a clerk in his father's store at East Finley, and was also for some time a salesman in a dry goods store at Pittsburgh; but on leaving college turned his attention to journalistic work. In 1884 he bought one-half interest in the Waynesburg *Republican*, in company with W. G. W. Day. Mr. Day retired in 1885, since which time Mr. Knox has edited and had charge of the paper. He is a Republican, and edits the only Republican newspaper in the county. On September 15, 1886, he was married to Miss Theodosia B., daughter of G. W. G. and Carrie (Throckmorton) Waddell. Mrs. Knox is a graduate of Waynesburg College, in the class of 1884. She is of English descent, and a member of the Cumberland Presbyterian

Church. Mr. Knox is a member of the Methodist Episcopal Church, in which he is secretary of the board of trustees.

P. A. KNOX, attorney, Waynesburg, Penn., was born in Bentleysville, Washington County, November 17, 1842. He is a son of William and Rosannah (Clark) Knox. His parents, who were natives of Washington County, Penn., were of Scotch and Irish origin. His father was a carpenter and mill-wright by occupation, and spent most of his life in Washington, Allegheny and Greene counties. In 1848 he went to Allegheny County, and in 1849 removed to Greene County and settled in Carmichaels, where he resided until his death, June 4, 1884. He was the father of three children, of whom P. A. Knox is the second. Mr. Knox received his earliest education at the public schools and at Greene Academy, and subsequently attended Waynesburg College, where he graduated in 1864 in the regular classical course. He began teaching school in 1858, when not quite sixteen years of age, and taught almost every winter until 1868. In 1866 he began the study of law with Messrs. Wyly and Buchanan. He was admitted to the bar in 1868, and commenced the practice of law in Waynesburg the following year. In March, 1869, he was appointed to succeed Hon. J. B. Donley as register in bankruptcy for the twenty-fourth district, which was then composed of Greene, Washington, Beaver and Lawrence counties. Mr. Knox, who is a Republican, holds the office of United States Commissioner by ap pointment. He was married in 1868 to Miss Martha H., daughter of James P. Parker. Their children are—Luella, William Parker, James Albert and John Clark Knox.

W. T. LANTZ, cashier of the Farmers and Drovers National Bank of Waynesburg, is one of the substantial and enterprising citizens of Greene County. He was born in Blacksville, West Virginia, October 25, 1842. His parents, William and Sarah (Thomas) Lantz, were also natives of West Virginia. Their family consisted of nine children, of whom four are living. Mr. W. T. Lantz is the sixth and was reared in Blacksville where he obtained his early education, and afterward attended the college in Waynesburg. In 1872 he opened a store in Waynesburg, and began taking an active interest in the enterprises of the county—among which was the building of the Waynesburg & Washington Railroad. Mr. Lantz was a member of the building committee with S. W. Scott, Jacob Swart and others, and was also a director of the road. These gentlemen are deserving of credit for the active interest they manifested in that enterprise. Again we find Mr. Lantz and others taking an active interest in building the Waynesburg Roller Mills. In 1876 he was elected president of the Waynesburg Agricultural Association, and in 1878 he was elected to his present position in the Farmers and Drovers Bank. He is one of the trustees of the college, and a member of the I. O. O. F. Mr. Lantz was united in marriage in Waynesburg with Miss Harriet, daughter of James A. Buchanan, a prominent attorney of the Greene County bar. They have one son, an intelligent and promising young man, named James for his grandfather. Mrs. Lantz is a consistent member of the Presbyterian Church.

J. S. LEMLEY, sheriff of Greene County, Penn., was born in Springhill Township, this county, March 22, 1845. He is a son of Israel and Mazy (White) Lemley, natives of this county, who were of German origin. His father was a farmer, and died at the early age of thirty-three. Mr. Lemley was the youngest in a family of four children—two boys and two girls. His ancestors were among the early farmers of Springhill Township. He was reared on the farm, attended the common school, and was a farmer by occupation. Mr. Lemley is a Democrat, and was elected sheriff of the county in 1885. He was justice of the peace while a resident of Whitely Township. In 1867 Mr. Lemley married Jane, daughter of David Lapping. Mrs. Lemley is of Irish descent. They have one child, a daughter, Lizzie. Mr. and Mrs. Lemley and their daughter are members of the Methodist Episcopal Church.

MORRIS LEVINO, merchant, of the firm of Levino Brothers, was born in Germany, June 20, 1863. His parents, Alexander and Fannie (Helburn) Levino, were also natives of Germany. Mr. Levino's father was a teacher in Germany, spending his life in that profession in which he was very successful. Mr. Morris Levino, the youngest in the family of four children, came to America in 1877, and clerked for three months in New York City. He then went to Lewisburg, Penn., where he was employed as a salesman for a period of two years. In 1880 he became the junior member of the firm of A. Levino & Brother, of Waynesburg. In 1882 they established a branch store at Mercer, Penn., and have been very successful in the business. The subject of our sketch has charge of the Waynesburg store, where may be found everything usually found in a first-class clothing house. Mr. Levino was united in marriage, January 18, 1888, with Miss Sophie Stern. She was born in New York City, February 17, 1868, and is the daughter of Herman Stern, of Allegheny, Penn.

HON. JAMES LINDSEY, deceased, was an attorney and counselor at law. He was born near Jefferson Borough, November 21, 1827, and was a son of John and Anne (Collins) Lindsey, who were natives of Greene County, and of Scotch-Irish extraction. His father was a farmer and subsequently sheriff and prothonotary and spent his life in this county. Judge Lindsey was the oldest in a family of eleven children, and was reared on a farm in Jefferson Township. He was educated at the Greene Academy in Cumberland Township, and studied law in Waynesburg, where he practiced his chosen profession until 1863, when he was elected President Judge of the fourteenth judicial district, then composed of Washington, Fayette and Greene Counties. He was a Democrat and a successful business man and was noted for his honesty and integrity as well as for his scholarly attainments. In 1855 Judge Lindsey was united in marriage with Miss Sarah, daughter of Dr. Arthur Inghram, and a sister to the President Judge of the fourteenth judicial district, Hon. James Inghram. He died at the early age of thirty-seven years. To Mr. and Mrs. Lindsey were born four children. Arthur I., the oldest, was born at Waynesburg, July 10, 1856. He was educated in Waynesburg College, and in 1874 began clerking in the F. & D. National Bank of Waynesburg, in which he is now assistant cashier. He is a Democrat, and is among the most prominent young men of the county. The three remaining children are William W. and John H., who are in the West, and Annie L. Judge Lindsey was a Presbyterian, and his widow is a member of the Methodist Episcopal Church.

H. H. LINDSEY, merchant, who was born in Jefferson Borough, this county, October 27, 1823, is a son of James and Catharine (Shroyer) Lindsey. His parents were also natives of Greene County, and of Scotch-Irish descent. Mr. Lindsey's grandfather, James Lindsey, built the first brick hotel in Jefferson Borough, where he spent the remainder of his life. Mr. Hiram Lindsey was the second in a family of three children and was reared in Jefferson where he attended school. At the age of sixteen he began to clerk in a store and was engaged as a salesman till 1850, when he opened a general store and continued in that business for twenty-five years. In 1869 Mr. Lindsey was elected prothonotary of the county, served one term and was re-elected in 1872. In 1876 he removed to Chicago, Illinois. Returning to Waynesburg in 1881, he has since been engaged in the mercantile business. In 1847 Mr. Lindsey married Miss Sarah, daughter of Philip Minor. Mrs. Lindsey is a native of Greene County, and of Welsh origin. Their children are—William L., for the last twenty-one years with J. V. Farwell & Co., Chicago, Ill. James M. who is a clerk in the United States revenue office at Pittsburgh, Penn.; Laura, wife of Robert D. Myers, of Chicago; Margaret, wife of L. L. Minor, Esq., of Uniontown, Penn.; Anna, and George B., who is with Farwell & Co., of Chicago. The deceased are Helen, wife of W. A. Bane, and Jessie. Mr. Lindsey is a member of the I. O. O. F. and A. Y. M., and his wife is a faithful member of the Presbyterian Church. They are among the representative citizens of Waynesburg, Penn.

WILLIAM LIPPENCOTT, SR., farmer, Waynesburg, Penn., was born in Franklin Township, this county, October 14, 1812. He is a son of Uriah and Nancy Lippencott, natives of New Jersey, and of English descent. Mr. William Lippencott's grandfather was among the earliest settlers of Greene County, and engaged in farming and stock growing. He gave his son Uriah instructions in the art of husbandry—a business he followed all his life, except the time he spent in teaching school. His death occurred in 1855. William Lippencott is the fifth in a family of eight children, and was reared on the farm where he and his family reside. Like his ancestors, he chose farming and stock growing as a business and has been very successful. His home farm contains 400 acres of valuable land. Mr. Lippencott was united in marriage, in 1832, with Rachel, daughter of George and Margaret (Bowen) Ullom, and they are the parents of five children, viz., Uriah, Margaret, Melissa, Martha and Maria. Mrs. Lippencott died in 1848. In 1849 Mr. Lippencott married Rebecca, daughter of Sylvanus and Rachel (Pew) Smith, natives of New Jersey, and of English lineage. Their children are—Smith, A. J., Elisha, Rachel A., B. F. and Sylvanus I. Mr. Lippencott has filled the offices of assessor, director of the poor and school director. Mrs. Lippencott is a consistent member of the Methodist Protestant Church.

H. C. LUCAS, druggist, was born at Hopewell, Greene County, Penn., August 23, 1859, and is a son of Samuel and Maria (Nicely) Lucas. His parents were born in Pennsylvania—the former in Washington County, and the latter in Greene. They were of Scotch-Irish origin. His father was a merchant and carried on business in this county for several years. He conducted a general mercantile business in Waynesburg, died at Kenton, Ohio in 1863. Of his family of six children, Harry C., is the fifth. But three of the children are now living. Mr. Lucas, the subject of this sketch, spent most of his early life with his grandparents in Ross County, Ohio, on the farm where he attended the district schools. He was afterwards a student in Waynesburg College for three years. In 1876 he went into a store to learn his present business, and was a faithful student. In 1882 he accepted a position as prescription clerk in a large drug store at Pittsburg, Penn., and remained there for two years, closely confining himself to his work. He returned to Waynesburg in 1884 and opened a drug store on Main street. As a business man Mr. Lucas is spoken of, by those who know him best, as a high-minded, honorable gentleman. He is a Republican, and an active member of the Presbyterian Church.

A. B. MILLER, D. D., LL. D., now president of Waynesburg College, was born near Brownsville, Fayette County, Penn., October 16, 1829. His parents, Moses and Mary (Knight) Miller, were respectively of German and English descent. The subject of this sketch was the fourth of ten children, eight of whom grew up, seven being still alive and in active life. His school opportunities in boy-

hood were very meagre, because of a disscusion which closed the
district school for several years, during which his youth was spent on
a farm where his parents resided until his father's death in 1859. In
1847 he entered Greene Academy, at Carmichaels, Penn., spending
there three summers, and teaching in the winters, his first effort being near Greenfield, Washington County, Penn., which proved so
successful as to place at his option four terms in the school of his
home district. A few months before twenty-one he was licensed to
preach by Union Presbytery of the Cumberland Presbyterian Church,
his first field being Masontown, Penn., where, within a few months
he secured the erection of a house of worship, his first preaching being in a school-house. In the autumn of 1851, by earnest entreaty,
he gained the consent of his presbytery for his return to school, and
entered Waynesburg College at the very opening of the institution
in the first building. At his graduation in 1853 he was elected
Professor of Mathematics in his Alma Mater, and in 1858 was advanced to the position of President, which he has occupied continuously. It is perhaps within the bounds of truth and justice to say
that, all things considered, the success of Waynesburg College has
been so remarkable as to present few parallels. It has now property
and endowment fund valued at considerably over $100,000, all ac-
quired little by little through persistent effort covering many years.
The new college edifice is capacious, substantial, and a marvel of
architectural beauty, of which the St. Louis *Observer* perhaps justly
says, in referring to Dr. Miller's recent call to a University in Illinois, that " all who are acquainted with the facts will agree that this
building would not have been there but for the untiring labors of
Dr. Miller." The alumni of the college now number hundreds,
many of them being men and women of distinction in their spheres
of useful work. In connection with his college work Dr. Miller
preached regularly to the Waynesburg Cumberland Presbyterian
Church for ten years, and for several years owned and published the
Cumberland Presbyterian while preaching twice of Sundays and
teaching daily six hours in the college, and supplementing all this,
while largely managing the financial affairs of the college, with an
immense amount of lecturing for teachers' institutes, on temperance,
etc., and with all this maintaining such health as to be spoken of as
" the man who is never sick." In 1855 he married Margaret K.
Bell, then principal of the female department of Waynesburg College, a position she held until her death, in April, 1874, her labors
being so efficient, and her life so noble, as to leave among the people
who knew her an admiration that is little short of worship. From
this marriage came eight children, of whom seven still survive, the
death of one resulting from an accident in infancy. The oldest is
the well known Mrs. Lide Simpson, wife of Dr. Theodore P. Simp-

son, of Beaver Falls, Penn. The second daughter, Lucy, is the wife of Prof. W. M. Beach, late president of Odessa College, Missouri, now a student in Jefferson Medical College. The oldest son, Lieut. Albert B. Miller, is pursuing medical studies, and will enter Jefferson College in the autumn; and the younger children, Miss Haddie, Miss Jessie, Howard B. and Alfred Tennyson are at home with their father, the home management being now in the hands of Mrs. Jennie (Wilson) Miller, wife of Albert B. If success and perseverance are evidence of ability, it cannot be doubted that Dr. Miller is a man of marked endowment in all his lines of effort, to which he adds that of almost boundless capacity to work, which someone has declared to be itself genius. While he has certainly not earned the reputation of having enriched himself, his long continued and arduous labors have enriched many with high qualifications for success and usefulness, and will leave the people of Waynesburg and Greene County the legacy of Waynesburg College.

ISAAC MITCHELL, retired farmer and resident of Waynesburg, was born in Washington Township, Greene County, Penn., September 9, 1816. His parents were Shadrick and Margaret (Rinehart) Mitchell. The former was a native of Maryland and the latter of Greene County, Penn. They were of English and German ancestry. Mr. Shadrick Mitchell was a farmer and stone-mason, and in early life followed his trade. He purchased land in what is now Washington Township in 1799, and settled and remained there until his death, which occurred in 1863. He was then ninety-seven years old. The farm he purchased is still in the possession of the family. He was the father of five daughters and five sons, of whom Mr. Isaac Mitchell is the youngest. He was reared in Washington Township, on the farm that has been in possession of the family for eighty-nine years. He made farming his business and has been very successful, owning at present 300 acres of fine land besides other property. He moved to Waynesburg in 1877, since which time he has been living a retired life. Mr. Mitchell's political views are Democratic, and he served two terms as overseer of the poor of Greene County. Mr. Mitchell was united in marriage October 4, 1838, with Elizabeth Barnes, whose parents were Jacob and Phœbe (Crayne) Barnes. Mr. and Mrs. Mitchell are the parents of six children—Margaret P., Mary E., Lucy, Thomas, George and Ross. Mrs. Mitchell is a consistent member of the Cumberland Presbyterian Church.

T. P. MOFFETT, merchant tailor, Waynesburg, Penn., was born at Carmichaels, Penn., December 8, 1854. He is a son of Richard and Rebecca (Jackson) Moffett, who were of Scotch and English extraction. His mother was a native of this county. His father, a native of Maryland, was a merchant tailor, and for many years carried on a successful business at Carmichaels. His family consisted of four children—all boys—of whom the subject of this sketch is the second. He was reared in Carmichaels and educated in Greene Academy. He very naturally learned to be a tailor with his father, serving a regular apprenticeship. He afterwards learned cutting with the well known J. B. West, of New York City. Mr. Moffett engaged in business in West Elizabeth for a period of three years. In 1877 he commenced business in Waynesburg, where he does first-class work, keeps good materials and always guarantees satisfaction to his many customers. Mr. Moffett was united in marriage in 1877 with Emma R., daughter of Abner W. Beddell. Mrs. Moffett is a native of Allegheny County, Penn., and a member of the Cumberland Presbyterian Church at Waynesburg. They have two children —Edwin Richard and Fannie Blanche. Mr. Moffett is a Republican, and a member of the Knights of Honor.

JOHN A. MOORE, liveryman, of the firm of Moore & Hill, was born in Whiteley Township, this county, June 9, 1848, and is a son of Thomas and Rachel (Maple) Moore. His mother was born in Maryland and was of English extraction. His father, who was a farmer all his life, was of Irish lineage, and a native of Greene County. His family consisted of ten children, eight of whom grew to maturity. Mr. Moore attended the district schools of Whiteley Township, and worked on a farm until he became of age, then taught school. He then began clerking in a general store, and remained there three years. Mr. Moore subsequently engaged in selling buggies and continued that business for a period of eight years. In 1885, in company with F. M. Patterson, he engaged in his present business in Waynesburg, where they keep a first-class livery stable and have a fair share of the patronage. Mr. Patterson, in 1888, sold his interest to Mr. S. M. Hill. Mr. Moore was united in marriage, October 6, 1872, with Miss Eliza M., daughter of Eaton Rose, and they have one child—Golda Myrtle. Mr. and Mrs. Moore are members of the Methodist Episcopal Church South. He is a Democrat, and a member of the I. O. O. F.

WILLIAM H. MORRIS, farmer and stock-dealer, Waynesburg, Penn., was born in this county April 23, 1847, and is a son of Jacob and Nancy (Jewel) Morris. His father is an active, energetic business man and prominent farmer of Greene County, and has succeeded in accumulating a fair share of this world's goods. His family consists of nine children, of whom William H. is next to the oldest. He was reared on the farm with his parents, and after receiving a limited education in the district schools started out in life as a huckster. He subsequently started a general store at Holbrook, Penn., where he continued in business until 1878, then bought his present farm where he resides in Franklin Township. In 1873 Mr. Morris married Miss Sallie, daughter of Benjamin Huffman, and they have seven children, viz: Milton, Emanuel, Jacob, Anna, Frank, Guy and Nannie. Mr. Morris is a Republican. His wife is a devoted member of the Baptist Church.

HON. ROBERT A. McCONNELL, attorney at law, Waynesburg, Greene County, Penn., was born October 29, 1826, at New London, ten miles south of Lynchburg, Virginia. He is the son of James and Elizabeth (Luckey) McConnell, who were natives of Franklin County, Penn., and of Scotch-Irish lineage. The subject of our sketch came from the pure Celtic stock, his great-grandfather, Robert McConnell, being a native of County Antrim, Ireland, and born in 1695. His ancestors went from Scotland to the Green Isle in the Sixteenth century. Robert McConnell and wife emigrated to the American colonies, settling in Franklin County, Penn., where he died in 1770. The members of the family have occupied many exalted positions and offices of trust. They have participated in all the wars of America. James McConnell, grandfather of Robert A., served as a captain through the Revolutionary war. After the close of the war he returned to Franklin County, where he served as justice of the peace and as county commissioner for several years. From 1804 to 1806 he was a member of the State Legislature of Pennsylvania. Robert A. McConnell's father, James McConnell, was born in Franklin County, Penn., October 9, 1784, being the fourth son in a family of twelve children. In 1808 he was united in marriage with Elizabeth Luckey, who was born near Winchester, Virginia, April 5, 1785. Their children numbered eleven, of whom Hon. Robert McConnell is the tenth. The family have usually been Presbyterians. James McConnell graduated at Jefferson College, in 1805, and was admitted to the bar in 1810. On account of failing health he had to abandon his profession and subsequently engaged in teaching. Having come to Greene County in 1828 and resided on a farm in Morris Township, where Robert A., the subject of our sketch was reared. He attended the common schools and in 1845 entered the West Alexander Academy. He subsequently attended Washington College where he graduated in 1851. He then began the study of law at Waynesburg, in the office of Hon. C. A. Black and John Phelan. He was admitted to the practice in 1854 and was elected district attorney in 1858, serving six years. In 1870 he was elected to the State Legislature, where he introduced a number of important bills and was a strong advocate of local option. In 1872, when the members of the Legislature made the Speaker a present of $500 worth of silverware, Mr. McConnell was selected to make the presentation speech. On January 5, 1888, he was united in marriage with Miss Sallie E. Arrison, of Waynesburg, Penn. Mr. McConnell is a Democrat, and an elder and useful member of the Presbyterian Church. He is a member of the board of trustees of Waynesburg College. Since the death of his brother, Joseph L. McConnell, he has been employed in settling up the estate.

JOSEPH L. McCONNELL (deceased), surveyor and civil engineer, who was born in Virginia, August 25, 1814, was a son of Jamas and Elizabeth (Luckey) McConnell, being the fourth in their family of eleven children. His early childhood was spent in Virginia, but at the age of fourteen years he came with his parents to Greene County, Penn. He received a good English education and devoted much of his time to the study of surveying. He first began surveying in 1836 and followed that as a business for many years. He also made a map of the county which is very correct. Mr. McConnell was a very clever and genial man and had a large acquaintance throughout the county. He was married, May 11, 1859, to Miss Anna Luckey, and died January 31, 1875. He was a Democrat and he and his wife were members of the Presbyterian Church.

SAMUEL J. McNAY.—Among the prominent and wealthy farmers of Greene County we mention the name of Samuel J. McNay. Mr. McNay was born December 11, 1821, on the farm in Franklin Township where he now resides. His parents, James and Anna (Dickenson) McNay, were natives of Pennsylvania and were among the pioneers of the State. Mr. McNay is the second of a family of eleven children—eight sons and three daughters. He was reared on the farm and attended the common schools. Early in life he chose farming as his business, in which he has met with marked success and is the owner of 1,329 acres of land. For a number of years he has operated a saw-mill, and has done most of his own work. In 1845 Mr. McNay married Miss Priscilla Motford and they were the parents of six children, only two of whom are living—Melissa, wife of John Baldwin, and Lucy, wife of George Knox. Mrs. McNay died in 1875, a faithful, loving wife and devoted mother. Mr. McNay was again united in marriage, in 1882, with Miss Mary J., daughter of Jesse Adams, a Cumberland Presbyterian minister. They are the parents of two children—Luella G. and Jessie. Mr. and Mrs. McNay are members of the Cumberland Presbyterian Church, in which he has been elder for many years. He is a Democrat, and has served as school director in his township.

JESSE B. ORNDOFF, farmer and stock-grower, Waynesburg, Penn., was born in Greene County, Pennsylvania, October 6, 1857, and is a son of Jesse and Susan (Wear) Orndoff. His father was also a native of this county, and his mother was born in Virginia. His father is a prominent farmer of Center Township, where Jesse was reared and received his early education. Mr. Orndoff is one of the most industrious farmers of Franklin Township, where he owns a well improved farm. He was united in marriage, in 1886, with

Miss Mary L., daughter of Thomas and Susannah (Loar) Hughes. Mrs. Orndoff is of Dutch and Irish ancestry. They have one child. Mr. Orndoff is a Democrat, and one of the representative young men of the county.

NATHANIEL PARSHALL deceased, was born in Fayette County, Penn., February 12, 1824, and died in 1881. He was a son of James and Hannah (Coldren) Parshall. His father was a farmer by occupation, and reared a family of eleven children. Nathaniel was the second and was reared in Fayette County, where he attended the district schools. When twenty years of age (1844), he came to Greene County and worked at the cooper's trade, in connection with farming, for a time, but subsequently worked at the carpenter's trade. In 1858 Mr. Parshall married Miss Priscilla Delaney, and they were the parents of five children—three boys and two girls— Charles T., Hannah, wife of Elmer Keenan; Sarah, wife of Joseph Mason; Alpheus and Isaac S. Mr. and Mrs. Parshall were members of the Baptist Church, in which he served as deacon for thirty years. He was a highly respected citizen and his death was mourned by all who knew him.

W. W. PATTERSON, register and recorder of Greene County, Penn., was born in Whiteley Township, this county, September 17, 1855. He is a son of James and Susan (Groves) Patterson, who were of Scotch-Irish descent. His ancestors were among the pioneer settlers of Whiteley Township, and were usually farmers. Mr. Patterson was reared on the farm, attending the common schools in the county, and also Waynesburg College. For a few years he devoted himself to teaching, having taught seven terms in this county. He has held his present position in the county for seven years. He is a Democrat, and has served on the school board of Waynesburg. In 1885 Mr. Patterson married Miss Edith N. Meek, a consistent member of the Baptist Church. Mrs. Patterson's father served one term as county treasurer, and is a prominent farmer of Jackson Township.

REV. ALBERT E. PATTERSON, of the firm of Rinehart & Patterson, owners of the Keystone Marble Works at Waynesburg, Penn., was born in Center Township, Greene County, Penn., March 14, 1860. He is a son of James and Mary J. (Parshall) Patterson, who were natives of Pennsylvania, and of Scotch and French origin. His father, who was a farmer all his life, was twice married. His first wife's maiden name was Julia Ann Quick. Of his six children, four are children of the first wife and two of the second. Rev. Albert E. is the youngest. He was reared on the farm and received his education at Monongahela College, with a view of entering the ministry. He received a license in 1884, and was for some time a supply for the Bates Fork Baptist Church. In 1886 Rev. Patterson was married, near Uniontown, West Virginia, to Miss Elvira

Glover. Mr. Patterson expects to devote his life to the ministry, but will for a time engage in his present business, in which he is very successful.

HON. ALEXANDER PATTON, deceased, was born in Washington County, Penn., in 1819, and was the son of Joseph Patton, a native of Ireland. His education was limited, but by energy and pluck he was enabled to begin the study of medicine at Cannonsburg, where he finally completed his studies. He began the practice of his chosen profession at Waynesburg, remaining there only a few years. He then removed to Clarksville, Penn., where his genial and gentlemanly demeanor and professional skill soon won for him an extensive practice. He remained in Clarksville until 1865, when he moved to Auburn, near Jefferson, where he died in 1884. He was a successful physician, and had many friends in Greene County. For many years he was an acknowledged leader in the Democratic party in Greene County, and in 1863 and 1864 he was elected to represent the county in the assembly. In 1882 he was elected State Senator. He was an active politician, and able to carry almost every vote in his township. He was married in Greene County in 1845 to Miss Ann, daughter of Abraham and Mary (Carter) Burson. Mrs. Patton's parents were of Scotch-Irish descent and natives of Bucks County, Penn. Mr. and Mrs. Patton's family consisted of nine children. Two of their sons are now residents of Waynesburg; one, Joseph, is an attorney and counselor at law; and the other, A. B., is a physician and surgeon. Hon. Mr. Patton was one of Greene County's most highly esteemed citizens.

JOSEPH PATTON, attorney and counselor at law, was born in Clarksville, Penn., August 4, 1855. He is a son of Hon. Alexander and Ann (Burson) Patton. His mother was a native of this county, and his father was born in Washington, Penn. Mr. Patton, the sixth in a family of nine children, was reared on a farm in Jefferson Township and attended the Monongahela College. He studied law at Waynesburg, where he was admitted to the bar in April, 1880. He has met with more than average success in the practice of law. He was married in January, 1884, to Miss Ellen, daughter of W. T. Webb, justice of the peace at Waynesburg. Mr. Patton's father was born in Waynesburg February 21, 1840, and is the son of W. T. E. Webb, Esq., deceased. Mr. and Mrs. Patton have one child— William A. Mr. Patton is a Democrat in politics.

WILLIAM THOMPSON HAYS PAULEY, editor and proprietor of the Waynesburg *Messenger*, was born in Youngstown, Ohio, February 6, 1820, and is a son of Thomas and Sarah (Hays) Pauley, who were of Irish and English descent. His father, who was a farmer, was born in Pennsylvania, as was his mother also. Mr. Pauley is the second in a family of three sons. He lived in Youngstown,

Ohio, until he was twelve years old. His father died in 1830, and two years later he came to Waynesburg and learned the printer's trade. He has been in the newspaper business ever since he was thirteen years of age, except while at school, and the greater part of that time he spent in the Waynesburg *Messenger* office, where he learned his trade. He went to Oxford, Ohio, to school in 1838, and remained four years. In 1842 he was employed by Major Hays to publish the Waynesburg *Messenger* until 1844, when he purchased the paper, which had been established in 1813, by Dr. Duston. Mr. Pauley is a Democrat, and his paper has been the supporter of all regularly nominated Democratic candidates in the county, state and nation. In 1847 he was elected county treasurer and served one term. He was married in 1845 to Miss Mary Jennings, who died September 2, 1887. Their children are—Sarah E., wife of Isaac Bell; James J., of the *Messenger;* Benjamin J., a farmer; John F., a printer, and Thomas C. (deceased). Mr. Pauley is a member of the Masonic fraternity and a Sir Knight Templar. He has been connected with the *Messenger* in some capacity, with the exception of the four years spent in Oxford, ever since the 14th day of May, 1833.

ZADOCK WALKER PHELAN, manufacturer, foundryman and machinist, is a member of the firm of Bower & Phelan, Waynesburg, Penn., where he was born June 21, 1838. He is a son of John and Jane (Walker) Phelan. His mother was born in Fayette County, Penn. His father, a native of Greene County, was an attorney by profession, practiced in Waynesburg for many years and represented his county in the State Legislature. His family consists of five sons and one daughter. Z. W., the third in the family, was reared in Waynesburg and educated in the college. He learned the cabinetmaker's trade and carried on the furniture business in Waynesburg; then went to Kansas and shared the struggles of that young State, and in 1884 he began his present business. Mr. Phelan's wife was Miss Harriet, daughter of J. Wesley Chambers of Washington County, Penn. They have three children—Anna W., John Charles and Zadock Walker. Mr. and Mrs. Phelan are members of the Methodist Episcopal Church, in which he has held many important positions. He is a strong advocate of the temperance cause and votes the Prohibition ticket. He was the first county chairman of the party, and a candidate on the first ticket issued by the party.

R. H. PHELAN, attorney and counsellor at law, was born at Waynesburg, February 21, 1836, and is a son of Hon. John and Jane (Walker) Phelan. His mother was a native of Maryland, and was of English and Irish descent. His father, who was an attorney, was born in this county, of which he was prothonotary for about twelve years. He was elected a member of the State Legislature in 1867, and served two terms. He died August 31, 1874. R. H.

37

Phelan is the second in a family of six children. He was reared in Waynesburg and attended the common school and college. He went to the territory of Kansas in 1854 and remained until 1861, when he returned to Waynesburg and subsequently studied law in the office of his father and Hon. C. A. Black. He was admitted to the bar in 1867, and has been in active practice ever since. Mr. Phelan is a Democrat. He has been a member of the town council, and is a trustree of the Presbyterian Church. His grandfather, Richard H. Phelan, was born in Ireland, and case to Greene County, Penn., at an early date. He served on the first grand jury in 1796. R. H. Phelan is president of Green Mount Cemetery Company, treasurer of the Waynesburg Park Company, and a director in the Farmers' and Drovers' National Bank of Waynesburg.

JOHN R. PIPES, clerk of the courts of Greene County, Penn., was born in Morrisville, Penn., March 25, 1855, and is a son of James and Elvira (Rinehart) Pipes. His parents were natives of Franklin Township, and of English extraction. His father, who was a farmer all his life, died September 5, 1881. The subject of our sketch was reared in Franklin Township, attended the common school and the Monongahela College at Jefferson, Penn. He first engaged in teaching as an occupation, teaching in the winter for five years and mining coal in the summer. Mr. Pipes is a Democrat, and was elected to his present position in 1884. In 1882 he was united in marriage with Miss. Melinda, daughter of William Pitcock, one of the early pioneers of the county. Mr. and Mrs. Pipes have two children—Mary Emma and Daisy. Mr. and Mrs. Pipes are members of the Methodist Protestant Church, in which he has held many offices, and also served as superintendent of the Sabbath-school. He is a member of the I. O. O. F. His father was born in 1800 and his mother in 1818. She is still living, making her home with John R. in Waynesburg, Penn.

D. B. PRATT, farmer and stock-grower, Waynesburg, Penn., was born in Franklin Township, Greene County, Penn., December 25, 1838. He is a son of William Pratt, also a prominent farmer in this township, who was born in Fayette County, Penn., October 13, 1814. His parents were James and Sallie (Boner) Pratt, also natives of Fayette County, and of English lineage. William Pratt owned a well improved farm of 200 acres in Franklin Township, where he died in 1874. He was a blacksmith by trade, in which he engaged until 1854 when he began farming. He spent most of his life in Greene County, where he was united in marriage, in 1838, with Miss Harriet, daughter of Joshua and Catharine (Livengood) Thomas. Her father was born near Philadelphia, Penn., and was of Dutch ancestry. Mrs. Pratt was born in Center Township, this county, June 2, 1820, and was the seventh in a family of fifteen children. D.

B. Pratt, the subject of this sketch, is a man of tireless zeal and unusual energy, by means of which he has been very successful in his chosen pursuit, and owns a well improved farm of 175 acres. On August 25, 1870, he married Margaret, daughter of William and Sarah (Bodkin) Smith, who were of English and Irish lineage. Her mother was a native of Pennsylvania. Her father was born in New Jersey, and died in 1874. They were the parents of sixteen children, of whom Mrs. Pratt is the youngest. To Mr. and Mrs. Pratt have been born two sons—William Harvey and Lindsley Inghram. Their mother is a member of the Baptist Church. Mr. Pratt is a Democrat and a member of the I. O. O. F. He has served as school director and auditor of his township.

ANDREW ARMSTRONG PURMAN, attorney and counselor at law, was born on Short Creek, in Ohio County, Virginia (now West Virginia), April 8, 1823. He is a son of John and Barbara (Burns) Purman. His parents were natives of Pennsylvania, and of German and Scotch extraction. His father was a farmer and came to Greene County in 1833, settling on a farm in Richhill Township. Later in life he moved to Shelby County, Indiana, where he died in 1838. His family consisted of nine children, of whom the subject of this sketch is the third son. A. A. Purman, Esq., the subject of our sketch, spent his early life with his parents on the farm, where he first went to subscription school. He was afterwards a student in a select school in Waynesburg, and at the founding of Waynesburg College he entered it as one of its first students. He began the study of law in Waynesburg in 1847, in the office of Hon. Samuel Cleavenger, and at the death of Mr. Cleavenger, 1848, finished the course with Lewis Roberts, Esq., and was admitted to the bar in May, 1849. He has devoted his life to the practice of his chosen profession. In 1856 Mr. Purman was elected district attorney, serving three years. In 1869 he was elected State Senator from Greene, Fayette and Westmoreland counties, and served in the session of 1871 as chairman of the finance committee. He was elected in the year 1872, on the Democratic ticket, a delegate at large to the constitutional convention of 1872-1873, and served on the committee on legislation and corporation. Mr. Purman was a school director for fifteen years, and served for several years as a member of the borough council. He is a Democrat, and commenced public speaking for the party in 1844, for Polk and Dallas, has spoken in every presidential campaign since, and was offered the nomination for Lieutenant-Governor of Pennsylvania in 1874. In 1865 he came within one vote of being nominated President Judge of the Fourteenth Judicial District. Mr. Purman was united in marriage June 26, 1856, with Miss Mary Ann, daughter of Thomas and Elizabeth (Morris) Russell. Of their nine children seven are now living. They are Thamas R., John, a physician and surgeon; Lida, wife of B. R. Williams, of Sharon, Penn.; James J., a law student; Alexander E., Elizabeth M. and A. A. Jr. Mr. Purman's grandfather, James Burns, was a soldier in the Revolutionary war. Mr. and Mrs. Purman are members of the Baptist Church, in which he has held many official positions. He is and has been president of the board of trustees of Monongahela College at Jefferson ever since its organization in 1867.

Z. C. RAGAN, of the firm of Ragan & Evans, editors and proprietors of the Waynesburg *Independent*, was born in Zanesville, Ohio, July 14, 1833, and is a son of Joab and Mary (Stull) Ragan. His mother was born in Kentucky, and his father in Beaver County, Penn. They were of Scotch-Irish descent. His father, who died at the early age of thirty-three, was a minister of the Methodist Protestant Church, and served as president of the conference. He was a self-made man and an able linguist, speaking and writing four languages. Z. C. Ragan is an only child. He was brought to Waynesburg in 1840, where he was reared, and partially educated in Waynesburg College. Early in life he learned the printing business, a calling he has followed the greater part of his life. He started a paper in Waynesburg in 1872, in company with J. W. Axtell, called the Waynesburg *Independent*, which has a circulation of over 3,000 copies per week. The financial success of the paper has been largely due to Mr. Ragan's untiring efforts. He was for seven years a member of the board of trustees in Waynesburg College, and is a prominent member of the Knights of Honor. In 1861 he enlisted in Company F, Eighty-fifth Pennsylvania Volunteer Infantry, and was discharged in 1864. He served as Sergeant, and had charge of his company when it was mustered out. Mr. Ragan was united in marriage, in 1858, with Miss Anna M., daughter of Thomas Hill, a farmer of Greene County. Their children are—Emma L., a graduate of Waynesburg College, and wife of W. S. Pipes; and Minnie E., a student in the college. Mrs. Pipes was for three years a teacher in Enfield College, Illinois. The family are members of the Cumberland Presbyterian Church, in which Mr. Ragan is an elder, and was superintendent of the Sabbath-school over eight years.

JAMES F. RANDOLPH, a farmer and stock-grower of Franklin Township, was born in Jefferson Borough, Greene County, Penn., April 23, 1832. He is a son of Isaac and Sarah (Adamson) Randolph, who came from New Jersey, their native State, and settled in Greene County, Penn., in 1795, on a farm where they spent the remainder of their lives. They reared a family of ten children, eight of whom grew to maturity. James F., the third in the family, was reared on the farm with his parents, and attended the district school. He has successfully engaged in farming as a business, and is the owner of some fine land in this county. In 1855 Mr. Randolph married Elizabeth, daughter of William Braden, who is an ex-associate judge, and a prominent citizen of this county. To M.. and Mrs. Randolph were born eight children—Sarah M., wife of Smith Adamson; Mary, wife of Isaiah Gordon; Rachel, wife of Jackson Pratt; Lucy, Isaac L., William, Lizzie and Thomas. Mr. Randolph is a Democrat. He and wife are prominent members of the Cumberland Presbyterian Church.

J. A. F. RANDOLPH, insurance and real estate agent, Waynesburg, Penn., was born in Jefferson Township, this county, March 18, 1851, and is a son of Abraham F. and Emily A. (Adamson) Randolph, also natives of this county. Abraham F. Randolph was a son of James F. Randolph, a native of Middlesex County, N. J., and member of the Society of Friends. He came to Greene County, Penn., in 1795, and remained all his life on the farm where Abraham F. was born. The farm is still in possession of the family. Abraham F. and Emily A. Randolph were married in this county, June 18, 1833, where they died, the former December 8, 1866, and the latter March 9, 1885. They were the parents of four children, two of whom are living—William H. F. and James A. F. The deceased are an infant, and Sarah L., wife of C. C. Strawn. The subject of our sketch was united in marriage, January 9, 1888, with Miss Emma F. Johnson, who was born September 26, 1859. She is a daughter of William R. and Minerva E. (Fleming) Johnson, the former a native of this county, and the latter of West Virginia. Mr. Randolph acquired his education in the common schools and Waynesburg College. He remained at home until twenty-one years of age, then taught school for a period of five years. He first engaged in his present business in 1880. He represents some of the best insurance companies of the United States, and also deals extensively in real estate. Mr. Randolph is a member of the board of trust of the Pennsylvania Synod of the Cumberland Presbyterian Church, and treasurer of the endowment fund for support of Waynesburg College. He and his wife are members of the Cumberland Presbyterian Church. He is at present city clerk.

JOSEPH W. RAY.—The subject of this sketch, Joseph W. Ray, is the eldest son of James E. and Margaret (Leonard) Ray, and was born May 25, 1849, in Morris Township, Greene County. His father, who is now (July, 1888) in his eightieth year, was born in Morris County, N. J., and his mother in Trumbull County, Ohio. His parents, immediately upon their marriage, settled in Washington County, Penn., but removed therefrom April 1, 1849, to a farm in Greene County, where they have ever since resided. They gave him the advantage of such educational facilities as the common schools of that time and section afforded. At nineteen years of age he secured employment as a teacher, a calling to which he devoted several years.   In 1871 he became a student of Waynesburg College, and was graduated by that institution in the class of 1874. About this time he commenced the study of law, and was admitted to the bar of his native county in June, 1876.   Two years later, or April 1, 1878, having associated himself with H. B. Axtell, Esq., they opened an office in Waynesbnrg, under the firm name of Ray & Axtell, since which time he has been actively engaged in the practice of his profession.   He was admitted to practice in the Supreme Court of the State in 1883.   In politics Mr. Ray is a Republican. He was chairman, for three years, of the Republican County Committee of Greene County.   He has represented the county in a State Convention, and was an alternate delegate to the Republican National Convention of 1880.   He has twice been the nominee of his party for office.   In 1884 he ran for Congress against Hon. Charles E. Boyle, the Democratic candidate, in what was then the twenty-first district, composed of the counties of Fayette, Greene and Westmoreland.   Although defeated by 2,500 votes, this was much the smallest Democratic majority the district ever gave, up to that time. In 1886 he was nominated for the State Senate, in the fortieth senatorial district, composed of Fayette and Greene counties, having for his Democratic competitor Hon. Thomas B. Schnatterly.   The official returns gave Mr. Schnatterly 8,438 votes, and Mr. Ray 8,256 votes, a reduction of the usual Democratic majority of more than 2,000 in the district to 182.   Mr. Ray was married May 18, 1878, to Miss Henrietta Iams, a daughter of the late Thomas Iams, of Morris Township, Greene County.   Since their marriage they have resided in Waynesburg, and have four children, two girls and two boys.

WILLIAM RHODES, farmer, Waynesburg, Penn.; who was born in Franklin Township, July 12, 1818, is a son of William and Nancy (Rinehart) Rhodes, who were of German extraction.   His father was a native of this county, and a farmer all his life.   The Rhodes family have usually been farmers.   William Rhodes is an only child.   He was born in a house where the poor-house now stands. The subject of this sketch received his early education in the district schools of Franklin Township.   He has been a successful farmer, and owns 300 acres of good farming land.   He remained on the farm with his parents until 1852, when he married Miss Jane, daughter of William and Elizabeth (Shull) Shriver.   Her parents were natives of this county, and of Dutch and Irish lineage.   To Mr. and Mrs. Rhodes were born seven children—Lizzie, Rettie J., wife of Rinehart Gwynn; George F., Belle H., Ida D., Willie B. and Charley.   Mr. Rhodes is steward in the Methodist Church, is a member of the Masonic fraternity and the I. O. O. F.   The following sketch of William Rhodes' grandfather will be of interest to many readers: William Rhodes was born at Newport, R. I., about 1759.   He went to sea at sixteen and remained a sailor for sixteen years. With many vicissitudes his career seems checkered. From his manuscript journals we find him a prisoner in the French prison from 1778 to 1780, and on his very next voyage from London in May was recaptured, but liberated through the influence of American friends, as an American citizen. In October of 1780 he sailed for Barbadoes with a large fleet of merchant ships, convoyed by ten line of battle ships. The next year he was once more captured by the French and again liberated. Again he was a prisoner in New York, being captured by the English, and exchanged after five months' confinement. In 1784 he was wrecked off Cape Cod, and the following year (1785) he heard for the first time of the Ohio settlement. About 1787, his father dying, William Rhodes' attention was directed to the settlements west of the Alleghany Mountains, and on the 18th of January, 1788, reached the old Redstone Fort (now Brownsville) in Fayette County. After peddling, and keeping store at Jackson's Fort (then Washington County), he bought, in 1791, a plantation (where his son, James R. Rhodes, now resides), married and began farming. In his own words: "Settled for life, I hope. Here I began jogging for life and family, not in the least discouraged in my new profession." The manuscript is rather amusing and interesting, illustrated by drawings of his own, of ships, scenery, women, men, birds, fishes and animals, according to the fancy of this backwoods artist.

S. S. RINEHART, merchant, Waynesburg, Penn., son of Samuel and Mary (Zook) Rinehart, was born in this county February 16, 1848. His mother was also a native of this county, and his father was born in Ohio. They were of German and Irish extraction. His father was a farmer and coal miner, and reared a family of nine children, of whom the subject of this sketch is the fourth. He was reared in Franklin Township, attended the common schools, and in early life learned the harness maker's trade. He engaged in that business in Waynesburg until 1872, when he commenced clerking in a store. He was employed as a salesman until 1878, when he began business for himself at Morrisville, Penn., and has met with success. Mr. Rinehart was united in marriage October 7, 1872, with Mary Ella Lippencott, a native of this county. Their children are—Mattie, Nettie, Eddie H. and Hermon. Mr. Rinehart is a Democrat in politics.

JAMES R. RINEHART, Professor of Languages in Waynesburg College, was born at Woodsfield, Monroe County, Ohio, in October, 1832, and is a son of Simon and Hannah (Morris) Rinehart, natives of Greene County, Penn. His father was of German and Irish extraction. Prof. Rinehart's great-grandfather, who was a farmer, was among the early settlers of this county, and was killed by the Indians. His grandfather, Barnett Rinehart, was born September 8, 1777, in this county. His maternal grandparents were natives of Monmouth County, New Jersey, and were of Scotch and German descent. The Rinehart family have, as a rule, been farmers and very successful in business. Several members of the family have entered the professions and have met with unusual success. Prof. Rinehart's father was a blacksmith by trade. He was clerk for the county commissioners for several years, and also served as justice of the peace. He reared a family of four children, of whom the Professor is the third. He was educated in Greene County, graduating in the regular classical course at Waynesburg College. He then took up the study of law and was admitted to the bar in 1857. He began the practice of his profession in Clinton, Illinois, and after a short time went to St. Louis, Missouri, where he remained until 1860, then returning to Greene County, Penn. In 1887 he accepted his present position as instructor in Waynesburg College, and has filled the same continuously since that time. Prof. Rinehart was married in 1873 to Miss Ida, daughter of Hon. Patrick Donley, of Mt. Morris, Penn. Their children are—Patrick Donley and Margaret Morris. The Professor is a member of the Masonic Fraternity.

PROF. A. I. P. RINEHART, superintendent of the public schools of Waynesburg, Penn., is among the prominent instructors of the county, and a man of marked ability as a teacher. He was born in Franklin Township, this county, April 17, 1860, and is the son of William and Elizabeth (Porter) Rinehart, who were of English and German descent. His parents were natives of Greene County, and descendants of its early settlers. His father was a farmer, and of his family of nine children Prof. Rinehart is the oldest. He received his early education in the common schools and afterwards took a regular course in the Edinboro State Normal School, graduating in 1883. He has since engaged in teaching as a profession, and his work has been confined to Greene County, with the exception of two years that he was principal in the High School at Freeport, Armstrong County, Penn. In 1885 he was elected to his present position of principal of schools in Waynesburg. During vacation he has frequently instructed other teachers of the county. In 1888 he taught a very successful term in Jackson Township, his pupils being principally those who had themselves been teachers. Prof. Rinehart is a genial, pleasant gentleman, and is held in high esteem by the teachers of Greene County.

J. G. RITCHIE, Chicago, Illinois, was born in Cumberland Township, Greene County, Penn., June 27, 1834. His parents were Col. Newton J. and Anna (Gwynn) Ritchie, natives of Pennsylvania, both now deceased. They were the parents of four children, of whom two are living—Mrs. William Smith and the subject of this sketch. He was united in marriage February 10, 1876, with Miss Philinda

Andrew, who was born in Richland County, Ohio, April 18, 1847. Her parents were William and Mary J. (McConnell) Andrew, the former a native of Washington County, Penn., and the latter of Virginia. Mr. Andrew departed this life in 1850, and his widow in 1863. They were the parents of five children, four of whom are living, viz.: Elizabeth, wife of Samuel Bonar; Louisa, wife of John Chambers; Mary J., widow of Dr. F. M. Denny, and Mrs. J. G. Ritchie. The deceased was James A., who was killed in the late war. Mr. and Mrs. Ritchie are the parents of one daughter—Anna M., born in Waynesburg, Penn., February 19, 1878. Mr. Ritchie acquired his education in the common schools and Greene Academy at Carmichaels, Penn. He subsequently taught for a number of years, then read law with E. M. Sayers. After his admission to the bar he practiced in partnership with A. A. Purman, Esq. Mr. Ritchie served as District Attorney for Greene County, after which he engaged in the hardware business for five years with his brother-in-law, William P. Smith, in Waynesburg. He next turned his attention to the W. & W. R. R. enterprise, in which he took an active interest and was one of those most instrumental in procuring the road to Waynesburg. He served as first president of the road, was also superintendent, and is still one of the directors. In 1887 he went to Chicago, and in company with J. S. Wolf, has been engaged in the real estate business. He and his wife own property in Greene County, Penn., Richland County, Ohio, and in Chicago. They are consistent members of the Presbyterian Church,

MORGAN ROSS, dealer in wagons, carriages and harness, Waynesburg, Penn., was born in Center Township, this county, February 22, 1844. He is a son of Peabody Atkinson and Maria (Matthews) Ross. His parents were natives of Pennsylvania, and of Scotch-Irish origin. His father was for some time a manufacturer, but devoted most of his life to farming. His family consisted of eight children, of whom the subject of this sketch is the oldest living. Until he was twenty-one years old Mr. Ross remained on the farm with his parents in Center Township, where he attended the district school. In 1865 he came to Waynesburg and learned the carriage and wagon-maker's trade, subsequently engaging in that business until 1883, the year in which his first wife, Maggie Throckmorton Ross died. Mr. Ross has one child, Charles, born July 4th, 1879. He was married the second time in 1885. Mr. Ross is a Democrat, and a member of the I. O. O. F.

JOSEPH B. ROSS, manufacturer, of the firm of McGlumphy & Ross, Waynesburg, Penn., was born in Dunkard Township, Greene County, Penn., January 24, 1844. His parents, Thomas and Eliza (Bailey) Ross, were natives of Fayette County, and of German origin. His father was a cabinet-maker by trade, to which he devoted the early part of his life. In later years he retired to the quiet of the farm, where he spent the remaining portion of his life. His family consisted of five children—three daughters and five sons, of whom Joseph B. is the second. He was reared in Cumberland Township, where he attended the common schools and early in life learned the manufacturing of woolen goods. He was employed in that business at Clarksville, Penn., until 1873, when he bought land near Waynesburg and engaged in farming from 1876 to 1879. Mr. Ross was then proprietor of a grocery and meat-market for two years, when he bought the old planing-mill and started his present business. In 1873 Mr. Ross married Susan, daughter of Samuel Luse, a prominent and successful farmer of Franklin Township. They have three children—Charles L., Walter S. and Franklin. Mr. Ross is a Republican. His grandfather, Thomas Ross, was one of the pioneers of Greene County.

HON. ABNER ROSS, ex-Senator, is a merchant by occupation. He was born in Washington Township, this county, March 30, 1838, and is a son of Benjamin and Hannah (Johns) Ross, also natives of this county. His grandfather, Timothy Ross, was among the early pioneer farmers of the county. Mr. Ross is the fourth in a family of twelve children, eight of whom grew to maturity. He was reared on the home farm, and his early education was obtained at an Academy in Fayette County, Penn. He afterwards spent some time in Waynesburg College. Mr. Ross chose farming as a business in which he engaged until he was elected sheriff of the county in 1870. He held that office for three years, then engaged in the mercantile business in Waynesburg until 1884, when he was elected State Senator and served two years, was elected to fill the unexpired time of Senator Patton. He has since continued in the boot and shoe business which he established in 1882. In 1863 Mr. Ross married Margaret P., daughter of Isaac Mitchell. Mrs. Ross is also a native of this county, to which her grandfather came at an early date and lived to the advanced age of ninety-six years. Mr. and Mrs. Ross are the parents of four children—Albert Lee, Benjamin F. and Isaac Wilbert. Jennie E. died July 14, 1885, aged fifteen years. Mr. Ross is a Democrat. He and his wife are members of the Baptist Church.

J. H. ROGERS, photographer, was born December 11, 1831, near the place where the Union depot now stands in the city of Pittsburgh, Penn. His parents are James R. Rogers, born in 1805, and Sarah O. Rogers, born in 1812. They were both natives of Pennsylvania. They were married in 1830, afterward settling in Pittsburgh where they remained for six years. Mr. James Rogers was a carpenter and contractor and resided in several different towns after leaving Pittsburgh. He resided for a time in Bealsville, Penn., where Mrs. Sarah O. Rogers died. Mr. Rogers afterwards married Mary Price and moved to Clover Hill, and from there to Brownsville, Penn. He then moved near Mount Pleasant, Ohio, and finally to Indiana, where they reside at the present. By the first marriage there were ten children, of whom Mr. J. H. Rogers is the oldest. Of these five are living. The subject of our sketch was united in marriage, October 31, 1854, with Charlotte V. Rearhard, who was born in Uniontown, Fayette County, Penn., January 3, 1833, and is a daughter of Conrad and Elizabeth Rearhard, natives of Pennsylvania. Her father was born in 1787, and departed this life December 5, 1870. Mrs. Rearhard was born in 1792, and died May 24, 1888. Mr. and Mrs. Rogers have six children, five of whom are living; viz., Sarah E., Emma J., Anna V., Craig S. and James H. Frank is deceased. Mr. Rogers acquired his education in the common schools, after which he learned the carpenter's trade with his father and worked at that business till 1861. He then began studying photography with J. S. Young, of Washington, Penn. He finished the study in two years and opened a gallery in Bealsville. After remaining there about nine months he carried on a successful business at Brownsville for a period of eight years. He then returned to Washington and purchased the gallery owned by J. S. Young. He remained there for eight years, then purchased a farm in Amwell Township, Washington County, on the W. & W. Railroad, consisting of one hundred acres. He remained on his farm three years, then moved to Waynesburg, opened a gallery and has been very successful in his business. He makes photographs of all kinds and sizes, making a specialty of copying and enlarging pictures. Mr. Rogers is a member of the Knights of Honor, and both he and his wife are members of the C. P. Church.

REV. W. M. RYAN was born March 7, 1848 near West Alexander, Washington County, Pennsylvania. His parents, Joseph and Isabella Ryan, still reside in Washington County. His father has been a farmer all his life, hence the subject of this sketch was reared on a farm. He enjoyed the advantages of the public schools of his native county, and also a term or two in the Academy at West Alexander. After this he became a teacher, teaching for five years. In December, 1868, he made a profession of religion, and became a member of the Pleasant Grove Baptist Church. In 1871 he entered Waynesburg College, graduating in the class '74, in the classical course, after which he took a three year's course in Crozer Theological Seminary, at Chester, Pennsylvania. He was ordained as a gospel minister in September, 1877, since which time he has been engaged in the active duties of his profession. His first pastorate was with the Beulah and Bates Fork Baptist Churches of this County. From these churches he was called to the charge of the

Waynesburg Baptist Church, where he is now in the ninth year of pastorate. His labors in all these fields have been eminently successful. Mr. Ryan has been twice married; first, to Miss Nantie, daughter of Jesse Hill, August 24, 1876. She died June 21, 1880. He was again married May 17, 1883, to Miss Lizzie, daughter of Calvin Rush, of Morris Township, this County. Mr. Ryan's family now consists of himself, wife and four children; viz., Gertrude M., and Nantie Belle, by his first wife; and Isa Lee and Jessie J., by his second marriage.

E. M. SAYERS, attorney at law, Waynesburg, Penn., is one of the first and most active business men of the county. He was born in Waynesburg May 30, 1812. His father Ephriam Sayers, was a native of London County, Virginia, and his mother, Mary (Wood) Sayers, was born in Hartford County, Maryland. Both were of English ancestry. Ehpriam Sayers was a pioneer of Greene County, having in 1786 settled two miles east of the present site of Waynesburg borough, where he led an industrious life, and reared a family of four children—three sons and one daughter. The subject of this sketch was reared on a farm in Franklin Township, this county, and completed his education in Washington College, He read law in Waynesburg with the Hon. Samuel Cleavenger, and commenced the practice of his profession in his native town in 1835. He has met with marked success, which may be attributed to his more than ordinary business qualifications. He is the owner of a number of farms in Greene County, large tracts of land in the South and West, and considerable real estate in Waynesburg. He has been a member of the Republican party since its organization. Mr. Sayers was united in marriage with Miss Jane Adams, a daughter of Robert Adams, in 1839, she died in 1847. Their children are Henry C., a farmer and business man of Waynesburg; James E., a member of the Greene County bar—Thomas and Ezra, deceased. Mr. Sayers was united in marriage the second time, in 1852, with Miss Harriet W. Tanner, a native of Massachusetts. They are the parents of six children: Norman, a farmer of Franklin Township; Florence A., wife of Charles A. Martin; Mary, D. L., and two children who were burned to death when quite young. Mr. Sayers has given his children the advantages of a liberal education. His sons Henry C. and James E., were soldiers in the late war; and his uncle, Josiah Sayers, and his grandfather, William Sayers, were in the Revolutionary war, being present when Lord Cornwallis surrendered his army at Yorktown, Virginia. The farm settled by William Sayers the ancestor is still in possession of the family, and has been for about a hundred years.

JAMES E. SAYERS attorney at law of Waynesburg, Penn., where he was born May 30, 1845, is a son of E. M. and Jane

(Adams) Sayers, also natives of Waynesburg. His father is an attorney and counsellor at law. James E. was reared in Waynesburg, where he attended the common school and college. He was afterwards a student in the Ohio State University, and learned the printing trade when a boy. July 15, 1862, he enlisted in Co. F, 85th Penn. Vol. Infantry, as a private, was discharged at Richmond, Va., with the rank of Orderly Sergent on May 13, 1865. He was "in at the death," having fired his last gun at Appomattox C. H. Va., and having participated in twenty-two battles and skirmishes and three seiges—Charlestown, S. C., Petersburg and Richmond, Va. Returning from the army, his first business venture was as an editor. In 1866 he bought the Waynesburg *Republican*, of which paper he was editor and proprietor for nearly three years, when he again entered school and graduated, in 1870, in the law course in the Indiana State University. For four years thereafter he continued in journalistic work. In 1874 he began the practice of law in Waynesburg, where he has since remained. Politically Mr. Sayers is an earnest Republican. He was a delegate in the National Republican Convention of 1884, and was once the nominee of his party for Congress in the Twenty-first District. On June 16, 1868, Mr. Sayers married Anna A., daughter of Albert Allison, One of the first merchants of Waynesburg. Mr. and Mrs. Sayers are the parents of two children—Albert H. and Jane.

ROBERT A. SAYERS, chief burgess of Waynesburg, Penn., born May 27, 1841, is a son of William W. and Rebecca (Adams) Sayers, natives of this county. His father was born August 12, 1805, and died May 22, 1886. He was a brother of E. M. Sayers, Esq., and they were for years associated in the real estate business in Waynesburg. William's main occupation was the stone and marble business, in which he was a partner with Simon Rinehart, Esq., for many years. He was married in Waynesburg to Miss Rebecca, daughter of Robert Adams, who was a Whig and a Republican, and lived to be ninety-six years old. He was at one time register and recorder of Greene County. Robert A., the subject of our sketch, was reared in Waynesburg, where he was educated in the college. When the war broke out he left college and enlisted Nov. 4, 1861, in the 8th Penn. Reserves. His military career is worthy of record. He participated in severe battles; was taken prisoner and suffered all the horrors of prison life. He was wounded at the battle of Gaines Mill, in left thigh, and left on the battle-field for two weeks receiving no medical aid. He was then sent to Belle Isle, and subsequently to Libby prison, where he was paroled and sent home. He only remained until his wound was well enough, and went through a long siege of typhoid and malarial fever, when he again joined his regiment at Upton Hill, Virginia. At the close of his three years' service he returned home and engaged in the coal business for sixteen years. In 1883 he was appointed U. S. Store-keeper and Guager. Mr. Sayers was married in Potter County, Penn., January 21, 1869, to Miss Florence Stevens, whose parents were born in Vermont. Mr. and Mrs. Sayers have one child—Fendora, now a student at Oberlin College, Ohio. Mr. and Mrs. Sayers and daughter are members of the Presbyterian Church. He is a Republican and a member of the G. A. R. Post, No. 367, Department of Pennsylvania.

HENRY C. SAYERS is among the successful busines men of Greene County. He has made farming his chief pursuit and has also dealt extensively in stock and real estate. He began business early in life, being the oldest son of E. M. Sayers, Esq. Mr. Sayers was born in Waynesburg, November 21, 1840. Here he grew to manhood and was a student at the first session of the college. He went to Iowa in 1859 and engaged in buying and shipping stock to Chicago, Illinois. He returned to Waynesburg in 1861, and August 11, 1862, he enlisted in Company G, Fifteenth Pennsylvania Cavalry. This was an independent regiment which acted as body guard to General Rosecrans. Among the battles in which he engaged were the following: Antietam, Murfreesboro, Chickamauga, Tullahama and Rome, Georgia, pursuit of Longstreet through Tennessee by way of Knoxville to North Carolina, and then had quite a skirmish with the Indians. In 1863 he was captured by General Wheeler's Cavalry and marched with Wheeler's command for some time before being paroled. After joining his regiment he was for a time detailed as a courier to carry despatches to the front facing the enemy. At the close of the war Mr. Sayers returned to Waynesburg, where he has been successfully engaged in business. He was united in marriage, in 1867, with Miss Clementine, daughter of Samuel Rush. Mrs. Sayers is a native of this county, and of English descent. Their children are—Ella Jane, C. E. and Henry C., Jr. Mrs. Sayers is a member of the C. P. Church. Mr. Sayers is a Republican, was constable of the county, two terms and has served as a member of the school board of Waynesburg. He is a member of the Masonic fraternity. Mr. Sayers was formerly a member of the Templeton Post of Washington, Penn., but now belongs to Col. J. F. McCullough Post, of Waynesburg, of which he has been commander, and was an alternate delegate to the Twenty-first National Encampment at St. Louis, Mo.

J. M. SCOTT, farmer and stock-grower, and U. S. store-keeper and gauger in the twenty-third collective district of Pennsylvania, was born in Jefferson Township, Greene County, Penn., December 10, 1844, and is a son of William P. and Sarah (Long) Scott. His father and grandfather were farmers. His grandfather, James Scott, came from Baltimore, Md., to Greene County, Penn., among the early settlers of Jefferson Township. J. M. Scott's grandmother, Scott, was ninety-eight years of age; her maiden name was Margaret Kincaid, she died April 1, 1888. The subject of our sketch is the oldest in a family of seven children, all of whom are living and married. He was reared on the farm, attended the district school in Jefferson Township and Waynesburg College. He taught school in early life, but has made farming his main pursuit, and is a resident of Franklin Township. In 1871 Mr. Scott marrried Miss Margaret, daughter of Hiram Rinehart. Their children are—Harry, Henry and Jesse. Mrs. Scott is a member of the Methodist Episcopal Church. Mr. Scott is a Democrat, and a member of I. O. O. F., and is a member of the encampment. He is also a Master Mason.

S. W. SCOTT, wool and grain merchant, was born in Washington County, June 26, 1835, and is a son of William and Abigail (Wood) Scott, natives of Washington County, Penn. His father was Scotch and his mother was of English and Irish origin. His father who was a farmer nearly all his life died in 1878. His family consisted of eight children. The subject of our sketch was reared in Greene County, to which his parents removed in 1839. He attended the public schools and Waynesburg College. He learned the carpenter's trade at which he worked for six years. Mr. Scott then began dealing in wool and has been extensively engaged in that business since 1863. He is prominent among the successful business men of Waynesburg. Mr. Scott, who is a Republican, was appointed Deputy U. S. Revenue Collector in 1864, and served until 1866. He was re-appointed in 1869 and served until 1874. Mr. Scott was married in 1865 to Miss Frances, daughter of Thomas Hill. Their children are—Ella B., wife of A. P. Dickey, Esq., of Waynesburg; William E., Nannie, Fannie and Samuel W. Mr. and Mrs. Scott are members of the Methodist Episcopal Church, in which he is a trustee.

W. G. SCOTT, Professor of Mathematics of Waynesburg College, was born in Washington County, Penn., December 11, 1832. His parents were William and Abigail (Wood) Scott, also natives of Washington County, and of Scotch and English ancestry. They were married in Washington County, where they remained until 1839, at which time they removed to Greene County, where they remained until their death. Mr. Scott departed this life in 1878, and his widow in 1880. They were the parents of nine children, eight still living. Prof. W. G. Scott is the oldest and was united in marriage, April 17, 1862, with Miss Mary Sutton, who was born in England, being the daughter of the Rev. R. H. and Martha (Cowen) Sutton, now residents of Waynesburg. To Mr. and Mrs. Scott have been born three children—Mattie E., wife of Rev. J. H. Lucas; Minnie M., wife of J. N. Norris, and Gail. Prof. Scott acquired his earliest education in the old-fashioned log school-house and afterwards attended Waynesburg College, where he graduated in the year 1867. After teaching one year in Greene Academy, he was elected to the chair of mathematics of Waynesburg College, and has filed the position ever since. He has also been engaged in the mercantile business since 1867, being now sole proprietor of the store opened by him and his father in that year. It is one of the leading stores in Waynesburg, receiving a large patronage from the town and vicinity.

E. H. SHIPLEY, druggist, was born in Uniontown, Fayette County, Pennsylvania, November 3, 1864, and is a son of Julius and Eliza (Hair) Shipley. His parents were also natives of Fayette County, and of English descent. His father was a civil engineer, and is now deceased. The subject of our sketch is the second in a family of three children. He was reared in a Uniontown, where he attended school. He afterwards clerked in a drug store for a period of three years. Mr. Shipley came to Waynesburg in 1881, clerked in a drug store for two years, then opened up his present business, in which he has been very liberally patronized by the people of Waynesburg and vicinity. He is a Democrat in politics. On January 23, 1888, Mr. Shipley married Miss Anna L., daughter of Captain J. R. and Nancy (Bayard) Hewitt. Mrs. Shipley is a native of this county, born July 7, 1865.

A. F. SILVEUS, attorney at law, Waynesburg, Penn., was born near Jackson Centre, Mercer County, on the 5th of December, 1851. He is the son of Henry B. and Rachael (Taylor) Silveus, who were natives of Greene County, and were of German and English origin. His father, a farmer and stock-grower, was elected sheriff of Greene County in 1867, and served the term of three years. The son was the fourth in a family of eight children, five sons and three daughters. He was reared upon the farm, attended the common schools, and when his father was elected sheriff he served as deputy. He subsequently taught school, and became a student at Waynesburg College, from which he graduated in 1873. He then resumed teaching, and in 1875 was elected superintendent of the schools of Greene County. For two terms he taught in Waynesburg College, giving special attention to the normal classes. He read law with Hon. A. A. Purman, was admitted to practice in 1878, and opened an office at Waynesburg, where he has practiced since. He has served as a school director. He was married in 1877 to Miss Lida, daughter of John T. Hook. Both are members of the Cumberland Presbyterian Church. They have two children—Jessie and John T. In politics Mr. Silveus is a Democrat.

REV. J. L. SIMPSON, a retired Methodist minister, was born in Virginia, January 6, 1822. He is a son of William and Mary Ann (Leech) Simpson, who were of English and Irish descent. His father was a boot-maker. Rev. J. L. Simpson is the second in a family of eight children. He received a collegiate course in West Virginia, and also served a regular apprenticeship at the saddler's trade. He entered the ministry in his twenty-second year, in which field he has successfully labored ever since. He was first licensed in 1844 and was appointed as an assistant in Pittsburgh, Penn. In 1846 he came to Waynesburg and took charge of a circuit, but subsequently went to Virginia, where he engaged in the ministry until 1862. When a large number of the young men in his church and congregation enlisted in the army and insisted on his going with them, he enlisted and was elected Captain of their company. They were assigned to the Fourth Virginia Cavalry. Captain Simpson was elected chaplin of the regiment and served two years in that capacity. At the close of the war he again entered the ministry and went to Wisconsin, where he took charge of the Methodist Protestant Church at Beliot for two years. In 1854 he was married to Miss Mary J., daughter of Thomas and Nannie Black. Her parents were natives of West Virginia, and of Scotch and English descent. Mr. and Mrs. Simpson have six children, three of whom are living—Anna May, wife of Harvey Clifford, of Wisconsin; Mary L. and George B. The deceased are Charles R., Helen V. and Carrie Olive. The family are members of the Methodist Protestant Church. Mr. Simpson is a Republican, and has met with more than average success as a minister of the gospel.

A. C. SMALLEY, chief of police, was born in Waynesburg, September 10, 1843. His parents, E. P. and Catherine (Rinehart) Smalley, were also natives of Waynesburg. His father was born in 1805, and died in 1885. The subject of this sketch is the oldest in a family of three children—two sons and a daughter. He attended the public school and Waynesburg College. Mr. Smalley learned the chairmaker's trade and carried on the business in Waynesburg for a time. In 1862 he enlisted in Company H, in the One-Hundred and Twenty-Third Pennsylvania Volunteer Infantry and served his term of enlistment. On returning home, he resumed chair making and carried on the business until he embarked in the mercantile trade. On account of failing health he retired from business in 1883, sold out in 1887 and was appointed chief of police, which position he still holds. In 1868 Mr. Smalley was married to Mary E., daughter of Absalom Hedge. She is also a native of this county, and of English lineage. Mr. and Mrs. Smalley are members of the Baptist Church, in which he is trustee and treasurer of the Sabbath-school. He belongs to the G. A. R. Post, No. 367, Department of Pennsylvania, of which he has been quartermaster, and is also a Master Mason.

J. M. SMITH, saddle and harness manufacturer, was born at Carmichaels, Penn., November 18, 1845, and is a son of H. A. and

Mary E. (McGee) Smith. His grandfather, J. H. McGee, was a wealthy merchant at Carmichaels, where he also engaged extensively in the coal business. Mr. Smith's father was also a saddle and harness manufacturer and carried on a successful business at Carmichaels for many years, was also post-master for sixteen years. The subject of our sketch is the oldest of a family of five children—four sons and one daughter. He was reared in this county, receiving his education in the old Greene Academy at Carmichaels. Mr. Smith earned harness making with his father and has been engaged in that business since 1867. In 1864 he enlisted in the Twenty-Second Regiment of Pennsylvania Cavalry, or Ringold Cavalry, and was with General Sheridan on his famous ride from Winchester. He then went West for eight years, returning to Waynesburg in 1875, when he engaged in his present business and has met with average success. Mr. Smith was united in marriage, September 19, 1876, with Melissa Donley, whose ancestors were among the early Irish settlers of Pennsylvania, and among the first to find a home in Greene County. Mr. and Mrs. Smith have four children—Harry, Joseph R. D., Donley McGee and Catharine D. Mr. Smith is a Republican and has been a member of the town council three terms. He is Captain of the Waynesburg Blues—Company K, Tenth Regiment, N. G. P., and a member of the G. A. R. Post of Waynesburg.

JAMES B. SMITH, county surveyor, was born in Center Township, August 16, 1846, and is a son of Edmund and Elizabeth (Adamson) Smith. They were also natives of this county, and of English origin. His father was a farmer all his life, and died in February, 1887. Of his family of eight children six are now living, of whom James B. is the third. He was reared in Greene County, attending the common school and the Millsboro Normal school. He gave especial attention to the study of surveying and civil engineering and has devoted most of his time to that business, having served as county surveyor for several years. Since 1880 he has been principally engaged in civil engineering. In September, 1868, Mr. Smith married Miss Elizabeth M., daughter of Samuel Throckmorton, and they have one child, Albert Bunyan.

D. A. SPRAGG, U. S. Revenue Collector of the twenty-third district, Greene County, Penn., was born January 28, 1835. He is a son of Jeremiah and Sarah (Shriver) Spragg, natives of this county. His ancestors were among the earliest English farmers of Wayne Township. The original farm is still in possession of the family. Mr. Spragg's father died in 1877. Of his family of three children the subject of our sketch is the second. He was reared on the farm in Wayne Township, attending the district school. He chose farming as an occupation, but followed it only a short time.

At the age of thirty-two he opened a store at Spraggsville. He was elected sheriff of the county in 1882 and held the office three years. In April, 1886, he was appointed to his present position. In 1860 Mr. Spragg married Elizabeth, daughter of John Gibbons. Mrs. Spragg is also a native of this county, and of English extraction. Their children are—Sidney D., wife of C. T. Wise, and Herman. Mr. Spragg is a Democrat, and a member of the I. O. O. F., in which order he has taken all the degrees.

T. ROSS SPROAT, farmer and stock-grower, who was born in West Virginia, January 7, 1842, is a son of James and Susan (Johnson) Sproat. His mother was born in Washington County, Penn. His father, a native of Greene County, and a farmer and carpenter by occupation, settled in Whiteley Township in 1844, and died in 1849. Mr. Sproat's grandfather was David Sproat, a native of Virginia. At his father's death Ross was obliged to make his home among strangers, and received but a limited education in the district schools. He started out in life, however, with a determination to succeed and, by means of his energy and close application to his work, he has secured a good farm of one-hundred and fifty-nine acres, where he resides near Waynesburg, Penn. In 1862 Mr. Sproat enlisted in Company K, Eighteenth Pennsylvania Cavalry. He was discharged in 1863, having taken sick at the battle of Stone River and never again being able for duty. In 1869, he married Miss Harriet, daughter of Joseph and Charlotte (Rinehart) Ankrom. Her parents were natives of this county—her father was born in 1807 and is still living. Mr. and Mrs. Sproat are the parents of seven children—Charlotte, Joseph, Susan, Eva V., Wilbert, Jesse and May. Their parents are members of the Methodist Episcopal Church, in which Mr. Sproat has been class-leader, and superintendent of the Sabbath-school.

M. L. STROSNIDER, manufacturer of woolen goods, Waynesburg, Penn., was born in West Virginia, June 11, 1847, and is a son of Moses and Mary (Thompson) Strosnider. They were natives of Greene County, Penn., and of German and Scotch-Irish extraction. His father was a wheelwright by trade. M. L. Strosnider is next to the youngest of ten children, was reared in West Virginia, and received his education in Waynesburg College. He first began manufacturing in Blacksville, W. Va., in 1870, where he continued until 1884. In that year he established the woolen-mills at Waynesburg, where he has since successfully engaged in that business. Mr. Strosnider was united in marriage May 19, 1875, with Caroline, daughter of Alexander Wallace, and they have had three children, viz.—James W., Harley L. and Flora, of which two are living. Mr. and Mrs. Strosnider are members of the Methodist Episcopal Church. He is a Democrat, and a member of the Knights of Honor.

CAPT. W. H. STOY was born at Brownsville, Penn., February 12, 1815, and is a son of Henry W. and Catharine (Cook) Stoy. His mother was born at Hagerstown, Maryland, and his father at Lebanon, Penn. They were of Dutch and English descent. His father received a medical education in Germany. His grandfather was a graduate of Heidleberg College, and was sent to this country by the King of Germany as a foreign minister. Captain Stoy's father came to Brownsville in 1807 and practiced medicine for forty-five years. Captain Stoy had a natural inclination for music, which he wisely cultivated, and for fifty years he has been a teacher and composer. He has twenty bands in different towns and cities for which he furnishes music. In 1861 he enlisted and served in the Union army as leader of the band for the Eighth Pennsylvania Reserves. He served until the bands were discharged by general order, when he returned to Waynesburg, where he has since resided. He was married in 1844 to Margaret, daughter of Allen Biggs. Mrs. Stoy was born in Ohio County, W. Va., in 1826. Their children are all married except the youngest. They are—Mary, wife of J. P. Sullivan; Charlotte, wife of George Albertson; Catharine, wife of I. B. Raisor; Henry W., a printer; Gustavus, a drug clerk; Dollie, wife of T. J. Hawkins; Lillie, wife of D. M. Morrison; Jennie, widow of W. F. Clayton; George B., who married Miss Anna Robison, of Bealsville, in 1888; and Frank, a tailor in Pittsburgh, Penn. Captain Stoy is a prominent member of the Masonic fraternity and a Sir Knight Templar. Gustavus, his second son, was born in Washington, Penn., August 26, 1854. He was reared in Waynesburg, where he attended school and also learned telegraphy. At the present time he is salesman and prescription clerk for H. S. Blachly, of Waynesburg. He was married in 1884 to Miss Ruth Robinson, a native of West Moreland County, Penn., and a niece of Hon. R. S. Robinson.

GEORGE TAYLOR, a successful farmer and stock-grower of Franklin Township, was born in Washington Township, this county, February 16, 1832. His parents were William and Jane (Crane) Taylor, also natives of this county. His father's family consisted of three children, of whom George is the oldest. He was reared in Washington Township, where he received his education, and early in life began farming. He is now the owner of 318 acres of good farming land in Greene County. In 1858 Mr. Taylor married Miss Dorcas, daughter of William Grimes. Mrs. Taylor was born in Franklin Township in 1831, and is a sister of H. M. Grimes, a prominent farmer. Mr. and Mrs. Taylor have a family of eight children—Margaret Maria, wife of J. Huffman; Elizabeth Mary, wife of Thomas Robinson; William G., George W., C. F., Daniel C., Ella and Dorcas Anna. Mr. Taylor is a Democrat, and has served on the school board of his district.

JUSTUS FORDYCE TEMPLE, ex-auditor general of the State of Pennsylvania, was born in this county February 13, 1824, and is a son of John and Elizabeth (Douglas) Temple. His parents were natives of Pennsylvania, and of English extraction. His father, an inn-keeper, was also a drover, and dealt in stock extensively. General Temple was the oldest in a family of four children, and was reared in Greene County, where he attended the common schools. Early in life he learned the cooper's trade, at which he worked for four years. He then taught school and took an active part in the teachers' institutes. In 1854, General Temple, who is a Democrat, was elected county auditor, and in 1857 was elected register and recorder, which office he held for six years. He was then elected prothonotary of the county and served for six years in that office. He then took up the study of law and was admitted to the bar in 1869, remaining in active practice until 1874, when he was elected State auditor general, where he served with honor for three years. He then resumed the practice of law. General Temple was at one time somewhat of a musician, and considered by the boys in blue as an expert fifer. He takes an active interest in the schools, and has served as a member of the school board. He was an active mover in the erection of the new college building at Waynesburg, and gave liberally to the enterprise. General Temple was married in 1851 to Miss Nancy Ann Schroy, who died in 1875. Their children are— Mary, wife of William J. Bayard; Nevada, wife of William G. Osgoodby; James B. and Anna Belle, wife of Joseph O'Neill. In 1877 the General married Katherine, daughter of Michael Salmon. General Temple is a prominent member of the I. O. O. F. He has been Deputy Grand Master, and is also a member of the Masonic fraternity.

JOHN P. TEAGARDEN, attorney at law, was born at the old Teagarden homestead in Richhill Township, Greene County, Penn. His father was Colonel Isaac Teagarden. His mother's maiden name was Sarah A. Parker. The family is of Prussian origin, and the ancestry is traced back many generations. Abraham Teagarden was an educated civil engineer, and came from Prussia to America in 1744, locating first at Philadelphia, Penn., where in 1745 he married Miss Mary Parker, of English birth. Their oldest child, William Teagarden, was born in Philadelphia on the 17th day of January, 1746. Some time after this Abraham Teagarden, with his family, moved to Western Pennsylvania. He was one of the first white men who attempted to make a settlement in this part of the State. Tradition tells of the many thrilling adventures he and his family had with the Indians. William Teagarden was married to Bethia

Craig, of Maryland. Shortly after this Abraham and William Teagarden, and two other families named Hughes and Hupp, made the first settlement attempted in the limits of Greene County, near where Clarksville now stands. Old Fort Red Stone, near Brownsville, was the nearest fort or place of refuge from the savage marauders. William Teagarden and his wife, had, one occasion taken refuge in old Fort Redstone, and it was there, on March 6, 1775, that Abraham Teagarden, grandfather of John P. Teagarden, was born. Abraham Teagarden secured a liberal education for those days. During the Indian wars following, he enlisted as a private soldier in General Wayne's army, and remained in the field until peace was restored. He married Nancy McGuier, and immediately moved to lands he had located in Richhill Township and in West Finley Township, Washington County. His first house was on the old Teagarden homestead in Richhill Township. Twelve children were born to them, the third being Isaac, the father of John P. Teagarden. Isaac Teagarden was born April 12, 1807. He was a mill-wright by occupation, and built many of the mills in this and Washington County. When the slavery question arose he was among the first to array himself on the side of liberty and equal rights. He assisted in the organization of the so-called Abolition party and cast one of the first votes for that party in this county. He voted for Birney, the Freesoil candidate for President, and continued to act with the party of freedom, voting for all its candidates, until the organization of the Republican party in 1856, when he connected himself with that party, and remained steadfast to its principles till the time of his death, June 20, 1886. He was elected Colonel of the Forty-sixth Pennsylvannia Militia and was commissioned Colonel by Governor Ritner in 1838, for three years. When the war of the late Rebellion came, he, at the advanced age of fifty-four, enlisted in Company F, Eighty-fith Pennsylvania Volunteers. He participated with his regiment in the battles of the Peninsula and before Yorktown. He was a member of the Christian Church. His family consisted of four children—Phœbe Jane, Charity Louise, John Parker and Thomas L., the latter having died early in childhood. Phœbe Jane Teagarden was one of the prominent teachers of the county, but she abandoned that profession and commenced the study of medicine, which she completed in a three years' course at the Woman's Medical College at Philadelphia, graduating from that institution in the class of 1882. She then immediately commenced the practice of medicine at Waynesburg, where she now has a large and lucrative practice. Charity Louise Teagarden is also a teacher of prominence, and is at present a teacher in the Union school of Waynesburg, a position she has held for the past twelve years. John P. Teagarden commenced life as a teacher. In 1869 he went to Iowa to teach school, and in the fall of that year commenced the study of law under the tutorship of W. W. Haskel, of the Oskaloosa, Mahaska County bar, and was admitted to practice in the several courts of Iowa in 1871. He returned to the home of his parents in Richhill Township, and in 1872 the entire family moved to Waynesburg. He was admitted to practice at the Greene County bar in 1872, and later to the Supreme Court of Pennsylvania and the United States Courts, and has continued in the practice ever since. He is a Republican in politics, and has always taken an active interest in political affairs. In 1878 he was tendered the Republican nomination for State Senate in the Fortieth Senatorial District composed of Greene and Fayette counties; and while he was defeated, yet he materially reduced the large Democratic majority in the district. In 1880 he was elected Presidential elector and cast one of Pennsylvania's votes for General James A. Garfield for President. He served two years as Secretary and three years as Chairman of the Republican County Committee. He was elected burgess of Waynesburg borough two terms, was a member of council two terms, and is a prominent member of the I. O. O. F. of this county. He was married in 1885 to Miss Mary E. Davis, of Waynesburg.

JOB THROCKMORTON, a farmer and stock-grower of Oak Forest, Penn., was born in Greene County December 17, 1809. His father and mother were Joseph and Catharine (Hulsart) Throckmorton, natives of New Jersey, and of English origin. His father, who was a farmer all his life, came to Greene County in 1809, and settled two miles west of Waynesburg, Penn. His family consisted of ten children, five daughters and five sons, of whom Job was the oldest, and was reared on the farm with is parents. Early in life he learned the tailor's trade and engaged in that business for seventeen years. He then bought his first farm, in 1835, and has since devoted his time wholly to farming. His home farm contains 109 acres of valuable land. Mr. Throckmorton was united in marriage with Sarah Fry, who is of German extraction. Her grandparents were among the earliest settlers of this county. Her father was a farmer and lived to be over forty-five years old. Mr. and Mrs. Throckmorton's children are—George, a farmer; Catharine, wife of John Maple; Joseph R., a farmer; and Franklin B., a carpenter. Mrs. Maple, the only daughter, died February 17, 1885, and her husband died February 18th of the same month and year, and both were buried in one grave at the same time. Mr. and Mrs. Throckmorton are members of the M. E. Church, in which he has held various official positions. He has been a life-long Democrat, and has held most of the offices in Franklin Township. Mr. Throckmorton is greatly interested in school matters, and has served as school director for a number of years.

F. B. THROCKMORTON, secretary of the Waynesburg Roller Mill Company, was born in Franklin Township, Greene County, Penn., October 12, 1852. He is a son of Job and Sarah (Fry) Throckmorton, the former a native of Pennsylvania and the latter of New Jersey. They were of English descent. His father was a tailor by trade and followed that business in early life, but later he retired to the farm where he now resides in Franklin Township. F. B. Throckmorton is the youngest in a family of four children and was reared in Franklin Township, where he attended the district schools. Early in life he learned the cooper's trade which he followed until 1885, when he was employed by the roller mill company at Waynesburg. In 1872 Mr. Throckmorton married Sarah A., daughter of William Johnson. Their children are Ada B., Jesse E., George Albert and William. Mr. and Mrs. Throckmorton are members of the Methodist Episcopal Church, of which he is trustee. He is a Democrat and has served as township assessor. He is chaplain of the Royal Arcanum at Waynesburg.

J. T. ULLOM, physician and surgeon, of Waynesburg, Penn., was born in Center Township, Greene County, Penn., April 11, 1847. He is a son of D. T. and Anna (Johnson) Ullom, natives of this county, and of German and Irish lineage. His ancestors were among the earliest settlers of the county. Dr. Ullom is a member of a family of twelve children, nine of whom grew to maturity. He was reared on the farm and attended Waynesburg College. He began the study of medicine in 1866, with Dr. S. L. Blachly, at Sparta, Washington County, Penn. In 1868 he attended lectures at Charity Hospital Medical College at Cleveland, Ohio. In 1869 he entered Jefferson Medical College at Philadelphia, and graduated in 1870. He at once began the practice of his profession in Rogersville, Greene County, where he continued for seventeen years. He came to Waynesburg in 1887 and formed his present partnership with Dr. J. T. Iams. Dr. Ullom was married in Rogersville, January 8, 1875, to Anna, daughter of George Sellers. She is also a native of this county, and of English descent. Their children are—Blanche and Frank S. Dr. and Mrs. Ullom are members of the Methodist Protestant Church. He is a member of the Masonic fraternity. He has been president of the County Medical Society, and in 1887 was elected first vice-president of the State Medical Society.

W. S. VANDRUFF, surveyor, born in Perry Township, this county, May 18, 1852, is a son of John and Rachel (Maple) Vandruff, natives of Greene County. They own a well-improved farm of 119 acres in Perry Township, where Mr. W. S. Vandruff was born. He is the oldest in a family of ten children, and was reared on the farm, attending the common schools of the county. When he reached his majority, he began working by the month on a farm. At the age of twenty-three he learned the carpenter's trade, at which he worked until 1880. While working at his trade he studied surveying, and is now considered a competent surveyor. He also draws maps with great speed and accuracy. In 1887 Mr. Vandruff erected a neat and substantial residence in Waynesburg, where he now lives. He owns a small farm in Perry Township, where he has given considerable attention to bee culture. Mr. Vandruff, who is a man of more than ordinary ability, is a great reader and has a bright future before him. He was married in 1876 to Matilda, daughter of John and Dorotha (Haines) Fox, natives of this county. Mr. and Mrs. Vandruff are the parents of two children—Ross Elliott and Ottly Earl. They are members of the Methodist Episcopal Church.

D. S. WALTON, attorney, and member of the firm of Wyly, Buchanan & Walton, was born at Ryerson's Station, Greene County, Penn., May 17, 1853. His parents were D. M. and Mary M. (Drake) Walton, the former a native of Washington County, Penn., and the latter of Philadelphia. They were married in Clarksville, this county, and settled in the city of Pittsburgh, where they were burned out in 1845. They then returned to Clarksville, and in 1850 moved to Ryerson's Station. Mrs. Walton departed this life in 1859. Nine years after her death Mr. Walton moved with his family to Oskaloosa, Iowa, where he has since resided. The family consisted of ten children, of whom three are living. Mr. D. S. Walton, who is next to the youngest, acquired his education in the common schools and in the colleges at Oskaloosa and Waynesburg. He read law with Wyly and Buchanan, of Waynesburg, and Judge Rinehart, of Oskaloosa. He was admitted to the bar in Iowa, November 17, 1874, practiced one year, and came to Waynesburg, entering the firm of which he is still a member. Mr. Walton is a member of the Masonic fraternity, and has filled several offices of trust in Waynesburg. He has been a member of the borough council, a member of the school board, and in 1884 was burgess of the borough. He has been a trustee of the college for twelve years, and is now president of the board. Mr. Walton was united in marriage, March 18, 1873, with Miss Mary A., daughter of James A. J. Buchanan, and they are the parents of one child, Jimmie B., a bright and interesting son, who was born March 27, 1874, and departed this life April 17, 1888.

GEORGE W. WISECARVER, farmer, Waynesburg, Penn.—Among the representative business men of Greene County, we take pleasure in mentioning the name of George W. Wisecarver, who was born in Whiteley Township, this county, July 22, 1813. His parents were George and Catharine (Orndorf) Wisecarver, natives of Frederick County, Va., and of English and German descent. The former was born in 1756. Mrs. Wisecarver was several years younger.

They came to Greene County in 1800, settled in Whiteley Township and remained until their death. They were the parents of nine children, all of whom lived to be over seventy years of age. Of these six are living, the youngest now past the seventieth mile-stone. George W. Wisecarver's early life was spent with his parents on the farm in Whiteley Township, and on account of the thinly settled country his opportunities for an education were very limited, and he received but four months' schooling. His father did not succeed in accumulating very much of this world's goods, and was obliged to have his children raised by strangers. At the age of sixteen George started out in life for himself, and has succeeded so well that at one time he was the owner of 4,000 acres of good land in Greene County, the most of which he has divided with his family. It is very interesting to hear Mr. Wisecarver relate the many things that have transpired from the time he did his first day's work in the county for himself, up to the present, when we find him among the wealthiest men of Greene County. The pay for the first day's work was a fish-hook, and we would presume that he did not like work by the day, as he soon found employment by the month at very low wages, and for his first month's work received from his employer, Samuel Nelson, one pair of shoes valued at $1.50. At that time $4 was considered good pay for a month's work. Mr. Wisecarver learned the cooper's trade, which he followed in connection with his farming. Most of the time for twelve years he worked eighteen hours out of every twenty-four, and for seven years he made enough at night at his trade to pay two men for their work through the next day. In 1843 he bought a farm of 210 acres in Washington Township. In 1849 his shop and coopering tools were destroyed by fire. Since then he has devoted most of his time to farming, dealing in real estate and raising live stock. In 1854 Mr. Wisecarver went to Iowa and entered 2,000 acres of land. In 1857 he bought 330 acres more in Greene County, and in the same year he traded his land in Iowa for 500 acres in Richhill Township, this county, giving the difference in cash. He traded most of his land in Iowa for land in Pennsylvania. By good management and industry he added many acres to these purchases, and has cleared over 1,000 acres in this county. Mr. Wisecarver, like the majority of business men, has had his share of bad luck, and has paid over $45,000 for security and otherwise, from which he derived but little benefit; but being more of a believer in pluck than luck, he has succeeded notwithstanding his losses. He was united in marriage, May 1, 1843, with Priscilla, daughter of Jacob and Phœbe (Crayne) Barnes. To Mr. and Mrs. Wisecarver have been born eight children, viz: Nancy, who has been twice married, first to Norman Worley, deceased, her present husband being Maj. Benjamin Herrington; Caroline, wife of Amos A. Allison;

Frank P., of Philadelphia; Timothy J., a large land-owner in this county; Margaret M., wife of Jesse Wise, a young attorney of the Waynesburg bar; and Virginia, a very estimable young lady. The deceased are Phœbe J. and Elizabeth. Mr. Wisecarver's father served as wagon-master under Gen. Washington, and drew a pension until his death. He was present when Lord Cornwallis surrendered·

REV. JOEL J. WOOD, farmer and stock-grower, Waynesburg, Penn.—The subject of this sketch is one of the few Methodist ministers who have been financially successful. He owns over four hundred acres of land in Greene County, and also has land in the State of Iowa. Mr. Wood, who is of English extraction, was born in Whiteley Township this county, in 1814, and is the third son of Edward Wood, also a native of Greene County. Rev. Mr. Wood attended the old Greene Academy at Carmichaels, Penn., and obtained a good English education, together with a fair knowledge of the languages. Early in life he made a profession of religion. He taught school a few months, but subsequently accepted a circuit in the Pittsburg conference, and was actively engaged as a minister over twenty-five years. He was always faithful to his charge and allowed nothing to interfere with his appointments. He has met with marked success in building church houses and has been to a great extent instrumental in building up the Methodist Protestant Church. Since 1866 Mr. Wood has engaged in farming. He has been twice married. His present wife, whom he married in 1864, was Miss Maggie E. Boyd, of Washington County, Penn. He was first married at Fairmount, West Virginia, to Mary Ann, second daughter of Rev. A. A. Shinn, D. D., who was one of the organizers of the Methodist Protestant Church. Mrs. Wood died in 1852. They had two children, one now living—Asa R., a prominent business man of Washington, Penn. By his second marriage Mr. Wood is the father of three children—Mary E., Phœbe A. and Harriet Frances.

HIRAM C. WOOD, wool and stock-dealer, was born in Franklin Township, Greene County, Penn., April 11, 1851. He is a son of John D. and Sevela (Barnes) Wood. His mother was a native of New Jersey. His father, who was born in Greene County, Penn., was an extensive dealer in wool and stock, and died September 26, 1876. He was also a physician of the Eclectic School and had an extensive practice. Mr. Hiram C. Wood is the youngest of six children living. He received his education in the common schools of Greene County. He very naturally took up the business of his father and was his partner in stock-dealing for several years. He owns a fine farm of one hundred and seventy-five acres in Franklin Township. In February, 1873, Mr. Wood was united in marriage with Sarah J., daughter of Corbly Orndoff, ex-county commissisner, and they are the parents of three children—John F., Nora M. and

Mattie C.   Mr. and Mrs. Wood are members of the Methodist Episcopal Church.   He is a Democrat, and a member of the I. O. O. F. Lodge at Oak Forest, Penn.; also a member of the Waynesburg Council, No. 550, Royal Arcanum.   He was a member of the firm of John Hesket & Co., commission merchants for the sale of live stock at the Central Stock Yards, Pittsburg, Penn.

HENRY ZIMMERMAN.—The writer takes great pleasure in giving a sketch of the life of Henry Zimmerman, of Franklin Township, one of the oldest citizens of Greene County, born November 23, in the year 1813.   He has witnessed great strides in the progress and improvement of the county.   He has seen the wilderness metamorphosed into highly cultivated and rich farming lands, covered with pleasant homes and inhabited by a prosperous and intelligent people.   His parents, who were of English and German descent, came to Greene County in 1809, and resided in Whiteley Township twenty-five years, then they took up five hundred acres of land in Franklin Township, on which they resided until their death. Henry was a member of a family of nine children, all boys; and his father lived to see the day—the proudest of his life—when he and his nine sons could march to the polls in solid phalanx and cast ten democratic votes.   At present writing (1888), however, but two of his sons are living—the subject of our sketch and Robert Zimmerman, of Wayne Township.   In his youth Henry Zimmerman learned the trade of stone masonry, which he has followed through life, together with farming, being the owner of a fine farm of one hundred and twenty-five acres in Franklin Township.   His California peaches are the finest ever brought to market in this part of the country, and he takes great pride in his orchard of over eight hundred trees.   Mr. Zimmerman was united in marriage, September 29, 1839, with Mary Ellen, daughter of William and Ellen (Hood) Seals, who were of Irish and English ancestry.   Mrs. Zimmerman is a grand-daughter of James Seals, who was a Colonel in the Revolutionary war.   To Mr. and Mrs. Zimmerman were born two children—Ellen J. and James B., who was born in 1856, and in 1879 married Jane A., daughter of Robert and Elizabeth Tewksberry. Their children are W. S., Robert H. and Gilbert T. R.   Ellen J. was united in marriage with J. S. Herrington, and they were the parents of two children—Mary C. (deceased) and Emma A.

R. S. ZOLLARS, farmer and stock-grower, Waynesburg, Penn., was born in this county July 4, 1835.   He is a son of Neal and Elizabeth (Spencer) Zollars, natives of Pennsylvania, and of French and Dutch extraction.   His father, a farmer, came to this county in 1834.   Richard, the oldest of his six children, was reared on the farm, and received his earliest education in the district school.   He subsequently attended Waynesburg College, and for three years clerked in a dry goods store. In 1862 he enlisted in Company F, First Pennsylvania Cavalry, and served until the close of the war. Returning to his native county, he has since successfully devoted his time to farming. Mr. Zollars was united in marriage in 1882, with Miss Mary, daughter of Caldwell Orr. Mrs. Zollars was born and raised in this county, and is a zealous member of the M. E. Church. Her husband is a Republican, and served one term as coroner of the county. He is a prominent member of the I. O. O. F. and the G. A. R. Post.

GILMORE TOWNSHIP.

WILLIAM CLOVIS, a farmer and stock-grower of Greene County, Penn., was born in Monongalia County, West Virginia, September 9, 1825. His parents, Matthias and Nancy (Barr) Clovis, were natives of eastern Pennsylvania, and of German extraction. His father was a shoemaker by trade, and spent most of his life in Greene County. He died in 1861. William is the ninth in a family of twelve children. He received his education in this county, and early in life learned the miller's trade and engaged in that business for sixteen years. He has since been farming and dealing extensively in stock. He has lived in Gilmore Township since 1864. Mr. Clovis has made a success of his business, and has a wide circle of friends in Greene County. He is a Republican in politics, and was elected county commissioner in 1888. His home farm contains two hundred and eighty-seven acres of good land. William Clovis was united in marriage, in West Virginia, with Miss Rebecca, daughter of Robert and Margaret (Hinkens) Chalfant, who were of English and German lineage. Mr. and Mrs. Clovis have a family of twelve children, eleven of whom are living—Jacob C., a farmer and miller; Marion J., a farmer; John H., a merchant; L. B., a stock-dealer; Frances E., widow of Phenix Meighen; A. E., a merchant; Peter, Samuel S. and Robert M., farmers; Dora Belle and Oscar W. Their parents are members of the M. E. Church, in which Mr. Clovis is steward, trustee and class-leader. He also takes an active interest in the Sabbath school. He has served as justice of the peace for a period of ten years.

JEFFERSON DYE, hotel-keeper at Jolleytown, Penn., is a descendant of the earliest settlers of this county, and of English and German extraction. His father was a farmer and miller by occupation.

Mr. Dye comes of a large family, of which there are representatives now located in various parts of the United States. He was born November 16, 1844, a son of Minor and Rachel (Caine) Dye. His mother was born in Loudoun County, Virginia, and was of German and English lineage. Jefferson was reared in Greene County, Penn., where he attended the common schools. He was with his father in the mill until he went to the war, in 1861. He enlisted in Company F, Seventh West Virginia Infantry, and was a non-commissioned officer. He was in many serious engagements; among others, the battles of Antietam, Chancellorsville and Gettysburg. Mr. Dye was a brave soldier, and at the battle of Antietam when his regiment was relieved by a regiment of Meagher's Irish Brigade, he did not retire from the field with his regiment, but went in with the Irish Brigade. After exhausting all his ammunition he replenished his cartridge box from the box of a wounded comrade of Company H. At the close of the war he returned to Jolleytown, where he has been proprietor of a hotel and undertaking shop since 1872, and recently engaged in merchandising. He was married in this county, February 9, 1871, to Rebecca A., daughter of Henry Shriver. Mrs. Dye was born in Monongalia County, W. Va. She was appointed postmistress under President Cleveland's administration. To Mr. and Mrs. Dye were born five children, four of whom are living—Eva, Charles, Frank, Fannie and Mary (deceased). Mr. Dye's first wife was Mary J. Mc-Cans. They had one daughter—Harriet. Mr. and Mrs. Dye are members of the Methodist Episcopal Church. He was elected justice of the peace in 1882, re-elected in 1887; is a member of the I. O. O. F. and G. A. R. Post No. 367, J. F. McCullough, Waynesburg, Penn.

JACOB M. EAKIN, who is a farmer and stock-grower of Gilmore Township, was born in Monongalia County, West Virginia, September 1, 1827, and is a son of Justus and Mary (Myers) Eakin, who were of Dutch and Scotch-Irish extraction. His mother was born at Garard's Fort, this county. His father, a native of Virginia, was a cooper by trade, came to Greene County in early life, and died in 1870. His grandfather, William Eakin, was a carpenter, and located for many years at the old glass works at Greensboro, Penn. Jacob's grandfather was a soldier in the Revolutionary war, and died in Virginia. Jacob M. is the eighth of a family of ten children. He was reared in West Virginia and remained there until August, 1844. He then removed to Greene County, Penn., where he has been a very successful farmer, and is the owner of 600 acres of valuable land in this county. Mr. Eakin has been twice married, his first wife being Miss Mary, a daughter of Erastus and Mary (Barnes) Woodruff. Her parents were natives of Delaware, and of English descent. To Mr. and Mrs. Eakin were born four children—Phœbe

J., wife of David Staggers; Sarah, wife of Marion Clovis; Athaliah, wife of Jacob Clovis, and J. Pierce, the only son. He was born in Gilmore Township, May 31, 1856, where he spent his early manhood. He was married in West Virginia, near Morgantown, January 29, 1880, to Mattie, daughter of Colonel Reuben Finnell, and they have three children—Jacob Myres, Mary Bodley and Robert Leemoyne. Mrs. Jacob Eakin died in 1856. Two years later Mr. Eakin married Miss Fannie, daughter of William and Nancy Lemmon, and they are the parents of one child—Mary E., who is the wife of O. J. Brown, of Mt. Morris, Penn.

JOHN G. FORDYCE, farmer and stock-grower, born in Gilmore Township, February 14, 1841, is a son of Corbly and Jane (Bailey) Fordyce. His parents were also natives of this county, and of English extraction. His father, who was a farmer and stock-grower all his life, was reared in Greene County. He died in 1862, leaving a family of twelve children, of whom John G. is the sixth. He was reared in Gilmore Township, on the farm where his brother resides. He received a common-school education, then engaged in farming as an occupation, and is now one of the most successful farmers in the county. He owns 400 acres of valuable land. In 1866 Mr. Fordyce married Jane Huffman, and they were the parents of two children—Dora and Charles. Mrs. Jane Fordyce died in 1877, a faithful member of the Methodist Episcopal Church. Mr. Fordyce was afterwards united in marriage, in 1878, with Miss Anna, daughter of Phillip and Lydia (Kennedy) Phillips, and they have one son— Phillip Corbly. Mr. and Mrs. Fordyce are prominent members of the Methodist Episcopal Church.

S. W. GILMORE, farmer and stock-grower, Jolleytown, Penn., was born in West Virginia May 24, 1842, and is a son of Peter and Ellen (Trowbridge) Gilmore. His parents were also natives of West Virginia, and of German and Irish lineage. His father, from whom Gilmore Township took its name, was a farmer during his life time, and died in West Virginia May 19, 1876. The subject of this sketch was the youngest in a family of five children. He was reared in Monongalia County, West Virginia, and received a common-school education. Mr. Gilmore has followed farming as his chief occupation, and is the owner of a good farm of 400 acres. He was first married January 13, 1873, to Hannah Taylor, daughter of George and Marinda (Garrison) Taylor. Of their five children, four are living, viz: William H., Oscar E., Martha M. and Marinda E. Their mother died September 30, 1881. Mr. Gilmore was again united in marriage, in 1883, with Elizabeth, daughter of John and Elizabeth (Sanders) White, and they are the parents of one child—John W. Mr. and Mrs. Gilmore are members of the Methodist Episcopal Church, in which he is class-leader and trustee. He has also been

superintendent of the Sabbath-school.   Mr. Gilmore is a Republican.
In 1862 he enlisted as a private in Company K, Fourteenth West
Virginia Infantry, and was promoted to the office of Second Lieu-
tenant.   He was wounded at the battle of Cloid Mountain.   He
served until the close of the war, and is now a member of G. A. R.
Post 550.

HON. JOHN HAGAN.—Among the most successful business
men of Greene County may be mentioned Hon. John Hagan, deceased.   He was born in County Londonderry, Ireland, and came to
America while very young.   He located at Pittsburgh, Penn., working at anything that came to hand, and was successful in everything
he undertook.   He had a taste for the mercantile trade, and when he
came to Greene County—more than half a century ago—he entered
into partnership with Patrick McCullough and carried on a general
store at Jolleytown, Penn.   At his death he owned over 700 acres
of land in Greene County.   His success was due mainly to his industry and a determination to succeed.   He died in 1873, shortly after
his election to the Legislature.   Mr. Hagan was united in marriage
in this county, in 1859, with Martha, daughter of Abner and Hannah (Morris) Garrison, and they had a family of five children, viz:
John Patrick, Charles L., a prominent attorney of West Virginia;
Clara May, Mary and Catherine.   The family are all members of the
Catholic Church.   Mrs. Hagan is now a resident of Ohio.   Her
mother was a sister of Major J. B. Morris, of Mt. Morris, Penn.

T. M. HENNEN, wool and stock-dealer and secretary of the
Philadelphia Oil Company, was born in Greene County, Penn., July
27, 1839.   He is a son of George and Jane (Munyon) Henner, who
were of Irish and English origin.   His father was a farmer and
stock-grower by occupation, and died September 13, 1885.   His
family consisted of eleven children, of whom the subject of this
sketch is the sixth.   He was reared in Gilmore Township and received a good English education.   Mr. Hennen first engaged in
farming and dealing in wool, in which business he has spent most
of his life.   In 1863 he became actively interested in the oil business in Dunkard Township, and when the Philadelphia Oil Company
was formed and commenced operations in Greene County he was
elected secretary.   He is the owner of a good farm of 165 acres,
where he now resides in Gilmore Township.   Mr. Hennen was
united in marriage in 1868 with Rachel, daughter of Thomas W.
Taylor, Esq., of this county, and they are the parents of three children—Frank W., George B. and Tinna A.   Mrs. Hennen is a
devoted member of the Baptist Church.   Her husband is a Democrat and secretary of the school board in his township.

JOHN LANTZ, farmer and stock-grower, Jolleytown, Penn.,
was born in Wayne Township, Greene County, Penn., May 8, 1829.

He is a son of Jacob and Delilah (Coen) Lantz, natives of this county, and of German and English lineage. His father was a farmer and stock-grower and a great hunter, born in Greene County in 1791. He was a soldier in the war of 1812, and died in 1858. His family consisted of five sons, of whom John is the fourth. He was reared on the home farm in Wayne Township, and has successfully engaged in farming as an occupation. He owns 350 acres of valuable land in Gilmore Township, where he has lived since 1850. Mr. Lantz was married in Greene County September 19, 1850, to Miss Sarah, daughter of Jacob and Charlotte Bradford, natives of this county, and of English descent. Mr. and Mrs. Lantz have a family of eleven children, ten of whom are living, viz.—William H. and M. J., merchants; A. B., a farmer; L. W., S. C., a carpenter; John, Delilah, Martha, Jacob and Alexander. Their mother is a member of the Methodist Episcopal Church. Mr. Lantz is a Republican, and has served as justice of the peace for fifteen years.

SALEM LEMMON, deceased, was born March 20, 1823, and died August 15, 1887. He was a farmer and stock-dealer and a successful business manager, being at the time of his death the owner of over 600 acres of land in Gilmore Township. Mr. Lemmon was the son of William and Nancy Lemmon, of this township. They were of Irish and German lineage. Mr. Lemmon was reared in this township, attended the common schools, and subsequently chose farming and stock dealing as his• business through life. He was twice united in marriage; first, with Mary (Babbit) Lemmon, and they were the parents of two children—William Milton, a farmer; and Harry, (deceased). Their mother died February 14, 1853. Mr. Lemmon's second wife, Maria (McCune) Lemmon, is still living. She was born in Dunkard Township, this county, and is a daughter of John and Mary McCune, who were of Irish origin. Mr. and Mrs. Lemmon were married December 25, 1859. Their children are Mary M., owner of a well improved farm in Gilmore Township, and a dressmaker by occupation; Sarah A., wife of Andrew Lantz; and Nancy V., wife of George Strawn. The family are all members of the Methodist Episcopal Church, in which Mr. Lemmon was steward and trustee. He was a Democrat, and served fifteen years as justice of the peace. He had just been re-elected, at the time of his death, to another term of five years.

W. M. LEMMON, farmer and stock-grower, who was born in Gilmore Township May 17, 1850, is a son of Salem and Mary (Babbit) Lemmon. His parents were also natives of this county, and of German and English descent. His father was a prominent farmer and stock-dealer, and was justice of the peace for many years in Gilmore Township. He was twice married. W. M. is the only child by the first marriage. He grew to manhood in this township, attended the common schools, and has engaged extensively in farming and stock growing. Mr. Lemmon is specially interested in fine horses, and is the owner of Diomede No. 1118 in France, and in America No. 2523. Diomede was brought from France and cost $2,000. Mr. Lemmon also owns a good farm of 150 acres. He was married in West Virginia August 30, 1874, to Clarissa J., daughter of Alexander and Rachel (Russell) Hennen. Mrs. Lemmon is a native of Virginia, and of English extraction. Their children are—Jesse Harry, Lydia Ellen, Mary Hally, Owen R. and Emma Alice. Mr. and Mrs. Lemmon are leading members in the Methodist Episcopal Church, in which he is steward and trustee.

SALATHIEL LEMMON, farmer and stock-grower, was born November 2, 1838, on the farm where he resides in Gilmore Township. He is a son of William and Nancy (Lemmon) Lemmon, who were of Irish and German origin. His mother was a native of this county. His father was born in Lancaster County, Penn. He was a farmer all his life, and died in this township in 1868. His family consisted of five children, of whom Salathiel is the youngest. He grew to manhood in this township, where he has been quite successful as a farmer, and is considered one of Greene's most prosperous citizens. He has also devoted some time to milling. Mr. Lemmon owns 450 acres of well improved land. He is a genial, agreeable gentleman, and has a wide circle of friends. He was united in the holy bonds of matrimony May, 15, 1860, with Miss Nancy, daughter of B. Renner, and they are the parents of six children—William J., Elizabeth E., wife of Lewis Cumpston; Barney R., Dora M., Charles M. and Rosa M. William, the oldest, was born in 1862, and reared on the farm with his parents. He was married in 1883 to Rosa May, daughter of Abraham Taylor, and they have one child—Abraham Salathiel. Elizabeth E. and Lewis Cumpston were married in 1883, and have three children—Bertie C., Goldie M. and Barney M. Mr. Lemmon votes the straight Democratic ticket. He takes an active interest in school affairs, and has been one of the board of directors for seven years.

PETER MEIGHEN, deceased, who was a pioneer farmer and stock-grower, was born in Wayne Township, Greene County Penn., September 25, 1809. He was the son of William and Elizabeth (Hughes) Meighen, the former a native of Ireland, and the latter of this county. Peter Meighen's grandfather Hughes came to Greene County in 1762, at sixteen years of age, and died in 1836. He was a farmer by occupation, as were most of the Hughes family in America. Some of them have engaged quite successfully in the mercantile business. The subject of our sketch died in 1867. Of his thirteen children ten are still living. Elizabeth, the oldest daughter, died in 1855. William H., the oldest son was born in this township in 1841. In 1861 he enlisted in Company F., Seventh West Virginia, Infantry. Afterwards re-enlisting, he served until close of the war. During his services he was Corporal, afterwards Sergeant, then promoted to First Lieutenant. Catherine, and Belinda are the two oldest daughters. James, deceased 1850. Felix, deceased 1884, was a prominent merchant of Jolleytown this Township. Susan, wife of Peter Bradley, a prominent merchant of New Freeport; Matthias is a partner of the firm of P. Bradley & Co. (New Freeport.) Priscilla, wife of Thomas C. Bradley, clerk in the Farmer's and Drover's National Bank of Waynesburg, Greene County, Penn ; Martha youngest daughter, teacher in the public schools this county. John, William, Dennis and Peter are prominent farmers and stock-raisers, they together, with their mother own seven hundred acres of land. Peter Meighen's widow is still living in Gilmore Township. She is a daughter of James Dye, who was born December 1, 1769. He was a hunter and pioneer farmer, and among the first to find the Corbley family after they had been murdered by the Indians at Garard's Fort.

PHILIP SHOUGH, farmer and stock-grower, son of Joseph and Catharine (Chisler) Shough, was born near Uniontown, Fayette County, Penn., August 10, 1809. His mother was a native of Maryland. His father, who was of German extraction, was born in Lancaster County, Penn., July 16, 1761, and died in Fayette County, Ohio. He was a farmer and gunsmith through life. Philip was the youngest of a family of thirteen children, all of whom reached maturity except one, who died at the age of seventeen. Mr. Shough was one of the few persons in Greene County who were so fortunate as to see General LaFayette during his last visit to America. Being a bound boy, he received but a limited education in the common schools. He was bound for five years to learn a trade, but has made farming his chief occupation, in which he has been very successful. At one time his possessions amounted to over seven hundred acres of land, but much of it has been given to his children. He now owns one hundred and fifty acres where he resides in Gilmore Township. He was united in marriage in Dunkard Township, January 15, 1832, with Matilda, daughter of George and Elizabeth (Long) Garrison. Mrs. Shough, who was of German origin, died January 18, 1885. Of their six children, four are living; Rebecca, wife of William Hoskinson; George W., a farmer; Sarah Ann, wife of Hiram Milliken; and Mattie. Josephus and Elizabeth are deceased. Mr. Shough is a Cumberland Presbyterian, of which church his deceased wife was a faithful member. Mr. Shough is a Republican in politics, and was a captain in the old militia. He takes an active interest in school affairs and has been a member of the board of directors in his township. G. W. Shough, his oldest son now living, was born March 16, 1839, and was reared in Gilmore Township on the old home farm. He has made farming his occupation, and is the owner of three hundred acres of land. He is married and the father of eleven children. He was a student at Waynesburg College when the war broke out in 1861, but enlisted in the Seventh Pennsylvania Volunteer Infantry, and was elected Lieutenant of the company. He was in many hotly contested battles—among others Gettysburg and Antietam.

JACOB L. SHRIVER, physician and surgeon, Jolleytown, Penn., was born in Whiteley Township, January 11, 1828. He is a son of William and Elizabeth (Shull) Shriver, who were also natives of this county, and of Irish and German origin. His father was a farmer all his life and died in 1880. His family consisted of nine children, of whom the Doctor is the oldest. He remained on the farm with his parents until he was eighteen years of age, and attended the district schools. He afterwards spent some time in the old Greene Academy at Carmichaels, and the College at Waynesburg, Penn. He studied medicine with Doctors Arthur Inghram and Alexander Shaw, of Waynesburg. Dr. Shriver first engaged in his chosen profession, in 1851, at Jolleytown, Penn., where he has had a large and lucrative practice, and is now the owner of considerable estate. He has a farm of two hundred and thirty acres in Gilmore Township. The Doctor is a registered member of the Greene County and State Medical Societies. He was united in marriage, December, 4, 1851, with Sarah, daughter of John and Sarah (Gardner) Goodwin, and they are the parents of nine children: Elizabeth Ann, wife of A. E. Clovis, a merchant at Jolleytown; John M., a physician; Josephine, wife of Morris J. Lantz; William G., who is in the real estate business in the West; Isaac N., a farmer; Sadie, wife of John Russell; J. F., Jessie May, and Mary Mattie. The Doctor is a member of the Methodist Episcopal Church, and has served as school director of his Township.

ABRAHAM TAYLOR, farmer and stock-grower, was born in Gilmore Township, this county April 1, 1839. His parents, Francis and Susannah (Baldwin) Taylor, were also natives of this county, and of English extraction, His father, who was a successful farmer, died in 1887. His family consisted of twelve children—four daughters and eight sons—of whom Abraham is the fifth. He was reared on the farm in Gilmore Township, and attended the district schools. He has been engaged as a farmer all his life, and owns seventy acres of good land where he resides. Mr. Taylor was united in marriage, August 20, 1864, with Eliza Ellen, daughter of Alexander and Maria (Clovis) Compston. Mr. and Mrs. Taylor have three children—Rosa May, wife of William Lemmon; Patrick Henry and John H. They are members of the Southern Methodist Church, in which Mr. Taylor is trustee. He is a Democrat in politics, and at the breaking out of the Rebellion, he promptly enlisted in Company F, Seventh West Virginia Infantry and served two years and nine days. He was in many battles and skirmishes, among which were the battles of Fredericksburg, Bull Run, Antietam, Chancellorsville and Gettysburg. He is a member of the G. A. R. Post 550.

GREENE TOWNSHIP.

W. C. BAILEY, farmer and stock-grower, who is descended from the early pioneers of Greene County, was born March 27, 1842, on Muddy Creek, this county, on the farm where his parents reside. He is a son of J. K. and Delilah (Craft) Bailey, who are natives of this county, and of German origin. W. C. is their fourth child. He was reared in Cumberland Township, and attended the common school and Greene Academy at Carmichaels, Penn. Mr. Bailey taught school for several years, but subsequently devoted his time wholly to farming and stock-growing, and owns 236 acres of good land near Whiteley P. O., Greene Township, this county. Mr. Bailey was united in marriage, January 15, 1874, with Miss Maggie, daughter of Richard and Emeline (Wise) Hawkins. She is of German and English origin. Mr. Bailey is a Republican. He and wife are active members of the Cumberland Presbyterian Church.

B. W. DENNY, M. D.. was born in Jefferson Borough, Greene County, Penn., September 17, 1836, and is a son of William and Rebecca (Litzenburg) Denny, natives of Pennsylvania. His father and grandfather, John Denny, were farmers. The latter came from England to America, and settled near Jefferson, Penn., where B. W. spent his youthful days and attended the common school. The Doctor attended Waynesburg College until he began the study of medicine in the office of Dr. W. D. Rogers, of Jefferson. In 1859 he entered the Medical College at Cleveland, Ohio, where he graduated in 1862. Then, instead of entering the practice of his profession, he raised a company for the service of his country. He was elected Captain of Company E, of the Ringold Cavalry, which afterwards became Company F, of the Twenty-second Regiment. Capt. Denny remained in command for three years, with the exception of about eight months when he was sent on detached service to Washington, D. C. Dr. and Mrs. Denny were at Washington at the time of the assassination of President Lincoln, and had intended going to Ford's Theatre that night; but fortunately, owing to the Doctor's indisposition, they were not present on that fatal occasion. At the close of the war he began the practice of medicine in Greene County, where he has been actively engaged in the profession ever since. Financially the Doctor has met with success, and owns a good farm where he resides in Greene Township. He was married October 8, 1862, to Miss Rachel, daughter of Samuel, and grand-daughter of James Braden. Her mother's maiden name was Hannah Ross. Mrs. Denny is of English and Irish descent. They have one child—Millie May. The family are faithful members of the Baptist Church, in which the Doctor is one of the trustees.

W. C. FLENNIKEN, merchant at Whiteley, Greene County, Penn., was born in Carmichaels, Penn., February 4, 1853. He is a son of James and Rachel (Kerr) Flenniken, natives of this county. His ancestors were among the earliest settlers of Greene County. Mr. Flenniken's father was a merchant and drover, and met with success in his business. For nearly half a century he was engaged in merchandising at Rice's Landing, Carmichaels, Jefferson and Ceylon, Penn., where he departed this life in 1886. Of his six children, three are now living, viz: Horace G., Emma J., wife of George McMillan, and W. C., the subject of this sketch. He was reared in this county, and early in life went as a clerk into his father's store, where he remained until he took an interest in the business with his father. They established the present business in 1879, and since his father's death W. C. has been sole proprietor. He was united in marriage, in 1873, with Miss Samantha, daughter of John Hughes. Their children are—Walter and Clyde. Mr. and Mrs. Flenniken are leading members of the Baptist Church.

STEPHENSON GARARD, farmer and stock-grower, P. O. Willow Tree, was born at Taylortown, Dunkard Township, Greene County, Penn., May 18, 1828, and is a son of Jonathan and Ann (Gregg) Garard. His father, who was a farmer, stock-grower and manufacturer, served ten years on the bench as associate judge of this county, where he died. His family consisted of five children, of whom Stephenson was next to the youngest. He was reared in Greene County, where he attended the subscription schools. In 1854 he bought a farm and has since very successfully devoted his time and talent to farming and stock-growing. Mr. Garard is the owner of about 500 acres of valuable land. On his home farm are the Garard oil wells, Nos. 1, 2 and 3, all producing wells. In 1850 Mr. Garard was united in marriage with Mary A., daughter of William Robinson. Mrs. Garard is of English descent. Their children are—Elizabeth, wife of John Minor; Emma M., wife of Albert Dowlin; Flora B., wife of G. W. W. Blair; Jesse L., A. Y.,

Anna and Rachel, all of whom, with one exception, are members of the Goshen Baptist Church, in which Mr. Garard serves as deacon. Mr. and Mrs. Garard come from two of the representative families of the pioneer settlers of Greene County, and are highly respected citizens.

CHARLES KEENER, farmer and stock-grower, P. O. Willow Tree, was born October 8, 1827, on the farm where he resides. He is a son of Robert and Elizabeth (Eberhart) Keener, natives of this county. His father, who is a successful farmer, has reached the advanced age of eighty-five years. He has reared a family of seven children, four of whom are living. Of these, Charles is the oldest. He was reared on the farm and received his education in one of the old-fashioned log school-houses of the district. Charles wisely chose his father's occupation, and by industry and economy has increased his father's farm from 180 to 233 acres of well-improved land. Mr. Keener was married October 16, 1857, to Miss Tabitha E., daughter of Charles Stewart. Mrs. Keener is a native of Virginia. Their children are—Robert C., Aaron, L. L., C. E., F. H., James W. and Thorton F. Mr. and Mrs. Keener are faithful members of the Methodist Episcopal Church, in which he is a steward. He is a Democrat in politics, has been school director, supervisor of Greene Township, and inspector of elections.

HON. ANDREW LANTZ, farmer and stock-grower, Whiteley, Penn., was born in Greene Township, this county, May 8, 1839. His parents, John and Jane (Wildman) Lantz, were natives of Greene County, and of English and German descent. His father, who was a farmer and stock-grower, was a man of marked business ability, and at the time of his death, in 1876, was the owner of 2,000 acres of land. Andrew has 1,400 acres. He was reared on the home farm and attended the district schools. Being the only child who grew to maturity, his father carefully instructed him in all kinds of work and the proper transaction of business. In 1860 Mr. Lantz married Miss Lucretia, daughter of George Lemley. Mrs. Lantz is of English descent. Their children are—John F., David E., Charley and Ada Alice. Mr. and Mrs. Lantz are active members in the Methodist Episcopal Church, in which he is trustee. In politics Mr. Lantz is a Democrat, and has served as justice of the peace for ten years in Greene County. He takes an active interest in educational affairs, and has served as school director for a number of terms. In 1882 he was elected to the Legislature, and was an active member during the two terms he was connected with that body.

JOHN F. LANTZ, farmer and stock-grower, Lone Star, Penn., was born October 10, 1861, in the township where he now resides. He is the oldest son of Hon. Andrew Lantz, of Greene Township, whose biographical sketch appears in this volume. John was reared on the farm and obtained his early education in the district schools. He subsequently took a regular course of instruction at Iron City College, Pittsburg, Penn., where he graduated in 1881. Mr. Lantz has a good farm of 201 acres well adapted to the raising of stock, in which he engages extensively, making fine cattle a specialty. In 1882, Mr. Lantz was united in marriage with Sarah, daughter of Imri Taylor, who is a merchant and farmer in Whiteley Township. Mr. Lantz is a Democrat in politics. His wife is a faithful member of the Methodist Episcopal Church.

GEORGE W. LANTZ, farmer and stock-grower, was born in Greene Township, March 24, 1844. He attended the district school, and has been engaged in his present occupation from his youth. In 1886 he engaged in the lumber business in company with Abner Munnell, and is owner and proprietor of a large planing and saw-mill, at Greensboro, Penn. Mr. Lantz is a son of Jacob and Cassandra (South) Lantz, natives of this county. His father, who was a success-ful farmer, died in 1861. Mr. Lot Lantz, George's grandfather, was at one time elected brigade inspector of the militia of the county, and was a pioneer of Greene County. He was a wealthy stock-drover and engaged extensively in pork packing, making heavy ship-ments to Baltimore. He also carried on a distillery for years. September 4, 1870, George Lantz married Miss Mary, daughter of Joseph Tannehill, and they were the parents of the following children: Laura V. Chandas, Hughes and James. Lessie being deceased. A remarkable fact exists in the history of these children. Lessie, born July 14, 1878, who lived to be two years of age, was born just six-teen days after her brother Hughes, who was born June 29, 1878 Mrs. Lantz was a devoted member of the Baptist Church. She de-parted this life August 19, 1888, she and her babe were buried in the same coffin. Mr. Lantz is a Democrat in politics, has served as justice of the peace in Greene Township, and is now postmaster at Willow Tree, Penn.

P. A. MYERS, hotel keeper, Whiteley, Penn., is a descendant of Rev. John Corbly, one of the pioneer settlers of Greene County. He was born near Garard's Fort, Penn., April 2, 1836. His parents are Alfred and Jane J. (Evans) Myers, who were of German and Welsh origin. Mr. Meyers is the oldest in a family of six children, was reared on a farm, received a common school education, and has been a successful business man. His boyhood days were spent with his uncle, an extensive cattle-dealer. When but fourteen years of age would help his uncle drive large droves of cattle, and conduct them overland to the Philadelphia markets, making as many as two or three trips a year. The greater part of his later years has been devoted to farming. While a young man he taught school for sev-eral terms, and has ever manifested an active interest in educational affairs. In politics he is a Republican. He has held various township offices—among others school director and justice of the peace. On November 1, 1857, Mr. Myers married Miss Louisa M., daughter of David and Mary Roberts, who were of Welsh and English descent. Her father, who was a farmer of Dunkard Township, died in 1885, at the advanced age of eighty-five years. Mr. and Mrs. Myers have two children and four grandchildren. Their children are—Buena V., wife of W. H. Bark, Esq., of Waynesburg, Penn.; and Pleasant J., wife of M. E. Garard, of Greene Township. Mr. and Mrs. Myers are prominent members of the Baptist Church.

JACOB REAMER, retired farmer and stock-grower, of Greene Township, was born in Monongahela Township, this county, January 16, 1814. He is a son of Jacob and Margaret (Black) Reamer, who were natives of Pennsylvania, and of German origin. His father, who was a farmer and distiller, spent most of his life in Greene County, and died in 1852. His family consisted of five children, of whom Jacob is the third. He was reared on the home farm, and received his education in the district schools. He has met with average success in his chosen occupation, and at present is the owner of a well improved farm of ninety-four acres, near Garard's Fort, this county. Mr. Reamer was united in marriage, in 1840, with Miss Louisa, daughter of John and Ortha Myers. They were Quakers and of English descent. Mr. Reamer is a Democrat in politics. He manifests great interest in educational matters, and has served as school director in his township. Mr. and Mrs. Reamer are leading members in the Goshen Baptist Church.

J. B. ROBERTS, farmer and stock-grower, Whiteley, Penn., was born in Greene Township, this county, March 18, 1832. His parents, Joseph and Jane (Johnson) Roberts, were natives of Greene County, and of Welsh descent. His father, who was a farmer by occupation, reared a family of eleven children, of whom J. B. is the ninth. He was reared on the farm and attended the subscription schools. He chose farming and stock-growing as his occupation, and has met with average success, owning at present a good farm of 150 acres. Mr. Roberts was united in marriage, December 31, 1879, with Elizabeth, daughter of James and Elizabeth (Clark) Henderson. Mrs. Roberts is a faithful member of the Methodist Episcopal Church. Her parents were natives of Greene County, and of English descent. At the time Mr. and Mrs. Roberts were married, she was the widow of Henry Lantz. Mr. Roberts is an enthusiastic Democrat, and a member of the I. O. O. F.

T. H. SEDGEWICK, M. D., of Whiteley, Greene County, Penn., was born at Rice's Landing, Penn., April 20, 1852, and is the son of Hon. Joseph and Elizabeth (Hawthorne) Sedgewick, who were of English and Irish descent. His mother was born in Washington County. His father, who was a natives of Virginia, served two terms as a member of the Legislature from Greene County. He was a commission merchant by occupation, in which business he engaged for many years at Rice's Landing, Penn., having first come to this county when seventeen years of age. He died in 1882. He was twice married and was the father of eight children. Dr. Sedgewick is the second child by the last marriage, and was reared at Rice's Landing, where he received his early education. He subsequently attended Monongahela College until he began the study of medicine in the office of Dr. T. H. Sharpnack, of Jefferson Borough. He then took a regular course in the Jefferson Medical College at Philadelphia, where he graduated in 1877. He entered the practice of medicine the same year in Greene County, and has since devoted all his time to his profession. In 1880 he settled in Whiteley, where his professional skill and remarkable energy soon won for him a good practice. That he might be better prepared for the practice of his profession, the Doctor took a post graduate course at New York City in 1888. He is a man of large stature and marked physical abilities which, coupled with his great industry and determination, eminently qualify him for the duties he has assumed. He was married at Rice's Landing, December 25, 1873, to Miss Lucinda, daughter of John Dowlin, a wealthy farmer of this county. They have two children—Joseph and John. The Doctor is a Democrat, and he and Mrs. Sedgewick are prominent members of the Baptist Church.

BENJAMIN SOUTH, farmer and stock-grower, P. O. Willow Tree was born in Greene Township, Greene County, Penn., January 16, 1819. He is a son of Enoch and Ruth (Gregg) South, who were of English descent. His mother was a native of Delaware. His father, who was a native of New Jersey, came to Greene County, Penn., in 1794, where he died in 1863. His family consisted of eleven children,—nine girls and two boys, of whom Benjamin was the sixth. He was reared in Dunkard Township, receiving his education in the subscription schools. Mr. South was a stone-mason early in life, and also worked for some time at the blacksmith's trade. In later years he has given his attention to farming, and by means of his untiring zeal and industry, is now the owner of 315 acres of well improved land. In 1842 Mr. South married Matilda Gapen, who is of English descent, and a daughter of Stephen and Rebecca (Snyder) Gapen. Their union has been blessed with seven children, four sons and three daughters—Maria, wife of D. Sikes; Melinda, widow of E. Alexander; Enoch C., a farmer; Stephen, a carpenter; Olive; Ortha, wife of Noah Minor; and Otho M., a school teacher. In politics Mr. south is a Democrat. He takes an active interest in educational affairs, and has served as school director for a number of years.

JOSEPH VANCE, farmer and stock-grower, was born in Greene County, Penn., January, 28, 1838, and is a son of Joseph and Margeret (Divens) Vance. His parents were natives of Pennsylvania, and of Irish and German origin. His father was born in Greene Township, in 1795, and lived to the advanced age of seventy-eight years. He was a farmer, stock-grower and stone-mason. His family consisted of ten children, of whom Joseph is the youngest. He has been reared in this township, where he received a common school education. Having chosen farming as his occupation, he has given it all his care and attention, and is the owner of a nice farm of eighty acres where he resides near Willow Tree, this county. The subject of our sketch was married in this township, in 1884, to Miss Martha Ann, daughter of Coverdel Cole, of Virginia. Mr. Vance is a Democrat in politics, and a highly respected citizen.

JEFFERSON TOWNSHIP AND JEFFERSON BOROUGH.

A. F. AMMONS, Khedive, Penn., one of the substantial farmers of Jefferson Township, was born in Perry Township, Greene County, April 20, 1824. He is a son of Abraham and Mary (Frost) Ammons. His mother was a native of Fayette County, Penn., and his father of Greene County, where they were married and spent the greater part of their lives, moving to West Virginia a few years before their death. Mr. Abraham Ammons died in 1833; his widow was afterwards united in marriage with Jerry Wright, now deceased. In 1847, January 21, A. F. Ammons married Rebecca Wade, who was born in West Virginia, January 15, 1828. She is a daughter of Sylva and Catharine (Dusonberry) Wade, and is a consistent member of the Cumberland Presbyterian Church. Her parents were also natives of West Virginia, where they were married and remained until Mr. Wade's death, March 31, 1850; his widow is still living. Mr. and Mrs. Ammons have nine children, six living—Mary, wife of Benjamin Fox; Perry, Douglas, Forney, Frank and Nettie; the deceased are—Jasper, William and Louvernia. Mr. Ammons was raised on a farm and worked by the month until nineteen years of age; then learned the carpenter trade which he followed for sixteen years. He afterwards engaged in farming and stock-dealing and, by great industry and good management, has secured a nice home for himself and family and a fine farm of 315 acres of improved land in Greene County. He filled the office of justice of the peace in Perry Township five years, served as school director eight years, and was assessor one year. Since moving to Jefferson Township, he has filled the office of justice of the peace for twelve years, and has voted the Democratic ticket all the time and still is for Cleveland, Thurman and the Mills bill.

N. M. BANE, retired farmer, P. O. Jefferson, was born in Washington County, Penn., February 27, 1818, a son of Abraham and Elizabeth (Venom) Bane, who were natives of Washington County, where they were married, settled and remained all their lives. Their son, N. M., is the only one of their nine children now living. He was united in marriage, November 21, 1844, with Mary McClenathan, who was born in Washington County, Penn., October 22, 1822, a daughter of William and Mary (Coulson) McClenathan. Her parents were also natives of Washington County, where they were married and remained through life. They were the parents of eleven children, five living. Mr. and Mrs. Bane's family consists of five children, two of whom are living—Jennie, wife of David Crayne, and John L., who married Mary E. Neal. The deceased are—Eveline, Thomas S. and James M. Mr. Bane owns 150 acres of land in Washington County, Penn., also some land and property in Greene County. He and wife are faithful members of the Baptist Church.

SAMUEL BAYARD, farmer, P. O. Rice's Landing, was born in Centre Township, Greene County, Penn., January 4, 1819, a son of William and Nancy Bayard (*nee* Scott). The former was born in Washington County and the latter in Greene County, Penn., where they were married, settling in Centre Township, where they remained until 1826; they then moved to Whiteley Township, where Mrs. Bayard died in 1840. Her husband died in Jefferson Township in 1860. They were the parents of three children—John S., Thomas W., and Samuel. March 3, 1839, Samuel Bayard married Miss Lucinda Randolph, born in Jefferson Township in 1818, a daughter of Jonah F. and Leah Randolph (*nee* Leonard). By this marriage Mr. Bayard is the father of two children—J. Randolph, who married Martha E. Oliver, they are the parents of two living children, Frank and Lon L.; Nancy, who is the wife of Capt. J. R. Hewitt, their children are Anna, who married E. H. Shipley, and William B. Mrs. Bayard departed this life July 3, 1845. August 18, 1846, Mr. Bayard was again united in marriage, with Rebecca A. Randolph, who was born in Jefferson Township, February 24, 1820, a daughter of Jacob and Ruth (Bailey) Randolph, and a faithful member of the Cumberland Presbyterian Church. Her father was a native of New Jersey and her mother of Pennsylvania; both are now deceased. By his second marriage Mr. Bayard is the father of three children—

William J., who married Mary Temple and is the father of J. Temple Bayard; Lucy R. and John A., who married Permelia Lucas and is now the father of two children—Lettie and Samuel. Mr. Bayard is one of the most highly respected farmers in his neighborhood, and owns 200 acres of land where he and family reside.

J. C. BURSON, farmer, Clarksville, Penn., was born September 27, 1825, in the house now occupied by himself and family. His father, Abraham Burson, was born on the farm which J. C. now owns in Jefferson Township. His mother was born in Washington County, Penn. After marriage they settled in Greene County, and remained until their death; Mrs. Burson died in 1839, July 17. Her husband afterwards married Hannah Crawford, now deceased; and he died in 1886. By the first marriage there are four children, three of whom are living. Mr. J. C. Burson was united in marriage, December 30, 1849, with Rebecca Reynolds, who was born in Jefferson Township, December 24, 1827. Her parents, John and Jane (Kincaid) Reynolds, were natives of Greene County, where they resided till death: Mrs. Reynolds died October 12, 1839. Mr. Reynolds afterwards married Priscilla Gwynn (nee Long), deceased. He departed this life February 20, 1882. To Mr. and Mrs. Burson have been born six children, five living—John R., who married Emily Leslie; David M., who married Emma Moredock; Abraham, who married Margaret Greenlee; Alexander P. and James O.; Abraham being deceased. Mr. Burson was raised on his present farm formerly owned by his father and grandfather; it consists of 200 acres. Mr. Burson has filled the offices of school director and overseer of the poor, and has been a member of the Masonic fraternity for about thirty-seven years.

WILLIAM COTTERREL, saddler and harness-maker, was born in New Jersey in 1772; he married Isabela Livingston, also a native of New Jersey. They settled in Jefferson, Greene County, Penn., about 1796, and lived there until the year 1824, when they moved to Waynesburg; he there followed his trade until his death in 1836. His wife died in 1826. They raised four childern—John, William, Isabela and Martha. Isabela died in 1844. Martha married Clark Ely, and died young; left one daughter, Isabel, who married David Babbit, and died without issue; William married Frances Minor, who died and left one daughter, Elizabeth, who married David Taylor. She died and left one daughter, Lee Taylor. William married for his second wife Mrs. Sarah Bane (formerly Sellers). He followed the tanning business for a number of years in Waynesburg, and died January, 1886, aged seventy-four years. His widow still survives at an advanced age. John Cotterrel, Sr., was born in Jefferson, Greene County, September 25, 1802. At the age of fifteen years he went to Uniontown, Penn., and learned the tanning trade with John Miller. He came back home and worked for his father until 1824, when he started business for himself. In 1828 he married Permelia, daughter of John and Mary Milliken (natives of Ireland). They raised nine children—Isabela, John, Mary A., Permelia, William, Jonas, Elizabeth, Martha A. and George. Isabela married William Anderson, of Pittsburgh. She died and left one daughter, Laura Bell. Mary A. married Dr. James W. Hancher, of Ohio—are both dead. They raised seven children. Permelia is dead. William married Olive Gorden, of Washington, Penn. Jonas married Anna Short, of Claysville, Penn. Elizabeth married Joseph A. Bell. Martha A. married Jacob Haver. George now lives in Hiawatha, Brown County, Kansas. John Cotterrel, Jr., was born in Jefferson, Penn., November 29, 1832. He learned the tanning trade with his father, and married Priscilla Swan, daughter of Samuel and Priscilla (Crago) Swan; she died June 10, 1861, and left two daughters—Elmyra P. and Margaret A. Elmyra P. now resides in Iowa. Margaret A. married T. Reed McMinn. She died June 11, 1885; left one son, Robert C. John Cotterrel's present wife is Mary H., daughter of William and Harriet (Randolph) Davis, and they have a family of three children—John F., William D. and Joseph R. In politics Mr. Cotterrel is a Republican, and takes an active interest in farming, wool-growing and stock-raising and now owns a farm of 175 acres one mile southeast of Jefferson, Penn.

　　HUGH D. CREE, plasterer and contractor, was born in Greene County, September 11, 1840. He is a son of William and Ann (DeFrance) Cree, who were natives of Jefferson Township, and of French and Irish origin. Our subject's father, William Cree, was born in Greene County, May 18, 1796. By occupation he was a farmer, and in religion a Presbyterian, in which church he was an elder. Mr. Cree's father was a farmer, who died November 5, 1871. His family consisted of twelve children—eight sons and four daughters. Their mother was born in Greene County in 1802, and died in 1875. Hugh grew up on the farm with his parents, attended the district school, and chose farming as his business; but subsequently learned his present trade, which he has pursued with more than ordinary success. He was married April 26, 1862, to Mary Elizabeth, daughter of Isaiah and Nancy M. (Guseman) Dean, who were of Dutch descent. Mr. and Mrs. Cree have one child, a daughter—Elizabeth Ann, now wife of George B. Waychoff. Mr. Cree and wife are members of the Methodist Episcopal Church. In politics he is a Republican. In 1861 he enlisted as a member of Company F, First Pennsylvania Cavalry, and was discharged the same year for disability. His five brothers were all soldiers in the Union army, three of them being in from the beginning till its close.

JESSE DOWLIN, farmer, P. O. Khedive, was born in Cumberland Township, Greene County, Penn., March 21, 1830. He is a son of John and Elizabeth (Gwynn) Dowlin, natives of Pennsylvania. They were married in Greene County and made it their home until their death. He departed this life November 26, 1874, and she September 30, 1878. Eight of their nine children are now living. Jesse Dowlin was united in marriage, February 22, 1855, with Eliza A. Huston, born in Fayette County, Pennsylvania. Her parents were John and Hannah (Sproat) Huston, both of whom died in Greene County—her father, March 5, 1885, and her mother in 1886. In the earlier part of his life Mr. Dowlin taught school through the winter and worked on the farm in the summer. He has since devoted all his time to farming and, as a result of his faithful labors, now owns a fine farm of 117 acres on which are good buildings. He has served as school director of his township.

WILLIAM GOODWIN, farmer, P. O. Jefferson, was born in Washington County, Penn., June 16, 1822. He is a son of John and Sallie (Gardner) Goodwin, the former born in York County, Penn., and the latter in Washington County, where they were married and remained until 1830, at which time they moved to Center Township, Greene County, and lived there till Mrs. Goodwin's death in 1843. Mr. Goodwin afterwards married Mary Dalripple (nee Bell), now deceased. He died in 1859. William was united in marriage, February 26, 1847, with Nancy Wilson, born in Ireland March 7, 1827. Her parents, James and Martha (Craigmills) Wilson, were both born in Ireland, where they were married and emigrated to America in 1827, living first in Washington County, and then in Westmoreland County, where she died in 1830. Mr. Wilson then married Catharine McKee, now deceased; he died in 1878. Mr. and Mrs. Goodwin are the parents of ten children, eight of whom are living—Sarah E., John T., Mary, wife of R. H. Armstrong; Rachel, wife of W. S. Scott; Margaret J., Nancy A. B., William W. and Jessie M. The deceased are: Martha J. and an infant. Mr. Goodwin was reared on a farm, and is now regarded as one of the most substantial farmers in his township. He owns 350 acres of land in Greene County. He and wife are consistent and earnest Christians.

MARSHALL GWYNN, farmer, Khedive, Penn., a descendant of one of the pioneer families of Greene County, Penn., was born in Jefferson Township, March 9, 1826. His parents, James and Hester (Cree) Gwynn, were natives of Greene County and residents therein through life. They were the parents of five children, two of whom are living, viz: Joseph and Marshall. In 1861, November 29, Marshall married Kate Hill, born in Greene County September 3, 1835, daughter of Thomas and Nancy Hill (nee Roseberry), who were natives of Greene County, where they remained through life. Mr.

Hill died in 1876 and Mrs. Hill in 1880. They were the parents of eleven children, ten now living. Mr. and Mrs. Gwynn have seven children—Frank, Frances, Thomas, Jesse, Ida, Remembrance and Albert. Mr. Gwynn is a farmer and owns eighty-eight acres of land where he and family reside. He is a faithful member of the Cumberland Presbyterian Church.

JOHN HAVER, P. O. Jefferson, is one of the pioneers of the township, where he was born October 12, 1802. He is the son of George and Priscilla Haver (*nee* Villars); the former was born in New Jersey and the latter in Pennsylvania, where they were married in Greene County and remained all their lives. They were the parents of ten children, of whom four are living. John is the oldest and was united in marriage March 8, 1832, with Jane Rex, born in Jefferson Township March 25, 1815, a daughter of George and Jane (Black) Rex, deceased. Mr. and Mrs. Haver are the parents of eleven children, of these seven are living—George R., Priscilla, Mary E., Hiram, Jacob, Charles and James. The deceased are Sarah, John, Margaret and Emma. Their mother departed this life January 9, 1879. Mr. Haver is one of the retired farmers of Jefferson Township, and owns one hundred and fifty acres of land where he and his family reside. He has held a majority of the offices in his township. He belongs to the Cumberland Presbyterian Church, of which his deceased wife was also a member.

JACOB HAVER, farmer, P. O. Jefferson, son of John and Jane (Rex) Haver, was born in Jefferson Township, Greene County, Penn., September 13, 1846. His father is living, and his mother deceased. His wife was Miss Nettie Cotterel, also born in Jefferson Township, January 17, 1847, a daughter of John and Permelia Cotterel (*nee* Milliken), deceased. Mr. and Mrs. Jacob Haver were married January 30, 1871, and are the parents of six children, of whom five are living— John C., Jane R., Laura B., Joseph B. and Lizzie; William being deceased. Mr. Haver was raised on a farm and has made farming and stock-dealing his business through life. He owns a good farm in Jefferson Township, containing about two hundred acres, on which are good, substantial buildings.

CHARLES H. HAVER, farmer and stock-dealer, P. O. Jefferson, who was born in Jefferson Township January 22, 1820, is a son of John and Jane Haver (*nee* Rex). The former is living and the latter deceased. Mr. Haver was united in marriage January 22, 1880, with Isabella McClure, who was born in Dunkard Township, Greene County, Penn., in September 1859, a daughter of James and Susan (Brown) McClure. Mr. McClure departed this life August 8, 1886; his widow is still living. Mr. and Mrs. Haver are the parents of two children—James C., born September 28, 1881, and Owen W., born March 27, 1884. Mr. Haver was reared on a farm and has been engaged in farming and stock-dealing all his life. He owns valuable property in the borough of Jefferson.

ISAAC HAYS, farmer, Millsboro, Penn., is one of the pioneer farmers of Greene County, and was born in Morgan Township May 10, 1816, a son of David and Mary Hays, (*nee* Rush). His father was a native of Maryland and his mother of Greene County, Penn., where they were married and remained all their lives. David Hays died in 1827 and his widow in 1870. They were the parents of four children, only two of whom are now living—Jane, and Isaac, the subject of our sketch. His wife was Margaret A. Walton, who was born in Washington County, Penn., in 1823, a daughter of John and Sarah (Paul) Walton, deceased. Mr. and Mrs. Hays were married September 22, 1838, and had a family of ten children, four living—Sarah A., wife of Wesley Rinehart; Mary M., widow of Lafayette Vernon; Margaret J., wife of George R. Baker, and Emeline E. Of the deceased Henry C. was born September 27, 1844, and died January 11, 1882, and John W., born November 1847, and died May 25, 1862. Mr. Hays owns a fine farm of one hundred and fifty-five acres on which he and family now reside. Mrs. Hays departed this life February 13, 1872. She was a kind and affectionate mother, and a loving, faithful wife.

CHARLES HUGHES, retired farmer, P. O. Jefferson, is a descendant of one of the first settlers of Greene County, Penn. He was born August 22, 1816, a son of John and Mary (Rex) Hughes. His mother was a native of Lancaster County, and his father of Greene County, where they were married in Jefferson Township in 1794, lived there seven years, then moved to Morgan Township and spent the remainder of their days. Mr. John Hughes died in 1844, and his wife in 1849. They were the parents of twelve children, only two of whom are living—Maria, the widow of Joseph McNealy, and Charles. He was united in marriage September 21, 1843, with Catharine McEowen, a native of New Jersey, and daughter of George and Permelia (Coleman) McEowen, deceased. By this marriage Mr. Hughes is the father of five children, four living—John S., Mary E., wife of Hamilton Riggle, of Iowa; Permelia, wife of D. A. Bumgarner and Maria C., wife of B. F. Kendall. Amy is deceased. Mrs. Catharine Hughs departed this life June 13, 1856; and two years later, May 26, 1858, Mr. Hughes married Elizabeth Hill, who was born in Greene County July 14, 1829, a daughter of Samuel and Hannah Hill, both deceased. Mr. and Mrs. Charles Hughes are the parents of two children—Maggie and Anna M. Mrs. Elizabeth Hughes died November 27, 1887, a faithful member of the Cumberland Presbyterian Church, of which Mr. Hughes' former wife was also a consistent member. Like his ancestors, Mr. Hughes made farming his business through life, and owns 116

40

acres of land—his home farm. He filled the office of assistant assessor under appointment by the Government.

JOHN H. HUGHES, merchant, Jefferson, Penn., is a descendant of the early settlers of Greene County, and of Irish and English descent. His great-grandfather, Thomas Hughes, laid out the borough of Jefferson. His grandfather, John Hughes, was born in Jefferson, where our subject's great-grandfather settled in 1776; Barnett Hughes was born in 1819, and died in 1882. Two of his children are now living—George, a farmer; and John H., who was reared in Jefferson, attended the schools of Greene County, and early in life went into the dry goods business as salesman. In this capacity he worked for some years at Danville, Illinois, returning to Jefferson in 1871, when he established a general store, in which he has met with deserving success. Mr. John Hughes' wife was Mary, daughter of David and Lettie Bell. Their family consists of one son and one daughter—Barnett and Lettie, both now deceased. Mr. Hughes has served as a member of the town council of Jefferson Borough. In politics he is a Republican; his wife is a member of the Baptist Church.

ROBERT H. JORDAN, farmer, born in Washington Township, Greene County, Penn., is a son of Silas and Sarah (McCormick) Jordan. His parents were natives of Greene County, Penn., and of Irish and English lineage. His grandfather, John Jordan, was a pioneer mill-wright of this county. His father was also a mill-wright and carpenter. His family consisted of eight children, of whom Robert H. was the second. Robert was reared in Jefferson and received a common school education. Early in life he learned the carpenter trade, which occupation he followed for many years. He was twice married, his first wife being Harriet, daughter of John Daniels; she was a native of Ohio. By this union there were three children, all of whom died young. Mrs. Jordan died in 1873. Mr. Jordan was afterwards united in marriage, in 1874, with the widow of Gideon John, of Waynesburg, Penn. Mr. and Mrs. John's children were F. J. John, druggist; R. S., a jeweler at Waynesburg; and Harry J. at home in school. Their father was born in Washington County, Penn., and was of English descent; he died in 1870. Mr. and Mrs. Jordan have one child, James Leroy. Mr. Jordan is the owner of a farm of sixty-eight acres. He is a member of the town council and president of the school board of Jefferson Borough, also was at one time a member of the executive committee of the Monongahela College. He is an upright temperance man and one of the leading members in the Methodist Episcopal Church.

JOHN C. KENDALL, furniture dealer, Jefferson, Penn., was born in Smithfield, Fayette County, Penn., April 26, 1840. His parents were Samuel and Pauline (Custead) Kendall, who were of

German and English origin. His father was a Baptist minister; he died in 1872. His family consisted of twelve children, eleven of whom—nine sons and two daughters—attained the age of maturity. John is the oldest son, and was reared in Fayette County until ten years of age, when he came with his parents to Greene County. He went to school in Fayette County and at Waynesburg College; afterwards returning to Fayette County, where he learned the wagonmaker's trade, and followed it as a business for nine years. He taught school fifteen years, five years of that time in Illinois. In 1861 he married Catharine, daughter of John and Elizabeth Grimm, and by this marriage is the father of two children—Eva and John. The latter is a graduate of the Commercial College, of Springfield, Ill. Mrs. Kendall died in 1866. In 1876 he was next united in marriage with Hannah B., daughter of John and Maria (Loughman) Ross. At the time of her marriage Mrs. Kendall was the widow of the late Thomas Johns, and the mother of one child, Albert Leslie. Mr. and Mrs. Kendall have two children—Paul and Samuel. Mr. Kendall takes quite an active interest in educational matters, and is a member of the board of trustees of Monongahela College. They are both members of the Baptist Church, in which Mr. Kendall is a deacon, and has served as teacher and superintendent in the Sabbathschool.

ELI LONG, deceased, was born April 28, 1821, near Khedive P. O., on the farm now occupied by his heirs. His father and mother were Richard and Mary Long, who were natives of Pennsylvania, were married in the eastern part of the State, and came to Greene County, where they settled and remained until their death. Mr. Eli Long was united in marriage October 25, 1853, with Sarah Pryor, who was born in Belmont County, Ohio, July 27, 1831,—a daughter of Joshua and Susan Pryor, now deceased. To Mr. and Mrs. Long were born four children, of whom two are living—Lizzie L. and Albert C. The deceased are Vincent P. and Della. Mr. Long was reared on a farm, and made a great success of farming and stock dealing, possessing at the time of his death, October 1, 1881, 560 acres of land, which is now owned and managed by his son and daughter. Mrs. Long departed this life August 27, 1886. She and her husband were faithful members of the Cumberland Presbyterian Church, of which the son and daughter are also members.

MARTIN J. LOVE, farmer, P. O. Jefferson, one of the substantial citizens of Jefferson Township, was born in Greene County, Penn., March 11, 1826. His parents were Alfred and Ann Love (*nee* Piper), who were natives of England, where they were married and emigrated to America in 1819, coming to Greene County, Penn., where they remained until their death. Mrs. Love departed this life in 1853 and her husband in 1863. They were the parents of six children, four of whom are living.   Martin J. is the youngest, and was united in marriage November 5, 1857, with Harriet Rinehart, who was born in Greene County November 11, 1829.   She is a daughter of Jacob and Abigail (Huss) Rinehart, who were also natives of Greene County and residents therein through life.   Mrs. Rinehart died in 1841.   Mr. Rinehart afterwards married Elizabeth Hoge, now living; he died in 1874.   To Mr. and Mrs. Martin J. Love have been born nine children; of these five are living, viz.— Emma, George, Ruth, wife of Thomas Hughes; Kate, wife of Hugh Hamilton, and Charlie.   The deceased are Ella, wife of Dr. C. H. Pollock; Lizzie M., Milton J. R. and Millard F.   Mr. Love was raised on a farm, has made farming and stock dealing his business, and owns 300 acres of land where he and family live.   He and wife are consistent members of the Cumberland Presbyterian Church.

EWING McCLEARY, merchant, Jefferson, Penn.—Among the prominent business men of Greene County we mention the name of Ewing McCleary.   He was born in Fayette County, Penn., February 3, 1840, a son of William and Rebecca McCleary.   His parents were also natives of Fayette County.   His father was a merchant in early life, in later years a banker.   Ewing was the only son in a family of three children, and had the advantages of good schools, having attended both the High School and Academy at Uniontown, Penn.   In 1865 he was admitted as a partner in his father's store, in which he had been a salesman for several years.   In 1872 he came to Jefferson and established his present business. Here his long experience in the mercantile trade, and his polite and gentlemanly demeanor, soon won for him a good trade.   His store is an example of neatness, and in the arrangement and selection of goods he exhibits marked ability and good taste.   Mr. McCleary was married in Fayette County, Penn., to Miss Lizzie, daughter of P. G. and Martha (Burchinal) Sturgis.   Mrs. McCleary's father was a Baptist minister, and she is a faithful member of the Baptist Church.   In politics Mr. McCleary is a Democrat.

MICHAEL McGOVERN, deceased, a man highly respected for his many excellent qualities, was a prominent farmer and stockgrower in Jefferson Township, where he died in 1876 at the advanced age of eighty-four years.   He came to Jefferson Township when a young man, and made the tilling of the soil and raising stock the business of his life, which he pursued with more than ordinary energy.   As the fruits of his toils, he was the owner of two farms well stocked and improved.   He was quite happily married to Miss Lucinda Daken, who was born in Ohio, and of English origin.   She has spent most of her life in Greene County, Penn.   The union of Mr. and Mrs. McGovern proved a very pleasant one.   Their youngest child is J. E., who is now a full-grown man.   In politics Mr.

McGovern was a Democrat. He was a zealous member of the Catholic Church.

THOMAS R. McMINN, deceased, who was a saddler and harnessmaker, was born in Cumberland Township, Greene County, Penn., April 22, 1820. He was a son of Robert and Rachel (Rice) McMinn, of Irish and English origin. His father was born in Ireland, and was a school teacher by occupation; in later life he engaged in farming. Thomas McMinn was the youngest in a family of four children—Elizabeth, deceased, who was the wife of James Mahanna; Mary, the widow of James Pogue; Sarah, wife of John Curl; and Thomas R., who married Miss Elizabeth V., daughter of William Lee Pollock, of Pittsburgh, Penn. Mrs. McMinn is next to the youngest of a family of twelve children. The marriage of Mr. and Mrs. McMinn has been blessed with seven children, five of whom are living—Mary A., wife of John Rex; W. J., a saddler; Elizabeth L., Thomas Reed, a liveryman at Jefferson; and John C., a minister in the Methodist Episcopal Church. Robert L. and an infant are deceased. Mr. McMinn took great pride in fine horses and cattle, in which he dealt quite extensively during his life. He was a man of more than ordinary intellect, always foremost as a peacemaker, and beloved by everybody who had the pleasure of his acquaintance. In the language of all persons of that section with whom we have been able to converse, " his place can never be filled." Nothing can be said that would not be appropriate to the character of so honored a friend of the people. He started in life a poor boy, and by industry, honesty and integrity, he amassed considerable fortune, leaving every member of his family in comfortable circumstances. His widow is a devoted member of the Methodist Episcopal Church.

DANIEL MOREDOCK, farmer, Jefferson, Penn., was born in Jefferson Township, Greene County, March 29, 1820. His father, George Moredock, a native of Greene County, was three times married, his first wife being Priscilla Anderson, Daniel's mother, who was born January 10, 1798, with whom he lived in Jefferson Township until her death, May 16, 1841. He married for his second wife Mary (Moredock) Worthington, and for the third, Emily A. Randolph, now deceased. He departed this life in 1881. He was the father of twelve children, nine of whom are living. Daniel is the second, and was united in marriage, November 25, 1849, with Elizabeth Rex, who was born in Jefferson Township, August 23, 1834, a daughter of Charles and Mary (Hickman) Rex, deceased. By this marriage Mr. Moredock is the father of ten children, eight living, viz: Rex, Margaret, wife of Samuel Cox; Emma, wife of David Burson; Sarah, wife of Anderson Moredock; Anna, wife of William Daugherty; Edda, Elizabeth and Austin L. The deceased are George and James A. Their mother departed this life April 11, 1877.

August 26, 1885, Mr. Moredock married Rosa A. Stephens, who was born in Delaware. Mr. Moredock is an industrious and economical farmer and stock-dealer, and owns a nice home and good farm of 240 acres where he and family now live.

JEREMIAH PRICE, farmer, P. O. Rice's Landing, was born in Monongahela Township, Greene County, Penn., September 7, 1814. His parents, Michael and Mary (Evans) Price, were natives of Wales, where they were married and lived about one year, then emigrated to America, locating in Greene County, Penn., where they remained until Mr. Price's death, July 9, 1853. Mrs. Price died in June, 1870, being one hundred years and thirteen days old. They were the parents of six children, only two of whom are living—Michael, single, and Jeremiah, who was united in marriage, August 14, 1855, with Mary J. Goslin. She was born in Fayette County, Penn., September 17, 1821, and is a consistent member of the Cumberland Presbyterian Church. Her parents were Richard and Jane (Millison) Goslin, who were natives of Fayette County, Penn., and moved from there to Greene County, where they died. Richard Goslin was a soldier of the war of 1814. Mr. and Mrs. Price have three children, two living, viz: Oliver J. and George E. The deceased was Maria J., wife of Simon Sharpnack. Mr. Price is a farmer and quite a genius, having engaged at different times in blacksmithing, malting, and the practice of veterinary surgery. He and his brother Michael own 400 acres of good land in Greene County. Mr. Michael Price filled the office of auditor of the county one term, and has met with success as a farmer and school-teacher. The following is a copy of the naturalization papers of the parents of our subject: "Delaware District, ss. I,—Do Hereby Certify That, Michael Price wife & one child of Radnor, Shire—Himself aged 34 years, a Native of Wales Subject to King of Great, Brittain, and that, he intends residing in Newyork, an is regestered in the Office of the District Court in Testimony whereof, I, have hereunto set my hand and affixed the, Seal, of the District Court of the United, States For the, Delaware District at Wilmington this, 22d day of July—in the year of our Lord—one Thousand Eight Hundred and one. Thomas Stocton, Clerk, Delaware District."

GEORGE REX, farmer, P. O. Jefferson, is a descendant of one of the pioneer families of the township, and was born November 30, 1838, on the farm where he and family now reside. He is a son of Charles and Mary (Hickman) Rex. His father was born on the old Rex homestead in Jefferson Township, Greene County, July 1, 1801, and was a son of George and Margaret (Keppler) Rex, the former a native of England, and the latter of Germany. They emigrated to America, and were married in Pennsylvania, settling in Greene County, which at the time of their settlement was known as Washington County. Here they remained until their death. Mary Rex, George's mother, was born in Fayette County, Penn., January 19, 1801, a daughter of Solomon and Elizabeth Hickman, who were natives of Pennsylvania, and departed this life in Jefferson Borough. Charles and Mary Rex were the parents of seven children, three of whom are living, viz: Margaret, wife of W. F. Hughes, of Mount Pleasant, Iowa; John, a resident of Fairbury, Ill.; and George, the subject of our sketch. George was united in marriage, December 8, 1861, with Mary E. Strickler, born in Westmoreland County, January 5, 1843, and is a consistent member of the Presbyterian Church. Her parents are Isaac and Catharine (Heath) Strickler, natives of Fayette County, where they lived a few years, then moved to Westmoreland County, where they now reside. Mr. and Mrs. Rex have a family of ten children, eight living—Charles, Ella J., Edward B., Georgianna, Joseph A., Albert G., Mattie M. and Ernest. The deceased were Catharine and George. Mr. Rex, like his ancestors, has made farming the business of his life, and owns 125 acres of land, known as the old Rex homestead.

H. P. RINEHART, farmer, P. O. Waynesburg, was born in Franklin Township, Greene County, Penn., June 1, 1844. He is a son of Arthur and Rebecca (Roberts) Rinehart, who were natives of this county and residents therein until death. He departed this life April 6, 1872, and she January 5, 1873. They were the parents of thirteen children; seven are living, the youngest of whom is H. P., who was married June 28, 1866, having chosen as the sharer of his fortunes Miss Maria Bowers, who was born in Whiteley Township, February 22, 1844. Her parents were John and Elizabeth (Cowell) Bowers, also natives of Greene County, where they lived until 1869, at which time they moved to Taylor County, Iowa. Mrs. Bowers died February 14, 1877. Mr. Bowers is still living. Mr. and Mrs. Rinehart have had eight children—Charles W., Floe F., Jesse B., Mary L., John R., William W. and Maria K.; Maggie being deceased. Mr. Rinehart owns 123 acres of land where he and family live. He filled the office of director of the poor one term, also served on the school board of his township. He and wife are consistent members of the Methodist Protestant Church.

JAMES SCOTT, deceased, was one of the most successful and enterprising farmers of Jefferson Township. He was born October 6, 1822, on the farm where his family resides. His father and mother were James and Margaret (Kincaid) Scott. His father was a son of Mordecai and Kizzie (Potete) Scott, and came with his parents from Maryland to Greene County, Penn., where he married Margaret Kincaid, who was born in 1790, and departed this life in 1888. James was the fourth in their family of five children. He was united in marriage, May 19, 1853, with Mary A., daughter of William and

Elizabeth (Hedges) Spencer, who were natives of Washington County, Penn. Mr. Spencer came with his parents to Greene County when only two years of age. He was married in Washington County, returned with his wife to Greene County and remained until 1871, then moved to the State of Tennessee, where Mrs. Spencer died April 12, 1883. In the fall of the same year he again returned to Greene County, and has since made his home with his daughter, Mrs. James Scott. To Mr. and Mrs. Scott were born six children, five of whom are living. The oldest of these, Lizzie E., is the widow of I. N. McNay, the mother of one child, named Newton for his father; the second daughter is Anna S., wife of Dr. J. L. Millikin, of Greensboro, Penn., and the mother of one son, Joe P.; the others are William S., Emma K. and J. Newton. Margaret is deceased. Mr. Scott acquired hsi education in the common schools in Jefferson Township. Like his ancestors, he made farming and stock-raising his business, and owned 400 acres of land. He was a member of the Masonic fraternity, and belonged to the Cumberland Presbyterian Church, of which Mrs. Scott is also a devoted member. He remained on the old Scott homestead until his death, September 30, 1878.

MILTON S. SHAPE, farmer, Clarksville, Penn., was born in Greene County, July 29, 1835, a son of Jacob and Joanna Shape (nee Pettit), who were also natives of Greene County, where they were married, settled and remained until Mrs. Shape's death, which occurred in 1859. Her husband afterwards married Elizabeth Black (nee Walters), and they reside in Clarksville, Penn. Mr. Jacob Shape is the father of eight children, six now living. Milton S. is the oldest and was united in marriage, August 16, 1878, with Catharine A. Lancaster, who was born in Fayette County, Penn., February 10, 1844. Her parents, Bartholomew and Minerva (Fraley) Lancaster, were natives of Maryland, where they were married and then came to Greene County, Penn., in 1843, removing two years later to Fayette County, Penn., where they died. Mr. and Mrs. Milton Shape are the parents of four children, only one living, Hadashia B., born November 11, 1880. Mr. Shape is a carpenter by trade, which he followed for sixteen years. He then engaged in farming, and owns seventy-two acres of land. He enlisted in Company G, Fifteenth Pennsylvania Cavalry and served his country three years. He is a member of the Masonic fraternity and Mrs. Shape is a member of the Methodist Episcopal Church.

THOMAS SHARPNACK, farmer, Jefferson, Penn., was born in Cumberland Township, Greene County, June 30, 1827. He is a son of Peter and Mary (Alfree) Sharpnack, who were native of Greene County, where they were married and made their home until Mr. Sharpnack's death in 1845. Mrs. Sharpnack died in 1867. They were the parents of nine children, five now living. Of these

Thomas is the oldest and was united in marriage, June 27, 1852, with Elizabeth Craft, who was born in Fayette County, Penn., November 6, 1826. She is a daughter of Benjamin and Mary Craft, also natives of Fayette County. Her father died March 27, 1886; her mother is still living. They were the parents of fifteen children, nine living. To Mr. and Mrs. Sharpnack have been born five children, only one living, Simon. The deceased are George, Adaline, Benjamin and Peter. Mr. Sharpnack is a farmer and owns 166 acres of land where he and his family reside. Mrs. Sharpnack is a faithful member of the Cumberland Presbyterian Church.

T. H. SHARPNACK, M. D., born at Rice's Landing, Penn., November 20, 1843, is a son of William and Sarah (Neel) Sharpnack. His parents were natives of Greene County, Penn., and were of Scotch and German descent. His father is a farmer and stock-grower and resides in Cumberland Township, where he was born in June 9, 1810, a son of Samuel and Nancy (Crago) Sharpnack. The Doctor's grandmother, Nancy Sharpnack, was born in 1776 and lived to be eighty-four years old. His grandfather, Samuel, died in 1852 at the age of sixty-three. The Doctor's grandparents on his mother's side were Barney and Martha (Hughes) Neel. They were natives of Cumberland Township. Eleven of their children grew to maturity. The Doctor is the fourth in a family of nine children. He was reared in Jefferson Township, educated at Waynesburg College, and studied medicine with Dr. Laidley, of Carmichaels. He took the regular course in medicine at Jefferson Medical College, at Philadelphia, and graduated in 1872. He then entered his profession at Jefferson, where he has had a good practice since. The Doctor is a member of the Greene County Medical Society, and was sent as delegate to the State Medical Association. He has served as the physician of the Children's Home in this county, and is examining physician for three life insurance companies. He was married, June 23, 1870, to Cynthia, daughter of James and Hannah Moredock. They have four children—James M., William F., Gertrude H. and Thomas P. (deceased). Mrs. Sharpnack died August 16, 1877. The Doctor is a member of the Baptist Church; in politics he is a Democrat.

STIERS SHARPNACK, farmer, Jefferson, Penn., was born on the farm where he and his family reside, July 2, 1855. His parents were Thomas E. and Catharine (Haver) Sharpnack, who were natives of Greene County, Penn., where they were married, settled and remained until their death. He departed this life October 2, 1876, and she November 8, 1887. They were the parents of three children —Calvin, Andrew S. and Stiers, the subject of this sketch. He was united in marriage, April 14, 1877, with Jennie Hupp, born in Morgan Township, March 4, 1856, a daughter of Uriah and Marinda

Hupp (*nee* Cox).   Mrs. Sharpnack is a consistent member of the Disciple Church.   Her father was a native of Washington County, Penn., and her mother of Greene County, where they reside in Morgan Township.   Mr. and Mrs. Sharpnack have four children— John H., Minnie L., William H. and Harry A.   Mr. Sharpnack was raised on a farm and makes farming his business.   He owns 107 acres of land in Jefferson Township.

ALVA C. SHAW, merchant and burgess of Jefferson Borough, was born in Canaan Township, Morrow County, Ohio, March 4, 1844, a son of John and Mary A. (Bell) Shaw.   Their parents were of Scotch-Irish origin; they were Quakers and among the early settlers of Pennsylvania.   The Shaws have usually been farmers and merchants.   Alva's father, J. L. Shaw, was a farmer and stock-grower, born in Morrow County, Ohio, June 6, 1806.   He was a son of John and Polly (Luther) Shaw, and was the oldest in a family of six children.   He always met with marked success in business.   In 1877 he moved from Ohio to Jefferson, Penn., and engaged in selling farming implements.   He died in Jefferson Borough.   Of his six children, only three reached maturity.   Alva is the youngest and was educated at Delaware College, and Ohio Wesleyan University.   He started in life as a teacher, but was induced by his father to work on the farm till 1874 when he went to Lincoln, Nebraska, and engaged in the coal business till 1879.   He then came to Jefferson and began merchandising.   He was elected burgess in 1887.   He is a strong temperance man, and in politics is a Prohibitionist.   He is a member of the Methodist Episcopal Church, in which he is steward, trustee and teacher in the Sabbath-school.

SYLVANUS SMITH, M. D., Jefferson, Penn., was born in Franklin Township, Greene County, November 30, 1832, a son of Samuel and Elizabeth (Huss) Smith, they were natives of Pennsylvania and of German and English origin.   His father was born in Greene County, in 1796.   His grandfather, Sylvanus, a native of Monmouth County, New Jersey, came to Greene County, Penn., in 1793.   They were all farmers and members of the society of Friends. Dr. Smith's father died in 1879.   Of his four children, the Doctor is the youngest, and was reared on the farm with his parents in Franklin and Morgan townships.   He attended the district schools and studied medicine in Jefferson Borough, with Dr. W. D. Rogers. Here he commenced the practice of his chosen profession in 1862, has met with good success, and accumulated quite a competence from his practice.   June 1, 1862, he married Louisa Crayne, who is of English descent, and daughter of Miller Crayne.   Dr. and Mrs. Smith's children are—John S., a physician and druggist; Samuel M., a law student at Waynesburg; Elizabeth, C. Harry, Albert P. and Lucinda.   In politics the Doctor is a Democrat.   He is a member of the I. O. O. F., and a Sir Knight Templar of the Masonic Fraternity.

REV. CHARLES W. TILTON, pastor of the East Bethlehem Baptist Church in Washington County, was born in Washington County, Penn., November 21, 1815. He is the son of Enoch and Elizabeth (Wheatley) Tilton, natives of New Jersey. They were of Scotch, English and German ancestry. His father was a farmer, and his family consisted of thirteen children, eleven of whom grew to manhood and womanhood. Charles W., the eighth in the family, remained on the farm with his parents until fifteen years of age, and attended the district school. His parents then moved to Beaver County, after which he entered Frankfort Academy. Early in life he taught school as a business. In 1839 he joined the Pleasant Grove Baptist Church in Washington County. In 1840 he came to Jefferson, Penn., and has lived in this vicinity ever since. In 1843 he was ordained as a minister and has been an active worker in the Baptist Church up to the present time, having held over one hundred protracted meetings, resulting in the conversion of fully 2,000 persons, and baptized over 1,500 converts. For many years he has taken a deep interest in education, and labored in the interests of Monongahela College, having served as secretary of the board of trustees from the organization of the college, and as financial agent for several years past. He has been twice married, first to Miss Nancy Hoge, who died in 1858. Again in 1861 to Sarah Elizabeth Davidson, daughter of William Davidson, of Baltimore, and Margarett (Oliver) Davidson. In his last marriage they had four children— Enoch Randolph, Charles Louis, Nannie Clare and John Hunt— three of whom are graduates of Mononghela College. The oldest son, E. R., a graduate of Crozer Theological Seminary, is pastor of a Baptist Church in Evans City, Penn. The second son, C. L., graduated in the Western Reserve University of Cleveland, Ohio, and is a practicing physician in the State of Colorado. The youngest son is still at school.

F. B. WISE, druggist and postmaster, Jefferson, Penn., is a native of Morgan Township, Greene County, where he was born April 24, 1846. His parents, Solomon and Hannah Wise, were natives of Pennsylvania, and of German origin. His father has been a farmer all his life, and at present is in the cattle business in the West. Frank is the oldest in a family of seven children now living, and was educated at Waynesburg College. He taught school and farmed until 1872, when he engaged in the drug business in company with Dr. Sharpnack, of Jefferson, whose interest he bought in 1879 and established his present business. In 1870 he married Miss Lizzie, daughter of H. Johns, ex-sheriff of Greene County, and of English descent. Mr. and Mrs. Wise are members of the Baptist Church, in which he is clerk and superintendent of the Sabbath-school, and clerk of the Ten-Mile Baptist Association. He is a member of the board of trustees and secretary of the executive committee of Monongahela College. In politics Mr. Wise is a Democrat. He is a member of the town council, and was appointed postmaster in 1883.

JACKSON TOWNSHIP.

JAMES CARPENTER, farmer and stock-grower, Nettle Hill, Penn., was born in Franklin Township, Greene County, Penn., March 5, 1838. He is a son of Joseph and Elizabeth (Smith) Carpenter, natives of this county, and of English and German origin. His father is a farmer and now resides in Gilmore Township. Of his family of eleven children James is the third. James was drafted in the three years' draft of 1863, paid his conscript and received his discharge the same year. He was reared on a farm, receiving his education in the common schools of Jackson Township. He makes farming and stock-growing his chief pursuit, and owns 125 acres of well improved land where he resides. Mr. Carpenter was united in marriage, December 12, 1863, with Miss Mazy, daughter of Joseph and Rachel (Shriver) Kniseley, and their children are—J. C., a teacher; Robert E. Lee and John B. Mr. Carpenter is a Democrat. He and his wife are members of the Methodist Protestant Church.

WILLIAM GRAHAM, farmer and stock-grower, was born in Franklin Township, this county, March 29, 1828. He is a son of William and Margaret (Muckel) Graham, who are of Dutch descent. The Grahams are an industrious, energetic family. Some branches of the family spell the name Grimes, but the original name was Graham. William Graham's father was a blacksmith by occupation, but also engaged in farming, spending most of his life in Greene County. His family consisted of six children, of whom William is the third. He was reared on the farm in his native township, and attended the common school. He has made a very successful business man, devoting himself principally to farming and stock-growing. He owns 318 acres of well improved land where he resides, near Holbrook, Penn. He also owns land in other parts of the county, making in all 473 acres. On November 7, 1850, Mr. Graham married Charlotte, daughter of William and Sallie (Bodkin) Smith, who were of English and Dutch extraction. Mr. and Mrs.

Graham's children are—Sarah M., wife of Thomas Henning; James F., a farmer; William S., who is in Kansas; Lydia Ann, Mary Elizabeth, wife of John Morris; Cephas J., who is in Kansas; John A. and Spencer Milton, all farmers; and Japheth E. All the family, with one exception, are members of the Baptist Church. Mr. Graham is a Democrat and a member of the Democratic County Committee.

HARVEY ALLISON GRIMES, a farmer and stock-grower of Jackson Township, this county, was born May 9, 1857, on the farm where his father now resides. His parents, P. M. and Maria (Ridgeway) Grimes, are natives of Greene County, and of English origin. His father is a merchant and farmer, and one of the influential citizens of Jackson Township. Harvey A. Grimes is the fifth in a family of eight children. He was reared on a farm, attended the common schools, and early in life made choice of farming as his chief pursuit. His present farm consists of 120 acres of finely improved land. On January 29, 1876, Mr. Grimes was united in marriage with Martha D., daughter of George and Mary (Gump) Loar, of German origin. Her father was a minister in the Methodist Church. Mr. and Mrs. Grimes are the parents of three children —Ada May, Eva Maria and Luta Lena. Mr. Grimes is a Republican. He has served as school director in his district. He and wife are members of the Methodist Episcopal Church.

GEORGE W. GRIMES, farmer and stock-grower, who was born in Jackson Township, this county, June 8, 1859, is a son of P. M. and Maria (Ridgeway) Grimes, natives of Greene County. The subject of this sketch is the sixth in a family of eight children. He was reared on a farm and received his education in the common schools. He made choice of farming as his occupation, and has been very successful and is the owner of 108 acres of land where he resides, near White Cottage, Penn. Mr. Grimes was united in marriage, January 10, 1880, with Miss Ella, daughter of William and Nancy (Dunson) Roberts, who are of English descent. Mr. and Mrs. Grimes are the parents of three children—John H., James A. and William E. Mr. Grimes is a Republican. He and wife are members of the Methodist Episcopal Church. Mr. Grimes belongs to one of the oldest families in the township, his ancestors having been among the earliest settlers in the county.

P. M. GRIMES, merchant and farmer, was born in Franklin Township, this county, October 16, 1823. He is a a son of William and Margaret (Muckle) Grimes, who were born in New Jersey, and of German descent. His father, who was a successful farmer and mechanic, died in 1877, at the age of seventy-six years. His mother died in 1865, and was sixty-six years of age. Mr. P. M. Grimes was reared on the farm and received his education in the subscription schools. He has resided in Jackson Township since 1846, and at

White Cottage, Penn., since 1851. He opened a dry goods and grocery store there in 1855, and has been very successful in his business. Mr. Grimes bought 800 acres of land, and has given several hundred acres to his children. He has the reputation of being an honorable, high-minded gentleman, and has a wide circle of friends. Mr. Grimes is a Republican, and has served as justice of the peace for thirty-three years. He has been postmaster at White Cottage for many years, and is a prominent member of the I. O. O. F. and the Masonic fraternity. Mr. Grimes was united in marriage in 1841 with Maria, daughter of David and Lydia (Calahan) Ridgeway. Mrs. Grimes is of English and Irish extraction. Their children are —William, Allison, George, David, James, A. L. and Margaret, wife of William Millikin, a prominent farmer of Greene County; and Jane, wife of Perry Scott, a prominent farmer and Democrat. Mrs. Grimes is a member of the Methodist Episcopal Church.

JOHN GROVES, farmer and stock-grower, born in Whiteley Township, this county, in 1837, is a son of Jacob and Nancy (Orndoff) Groves, natives of Pennsylvania, and of German descent. His father was a farmer all his life and died in Greene County, in 1868. He reared a family of twelve children, of whom John is the ninth. He was reared in Whiteley Township near Newton, Penn. Early in life he chose farming as his chief pursuit and has met with marked success. He is the owner of a good farm of one hundred and ninety acres where he resides near Holbrook, Penn. By his own exertions Mr. Groves has succeeded in making himself independent. Mr. Groves married Nancy, daughter of Robert Dunson. She died in 1886—eighteen years after their marriage. They were the parents of three children—William T., Anna Belle, and Flora Viola. Mr. Groves is a Democrat, and has served as school director in his township. He belongs to the Disciple Church, of which his deceased wife was also a member.

WILLIAM HUFFMAN, farmer and stock-grower, White Cottage, Penn., was born December 27, 1850, on the farm which he now owns in Jackson Township, Greene County, Penn. He is a son of Peter and Elizabeth (Stagner) Huffman, who were natives of this county, and of English origin. His father died in 1885 at the advanced age of eighty-three years. Of his family of nine children William is the seventh. He was reared on his present farm in Jackson Township, and has made farming his business through life. He has been very successful and owns two hundred and six acres of land well stocked and improved. Mr. Huffman was united in marriage, November 27, 1870, with Miss Jennie, daughter of Corbly and Jane (Bailey) Fordyce. Mrs. Huffman's ancestors were among the pioneers of Greene County. They were of English origin. Mr.

Huffman is a Democrat. His wife is a member of the Methodist Protestant Church.

N. H. JOHNSON, farmer and stock-grower, was born February 1, 1829, on the Haines farm, east of Waynesburg; he resides near White Cottage, Penn. He is a son of William and Hester (Haines) Johnson, who were born in Pennsylvania and were of German and English origin. His father, who was a tanner by trade, died in Greene County, May 3, 1847. Of his family of six children the subject of this sketch is the second. He was reared on the farm and received a limited education in an old-fashioned log school-house with slab seats and paper windows. He has been a successful farmer and owns a fine farm of 230 acres of land in Jackson Township. Mr. Johnson was a poor boy and by industry and patient effort has made himself independent. He has been thrice married. His children now living are—William Henry, who is in the West; N. J., Mary, wife of Ambler Elliot; W. S., J. S. and E. J. His first wife's name was Charlotta Coen, second Elmira Burge, and third Susannah Wagonner.

LINDSEY KEENER, farmer and stock-grower, Pine Bank, Penn., was born April 30, 1836, in Jackson Township. He is a son of Peter and Susan (Stewart) Keener. His mother was born in Maryland and his father in Pennsylvania. They were of English extraction. His father spent his life in Greene County, and was a farmer by occupation. Mr. Keener is the youngest of nine children. He was reared on the home farm, attended the common schools and chose farming as his life work. He owns a good farm of 110 acres which he has acquired by patient toil and earnest effort being a self-made man, and anxious to succeed in life. In politics Mr. Keener is a Republican, and one of the representative men of the county.

ALEXANDER KIGER, farmer and stock-grower, was born in Whiteley Township, Greene County, Penn., and is a son of John and Sarah (McLaughlin) Kiger, who were of German and Irish descent. His father was a farmer all his life, and died in 1872. Of his family of ten children, the subject of this sketch is the eighth. He was reared on a farm in his native township, and attended the district school. Mr. Kiger has made a success of farming and is the owner of 173 acres of valuable land where he resides near Holbrook, in Jackson Township. Mr. Kiger was united in marriage, March 9, 1862, with Catharine, daughter of Isaac and Phoebe (Pope) Higgins, who were of Dutch and English origin. Mr. and Mrs. Kiger's children are—Jerome B., Elizabeth, John L., Newton, Belle and Sadie. Mr. and Mrs· Kiger are members of the Methodist Protestant Church. He is trustee and class-leader in the church and a teacher in the Sabbath-school. In politics he is a Democrat.

JACKSON KUGHN, farmer and stock-grower, was born in Wayne Township, Greene County, Penn., December 22, 1828. He is a son of Abraham and Elizabeth (Huffman) Kughn, who were of German and English ancestry. His mother was born in Maryland and his father in Greene County, Penn., where he died in 1861. Jackson Kughn is the oldest of eight children. He was reared in this county and received a good English education in the common schools. He chose farming as his occupation through life and is the owner of the farm of 121 acres where he now resides near Pine Bank, Penn. On May 27, 1859, Mr. Kughn married Eliza Jane, daughter of John and Sarah (Stewart) Thomas, who were of English origin. Mr. and Mrs. Kughn's children are—John L., Abraham, William Henry, George Morgan, Rachel Ellen and Mary Alice. Mr. Kughn is a Democrat. He and wife are members of the Baptist Church.

LESTER KUGHN, merchant and farmer, Pine Bank, Penn., was born in this county, May 12, 1841, and is a son of Abraham and Elizabeth (Huffman) Kughn. His father, who was of English and German ancestry, was born in Greene County, Penn., where he spent all his life as a farmer. The subject of our sketch is the fifth in a family of eight children. He was reared on the farm in Jackson Township, and received his education in the common schools. Early in life he learned the carpenter's trade, at which he worked for several years, and also farmed considerably. He owns a good farm where he resides in Jackson Township. Since 1884 he has been engaged in the mercantile business. In 1863 Mr. Kughn married Ellen, daughter of John and Mary (King) Cole, and their children are—George, a carpenter; Mary A. and Elizabeth Jane. Mr. and Mrs. Kughn are members of the Baptist Church, in which he is a deacon and has been superintendent of the Sabbath-school. Mr. Kughn is a Democrat, and has served justice of the peace in his township.

JAMES MEEK, farmer and stock-grower, was born in Greene County, Penn., April 3, 1821. He is a son of John and Elizabeth (Boyd) Meek, natives of Greene County, Penn. His father was of French descent and his mother of Scotch ancestry. His father was a farmer and died in 1877. He served his country in the war of 1812. His family consisted of ten children. The subject of this sketch is the oldest of the children. He was reared on the farm, and was a school teacher early in life. He has made farming his main occupation, and owns a farm of 225 acres of well improved land. Mr. Meek is a self-made man, having acquired his present possessions entirely through his own industry. He was united in marriage, October 20, 1842, with Miss Mary, daughter of Samuel and Bithiah (Sharp) Smith, who were of Scotch and Irish lineage. Mrs.

Meek was born in Millsboro, Washington County, Penn., July 10, 1824. They have ten children, eight now living, viz., Melinda, wife of George Jewell; Elizabeth, wife of Abner Johns; James R., a farmer; Sarah Jane, wife of S. Lang; Martha, wife of W. Aukrom; C. J., a farmer; Eddie, wife of W. W. Patterson, ex-county register and recorder; and Mary A. Mr. Meek is a member of the Baptist Church. He is a Democrat, and in 1869 was elected county treasurer. He has held most of the offices in his township, and has also served as auditor of the county. He is a member of the I. O. O. F. and the Masonic fraternity.

W. E. MILLIKEN, farmer and stock-grower, White Cottage, Penn., was born in Jefferson Borough, January 6, 1845. He is a son of John and Mary (Ketchem) Milliken, natives of Greene County, and of Irish lineage. His grandfather, Thomas Milliken, was one of the early settlers of the county, and a blacksmith by trade. Mr. Milliken's father is a farmer, and now resides in Washington County, Penn. The subject of this sketch was reared on a farm, receiving his education at the common schools. He has always been a farmer and owns a farm of 119 acres where he resides in Jackson Township. In 1866 Mr. Milliken married Margaret M., daughter of P. M. Grimes, one of the prominent farmers of Jackson Township. They are the parents of six children, viz., T. W., Maria Jane, James P., Mary Ellen, Lora Belle and Emma M. Mr. and Mrs. Milliken are members of the Methodist Protestant Church in which he is trustee and treasurer of the Sabbath-school. Mr. Milliken's oldest daughter is one of the stewards in the church and an active Sabbath-school teacher. Mr. Milliken is a Republican. In 1862 he enlisted in Company G, Eighteenth Pennsylvania Cavalry and was a non-commissioned officer. He was in the battles of Cedar Creek, Gettysburg, and was at Winchester when Gen. Sheridan made his famous ride. He is a member of the G. A. R. Post.

L. H. MITCHELL, farmer and stock-dealer, was born in Greene County, Penn., June 10, 1846. He is a son of Jackson and Catharine (Lemmon) Mitchell, who were of English and Irish lineage. His father, who was a farmer, died in this county in 1858 or 1859. Mr. L. H. Mitchell is one of a family of four children. He was reared on the farm and attended the common schools of the county. Mr. Mitchell has made his own way in the world. In 1867 his only possession was thirty dollars, and he now owns 360 acres of land well stocked and improved. He has engaged extensively in the culture of fish and has two large ponds. His success, which seems indeed wonderful, may be attributed wholly to his great industry and unbounded energy. He is a temperance man and votes the prohibition ticket. In 1867 Mr. Mitchell married Miss Julia Ann, daughter of Peter and Elizabeth (Stagnard) Huffman. Their chil-

41

dren are—J. B., E. I. and C. A., aged respectively (in 1888) twenty, fifteen and ten years. Mr. Mitchell and wife were born on the 10th day of June—he being just one year the older. They are members of the Methodist Protestant Church. In connection with his other business projects, Mr. Mitchell is one of the managers of the roller flour mill at Oak Forest, Penn. He was actively interested in the Granger movement for many years and served as Master of the Order or lecturer for twelve years.

RUFUS C. MITCHELL, farmer and stock-grower, who was born in Jackson Township, this county, August 23, 1851, is a son of Jesse and Dorcas (Long) Mitchell, who were of English lineage. His father followed farming as an occupation, and died September 5, 1870. The Mitchells have ever been noted for their energy and industry, and have usually been farmers by occupation. Jesse Mitchell was twice married and had in all eight children. The subject of our sketch is the third child by the last marriage. He is a self-made man, and has made a success of his farming and stock-growing, being the owner of 100 acres of well improved land near Holbrook, Penn. Mr. Mitchell was united in marriage, December 24, 1870, with Miss Hettie, daughter of Peter Huffman. Their children are—Cora Belle, Mary Luella, Charles B., Ada, May, Elizabeth and Ross N. Mr. Mitchell is a Democrat. His wife is a member of the Methodist Protestant Church.

A. J. MITCHELL, farmer and stock-grower, was born in Richhill Township, Greene County, Penn., April 23, 1837. He is the son of Jesse and Lydia (Kerr) Mitchell. His father was born in Allegheny County and his mother in Greene County. They were of Irish and English lineage. His father was a blacksmith in early life and in later years a farmer. Mr. A. J. Mitchell is the second in a family of eight children. He was reared on the farm and received a common school education. He has followed farming and stock growing as an occupation, has been very successful in his business, and owns a farm of 248 acres. At the breaking out of the war in 1861 he enlisted in Company F, Eighty-fifth Pennsylvania Volunteer Infantry, and served for three years. He is a member of the G. A. R. Post No. 552. In 1865 Mr. Mitchell married Harriet, daughter of Bateman and Hannah (Howard) Martin. Their children are —Sarah E., Jesse, Eliza M., Jonathan, Thomas Jefferson, James Madison, George McClellan, Martha A. and Clara Belle. Mr. Mitchell, who is a Democrat, has been an efficient member of the school board in his township.

JACOB MORRIS, farmer and stock-grower, Holbrook, Penn., was born in Greene County December 17, 1819. He is a son of Robert and Salona (Renner) Morris, natives of Greene County, and of German origin. His father, who was a mechanic and farmer, died in this county. Jacob Morris is the oldest in a family of six children, and is the only one now living. He never had the advantages of a common school education, and as a consequence never learned to read. He grew up on the farm and chose farming and stock-growing as his occupation. Mr. Morris has by industry and good business management succeeded in building a good home. By his own exertions he has come into possession of 450 acres of land, and has also done much for his children. He is careful in all his business transactions, and seldom makes an error. On March 6, 1845, Mr. Morris married Miss Nancy, daughter of William and Mary (Dunn) Jewell, who were natives of this county, and of English descent. Isaac Dunn, grandfather of Mrs. Morris, was a soldier in the Revolutionary war. He died in this county. The children of Mr. and Mrs. Morris are—Rufus, William Henry, Mary Ann, wife of William T. Grimes; Phœbe J., wife of J. McCosh; James M., Hannah, wife of David Grimes; Sarah M., Charity, wife of Samuel Smith; and Jacob J. Mr. and Mrs. Morris are members of the Baptist Church. In politics he is a Republican.

CAPTAIN JOHN SCOTT, retired farmer and stock-grower, was born in Center Township, this county, April 6, 1815. He is a son of John and Susannah (Nicewonger) Scott. His parents were descendants of the Quakers, his mother being a native of West Virginia, and his father of Greene County, Penn. His father died May 21, 1857, at the advanced age of seventy-three years; his mother died December 12, 1870, aged eighty-five. Their family consisted of nine children, of whom the subject of this sketch is the fourth. He was reared on the farm in Center Township and received his education in the common schools. He has met with marked success as a farmer, and owns 252 acres of finely improved land. Captain Scott was an active member of the militia in Greene County many years ago. He has made his own way in the world, starting a poor boy, and has succeeded in acquiring a good home for himself and family. He was united in marriage June 16, 1836, with Miss Charlotte Mason, who was born in this county May 3, 1817, and is the daughter of James and Mary (Sayers) Mason. Her mother was born in New Jersey and was of German descent; she died February 9, 1883, aged ninety-six years. Her father was a native of Ireland, and died June 12, 1869. Mr. and Mrs. Scott are the parents of the following named children: Mason and J. C., farmers; Mary, wife of William Orndoff; Oliver Perry, a farmer; Eliza Jane, wife of A. C. Carpenter; Sarah, wife of George Moore; and Matthias, deceased. Mrs. Scott is a member of the Baptist Church. Captain Scott has always taken great interest in school affairs, and has served as school director for many years. He is a member of the I. O. O. F. His children and grandchildren were all present at the fifteenth anniversary of their marriage, which was one of the happiest events transpiring in the neighborhood for many years.

HUGH SMITH, a descendant of the earliest settlers of Greene County, and among its most prominent citizens, was born on Smith Creek in Franklin Township, January 26, 1832. His grandfather, Thomas Smith, was the first settler on the creek which bears his name. Mr. Hugh Smith is a son of Vincent and Elizabeth (Bell) Smith, the former a native of this county and the latter of Virginia. His father, who was of Irish descent, was born in 1791 and died in 1884. His family consisted of ten children, of whom the subject of our sketch is the youngest of those now living. He was reared on the farm, and has made a successful farmer. He is the owner of a fine farm of 400 acres where he now resides. Mr. Smith was married in his native county to Miss Mary E., daughter of John and Jane (Hennen) Lemley. Mrs. Smith's parents were descendants of the early settlers of the county, and of German and English origin. Mr. and Mrs. Smith have two children—Clara and Maggie.

JOHNSON T. SMITH, deceased, who was an attorney and justice of the peace, was born in this county December 8, 1818, and was a son of Thomas and Catharine (Johnson) Smith. His father was a farmer, and Mr. Smith was reared on a farm in his native county, where he attended the common schools. He also engaged in the study of law, and served as justice of the peace for a period of twenty years. He was a successful business man, and at the time of his death, in 1870, he was the owner of 400 acres of land. He was married December 19, 1853, to Martha J., daughter of Silas and Eliza (Huffman) Barnes. Mrs. Smith is of English ancestry. Their children are Thomas H., Eliza, wife of J. W. Phillips; Silas B., Hiram G., John E. and Elizabeth Jane, wife of M. Peththel. In politics Mr. Smith was a Republican. His oldest son, Thomas H., is a farmer and stock-grower, and was born in this county February 8, 1854. He received a good common school education, and has made farming his favorite pursuit. He has the management of his mother's farm, in connection with his own 100 acres of valuable land. Thomas Smith was married in 1875 to Miss Charlotte, daughter of Richard Peththel. Their children are—Maggie, Lawrence, Garfield, Oscar, Gracie and Blanche. Mr. Smith is a Republican in politics.

ABRAHAM STAGGERS, farmer and stock-grower, Bristoria, Penn., was born in this county January 22, 1818. He is a son of Abraham and Catharine (Grim) Staggers, natives of Greene County, and of German descent. His ancestors were all of German extraction and among the first settlers of Greene County. Of a family of eight children, Abraham Staggers is the fourth. He was reared on a farm near Waynesburg, where he was born. He spent a considerable portion of his early life chopping wood and clearing timber. He has made a very successful farmer, and is the owner of 294½ acres of land where he resides. Mr. Staggers was united in marriage December 27, 1857, with Rebecca, daughter of Robert and Salona (Renner) Morris. Her parents were natives of Greene County, and of Dutch ancestry. The children of Mr. and Mrs. Staggers are Hannah, James and Sarah A. Mrs. Staggers, who was a member of the Church of God, died in Jackson Township in 1873. In politics Mr. Staggers is a Republican.

DAVID WEAVER, farmer and stock-grower, was born in Washington County, Penn., May 10, 1833. His parents were Jacob and Julia Ann (Jackman) Weaver, who were natives of Washington County, and of German and English lineage. Mr. Weaver's father died in 1886. His family consisted of nine children, of whom David Weaver is the oldest. From his early youth Mr. Weaver has been engaged in farming. He is a plasterer and house painter and takes contracts for mason work on large buildings. He has been successful in all his business affairs, and is the owner of 100 acres of land in Jackson township where he and his family reside. He was married on the 22d day of April, 1858, to Mary Jane, daughter of Thompson and Anna (Johnson) Ullom, who are of Dutch extraction. Mr. and Mrs. Weaver are the parents of eight children, viz.: Amanda, George M., Elizabeth, Thompson, Charles, Henry, James and Flora. Mr. Weaver is a Republican. In 1863 he enlisted in the Twenty-second Corps, Fifth Pennsylvania Artillery, and was in many important engagements. He is a member of the G. A. R. Post and the I. O. O. F.

HIRAM WEAVER, merchant and minister, Holbrook, Penn., was born in Jackson Township, this county, April 17, 1839. He is a son of Jacob and Julia Ann (Jackman) Weaver, natives of Washington County, Penn., and of English and German lineage. His father, who was a farmer and school-teacher, died in Greene County April 15, 1886. His family consisted of nine children, of whom Hiram is the fourth. He was reared on the farm and attended the common school. He learned plastering and house-painting, at which he worked until the war broke out. He then enlisted in Company F, Eighty-fifth Pennsylvania Volunteer Infantry, and was a non-commissioned officer. He served three years and twenty days and was in many serious engagements. In 1865 he established a saw-mill, and in 1871 started a general store in Jackson Township, where he has been in business ever since. In 1884 Mr. Weaver married Elizabeth, daughter of Peter Fry, who is of German descent. Mr. and Mrs. Weaver are members of the Christian Church, in which he has held several important offices. In 1858 he was licensed to preach, and has since been a local preacher. In politics he is a Republican.

JACOB WEAVER, merchant, Nettle Hill, Penn., was born on Ten Mile Creek, this county, January 26, 1844. He is a son of Jacob and Julia Ann (Jackman) Weaver, who were of German and English origin. His father was a farmer and school-teacher, and lived in Greene County for forty years. He died in 1886. His family consisted of nine children, of whom the subject of this sketch is the seventh. He was reared on the farm in Jackson Township, receiving his education in the common schools. He learned the blacksmith's trade near Waynesburg, and followed it as a business until 1861. He then enlisted in Company F, Eighty-fifty Pennsylvania Volunteer Infantry. He re-enlisted in 1864, in the Twenty-second Pennsylvania Cavalry, Company A., where he served until the close of the war. He was in the battles of Williamsburg, Fair Oaks, Bolivar Heights and Winchester. He was wounded at Fair Oaks, losing two fingers. After the war he bought a saw-mill, operating the latter for a period of five years. He then farmed until 1880, when he established his store at Nettle Hill. He carries a large stock of dry goods, clothing, groceries, hardware and queensware, and has a good country trade. Mr. Weaver has built his present store and a neat and substantial residence since 1886. He was united in marriage December 5, 1867, with Miss Elizabeth, a daughter of Abraham and Margaret (Shields) Hickman, who died in 1882. He was again married December 3, 1883, to Miss Eliza, a daughter of J. and Perrie (Headlee) Smith, and they have two children, Roscoe Conkling and Otta D. S. Mr. Weaver is a member of the G. A. R. Post, and is Quartermaster.

JOSEPH WEBSTER, farmer and stock-grower, Bristoria, Penn., was born in Greene County, Penn., January 25, 1830, and is a son of John and Elizabeth (Cowell) Webster. His father was born in New Jersey and his mother in Greene County, Penn. They were of English extraction. His father, who was a farmer, moved to Iowa during the latter part of his life. His family consisted of eleven children, of whom Joseph is the third. He was reared as a farmer and has been very successful in that occupation, owning 147 acres of land in Jackson Township. He also has spent considerable time at the carpenter's trade. In 1853 Mr. Webster was married in Washington County to Cynthia Ann Keys, who died in 1858. They were the parents of one child, Alexander Leroy. Mr. Webster was again united in marriage December 16, 1859, with Jane, daughter of John and Sarah (Gardner) Goodwin, whose parents were of German lineage. She was the widow of J. S. Hunt, deceased, and they were the parents of two children—a son and daughter. The son, J. G. Hunt, is a farmer and school-teacher. The children of Mr. and Mrs. Webster are J. C. and S. M.

The family are members of the Baptist Church, and Mr. and Mrs. Webster are teachers in the Sabbath-school. Mr. Webster is a prominent member of the I. O. O. F. He has served on the school board of his township.

HIRAM WHITE, farmer and stock-grower, Nettle Hill, Penn., was born in Greene County, May 1, 1840. He is a son of Isaac and Lydia (Tustin) White, who were of English descent. His father, who was a farmer, was a soldier in the late war, serving in the Seventh West Virginia Regiment. He was twice married, and there were three children by the first marriage. By the second marriage there were eight children, of whom Hiram White is the fifth. He was reared in Wayne Township, on the farm, and attended the district school in that township. Mr. White has been a successful farmer and is the owner of a farm of 147 acres of land where he resides in Jackson Township. In 1865 Mr. White married Mary Ann, daughter of Henry and Elizabeth (King) Cole, and their children are John Henry, Elizabeth, wife of Isaac Hughes; George, Thomas, Eliza, James M., Zella and Lucy. Mr. White is a Democrat, and in 1844 was elected county commissioner. In 1861 he enlisted in Company E, Second West Virginia Volunteer Infantry. He was a brave soldier and fought in many battles. In 1884 Mr. White was appointed reporter for the Greene County Agricultural Society. He took an active interest in the Granger movement, and for years was deputy of the county. He is P. C. of the G. A. R. Post, No. 552, at Nettle Hill.

DR. T. T. WILLIAMS, Nettle Hill, Penn., was born in Washington County, Penn., July 22, 1826. He is a son of David and Mary (Thomas) Williams, who were natives of Washington and Westmoreland counties. They were of English, Welsh and Irish descent. His father was a farmer, and died in 1859. His family consisted of five children, of whom the Doctor is the third. He was reared on the farm and attended the common schools. He was subsequently a student in the Academy of Monongahela City, Penn., where he studied the classics, sciences and literature, and while still a young man he taught school for several years, aggregating three and a half years of continuous teaching. He studied medicine while engaged in the profession of teaching, and attended a Medical Institute at New York City, where he graduated, and after his return engaged in the practice of his profession. He subsequently took other special courses in medicine and collateral sciences, attended the Jefferson Medical College at Philadelphia, Penn., and afterwards resumed for a brief period his practice at Monongahela City, Penn. In 1857 he came to Greene County and located at Rogersville, where he remained for a period of four years in successful medical practice, the first year practicing with Dr. D. W. Braden, now of Waynesburg, Penn., as partner. Since 1861 he has been in practice at Nettle Hill.

Dr. Williams was married September 7, 1858, to Miss Elizabeth, daughter of Samuel Crouse, near Rogersville. Mrs. Williams is of English, Scotch and German extraction. They are the parents of seven living children, viz: Layton B., a farmer; Mary Etta, wife of Prof. T. R. Stockdale; Caroline R., wife of W. Scott Johnson; Samuel T., Jennie E., Britta L. E. and Leonora Estella. Dr. Williams is a Democrat in politics, and at this writing holds the commission of postmaster at Nettle Hill, Penn.

JAMES WOOD, farmer and stock-grower, Holbrook, Penn., was born October 14, 1819, on the farm he now owns in Jackson Township, and is a son of Micajah and Jane (Mason) Wood, who were of English origin. His ancestors were among the earliest settlers of Greene County, where his father spent most of his life as a farmer, having lived to the advanced age of eighty-three years. Of his family of nine children, all grew to maturity. Besides the subject of our sketch, there is but one other member of the family now living—a brother who was born in 1806, and now residee in Morrow County, Ohio. James Wood has spent most of his life in Aleppo and Jackson townships. He received a common-school education in his early youth, has been a successful farmer, and owns 204 acres of well-improved land. On March 11, 1844, Mr. Wood married Mary Ann, daughter of Morgan and Elizabeth (Lippencott) Hoge. Their children are L. W. and Thomas, farmers; Elizabeth Jane, wife of Henry Church; L. H., a merchant, and Lucinda, wife of Z. G. Call. Mr. Wood is a Republican. He and wife are members of the Christian Church.

MONONGAHELA TOWNSHIP AND GREENSBORO BOROUGH.

H. K. ATCHISON, a retired potter, who was born in Elizabeth, N. J., August 5, 1820, is a son of Robert and Jane (Parshall) Atchison, who were of Irish descent. His father was born on the ocean while his parents were on their way to America. They settled in New Jersey, where Robert grew to manhood. He learned the potter's trade, which he followed in Newark, N. J., for many years. He subsequently moved to Elizabeth, where he died in 1883. The subject of this sketch was the second in a family of eight children, and was reared in Elizabeth, N. J., where he received his early education. He very naturally learned the potter's trade with his father, and was employed as a journeyman for several years. In 1855 he engaged in the business at New Geneva, Fayette County, Penn., and continued therein for six years. On September 20, 1861, he enlisted in the service of his country in Company G, Eighty-fifth Pennsylvania Volunteer Infantry, and was in the following battles: In front of Yorktown and Fair Oaks; Siege of Yorktown, Va.; Williamsburg, Va., May 5, 1862; Savage Station, May 24, 1862; Seven Points, May 31, 1862; Jones' Ford, June 28, 1862; S. W. Creek, S. C., December 13, 1863; Kingston, N. C., December 14, 1863; White Hall, N. C., December 16, 1863, and others. In 1864 Mr. Atchison was wounded in front of Petersburgh, and lost his right arm. Returning to Greensboro at the close of the war, he was appointed United States store-keeper in 1869, and served for a period of twelve years. He was united in marriage, May 14, 1846, with Susan, daughter of Henry and Susan (Billingsley) Stephens. Her mother was born in West Virginia,. and her father was a native of Greene County, Penn. They were of English and Scotch descent. Mr. and Mrs Atchison have nine children and fourteen grandchildren, all but three of whom are living. The children are—Anna, wife of John Rumble; James, Henry, Charley, Jane, wife of William Halliday; Mary J. and Joseph. Robert and Clarinda are deceased. Their mother is a faithful member of the Baptist Church.

JOHN W. BARB, farmer and stock-grower, Mapletown, Penn., was born in Monongalia County, W. Va., July 8, 1854. His parents, Gideon and Sarah (Webb) Barb, were natives of Old Virginia, and of German descent. In early life his father was a farmer. He subsequently became a manufacturer of boots and shoes, and came to Mapletown in 1866, where he engaged in that business until his death in 1875. John W. is the eleventh in a family of twelve children. He was reared in Mapletown, and attended the district school. He has followed farming as his occupation, and is the owner of a farm of 100 acres in Monongahela Township, where he resides. Mr. Barb was united in marriage, in 1876, with Louisa E., daughter of Alexander and Maria (Debolt) Mestrezat, who were of French descent. Mr. and Mrs. Barb's children are—Lilian, Minnie, Charles A., Lamar and William. Mr. Barb is a Democrat. His wife is a zealous member of the Baptist Church.

GEORGE F. BIRCH, M. D., deceased, was born in Washington County, Penn., August 9, 1824. His father, David Birch, who was a farmer and school-teacher, was born in Ireland. His mother, Lucretia Ellen (Vankirk) Birch, was a native of Washington County, Penn., and of English extraction. Dr. Birch was the oldest in a family of six children, and was reared on the farm with his parents. He attended the Washington and Jefferson College, where he graduated in the classical course. He studied medicine with Dr. Isaac

Reed, of Jefferson Borough, this county, and subsequently attended the Western Reserve Medical University at Cleveland, Ohio, where he graduated in 1852. In 1853 he first engaged in the practice of his profession in Greene County, where he spent the remainder of his life in active practice. His practice in Greensboro and vicinity was quite extensive from 1853 until his death, which occurred September 18, 1884. Dr. Birch took an active interest in education, and served as school director for twelve years. He was an active member of the I. O. O. F. and the Masonic fraternity. He was married in this county, February 17, 1854, to Miss Adelia, daughter of Benjamin and Margaret (Kramer) Jones, who were of Welsh and English origin. Dr. and Mrs. Birch were the parents of eight children—two daughters, both deceased, and six sons, four living: William David, a carriage trimmer; B. J., a physician; George F., a book-keeper, and Samuel B., who is registered as a drug clerk. The Doctor was a member of the Disciple Church, and his wife is a devoted Baptist. Their second son, B. J., who was born in Greensboro, attended the University at Morgantown, W. Va., and read medicine at Cleveland, Ohio, where he graduated in 1883. He also attended the Medico-Chirurgical College at Philadelphia, graduating in 1887, and has since been engaged in the drug business and the practice of his chosen profession, at Greensboro, Penn.

JAMES A. BLACK, farmer and stock-grower, who was born in Greensboro, Penn., May 19, 1822, is a son of Benjamin F. and Sophia (Gabler) Black. His parents were natives of Greensboro, and of German and Scotch descent. His father, the brother of Hon. C. A. Black, a prominent attorney of Waynesburg, Penn., was a merchant and justice of the peace in Greensboro, and served one term in the State Legislature. He died in his forty-second year, June 10, 1843, leaving a family of six children. James was the second and was reared in Greensboro. He has made farming his chief occupation, and owns his present farm near Greensboro and other valuable lands. In 1844 Mr. Black married Miss Ann, daughter of James and Sarah M. (Morris) Steele, and they have a family of eight children, viz.: Charles E., John S., Emma V., wife of Rev. Mr. Patterson, of Meadville, Penn.; Anna, wife of Rev. Mr. McGree; James A., B. F., Samuel and Asia, five of whom, with their mother, are faithful members of the Methodist Episcopal Church. Mr. Black has served as justice of the peace at Greensboro for over a quarter of a century, and was at one time Master in the Masonic lodge.

J. S. BLACK, farmer and coal merchant, Greensboro, Penn., was born in Greensboro, March 30, 1852. His parents were James and Sarah (Steele) Black, the former a native of Virginia and the latter of Greene County, Penn. The subject of this sketch is the fourth in a family of eight children. He was reared in Greensboro and attended the common school. His first occupation was that of farming. He then engaged in the coal business, which he has since carried on quite extensively. Mr. Black was married in Fayette County, Penn., December 12, 1876, to Miss Jessie Nicholson. Her parents were natives of Fayette County, and of English descent. Mr. and Mrs. Black have four children—Eunice Aden, Nina May, Bessie N. and Albert Crystie. Mr. Black is a Democrat, and belongs to the Methodist Church. His wife is a Presbyterian.

JAMES E. BLACKSHERE, farmer and stock-grower, Mapletown, Penn., was born in Monongahela Township, Greene County, Penn., April 15, 1832. His parents, Frank and Sarah Blackshere, who were natives of Delaware, came to Pennsylvania early in life and settled in Greene County. Mrs. Blackshere is still living, having reached the advanced age of eighty-five years. They had a family of four children, of whom James E. is the youngest. He was reared on the farm and attended the common schools of the township. Mr. Blackshere is a prosperous farmer and owns a fine farm of 450 acres where he now resides. In 1856 Mr. Blackshere married Eliza, daughter of William Gray, who was among the wealthiest men of Greene County. Mr. and Mrs. Blackshere's children are six in number.

A. V. BOUGHNER is a merchant and postmaster of Greensboro, Penn., where he was born in 1830. He is a son of Daniel and Mary (Vance) Boughner, being the youngest in their family of six sons and three daughters. Mr. Boughner was reared in Greensboro, where he received a common-school education, and had some advantages above the common schools. He learned the potter's trade, in which business he engaged for almost twenty-five years. He also carried on a store during that time, and since 1868 has given all his attention to merchandising. In 1857 Mr. Boughner married Perie Minor, who is of English descent. Their children are—Alice, wife of Harry C. Lemmon; Mary, Eunice, Sherman and Claude. Mr. Boughner is a Democrat in politics, and was appointed to his present position of postmaster in 1885. He and wife were zealous members of the Presbyterian Church, in which he is an official member. His wife died in 1880.

O. P. COOPER, merchant miller, Mapletown, Penn., was born in Preston County, Virginia, April 25, 1836, and is a son of John G. and Elizabeth (Kearns) Cooper, who were natives of Virginia, and of German origin. His father, who was a miller and hatter by occupation, died in 1868, in Fayette County, Penn., where he had resided for many years. His family consisted of eleven children, of whom O. P. is the seventh. He remained in Fayette County till he was ten years of age, then came to Greene County, and received his education from the common schools. Early in life Mr. Cooper learned the miller's trade, and spent most of his life in that business. His long experience and natural mechanical ability, coupled with his universally polite and gentlemanly demeanor, eminently qualify him for his chosen occupation. In 1885 he bought the old Minor mill in Monongahela Township, which he has refitted and greatly improved. Mr. Cooper was married in Greene County to a Miss Hildebrand, who was a native of this county, and of German descent. Their children are—Walter L., principal of schools at Alton, Penn.; John F., telegraph operator and agent on B. & O. R. R.; Joseph M., practical engineer; Jefferson, in government land office in Kansas; Lewis M., a miller; Oliver P., studying medicine; Harry E., at home. Mr. and Mrs. Cooper are prominent members of the Methodist Episcopal Church.

A. B. DONAWAY, a druggist of Greensboro, Penn., was born near Brownsville, Fayette County, Penn., April 3, 1849. He is a son of John and Margaret (Robinson) Donaway, who were of Irish and English descent. His father, who was a teamster, died in 1882. His mother is still living at the advanced age of eighty-seven years. They had a family of three sons and one daughter. A. B., the youngest of the family, was reared in Greensboro, where he learned the potter's trade and followed it as a business until 1872. He then engaged in the drug business, in which he has met with unusual success. In 1878 Mr. Donaway married Elizabeth, daughter of E. O. Ewing, and they have three children—Minor G., Katie and Warren. Mr. Donaway is a Democrat, has been a member of the town council of Greensboro, and served as street commissioner. He also belongs to the Royal Arcanum.

J. H. DULANY, merchant and postmaster, Mapletown, Penn., was born in Cumberland Township, this county, August 13, 1856. He is a son of Dennis and Elizabeth (Seaton) Dulany, natives of Greene County, and of English descent. His father is a tailor by occupation, in which he is now engaged at Garard's Fort, Penn. The subject of this sketch is the sixth in a family of seven children. He was reared in Greene County, where he attended the common schools. While at home he assisted his father in the nursery, of which he was proprietor. Attaining his majority, he engaged in merchandising at Mapletown, where he has the postoffice in connection with his large general store, and meets with success in his business. In 1884 Mr. Dulany married Miss Cecilla B., daughter of Elisha and Cynthia (Coleman) Walters, who were natives of Pennsylvania, and of English descent. Mr. and Mrs. Dulany have one child—Maud E. Mr. Dulany is a Republican in politics, and his wife is a devoted member of the Baptist Church.

SAMUEL DUNLAP, farmer and stock-grower, Mapletown, Pennsylvania, was born in Fayette County, Penn., June 2, 1837, and is a son of Andrew and Mary (Stone) Dunlap. His parents were of Scotch descent, but natives of Pennsylvania. His father came to Greene County in 1844 and settled in Monongahela Township, where Samuel now resides. He was successful through life as a farmer, and had been acting justice of the peace for twenty-five years—at the time of his death in 1888. His family consisted of two children—Elizabeth Ann, wife of H. K. Barb; and Samuel, the subject of this sketch. He obtained only a common-school education in this county, was reared on a farm and has made farming the business of his life. Mr. Dunlap's wife was Miss Martha A., daughter of William and Elizabeth (Hedge) Spencer, who were of English and German descent. Her father was born in Jefferson Borough, this county, in 1805. Mr. and Mrs. Dunlap have but one child—Harry L. Mr. Dunlap is a Democrat in politics, and his wife is a devoted member of the Presbyterian Church.

E. S. EVANS, farmer and stock-grower, Greensboro, Penn., was born January 27, 1845, and is a son of Evan and Rebecca (South) Evans, who were of Welsh and German origin. His father was a farmer and stock-grower by occupation, and met with marked success throughout his life. He was a deacon in the Greensboro Baptist Church. Enoch S. was reared on the farm and received his education from the common schools and Waynesburg College. His father left him in comfortable circumstances and he follows farming more from choice than necessity. Mr. Evans has resided for many years on his farm in Monongahela Township, where he makes a specialty of raising fine stock. He was united in marriage, in 1871, with Miss Ada Lawson, daughter of A. C. and Martha D. Pennington, who were of English origin. Mr. and Mrs. Evans have an interesting family of seven children—Carrie May, Pierre O., Nona O., Evan, A. C. P. Wilson, W. B. and Nellie B. In politics Mr. Evans is a Republican. He and his wife are faithful members of the Baptist Church, of which he is deacon.

ELIAS A. FLENNIKEN, proprietor of the Greensboro hotel and livery stable, was born June 2, 1824, and is a son of J. W. and Hettie A. (Wright) Flenniken, natives of this county. He is the oldest of a family of seven children, and was reared on his father's farm in Cumberland Township, where he received his early education. He afterwards attended school in the old Greene Academy at Carmichaels, Pennsylvania. His ancestors were among the pioneers of Greene County. For many years Mr. Flenniken has bought and sold horses and has been particularly interested in fast horses. For the last twenty years he has dealt extensively in wool. For two years he was captain of a steamer on the Monongahela River. In politics Mr. Flenniken is a Republican. In 1846 he married Mary Ann, daughter of William Kerr of Cumberland Township. Mr. and Mrs.

Flenniken's children are—Joseph D., Sarah J., widow of Byrass Thompson, deceased; Thomas, Belle, wife of George Stemets; John F., James, Elizabeth, wife of Oliver McClain; George N., Mary, and William. Mr. and Mrs. Flenniken have twenty-one grandchildren now living and one dead, being the only member of the family deceased.

A. K. GABLER, a retired farmer of Greensboro, Penn., was born May 29, 1821, at the old glass works near Greensboro, and is a son of Thomas and Wilhelmina (Kramer) Gabler. Mr. Gabler's ancestors, who were of German extraction, were pioneers in the glass business in this part of Pennsylvania and established the first glass works in Greene County. Thomas Gabler was born in Maryland in 1798 and died in 1875. His wife died in 1881, having reached the advanced age of eighty.two years. Their family consisted of nine children, six of whom are living—four sons and two daughters. Mr. A. K. Gabler is the oldest son. He was reared at the old glass works, received a common school education and chose farming as his occupation through life. In 1852 Mr. Gabler married Miss Maria, daughter of John Jones, of Greensboro, and they are the parents of two children—Benjamin and Thomas C., a prominent young attorney. Mr. and Mrs. Gabler are members of the Presbyterian Church. A. K. Gabler's brother, Kramer, who is also a farmer and stock-grower, was born and raised at the old glass works, where he received his early education, and learned the saddler's trade with his brother, J. W. Gabler, of Greensboro. He worked at the trade until 1882, when he commenced farming and has met with success. Mr. Gabler is a Republican in politics. August 31, 1862, he enlisted in Company A, in the One Hundred and Fortieth Regiment, Pennsylvania Volunteer Infantry. He was a non-commissioned officer, and served until the close of the war. He has also served one term as Officer of the Day in Greensboro, G. A. R. Post. The youngest brother is George, born in 1841, who is also a farmer, and like his brothers, a Republican in politics. His farm consists of eighty-six acres of well improved land in Monongahela Township. Mr. Gabler comes of a family noted for their energy and industry. They have ever been diligent in business, and have met with financial success.

J. W. GABLER, harness-maker and saddler, Greensboro, Penn. Among the successful business men of Greene County we mention the gentleman whose name heads this sketch. He was born in this county April, 3, 1825, and is a son of Thomas and Wilhelmina (Kramer) Gabler, who were of German and English descent. His mother was born in Fayette County, Penn. His father was born in Frederick City, Md., and was a glass-blower and manufacturer, and came from Pittsburg to Greensboro, where he engaged in that busi-

ness for many years. He died in 1879 at the age of seventy-seven.
The subject of this sketch was the third in a family of nine children.
He was reared in Greensboro, where he received his early education.
At the age of nineteen he learned the saddler's trade, to which he
devotes most of his time. He is also a manufacturer of harness, in
which he uses good material and does good work. Mr. Gabler has
been in business in Greensboro for nearly forty-five years, and by
means of his industry and careful investments, has secured a good
competence for himself and family. He has a half interest in the
Greensboro hotel, and is the owner of 350 acres of land and real
estate in Greensboro and elsewhere. Mr. Gabler was married in
Greensboro, December 21, 1858, to Amy, daughter of Daniel and
Mary (Vance) Boughner. Mrs. Gabler is of Irish and Dutch
descent. They have but one child—Myrtilla. Mr. Gabler is a Republican in poiitics, and in religion a Presbyterian, in which Church
he has been teacher and treasurer for a period of twenty years.

  J. R. GRAY, a farmer and merchant, of Gray's Landing, Penn.,
was born July 4, 1831, on the farm near Mapletown, in Monongahela Township, this county. He is a son of William and Catharine (Robinson) Gray, who were of English and Irish origin. His
father, who was a wealthy farmer and prominent business man, was engaged in the commission business in Baltimore, Md., for several years.
He died in 1885, having had a family of six children, two of whom are
deceased. The subject of this sketch was the oldest, and was reared
on the farm with his parents. He attended the common-school at
Mapletown, Penn., and spent two years at Waynesburg College.
Mr. Gray was first employed with his father in the distillery, of
which he is now proprietor. He has also engaged in farming and
owns 500 acres of land, in connection with a general store which
they established in 1858. On February 22, 1855, Mr. Gray married
Catharine, daughter of James and Catharine Huston. Their children
are—L. Alice, wife of O. M. Boughner; Selisia and Selena. Their
mother is a devoted member of the Presbyterian Church. Mr. Gray
is a Republican in politics. He ever manifests great interest in the
educational welfare of his township, and has served as school director
for twelve years.

  DR. WILSON GREENE, of New Geneva, Penn., was born in
Monongahela Township, Greene County, Penn., December 1, 1829.
His parents were Matthew and Rachel (Sycks) Greene. His father
was of English origin and his mother was of German origin. His
father was born February 17, 1806, in Monongahela Township, Greene
County, Penn., where he still resides and now in his old age is
often visited by his son who is ever considerate of his happiness.
The Doctor's mother, who died in 1869, was a member of the Sycks
family who came to Monongahela Township while the Indians were still

inhabitants. They with the Seltzers built a fort for protection on Dunkard Creek, where the first Dunkard oil field is. Daniel Sycks, an elder brother of Rachel, was born, on the farm where she died, December 8, 1788 and died July 16, 1888, and was the oldest man in the township. When Dr. Greene's grandparents, William and Rebecca (Larue) Greene, first came to Greene County they settled on a farm near Willow Tree, on Big Whiteley Creek. They were natives of Bucks County, Penn., and descendants of the pioneer Quakers, who came from England with William Penn. Dr. Greene is the second and only son of a family of four children. He was reared on a farm and at an early age he made choice of the practice of medicine as his profession. His medical education was obtained at the Cleveland Medical College, Cleveland, Ohio. In 1859 he he opened an office at Bristol, Perry County, Ohio, where he soon gained an enviable reputation as a practicing physician. In order to be near his aged parents he returned in 1864 to the scenes of his childhood and settled in Fayette County, on the banks of the Monongahela River, in New Geneva, within three miles of his old home. Here the Doctor soon won a large and lucrative practice in Greene and Fayette counties. He was united in marriage March 23, 1859, with Miss Pleasant M., daughter of Evan and Nancy (Myers) Evans. Mrs. Greene is a sister of L. K. Evans, editor of the "Three Rivers Tribune," Michigan, and is of Welsh descent. Her father was a successful farmer of Greene County and died in 1865. Dr. and Mrs. Greene have two children, who took a course in Monongahela College, Isa D., wife of O. J. Sturgis, editor of the *Republican Standard*, at Uniontown, Penn., and Willie W., who is a graduate of Duff's College, Pittsburg, Penn. Isa, the only daughter, received all the advantages of a good musical education and graduated at Dana's Musical Institute, of Warren, Ohio. Dr. Greene is a Republican in politics. He devotes all his time to his business and profession, in which he has proven himself one of the most prominent in the county. The family are prominent members of the Baptist Church.

JOHN JONES, of the firm of Hamilton & Jones, manufacturers of earthen ware and tile roofing at Greensboro, Penn., was born in Monongahela Township, Greene County, Penn. He is a son of Benjamin and Laura (Kramer) Jones, natives of this county, and of Welsh and German descent. Mr. Jones' father was a glass-blower by occupation. His family consisted of eight children, all of whom reached maturity. Mr. John Jones, the fifth was reared in Greene County, and attended the common schools. Early in life he learned the potter's trade at Greensboro, and engaged in the business until 1866, when he went into partnership with Mr. Hamilton. They employ about twenty-five men, and have contributed much to the improvement of the town.   In 1865 Mr. Jones married Miss Mary A., daughter of W. L. Hamilton, a prominent citizen of Greensboro. They are the parents of one child, Asia K.   Mrs. Jones is a member of the Presbyterian Church.   Mr. Jones is a Republican, and a member of the town council, of which he has served as treasurer. He enlisted under Captain Harper, of Carmichaels, Penn., in Company F, First Pennsylvania Cavalry.   He was wounded and taken prisoner at the battle of Warrington, Virginia, but managed to escape the first night.   Mr. Jones has been engaged in the pottery business since the close of the war.   He is Post Commander of the Alfred Shibler G. A. R. Post No. 119, of Greensboro.

T. P. KRAMER, a retired glass manufacturer of Greensboro, Penn., was born October 20, 1804, and is the son of Baltzer and Sarah (Phillips) Kramer.   His mother was the daughter of Hon. T. P. Phillips, who at an early age was a member of the Pennsylvania State Legislature.   He was a farmer by occupation and resided in Fayette County, near Greensboro for many years, and in his house was the first court held in Fayette County.   T. P. Kramer's grandfather, Baltzer Kramer, came from Germany to Maryland, and subsequently removed to Fayette County, Penn., and settled on a farm near New Geneva.   He was afterwards one of a party induced by Hon. Albert Gallatin to settle near Greensboro and establish a glass works, Mr. Gallatin taking one-half interest and furnishing the material.   The firm consisted of George Reppert, Lewis Reitz, Christian and Baltzer Kramer, Jr., and Adolphus Everhart, one of the men who carried Gen. LaFayette off the battle-field, and was recognized by the General when making his farewell visit to America.   Baltzer Kramer's family consisted of seven children, of whom T. P. Kramer's father, Baltzer, Jr., was the oldest.   He was born in Maryland in 1777, and in 1808 became a member of the glass company near Greensboro, where he died in 1852, leaving a family of six children.   The subject of this sketch is the oldest, and has been a resident of this county the most of his life.   He was sent to school at Cannonsburg, Penn., but ran away and refused to go to college, so his father allowed him to learn the glass-blowing trade, and he has followed that as a business for many years.   In 1834 Mr. Kramer married Sarah, daughter of George Harter.   Mrs. Kramer is of German and English extraction.   They had a family of ten children—S. E. B., Sarah M., Elizabeth Ann, William, May Ellen, George, Baltzer, John P., and Virtue and Edward R., deceased. Their mother died in 1884.   Mr. Kramer has been a member of the Methodist Episcopal Church for nearly sixty years.   He has always taken an active interest in the affairs of the church, and has served as class-leader, steward and trustee.   His children are all members of the church.   Mr. Kramer is a Republican and a strong advocate of

42

the temperance cause. Although in his eighty-fifth year, he is strong and vigorous in mind and body, seldom failing to walk from his home to Greensboro every day—a distance of more than a mile.

JOHN C. KRAMER, Greensboro, Greene County, Penn.—The subject of this sketch is a descendant of the early settlers of Greene County. He was born in Monongahela Township, September 15, 1838, and is a son of George R. and Louisa (Jones) Kramer, also natives of Monongahela Township. Mr. Kramer's mother was born in 1814, and was of German origin. His father, who was a farmer and glass-blower, was born in 1808 and died June 28, 1881. John Jones, Mr. Kramer's grandfather, was a farmer by occupation, and died at the age of forty-two. His grandfather Kramer was a glass-blower, and lived to a good old age. John C. is the second in a family of six children, and was reared on his father's farm where he received his early education. At an early age he learned glass-cutting and he is now employed in that business in Pittsburg. Mr. Kramer was married in Camden, New Jersey, May 26, 1870, to Sallie C., daughter of Joseph and Lydia (Caine) Southard. Her parents were natives of New Jersey, and of German extraction. Mrs. Kramer is the third in a family of eight children, and was reared in Camden New Jersey. Mr. and Mrs. Kramer are the parents of four children, viz.: William M., Franklin B., Louisa J. and George R. Mr. Kramer is a Republican in politics, and in religion a Presbyterian. He is also a prominent member of the Masonic fraternity.

JOHN P. KRAMER, potter by trade, is the youngest son of T. P. Kramer, was born at the glass-works February 7, 1854. He received a common-school education and learned the potter's trade, which he has followed as a business very successfully. Mr. Kramer was united in marriage June 26, 1876, with Miss Josephine, daughter of William and Frances (Black) Wolverton. Mrs. Kramer is of German lineage. They are the parents of six children, viz.: Harry, Estella, Harris, Clarence, Fannie and Sarah. Mr. Kramer is a Republican. He and his wife are zealous members of the Methodist Episcopal Church, in which he has served as steward and superintendent of the Sabbath-school.

PROF. GEORGE F. MARTIN, principal of schools at Greensboro, Penn., was born in the State of Mississippi, June 25, 1846. His parents are Daniel P. and Hannah (Reynolds) Martin, the former a native of Virginia and the latter of Mississippi. They were of English origin. His father was a cotton planter in early life, and subsequently engaged in farming and stock-raising in southern Kansas. His family consisted of six children, of whom George F. was the fourth. He was sent to a private school in Mississippi until his father lost his fortune, which was valued at one million dollars. At his father's suggestion George went North when fourteen years of age, and worked about two years for a sewing machine company at Elizabeth, New Jersey. He then spent two years in Yale College. Being obliged to leave the school for lack of funds, he taught for two years, and was given the position of principal of schools at Stoughton, Wisconsin—a place of about two thousand inhabitants. He remained there about four years, afterwards teaching in Wisconsin and Michigan. Returning South, Prof. Martin taught several years in West Virginia, and in 1880 was appointed by the State superintendent of schools to conduct an institute at Morgantown, W. Va. For the past eight years he has been identified with the schools of Greene County, Penn., and has assisted in conducting two summer normals at Waynesburg College. Prof. Martin is one of Greene's most able educators and makes frequent contributions to the leading school journals. He was united in marriage in Monongalia County, W. Va., with Miss Anna M., daughter of John Blosser. Mrs. Martin is of English descent. They are the parents of five children—Frank P., William R., Clara M., Florence M. and Elmer W. The Professor is a Democrat in politics, and a member of the Royal Arcanum.

JEAN LOUIS GUILLAUME (called William) MESTREZAT, retired farmer and stock-grower, was born in Mapletown, this county, May 11, 1809. His parents, Charles Alexander and Louisa (Dufresne) Mestrezat, were natives of France, and came to Greene County, Penn., in 1795, among the earliest settlers. They lived a short time near Carmichaels, in Cumberland Township, then settled in Mapletown and spent the remainder of their lives. Mr. Mestrezat died April 1, 1815, and his widow in 1849. They were the parents of eleven children, of whom Jean Louis Guillaume is the eighth. He was reared in Mapletown, and early in life learned the gunsmith trade. He subsequently carried on the mercantile business, and also engaged in farming to some extent. He owns 330 acres of valuable land. In 1843 Mr. Mestrezat married Mary Ann, daughter of Matthias and Hannah (Leslie) Hartley, who were of Irish lineage. Mr. and Mrs. Mestrezat have five children—C. A., Harriet M., widow of the late Samuel Hudson; S. L., a prominent attorney at Uniontown, Penn.; Charlotte Amanda, wife of Hon. M. John, of Colorado; and J. L. G., a cattle-dealer in the West. Mr. Mestrezat is a Democrat in politics. He has served as school director for fifteen years.

FREDERIC MESTREZAT, deceased, was born September 25, 1807, and was the son of Charles Alexander and Louisa Elizabeth (Dufrene) Mestrezat, natives of France, who came to America in 1793. Frederic was the sixth child and second son in a family of eleven children. He attended the select schools of Mapletown, which were taught by teachers hired by the parents, by the year and half year. He was one of the foremost men during his short life in securing good educational advantages for the town in which he resided. He learned the hatter's trade, and dealt extensively in wool and furs. April 4, 1833, Mr. Mestrezat married Miss Martha Hall, daughter of Lemuel and Sarah (Grove) Hall. Her parents were natives of Delaware, and of Scotch-Irish and German origin. To Mr. and Mrs. Mestrezat were born six children, four of whom are living—John A., a carpenter; Mary A., wife of B. F. Mercer; Aline A., wife of William W. Shaffer, and Caroline A. Charles Alexander, the oldest son, was educated in Morgantown, W. Va. He enlisted in Company E, Fourteenth Pennsylvania Cavalry, and was captured at the battle of White Sulphur Springs, August 27, 1863, while in active service for his country. He was taken to Belle Isle, Richmond, and from there was removed to Hospital No. 21 in Richmond, where he died March 27, 1864. Mr. Frederic Mestrezat was a Republican in politics. He was an earnest and faithful worker in the Sabbath-school and for the church, although he did not unite with the church until a short time before his death, when he became a member of the Presbyterian Church of Greensboro, where his wife had been a faithful member since her youth.

ROBERT MILLIKIN was born in Ireland in 1773, and died in 1869. He came to America in 1794, and took up a tract of about 800 acres of land, situated six miles northwest of Waynesburg, on Brown's Fork of South Ten-Mile Creek. Nearly all of the upper end of Greene County was at that time covered with forests. Mr. Millikin was a farmer by occupation, and was one of the substantial citizens among the early settlers of this county. He held the office of county commissioner, and was the master builder of the first brick court-house in Greene County. At the age of twenty-four he married Miss Mary, daughter of Lindsey Gray, of this county, and aunt of the late Dr. D. W. Gray, who for many years was in successful practice at Jacksonville, Richhill Township. At their wedding the principal feature in the marriage feast was a young fat bear which had been caught in the neighborhood. There were born to them six children, and their son David, who married Miss Lydia Rogers, was the father of thirteen children. The youngest of these is Dr. J. L. Millikin, of Greensboro, one of the leading physicians of the county. Dr. Millikin was born in Greene County, six miles north of Waynesburg, June 24, 1854. He received his early education in the district schools, and afterwards attended Waynesburg College. He was a successful teacher in the public schools for several years, and began the study of medicine with Dr. W. S. Throckmorton at Nineveh, Penn., in 1873, and subsequently took the regular course in the Jefferson Medical College at Philadelphia, graduating at that institution in March, 1878. He then practiced with Dr. Throckmorton for nearly two years, when he located at Carmichaels, Penn., and during one year of his residence there was in equal partnership with Dr. J.

B. Laidley, of that place. In 1884 Dr. Millikin located at Greensboro, Penn., where his professional skill and genial disposition soon won for him a large practice in the town and surrounding country. The Doctor is an active member of the Greene County Medical Society, and served one term as its president. He is a permanent member of the State Medical Society of Pennsylvania, and belongs to the I. O. O. F. and R. A. He is examining surgeon for three insurance companies and for the Royal Arcanum. He has a special fondness for surgery, and has performed several difficult operations. He frequently contributes articles to the medical journals, and is a strong advocate of the temperance cause. November 30, 1883, Dr. Millikin married Miss Anna, daughter of James Scott, of this county. They have one child—Joseph Pancoast.

OTHO W. MINOR, farmer and stock-grower, Greensboro, Penn., was born in Greene Township, this county, January 22, 1830. He is a son of John and Melinda (Lantz) Minor, natives of Greene County, and of English descent. His father, who followed the blacksmith's trade in early life, was in later years a farmer and merchant miller, owning and operating a grist-mill for many years in this county. He died in 1881, leaving a family of five children, viz: Frances, Mary, William, Rebecca A., and Otho, who is the second in the family. He was reared on the farm, attended the common schools, and has made farming his occupation through life. In 1859 Mr. Minor married Miss Lucinda, daughter of Hiram and Elizabeth (Hunt) Stephens. Mrs. Minor is of English and Irish descent. They have a family of five children—Sylvanus K., John W., Ellsworth, Sarepta, and Viola (deceased). Mr. Minor is a Democrat, and he and wife are leading members in the Baptist Church.

JOHN S. MINOR, carpenter and contractor, Mapletown, Penn., was born in Monongahela Township, Greene County, Penn., March 5, 1859. His parents, William and Martha (Robinson) Minor, were natives of this county, and of English descent. His father, who was a farmer by occupation, was killed by the falling of a tree, January 5, 1875. John S. is the oldest of a family of four children. He was reared on the home farm and received a common-school education. He remained at home with his parents until he was sixteen years of age, when he learned the carpenter's trade and has since followed it as an occupation. He was united in marriage, March 10, 1878, with Miss Flora, daughter of Dissisiway and Maria (Maple) South, who were of English and German origin. Mr. and Mrs. Minor have three children—Myrtie, Walter T. and Willie Ray. Mr. Minor is a Democrat in politics, and in religion a Methodist, of which church his wife is also a devoted member.

T. F. PENNINGTON, merchant, Greensboro, Penn., was born in Brownsville, Penn., June 11, 1853. He is a son of A. C. and

Martha D. (Fall) Pennington, who were natives of Pennsylvania and of English descent. His father was for several years a silversmith and justice of the peace in Greensboro, where he located in 1868. He also served as burgess of the borough. His family consisted of nine children, eight of whom are living. The subject of this sketch is the third, and was reared at Brownsville, where he received a good English education. Early in life he learned the tinner's trade, in which he engaged at Greensboro. In 1878 he bought the Greensboro foundry, which he has since operated in connection with a stove and tin-ware store. In 1887 he procured a patent for a new kind of fire front, which seems to prove quite a success. Mr. Pennington was married at Grafton, W. Va., in 1884, to Miss Mattie, daughter of Nathan and Catharine Means, who are of English descent. Mr. Pennington is a Democrat, and in 1888 was elected burgess of Greensboro. He is a member of the Royal Arcanum, and a strong advocate of the temperance cause. His wife is president of the Greensboro W. C. T. U. They are both members of the Methodist Episcopal Church, in which he is steward and Sabbath-school super- intendent.

J. Y. PROVINS, retired farmer, Greensboro, Penn., was born in Monongahela Township, this county, in 1813. He is a son of Benjamin Provins, who was a soldier in the war of 1812 and died soon after its close. Mr. Provins was reared on the farm by his grandfather, who was a soldier in the Revolutionary war, and a pio- neer farmer of Fayette County, Penn. The Provins family were strong, courageous and patriotic, and ever ready to respond to the country's call for help. Mr. Provins' grandfather, James Hartly, was for many years a prominent citizen of this county. The subject of this sketch attended school in the old log school-house for a few months in winter. He chose farming as his occupation and has met with marked success. He has made his way in the world unaided, his success being due largely to his business ability. He began as a farm laborer working by the month or day, but is now the owner of 300 acres of valuable land. Mr. Provins was united in marriage, in 1834, with Miss Melinda, daughter of John and Catharine (Knife) Sterling, of German origin. She died in 1884. Mr. Provins, who is a Democrat, manifests great interest in the educational affairs of his township and has served as a member of the school board.

SILAS ROSS, farmer and stock-grower, Greensboro, Penn., was born in Dunkard Township, this county, June 27, 1843. He is a son of Bowen and Anna (Gantz) Ross, who were of Scotch-Irish descent. His father, who was a farmer all his life, was a native of Fayette County and died in Greene County in 1880. His family consisted of twelve children, all but two of whom grew to maturity. Silas was the seventh in the family and was reared in Dunkard Township, where he attended the common schools. He chose farming as his business, and at present is the owner of 110 acres of well improved land where he resides. In 1868 Mr. Ross married Bunnie V., daughter of Alfred and Jane (Evans) Myers, and they are the parents of two children—Robert C. and Alfred M. Mr. Ross is a Republican. He takes a great interest in educational matters and has served on the school board in his district. Mr. and Mrs. Ross are zealous members of the Baptist Church.

ELI N. TITUS, farmer and stock-grower, Greensboro, Penn., was born in Dunkard Township, Greene County, Penn., January 22, 1844. He is a son of Eli and Sarah (Myers) Titus, natives of this county and among the families most noted in its history. Mr. Titus is the seventh in a family of eleven children. His parents reside in Dunkard Township, on the farm where Eli was reared and attended the district schools. He also took a thorough course of instruction in Iron City College at Pittsburg, Penn., and graduated in 1863. He then enlisted in the Fourteenth Pennsylvania Cavalry and was assigned to Company E of the One Hundred and Sixty-ninth Regiment. During his service with this regiment Mr. Titus was in forty battles and skirmishes, and at different times narrowly escaped death. He served as a non-commissioned officer, quartermaster-sergeant, and was discharged by general order at the close of the war. In 1866 Mr. Titus married Miss Miranda, daughter of John and Leah (Keener) Durr. Her father was a native of Fayette and her mother of Greene County, and they were of German origin. A year after his marriage Mr. Titus went to West Virginia and engaged in farming and stock dealing. In 1870 he returned to Greene County, Penn., and continued in the same business in which he has met with great success. His farm is well stocked and improved and his house is one of the most substantial in the county. He owns 245 acres of land in Dunkard and Monongahela townships. Mr. Titus is a Republican in politics, and was once sent as a senatorial delegate from Greene and Fayette counties to the Republican State Convention. He is also a member of the G. A. R. of Greensboro. The family are members of the Baptist Church, in which Mr. Titus takes an active interest and is one of the trustees of the Greensboro Baptist Church.

E. L. TITUS, farmer and stock-grower, Greensboro, Penn., was born in Dunkard Township, Greene County, Pennsylvania, December 26, 1845, and is a son of Eli and Sarah (Myers) Titus. His grandparents, Peter and Pleasant (Corbly) Myers, were among the earliest settlers of Greene County. His ancestors were of English descent and usually farmers by occupation. Mr. E. L. Titus is the eighth in a family of eleven children. He was reared in Greene County, attending the common schools in Dunkard Township. He afterwards spent some time at the State Normal School at California,

Penn. He made choice of farming and stock-growing as an occupation and has made it the business of his life. In 1875 Mr. Titus married Elizabeth Jane, daughter of Jesse Steele. Mrs. Titus is of English and Irish descent. They have a family of four children, viz., Arcy V., Oscar V., Scott and Charles Eli. In politics Mr. Titus is a Republican.

J. D. WELTNER, a farmer and stock-grower of Monongahela Township, this county, was born February 23, 1824, and is a son of John and Elizabeth (Dunaway) Weltner. His parents were natives of Greene County, Pennsylvania, and of Dutch and English descent. His father, who was also a farmer and stock-dealer, was twice married. J. D. Weltner was the second child by the first marriage and was reared on the home farm, attending the common schools of Greene and Fayette counties. He chose farming as a business and also dealt in stock to some extent. He spent two winters in this business in Pittsburg, Penn., and met with marked success. Mr. Weltner has also proved a success as a farmer and his children own 380 acres of well improved land in Monongahela Township, where he has resided since 1856. Here he always keeps a number of cattle, usually sending fifty or seventy-five head to the markets each year. In 1854 Mr. Weltner was united in marriage with Miss Margaret, daughter of William and Catharine (Robinson) Gray, natives of this county. Her father was a wealthy and influential business man and succeeded in accumulating a handsome fortune. To Mr. and Mrs. Weltner were born seven children, viz., Charles W., Daisie, Minnie, Perlie and Eunice Ann, and two deceased. In politics Mr. Weltner is a Republican. His wife died in 1882, a faithful member of the Presbyterian Church,

BENJAMIN G. WILLIAMS, farmer and stock-grower, Greensboro, Penn., was born March 19, 1863, and is a son of Charles and Melissa (Johnston) Williams, who were of Scotch and English extracton. His father, a farmer and speculator, who was born in 1835, died in 1885 at Greensboro, where he spent the last nineteen years of his life. Mrs. Williams died in 1878. They were the parents of three children—Hattie M., Laura May, wife of George C. Steele, a merchant of Morgantown, W. Va., and Benjamin, the subject of our sketch. He first attended school in Greensboro, and spent some time in the West Virginia University. He is registered as a law student at Waynesburg, Penn., and is pursuing his studies. Early in life Mr. Williams engaged in the drug business—first in Greensboro, then in Dunbar, Fayette County, where he remained three years. At his father's death he was appointed administrator of the estate. He has carefully looked after the farm of 200 acres and valuable coal mines, and is at present engaged in building a railway from the farm to the river, in order to ship the coal more conveniently. Mr. Williams is a Democrat in politics, and one of the most enterprising and successful young men of the county.

MORGAN TOWNSHIP.

JOSEPH ADAMSON, merchant, Lippincott, Penn., was born in Greene County, Penn., August 1, 1843. His parents were Thomas and Mary (Hoge) Adamson, the former deceased. In 1866, March 24, Joseph Adamson married Mary E. Bell, who was born in Morgan Township, July 19, 1849. She is a daughter of Henry and Deborah (Adamson) Bell. Her father is a resident of Washington County. Mrs. Bell died April 15, 1886. To Mr. and Mrs. Adamson have been born eight children, four living—Maggie H., wife of J. L. Pyle, of Waynesburg; John B., Henry L. and Letitia D. The deceased are William T., James L. and two infants. Mr. Adamson was reared on a farm and engaged in farming until 1881, at which time he began merchandising in Morgan Township. In addition to his large general store, he owns fifty acres of land where he and his family reside. He and wife are descendants of pioneer families of this county.

SMITH ADAMSON, farmer, P. O. Lippincott, was born in Franklin Township, this county, October 5, 1850, and is a son of Thomas and Mary Adamson (nee Hoge). His father was born in Greene County, October 5, 1816, and his mother in Centre Township, September 9, 1818. They were married December 24, 1840, in the same house where the widow resides. Mr. Adamson died February 14, 1856. They were the parents of five children—all of whom are living, except John, the eldest, who died October 23, 1863, in the State of Alabama, while in the service of his country during the Rebellion. The subject of this sketch was united in marriage, October 12, 1875, with Sarah M. Randolph. She was born in Jefferson Township, February 4, 1856, and is a daughter of James and Elizabeth (Braden) Randolph, residents of Franklin Township. Mr. and Mrs. Adamson are the parents of four children—Walter, Laura, and Thomas, living; and Nora, deceased. Mr. Adamson, who is an enterprising and successful farmer and stock dealer, owns a good farm of 142 acres. Mr. and Mrs. Adamson are faithful members of the Baptist Church.

J. R. BELL, farmer, Jefferson, Penn., was born in Morgan Township, this county, April 12, 1836. His parents were Morgan and Mary Bell (*nee* Richards). His father was also a native of Morgan Township. He was born December 24, 1808. Mrs. Bell was born in Chester County, Penn., March 14, 1804. They were married in Greene County, where they remained until Mrs. Bell's death, April 8, 1878, Her husband died February 5, 1880. They were the parents of eight children, four of whom are living. J. R. Bell is the fifth, and was united in marriage, September 3, 1863, with Miss Helen Davis, born in Greene Township, this county, August 23, 1839. She is a daughter of Henry J. and Amelia (Myers) Davis. Mr. Davis was born in Jefferson Township, September 27, 1800, and his wife was born in Greene Township, October 22, 1814. They were married in this county, where they remained until the death of Mr. Davis, November 6, 1862. His widow died at the home of her daughter in Morgan Township, April 9, 1871. To Mr. and Mrs. Davis were born three children, two now living. Mr. and Mrs. Bell have three children: Maggie A., wife of W. K. Scott; Mary E. and Henry D. Mr. Bell was raised on a farm and received valuable instructions from his father in the art of husbandry, which he has made his occupation through life. He acquired his education in the common schools and Waynesburg College, and engaged in teaching for a few years. He filled the office of auditor of the county one year, under the old constitution; was re-elected and served three years under the new. Mr. Bell and family are consistent members of the Baptist Church.

B. F. BELL, farmer, Lippincott, Penn., was born in Morgan Township, this county, February 20, 1840, and is a son of Henry and Deborah (Adamson) Bell. His parents were natives of Greene County, where they were married and remained until Mrs. Bell's death, April 15, 1886. Mr. Bell subsequently married Marinda Spriggs (*nee* Keys), and they now reside in Washington County. He is the father of four children. B. F. is the oldest of the three living. He was united in marriage, February 10, 1867, with Mary E. Adamson, who was born in Franklin Township, this county, August 27, 1846. Mrs. Bell is a daughter of Thomas and Sarah (Hoge) Adamson, natives of Greene County. Her mother is now deceased. To Mr. and Mrs. Bell have been born three children—Clementine, Samanthia and William. Mr. Bell was raised on a farm, and has engaged in farming from the time he first started out in life. He owns ninety-five acres of good land where he and family reside. He served his country in the late Rebellion, in Company B, Pennsylvania Heavy Artillery. Mr. and Mrs. Bell are faithful members of the Baptist Church.

S. H. BRADEN, farmer, P. O. Lippincott, is a native of Morgan Township, Greene County, Penn., where he was born June 7, 1831. His parents were William and Rachel (House) Braden. His father was born in Washington County, and his mother in Greene, where they were married and made their home until Mrs. Braden's death, in 1838. Her husband afterwards married Nancy Douglas, who died in 1842. Mr. Braden married for his third wife, Miss Margaret Gibson, who departed this life in 1881. Mr. Braden still resides in Franklin Township, this county. In 1856 Samuel H. Braden married Charlotte (Huss) Adamson, who was born in Greene County, May 16, 1826. She is a daughter of David and Delilah (Rinehart) Huss, natives of Washington and Greene counties, respectively. After marriage they settled in Greene County and remained until the death of Mr. Huss in 1871. Mrs. Huss then went West on a visit, where she died in 1876. Mr. Braden is the father of four children— Albert, who married Anna Shriver; Eva, Smith and Lizzie. Mr. Braden is one of the substantial and enterprising citizens of Morgan Township. He owns 140 acres of land where he and family reside. Mrs. Braden is a consistent member of the Baptist Church.

HENRY BUCKINGHAM, farmer, Clarksville, Penn., was born in Washington County, Penn., December 19, 1809. He is a son of Isaac and Hannah (Heaton) Buckingham. His father was born in Washington County, and his mother in Greene County, where they were married. They settled in Washington County, where they remained until their death. Mr. Buckingham died in 1833 and his widow in 1846. They were the parents of eight children, two living— Hannah, wife of John A. Greenlee; and Henry, the subject of our sketch. He was united in marriage, December 25, 1833, with Mary Morton, who was born in Washington County, October, 18, 1814. Mrs. Buckingham's father, Thomas Morton, was a native of Washington County, and her mother, Mary (Cree) Morton, was born in Greene County, where they died—Mr. Morton December 2, 1869, and his widow, June 6, 1880. To Mr. and Mrs. Buckingham have been born six children, five living—Isaac, Elizabeth, wife of Stephen Morton; Thomas C., Robert, Francis J., and Isabella J. (deceased). Mr. Buckingham was reared on a farm, and has been engaged in farming and stock dealing all his life. He and his son Isaac own 143 acres of land where the family reside. Mr. and Mrs. Buckingham are leading members in the Cumberland Presbyterian Church.

A. S. BURSON, merchant, Clarksville, Penn., is a descendant of one of the pioneers of that village, where he was born November 16, 1837. He is a son of Edward C. and Maria Burson (nee Stewart). The former was born in Columbiana County, Ohio, April 20, 1815, and the latter in Millsboro, Washington County, Penn., April 3, 1815. His parents were married June 7, 1836, in Clarksville, where they settled and remained until their death. Mrs. Burson died July 23, 1874, and her husband January 19, 1880. Of their six children, A. S. is the oldest. He was united in marriage December 19, 1866, with Mary A. Greenlee, who was born in Washington County September 11, 1839. She is a daughter of John and Mary (Balentine) Greenlee, the latter deceased. Mr. and Mrs. Burson have three children, two living—Harry L. and May; William S., deceased. Mr. Burson was reared in Clarksville, and early in life began merchandising with his father. He has continued in that business all his life, with the exception of five years in which he learned and worked at the carpenter trade. He owns a general store in Clarksville. He has filled the offices of auditor and school director of his township, and has served as postmaster for about six years. He has been a member of the Masonic fraternity for twenty-seven years. Mrs. Burson is a consistent member of the Methodist Episcopal Church.

CEPHAS CARY, retired farmer, Clarksville, Penn., is one of the pioneer farmers of Greene County. He was born in Washington Township, August 6, 1812. His parents, Able and Eunice Cary, (*nee* Woodruff), were natives of this county, where they were married and resided until their death. Mr. Cary died in 1820. Mrs. Cary was afterwards united in marriage with John McGinnis. She departed this life in 1833. Cephas Cary was united in marriage January 11, 1844, with Mary Mitchener, who was born in Jefferson Borough October 8, 1820. She is a daughter of Mercena and Mary (Black) Mitchener, the former a native of West Virginia and the latter of Maryland. They were married in Greene County, Penn., where they spent the remainder of their lives. Mrs. Mitchener died May 5, 1859, and Mr. Mitchener April 15, 1880. To Mr. and Mrs. Cary have been born five children, four living—Lizzie M., Sophrona, wife of Daniel Hoover; Mercena M. and Jesse W., and Sarah J. (deceased), who was the wife of Hiram Baker. Mr. Cary is a cabinet-maker by trade, but after marriage he engaged in farming. He owns 100 acres of land, besides valuable property in Clarksville. Mr. and Mrs. Cary are consistent members of the Methodist Episcopal Church; also each one of their children. J. W. is a minister laboring in the Pittsburg Conference.

JOHN CLAYTON, deceased, farmer and stock-dealer, Lippincott, Penn., was born in Morgan Township, Greene County, June 27, 1826. He is a son of William and Sarah Clayton (*nee* Mickins), who were natives of this county, where they resided until their death. William Clayton was born December 30, 1796, and died February 1, 1851. His wife was born January 15, 1798, and departed this life October 12, 1869. They were the parents of ten children, three daughters and seven sons, of whom John is the oldest. He was united in marriage January 20, 1853, with Miss Elizabeth, daughter of Hugh and Priscilla (Hoge) Montgomery. Mrs. Clayton was born in Morgan Township, October 14, 1833. Her father, who was a native of Harford County, Maryland, was one of the early settlers of Morgan Township, Greene County, Penn. He died in June, 1882. His widow is a native of this county, and resides in Waynesburg, Penn. Mr. John Clayton and wife are the parents of four children, two deceased—Priscilla and Samuel; and two living, Sarah A., wife of Benjamin F. Lippencott; and Maria, wife of J. L. Corbett. Mr. and Mrs. Corbett are the parents of five children. Mr. Clayton was raised on a farm, and owned at the time of his death, which occurred June 23, 1888, 400 acres of land in Morgan Township where the family lived. He has served his county as auditor one term, and was a member of the Masonic fraternity and I. O. O. F. Mrs. Clayton is a faithful member of the Baptist Church.

JOHN B. COX, farmer and stock-grower, Jefferson, Penn., was born in Morgan Township, this county, August 17, 1824. He is a son of Jesse and Dorcas (Bell) Cox, also natives of Morgan Township, where they were married and remained through life. Mr. Jesse Cox died in Greene County, Maryland, in 1826, and was buried in that State. His widow, who was afterwards married to Thomas Patterson, died in Iowa, while on a visit to her daughters in 1872. Mr. Patterson died near Carmichaels, Penn. John B., the subject of this sketch, was two years old when his father died. He lived with his grandfather, John Bell, until twenty-one years of age. He was then united in marriage April 17, 1845, with Maria Crayne, who was born in Morgan Township, April 29, 1825. Her parents were Samuel and Mary (Huss) Crayne, deceased. Mr. and Mrs. Cox are the parents of eight children, six of whom are living—Mary A., wife of T. C. Buckingham; Samuel C., Dorcas L., widow of Adam Horn; Emeline, wife of Joseph Gordon; Stephen and Frank. The deceased are John B. and Calvin. Mr. Cox was raised on a farm, and has been greatly prospered in his farming and stock-raising for many years. He owns 380 acres of fine land on Castile. He is a member of the I. O. O. F.

MILLER CRAYNE, farmer, Lippincott, Penn., who was born in Morgan Township April 22, 1817, is a son of Samuel and Mary Crayne (nee Huss). His mother was a native of Maryland, and his father was born in Greene County, Penn., where they were married and spent the remainder of their lives. Mr. Samuel Crayne departed this life October 27, 1853, and his wife June 14, 1865. They were the parents of ten children, eight living. Miller is the third, and was united in the holy bonds of matrimony May 14, 1840, with Miss Lucinda Bell. Mrs. Crayne was born in Greene County January 18, 1821. She is a daughter of John and Ann (Cox) Bell, also natives of this county, where they departed this life Mrs. Bell in 1871, and Mr. Bell in 1880. Mr. and Mrs. Crayne are the parents of four children, two of whom are living—Louisa, wife of Dr. Silveus Smith; and John B., who married Martha A. Lippencott. Elmey and an infant are deceased. Mr. Crayne was raised on a farm, and has been an industrious tiller of the soil all his life. He owns eighty acres of improved land where he and family live. Mr. and Mrs. Crayne are consistent members of the Baptist Church.

STEPHEN CRAYNE, farmer, Jefferson, Penn., is one of the pioneer farmers of Greene County, and was born in Washington, Township, January 4, 1813. He is a son of Samuel and Mary (Huss) Crayne, the oldest of their ten children. The subject of our sketch was united in the holy bonds of matrimony, March 18, 1834, with Miss Mary Bell, who was born in Morgan Township, May 26, 1816. Her parents were Isaac and Elizabeth (Herrod) Bell, natives of Greene County, where they remained until their death. Mr. and Mrs. Crayne are the parents of six children, four of whom are living— Isaac B., Rachel, wife of James Fulton; David, Anna M., wife of George Hughes, and Caroline and Martha, deceased. Mr. Crayne was reared on a farm. He is one of the best known and most industrious farmers in the township, and owns a good farm of 157 acres. Mr. and Mrs. Crayne are faithful members of the Baptist Church.

DAVID CRAYNE, farmer, Waynesburg, Penn., was born in Morgan Township, February 2, 1818. His parents were Samuel and Mary (Huss) Crayne. The former was a native of Greene County, and the latter of Maryland. They were the parents of ten children— four boys and six girls—of whom eight are living. David is the fourth in the family, and was united in marriage, December 8, 1841, with Caroline Harry. Mrs. Crayne was born in Morgan Township, March 8, 1825. Her parents, Jacob and Catharine (Buskirk) Harry, were natives of eastern Pennsylvania. They were married in Greene County, where they remained until their death. To Mr. and Mrs. Crayne have been born eight children, six of whom are living— Samuel, Jacob, Emily A., Thomas, Stephen and Joseph. The deceased were Martha and Mary C. Mr. Crayne was reared on a farm, and has been successful as a farmer and stock-dealer through life. He owns 276 acres of land where he and family reside. Mr. and Mrs. Crayne are members of the Methodist Protestant Church. He also belongs to the I. O. O. F.

SAMUEL FULTON, farmer, P. O. Castile, was born January 10, 1818, on the farm where he and family reside in Morgan Township. John Fulton, his father, was a native of Virginia, and his mother, Isabella (Barr) Fulton, was born in Ireland. They were married in Washington County, Penn., afterwards settling in Greene County, on the farm now owned by Samuel, where they remained through life. Only two of their nine children are living. In 1836

Samuel Fulton married Harriet Huss, a native of this county, and daughter of John and Elizabeth (Eaton) Huss. Mrs. Harriet Fulton died in the same year in which she was married. In 1838 Mr. Fulton was again united in marriage, his second wife being Miss Louellen McClelland, who was born in Washington Township, this county, in 1818. Her parents were John and Nancy (Montgomery) McClelland, deceased. Mr. Fulton is the father of eleven children, nine of whom are living—Eliza, Isabella, wife of Clark Denney; Cerry, James, Nancy, wife of James Tharp; Evan, Henrietta, wife of George Weaver; L. Herrod and William. The deceased are Albert and John. We take pleasure in mentioning Mr. Fulton among the pioneers of Morgan Township. He was raised on a farm, and after his second marriage moved to Richland County, Ohio. Remaining there about nine years, he returned to Morgan Township, Greene County, Penn., where he owns a nice farm of 245 acres. Mr. and Mrs. Fulton are consistent members of Cumberland Presbyterian Church.

JAMES GREENLEE, farmer, P. O. Castile, Penn., was born in Washington County, Penn., November 11, 1818, and is a son of Samuel and Nancy Greenlee (*nee* Gantz). His parents were natives of Fayette County, Penn., but moved to Washington County, Penn., where they remained until death. On March 25, 1851, Mr. Greenlee married Catharine Bell, a native of Greene County, and daughter of Levi H. and Sarah Bell (*nee* Fulton). By this marriage Mr. Greenlee is the father of five children, four living—James L., Margaret, wife of Abraham Burson; Samuel B. and William—and Levi, (deceased). Their mother died in 1863. In 1865 Mr. Greenlee married Catharine Fulton, a native of Washington County, and daughter of Stephen and Ruth Fulton (*nee* Cary). James and Mrs. Catharine Greenlee are the parents of three children, two living— Lewis and John B.—and Stephen, (deceased). Mrs. Greenlee died in 1882. On October 6, 1887, Mr. Greenlee married for his third wife, Eliza Armstrong (*nee* Gregg), daughter of Alfred Gregg. Mr. Greenlee was reared on a farm, and has made farming his business through life. He owns 164 acres of land where and family reside. His present wife and both the deceased were devoted members of the church.

JAMES GREENLEE, farmer, P. O. Clarksville, was born in Greene County, Penn., November 2, 1841. He is a son of John and Mary Greenlee (*nee* Balentine). His mother was a native of Scotland. His father was born in Washington County, Penn., where they were married. They afterwards settled in Greene County, where Mr. Greenlee has since remained. Mrs. Greenlee died in September, 1855. His second wife was Eliza J. Cain. Mr. James Greenlee was united in the holy bonds of matrimony, January 10,

1871, with Mary E. Arnold, who was born in Washington County, December 27, 1847. Mrs. Greenlee is a daughter of Michael and Harriet (Miller) Arnold, who reside in Clarksville. To Mr. and Mrs. James Greenlee have been born two children—Ida .V., born March 6, 1875; and John C., who was born June 15, 1872, and died December 11 of the same year. Mr. Greenlee was reared on a farm, and has made farming his business through life. He owns sixty acres of land in Morgan Township, and valuable property in Clarksville. He and wife are consistent members of the Cumberland Presbyterian Church.

HENRY GRIMES, farmer and stock-dealer, Lippincott, Penn., —Among the representative business men of Greene County, we take pleasure in giving the sketch of Henry Grimes, who was born in Centre Township, this county, September 4, 1820. He is a son of Peter and Mary (Sharon) Grimes. The former was born in New Jersey, February 17, 1789, and the latter near Baltimore, Maryland, February 5, 1786. They were married in Greene County where they remained through life. Four of their five children are now living. Henry Grimes was united in marriage, March 27, 1846, with Nancy McClelland, born in Washington Township, February 1, 1823, and a daughter of John and Nancy McClelland (nee Montgomery). To Mr. and Mrs. Grimes have been born five children, four living—Caleb, Carey, who married Lizzie S. Sellers; Samuel, who married Clara Adams; Mary E., wife of Samuel C. Hawkins, and Sarah J. (deceased). Mrs. Grimes departed this life September 18, 1873, a consistent member of the Baptist Church. Mr. Grimes was reared on a farm, and owns about 1,500 acres of land, 812 acres of which are in Greene County. When sixteen years of age, Mr. Grimes received $300, in gold from his father; and by means of industry and careful management in his farming and stock-dealing has accumulated quite a handsome fortune, being considered one of the wealthiest men in Greene County.

C. C. HARRY, farmer, Jefferson, Penn., was born September 13, 1831, in the house where he and his family live in Morgan Township. He is a son of Jacob and Catharine Harry (nee Van Buskirk.) The former was a native of Chester and the latter of Northampton County, Penn. They were married in Greene County, where they departed this life—Mr. Harry in 1834, and Mrs. Harry December 1, 1859. They were the parents of five children, of whom C. C. is the youngest. In 1857 Mr. Harry married Martha Houlsworth, a native of Greene County, and daughter of Hugh C. and Isabella Houlsworth, deceased. By this marriage Mr. Harry is the father of four children, two of whom are living—Catharine, wife of Andrew Rich, and Belle. The deceased are Emma and James. Their mother died March 4, 1868. Mr. Harry afterwards married

Elizabeth Bayard, October 11, 1877; she was born in Whitcley Township, November 26, 1844, and is a daughter of John S. and Malinda Bayard (*nee* Leonard). They were natives of this county, where they remained until Mrs. Bayard's death, March 26, 1883. Mr. Bayard is still living. Mr. and Mrs. Harry are the parents of two children —Charles C. and John B. Mr. Harry has been very successful in his farming and stock-dealing, and owns 325 acres of excellent land. He is a members of the I. O. O. °F. Mrs. Harry belongs to the Presbyterian Church, of which the deceased wife was also a devoted member.

WILLIAM HATFIELD, farmer, Morgan Township, Penn., was born in Whiteley Township, this county, February 4, 1848 His parents, George W. and Mary (Richie) Hatfield, are both living and reside in Whiteley Township. February 8, 1872, William Hatfield married Mary J. McClure, a native of Dunkard Township. Mrs. Hatfield was born September 2, 1843, and is a daughter of James and Susan (Brown) McClure. Mr. McClure died August 8, 1886; his widow is still living. Mr. and Mrs. Hatfield are the parents of two children—Ida L., born March 9, 1873, and Sudie M., born July 24, 1876. Mr. Hatfield was reared on a farm, and has been engaged in farming and stock-dealing through life. He owns about 163 acres of land where he and his family reside. Mr. Hatfield has been greatly prospered in his business, and is one of the leading citizens in his community. Mrs. Hatfield is a faithful member of the Baptist Church.

JOHN C. HAWKINS, farmer, Zollarsville, Penn., was born in Greene County, Penn., December 15, 1825, in the house now occupied by himself and family. He is a son of Richard and Cynthia Hawkins (*nee* Crawford). His father was born in Maryland, and his mother in Fayette County, Penn. They were married in Washington County where they remained until 1814, at which time they moved to Greene County and remained until their death. Mrs. Hawkins departed this life in July 1845, and her husband February 6, 1856. They were the parents of eleven children, four of whom are living. June 7, 1882, John C. Hawkins married Elizabeth McMurray, who was born in Washington County, December 5, 1846. She is a daughter of James and Catharine (Whitely) McMurray. Her father was a native of Ireland, and her mother was born in Allegheny County, Penn., where they remained a few years, then moved to Washington County. Here Mrs. McMurray died November 26, 1866; and Mr. McMurray, March 17, 1875. Mr. Hawkins has been engaged in farming and stock-dealing through life. His farm in Morgan Township contains about 289 acres of land in a high state of cultivation. Mr. and Mrs. Hawkins are consistent members of the Baptist Church.

43

R. C. HAWKINS, farmer and stock-dealer, Jefferson, Penn.; was born in Morgan Township, this county, November 14, 1814. He is a son of Richard and Cynthia (Crawford) Hawkins. The former was born in Maryland and the latter in Fayette County, Penn. They were united in marriage in Washington County, where they remained a few years then moved to Greene County and spent the rest of their lives. Mrs. Cynthia Hawkins departed this life in July 1845, and Mr. Hawkins in February, 1856. The subject of this sketch was united in marriage November 25, 1841, with Emeline Wise, who was born in Washington County, November 28, 1820. Her parents were Frederick and Elizabeth (Burson) Wise, native of Washington and Greene counties, respectively. They were married in Greene County, remained a short time, then moved to Washington County where Mr. Wise died in 1877, and Mrs. Wise in 1881. Mr. and Mrs. Hawkins are the parents of nine children, of whom seven are now living: Joseph W., Maggie V., wife of William C. Bailey; Thomas, Clara E., wife of William Bodley; William B., Tressa, wife of Charles T. Harvey, and Samuel C. The deceased are Frederick W. and James F. Mr. Hawkins was reared on a farm and has been engaged in farming and stock-dealing all his life. He owns the fine farm of 280 acres where he and his family reside. Mr. and Mrs. Hawkins are faithful members of the Cumberland Presbyterian Church.

J. F. HAWKINS, deceased, was born in Morgan Township, Greene County, Pennsylvania, April 13, 1845, and died May 1, 1888. He was a son of Richard C. and Emeline (Wise) Hawkins. His father is a native of this county, and his mother of Washington County, Penn., where they were married. They subsequently removed to Morgan Township, Greene County, where they still reside. J. F. is the third of their large family, and was united in marriage, March 3, 1870, with Anna E. Greenlee. Mrs. Hawkins was born in Morgan Township, September 10, 1846. She is a daughter of Jacob and Mary (Spencer) Greenlee, natives of Washington and Greene counties, respectively. They were married in Greene County, where they remained until Mr. Greenlee's death, August 20, 1887; his widow survives him. To Mr. and Mrs. Hawkins were born seven children, five of whom are living—Walter R., F. Bernice, Wilber J., Emma M. and Edna B. Warren K. and an infant are deceased. Mr. Hawkins was reared on a farm. Like his ancestors, he made farming and stock-dealing the busines of his life, owning at the time of his death 200 acres of well improved land where his family now reside. Mrs. Hawkins and W. R. are consistent members of the Baptist Church.

THOMAS J. HOLDER, farmer, P. O. Clarksville, was born in Greene County, Penn., July 27, 1827. He is a son of Abraham and

Jane (Cree) Holder. The former was born in Virginia and the latter in Greene County, Pennsylvania, where they settled after marriage and remained until their death. Mr. Abraham Holder died January 9, 1846, and his wife in 1866. They were the parents of seven children, four of whom are living. In 1851 Thomas J. Holder married Malinda Cox, who was born in Washington County, Penn., in 1831. Her parents, Andrew and Margaret (Hupp) Cox, were natives of Washington County, where they remained until the death of Mr. Cox. His widow is still living. To Mr. and Mrs. Holder have been born twelve children—Lebenas P., Margaret J., Calvin, Josephus, Permelia, Emma, L, Dora, Lizzie, Elmer, Laura, Charlie and William. Although a farmer by occupation, Mr. Holder is also quite a genius in his way, and can accomplish almost any kind of work he undertakes. He owns 131 acres of land, on which are good substantial buildings. He has filled the office of auditor of his township, has served as school directors, and is also a member of the Masonic fraternity.

O. C. HORNER, farmer, Clarksville, Penn., was born in Fayette County, Penn., March 15, 1839. He is a son of Hiram and Malinda (Reynolds) Horner, the former a native of Fayette County, and the latter of Greene. They were married in this county, but made their home in Fayette until Mr. Horner's death, which occurred in November, 1874. His widow is still living and resides on the old home farm. They were the parents of five children, of whom O. C. is the oldest living. He was united in marriage, October 15, 1864, with Amy Cox, born in Jefferson Township, January 2, 1843. Her parents, Christopher and Mary (Rush) Cox, were natives of this county, where they were married and remained through life. Mrs. Cox died in 1857, and her husband in 1861. Of their ten children, three are now living. Mr. and Mrs. Horner are the parents of eight children—James L., Sarah F., Anna M., Cora B., Hiram C., Emma A., William and Oliver G. Mr. Horner was reared on a farm, and makes a business of farming and stock-raising. He owns 170 acres of land where he and family reside. Mrs. Horner is a devoted member of the Disciple Church.

HENRY KEYS, farmer, P. O. Castile, was born in Morgan Township, Greene County, Penn., June 10, 1837. His parents were David and Mary Keys (nee McGinnis). The former was a native of Washington County, and the latter of Greene County. After marriage they settled in Washington County and remained a few years, afterwards removing to Morgan Township, Greene County, where they spent the remainder of their lives. David Keys departed this life in August, 1872, and his widow in August, 1884. They were the parents of ten children, six of whom are living. On January 14, 1875, Henry Keys was united in marriage with Amelia Litzenburg,

who was born in Morgan Township November 14, 1854. Mr. and
Mrs. Keys have an interesting family of children—John R.,
Mary O., Wesley H., Priscilla R. and George W. Mr. Keys devotes
his time principally to farming, and owns 104 acres of fine land
where he and family now reside. He enlisted in behalf of his country's cause, in Company F, One Hundred and Fourth Illinois, and
served one year. Mr. and Mrs. Keys are faithful members of the
Methodist Episcopal Church.

SAMUEL LEWIS, farmer, Castile, Penn., was born on the farm
where he and family reside in Morgan Township, this county. His
parents were John and Hannah (Arnold) Lewis, who spent all their
lives on the farm now occupied by their son. Seven of their nine
children survive them. In 1854 Samuel married Martha Blackledge
(*nee* Sharpnack). Her parents were natives of Greene County. Her
father was born October 15, 1797, and her mother February 14, 1801.
After marriage they settled in Jefferson Township and remained until
their death. Mr. Blackledge died November 5, 1870, and his widow
April 11, 1876. To Mr. and Mrs. Lewis have been born six children, three living—Stiers, Margaret and Levi. The deceased are—
Mary M., John and Ellsworth. Their mother departed this life in
1863. Mr. Lewis is a farmer by occupation, and owns 325 acres of
excellent land. In addition to the care of his land, he has also devoted considerable time to the raising of stock, and is one of the
most prosperous citizens of his township.

SAMUEL MONTGOMERY, farmer, P. O. Lippincott, Penn.,
is a descendant of one of the old families of Greene County, and was
born in Morgan Township, July 17, 1835. He is a son of Hugh and
Priscilla (Hoge) Montgomery. His father was a native of Maryland
and when but a child came with his parents to Greene County, Penn.,
where they were united in marriage. They remained in this county
until Mr. Montgomery's death, which occurred in 1882. His widow
survives him. Mr. Samuel Montgomery was twice married, his first
wife being Mary Stentz, a native of Fayette County, and daughter of
Thomas Stentz. By this marriage there are two children—Charles,
and Anna, who is the wife of Nelson Goslin. Mrs. Montgomery died
September 28, 1869. After her death, March 5, 1870, Mr. Montgomery married Cyrene Davis (*nee* Dales), who was born in Washington County January 16, 1837. They are the parents of five
children—Mary E., Priscilla, Lizzie, Hugh and John. Mr. Montgomery was raised on a farm and received many instructions from
his father in the art of husbandry. He owns 130 acres of land
where he and family reside. He filled the office of auditor of the
county one term. He is a member of the Masonic fraternity. Mrs.
Montgomery belongs to the Baptist Church, of which the deceased
wife was also a devoted member.

THOMAS H. MONTGOMERY, farmer and stock-dealer, Lippincott, Penn., was born in Morgan Township January 24, 1847, and is a descendant of one of the pioneer families of Greene County. His father and mother were Hugh and Priscilla (Hoge) Montgomery. The former was born in Maryland and the latter in Greene County, Penn., where they were united in marriage and remained until the father's death, June 14, 1882. His widow survives him. Thomas H. Montgomery was united in marriage, October 17, 1878, with Virginia E. Gordon, who was born in Franklin Township, April 14, 1853. Mrs. Montgomery is a daughter of Bazil and Maria (Inghram) Gordon, natives and residents of this county. Mr. and Mrs. Montgomery are the parents of four children—Walter C., born September 5, 1879; Bernice L., born May 14, 1881; Florence M., born May 5, 1883; and Pauline E., born August 23, 1886. Mr. Montgomery has always lived on a farm, and owns 185 acres of good land where he and family reside. He is a member of the Masonic fraternity, and is filling the office of justice of the peace in his township. He is a Baptist, and has held the office of deacon since 1879, and his wife is a member of the Methodist Protestant Church. Previous to marriage he was a teacher in the public schools.

SAMUEL MURRAY, farmer, P. O. Jefferson, Penn., was born in Fayette County, Penn., January 28, 1822. His father, Jacob Murray, was also a native of Fayette County; and his mother, whose maiden name was Susannah Aukerman, was born in Westmoreland County, where they were married. After marriage they settled in Fayette County and remained until their death—Mr. Murray dying in 1852, and his widow in 1886. They had twelve children, eleven of whom are living. On August 29, 1843, Samuel Murray married Agnes Fulkerth, who was born in Westmoreland County, Penn., October 31, 1821. Her parents were Joseph and Esther Fulkerth (*nee* Stauffer), deceased. Mr. Murray and wife are the parents of eleven children, seven living—Cyrus, David, Anna, Jennie, Elias A. F., Joseph H. and Isaac G.—and Susannah, Rachel, Jacob and an infant, deceased. Mr. Murray was raised on a farm, and has devoted his time principally to agricultural pursuits. He owns ninety acres of land where he and family reside. He and wife are faithful members of the Brethren Church.

ABLE McCULLOUGH, retired merchant, Clarksville, Penn., was born in Washington County, Penn., October 18, 1845. He is a son of Aaron and Naomi McCullough (*nee* Turner). His father was also a native of Washington County, and his mother was born in Greene County. After their marriage they settled in Washington County and remained until their death. They were the parents of four children, two living—William and Able, the subject of our sketch. He was united in the holy bonds of matrimony, September

17, 1871, with Leah·Craig (*nee* Horn), born in Washington County, April 29, 1841. She is a daughter of John and Mary Horn (*nee* Shape), residents of Washington County until their death. To Mr. and Mrs. McCullough have been born three children—Olin W., Martha E. and Naomi L. Mrs. McCullough, by her first marriage, is the mother of one child—Mary H., wife of Samuel Teagarden. Mr. McCullough has made farming and merchandising his business through life. He and wife are faithful members of the Methodist Episcopal Church.

J. C. POLLOCK, farmer, was born in Amwell Township, Washington County, Penn., September 5, 1824. His parents were Thomas and Cynthia (Carter) Pollock. The former was a native of Waynesburg, and the latter of Washington County, where they were married and remained until 1835. They then moved to Greene County, where Mr. Pollock died January 3, 1876. He served as commissioner of the county three years, representative of the county two terms, in 1841 and 1842, and associate judge one term. He and wife were the parents of eleven children, ten of whom are living—nine in this county. On November 8, 1854, J. C. Pollock was united in marriage with Miss Malissa Ailes, born in Washington County, Penn., January 27 1833. She is a daughter of Stephen and Mary (Nixon) Ailes, the former a native of Washington County, and the latter of Ireland. To Mr. and Mrs. Pollock have been born six children, three living—James M., William P., David L.—and Mary M., Stephen A. and an infant, deceased. Mr. Pollock was raised on a farm, and when twenty-one years of age he began merchandising with his father, in which he continued for three years. He afterwards served as a clerk four years, then engaged in purchasing stock and grain for a distillery. He worked in this capacity for six years, then engaged in farming and milling. He owns fifty acres of land and a half interest in a large flouring-mill. He belongs to the Masonic order, and he and wife are members of the Cumberland Presbyterian Church.

WILLIAM PYLE, hotel-keeper, Clarksville, Penn., was born in Washington County, Pennsylvania, November 10, 1838. He is a son of Joseph and Alberah (Thornburg) Pyle, natives of Pennsylvania. His parents were married in Washington County, where they remained a number of years and then lived in Morgan Township, Greene County, for a short time. In 1858 they returned to Washington County and remained until their death. Mrs. Joseph Pyle departed this life in 1861. Her husband afterwards married Catharine Kenann, who is still living. Mr. Pyle died in 1873. William is the only one of the family in this county. In 1859 he married Sarah Yonker, who was born in Washington County, August 10, 1842. Mrs. Pyle is a daughter of Noah and Elizabeth Yonker (*nee*

Watt). Her father was born in Pennsylvania, and her mother in Maryland. They were married in Washington County, Penn., and remained there until Mr. Yonker's death January 9, 1853. His widow remained in Washington County until 1859, at which time she came to Greene County and lived with her daughter, Mrs. William Pyle, until her death, which occurred December 25, 1872, while she was on a visit to Pittsburg, Penn. William Pyle and wife are the parents of eight children—Joseph, Samuel, Frank, Lizzie, Jesse, Emma and William T., living; and Lucy, deceased. Mr. Pyle was reared on a farm, and has devoted almost all his life to farming. He owns property in Clarksville, where he has been proprietor of a hotel for the past two years. He and Mrs. Pyle are faithful members of the Christian Church.

W. H. F. RANDOLPH, farmer, Lippincott, Penn., was born in Jefferson Township, this county, July 14, 1836. His parents Abraham F. and Emily A. (Adamson) Randolph, were natives and residents of Greene County until their death. His father died December 8, 1866, and Mrs. Randolph, March 9, 1885. They were the parents of three children, two living—J. A. F. and W. H. F.— and Sarah L., deceased. The subject of this sketch was united in marriage, November 25, 1855, with Mary A. Heaton, who was born Morgan Township, January 28 1834, and died April 30, 1888. She was a daughter of Daniel and Elizabeth (Woods) Heaton, the second of their six children, three of whom are now living. Mr. Heaton was born in Greene County, and Mrs. Heaton in New Jersey. They were married in Greene County, Penn., where they remained until their death. Mr. Heaton died August 21, 1856, and his wife January 26, 1877. To Mr. and Mrs. Randolph was born one daughter— Laura L., October 7, 1856. Mr. Randolph was reared on a farm and is a farmer and stock-grower by occupation. He owns a well improved farm of seventy-five acres where he now resides. The family belong to the Baptist Church, of which his deceased wife was also a devoted member.

W. D. ROGERS, physician, Jefferson Penn., was born near Beallsville, Washington County, Penn., April 5, 1816. His parents, Philip and Mary (Johns) Rogers, who were natives of Maryland, came to Washington County, Pennsylvania, about the year 1806; and remained there the rest of their lives. Mrs. Rogers died in 1838. Her husband subsequently married Mary Borom, who departed this life in 1869. Mr. Rogers died in 1870. He was the father of seven children, four of whom are living. Dr. Rogers is the only one of the family in Greene County. He was united in marriage, January 13, 1847, with Charlotte H. Black. Mrs. Rogers was born in Morgan Township, this county, November 26, 1820, and is a devoted member of the Presbyterian Church. Her parents were Honarale and Charlotte (Heaton) Black, who were among the first settlers of the county. Dr. and Mrs. Rogers are the parents of five children —Ellen D., wife of H. A. Russell, of Iowa; William B., who married Cora L. Rogers; John A., Mary L. and Norval P. The Doctor acquired his education in the common schools of his county and in the academy at Brownsville, Penn. In 1842 he began reading medicine with W. L. Wilson, M. D., of Beallsville, Penn. In 1835 he gradu ated from the Medical University of Marlyand, at Baltimore. Since that time he has been engaged in the practice of his profession, most of which has been in Greene County, where he and family have resided for many years, and where he owns a fine farm of about one hundred and ninety-five acres. During the late Rebellion, Dr. Rogers was examining surgeon of the first drafted men from this county, and afterwards appointed examining surgeon for pensioned soldiers. He was a delegate to the National Convention of 1872, at Philadelphia, Penn., which nominated Grant and Wilson for President and Vice-President of the United States.

JOHN ROSE, farmer, Lippincott, Penn., was born in Cumberland Township, this county, August 29, 1832, and is a son of David and Mary (Hewitt) Rose. His mother was a native of Washington County, and his father of Greene County, where they were married and remained until their death. After his wife's death, in 1874, Mr. Rose married Eliza Greenlee, who is still living. Mr. Rose died May 14, 1879. He was the father of thirteen children, eleven of whom are living. John, who was their second child, was united in marriage, August 27, 1855, with Priscilla A. Litzenburg. Mrs. Rose was born in Washington County, Penn., January 20, 1836. Her parents, William and Charlotte (Rush) Litzenburg, were natives of Greene County, where they resided a short time, then moved to Washington County and remained until their death. Mr. and Mrs. Rose had one child, W. H., born October 6, 1857, and died September 16, 1858. Mr. Rose is a farmer and owns one hundred and sixteen acres of fine land. He and wife are zealous members of the Cumberland Presbyterian Church.

JACOB RUSH, farmer, Jefferson, Penn., was born January 27, 1823, on his present farm in Morgan Township, this county. His father, Matthias Rush, was also born on the same farm now owned by Jacob and his mother, Sarah (Iams) Rush, who was a native of St. Charles County, Maryland. They were married in Greene County, Penn., and resided their until their death. Mr. Rush died in 1863, and his widow in 1874. They were the parents of two children—Jacob, and William, who married Martha Hughes, and resides in Clarksville, Penn. Jacob Rush was united in marriage, November 11, 1846, with Elizabeth Cox, born in Morgan Township, May 13, 1824. Her parents were William and Abigail (Rush) Cox, natives of Greene County, and residents therein until their death. To Mr. and Mrs. Rush have been born four children, viz: Sarah A., wife of Stephen M. Hill; Isabella, wife of A. C. Myers; Micca and Benjamin F., who married Abigail Cox, now deceased. Mr. Rush was reared on a farm, and has been very successful in farming and stock dealing throughout his life. His home farm contains 200 acres of valuable land. Mrs. Rush at the age of sixteen became a member of the Christian Church, to which she was very devoted until her death, December 17, 1887.

JAMES RUSH, deceased, was born in Virginia, in 1770, and came with his parents to Clarksville, Penn., when he was only four years of age. He remained there until his death in 1842. He married Priscilla Case, who was a native of Greene County, and departed this life in 1825. They were the parents of nine children, eight daughters and one son. Only two of these are living—Priscilla and Sarah A., widow of Fletcher Allman, who was born near Clarksville in 1812. Mr. and Mrs. Allman were the parents of seven children. Mr. Allman departed this life February 10, 1877. James Rush was a farmer during his lifetime, and at one time owned 1,300 acres of land, of which the Allman heirs own 135 acres. Miss Priscilla Rush lives with her nephew Fletcher Allman, in Clarksville, Penn., where she owns nice property. She comes of a highly respected family, and is greatly esteemed by a wide circle of friends.

W. B. STEWART, farmer, Clarksville, Penn., was born in Millsboro, Washington County, Penn., June 26, 1818. His parents, Alexander and Elizabeth (Metzlar) Stewart, were natives of Franklin County, Penn., where they were married. They made their home in Fulton County until 1813, then moved to Washington County, and in 1828 came to Greene County, where they remained until their death. Mrs. Stewart died in 1858, and her husband in 1862. They were the parents of eight children, of whom only three are living, viz.: Eliza L., widow of Francis Drake; Melvina, widow of H. P. Hurst; and W. B., the subject of this sketch. He was united in marriage, October 7, 1849, with Elizabeth Wise, who was born in Washington County, May 28, 1823. Her parents, Joseph and Parmelia (Barnard) Wise, were natives of Washington and residents their until their death. Mrs. Wise died in 1852. Mr. Wise subsequently married Julia Welch, who survives him. Mr. Wise died in 1875. Mr. and Mrs. Stewart are the parents of seven children, five living—Joseph W., Elizabeth, wife of William Orr; Emma, wife of William Hoge; William B., Jr. and John C.—and Alexander and Francis, deceased. Mr. Stewart is a tanner by trade, which he followed until twenty-five years of age. After that his time was variously employed until 1851, when he turned his attention to farming, in which he has successfully engaged ever since. He owns 144 acres of land where he and family reside.

He has belonged to the Masonic fraternity for about twenty years, and he and his wife are devoted members of the Baptist Church.

EDWARD VANKIRK, SR., retired farmer, Jefferson, Penn., was born in Washington County, Penn., October 14, 1813, and is a son of Arthur and Elizabeth (Parkinson) Vankirk. His father was a native of New Jersey, and his mother was born in Pennsylvania, where they were married, settling in Washington County. They remained there until 1835, lived in Greene County seven years, then returned to Washington County, where they remained until Mrs. Vankirk's death in 1847. Mr. Vankirk died in 1865. They were the parents of eight children, three of whom are living—Edward, Ralph and William. Edward was united in marriage, May 21, 1835, with Jane E. Blake, who was a native of Pennsylvania, and daughter of Samuel and Elizabeth (Carr) Blake. By this marriage Mr. Vankirk is the father of six children, only two of whom are living— Elizabeth, widow of W. H. Kline; and Emma, wife, of A. J. Barr. The deceased are Samuel, William, George and Anna J., who was the wife of Hugh Montgomery, one of the substantial citizens of Morgan Township. Mrs. Vankirk departed this life July 27, 1852, a devoted member of the Christian Church. After her death, December 13, 1853, Mr. Vankirk married Sarah A. Gantz, who was born in Washington County, Penn., March 20, 1829. Her parents were John and Christina Gantz, deceased. Mr. and Mrs. Vankirk are the parents of eight children, seven living—David, Edward, Thomas, Clark, Lucy, James, Bertha,—and John F., deceased. Mr. Vankirk was raised on a farm and met with great success as a farmer during his more active life. He owns 160 acres of land in this county, where he and family reside. Mr. and Mrs. Vankirk belong to the Baptist Church.

W. H. VIRGIN, farmer, Clarksville, Penn., was born in Millsboro, Washington County, Penn., November, 17, 1840. He is a son of Jesse and Ophillipphia (Huntsberry) Virgin, the former a native of Fayette County, Pennsylvania, and the latter of Maryland. After marriage his parents settled in Greene County, Penn., subsequently removing to Millsboro, where they remained until Mrs. Virgin's death in 1842. Her husband afterwards married Clarinda Hupp, who is still living. Mr. Virgin died in 1880. He was the father of five children, of whom the subject of this sketch is the second. He was united in marriage, December 13, 1864, with Mary A. Anderson, born in Belmont County, Ohio, September 4, 1837. She is a daughter of John R. and Maria (Perry) Anderson, the former a native of Greene County, Penn., and the latter of Guernsey County, Ohio. After marriage, Mrs. Virgin's parents settled in Belmont County, Ohio, and remained until Mrs. Anderson's death, in 1855. Mr. Anderson afterwards married Mary Wildman, and they reside in Harrison County, Ohio. To Mr. and Mrs. Virgin have been born four children—Elizabeth R., Lena M., Hannah V. and Jesse A. Mr. Virgin has always lived on a farm, and has made farming the principal occupation of his life. He owns nice property in Clarksville. He is filling the office of jury commissioner of the county, and has served as assessor and constable of his township. He enlisted in the service of his country, in Company D, Eighty-fifth Pennsylvania Volunteers, November 6, 1861, and served over three years, passing through a number of serious engagements. Mr. Virgin is a member of the G. A. R. Post, No. 265. Mrs. Virgin is a faithful member of the Cumberland Presbyterian Church.

AMOS WALTON, retired merchant, P. O. Clarksville, was born in Washington County, Penn., October 12, 1807. He is a son of John and Sarah (Paul) Walton, who were also natives of Washington County, and residents therein until their death. Mr. John Walton died October 6, 1834. His widow was afterwards united in marriage with Levi Burson, who died in 1863. Mrs. Burson departed this life in 1874. On March 11, 1830, Amos Walton married Sarah A. Stephenson, who was born in Clarksville in 1813. She is a daughter of Asa and Priscilla (Gregg) Stephenson. To Mr. and Mrs. Walton were born ten children, five of whom are living—Jesse, Louisa, widow of B. F. Swan; Priscilla, wife of Dr. James A. Sargent; Ellis B. and Isaac N. The deceased are John M., Joseph R., Amos G., Morgan M. and an infant. Though raised on a farm, Mr. Walton began merchandising when starting out in life for himself, and has continued in the business for fifty years. He owns 300 acres of land, and good property in Clarksville. Mr. Walton is an elder in the Cumberland Presbyterian Church, of which he has been a faithful member for forty-four years. Mrs. Walton died May 14, 1875.

HENRY WATSON, farmer, Lippincott, Penn., was born in West Bethlehem Township, Washington County, July 28, 1845. He is a son of John and Mary A. (Almost) Watson. His father was a native of Ireland. His mother was born in Greene County, Penn., where they were married. They afterwards removed to Washington County, and remained until their death. He died September 3, 1856, and she May 27, 1869. September 6, 1866, Henry Watson was united in marriage with Mary A. Weaver, who was born in Washington County, October 17, 1846. She is a daughter of Jacob and Sarah (Register) Weaver, residents of Morgan Township. To Mr. and Mrs. Watson have been born eight children—Jacob W., William H., Charles F., Clara S., John F., Ida B., Lucy A. and Mary E. Mr. Watson was reared on a farm, and owns ninety-six acres of fine land where he and family live. He and wife are prominent members of the Baptist Church.

MORRIS TOWNSHIP.

HUGH AULD, farmer and stock-grower, Nineveh, Penn., was born in Morris Township, Greene County, Penn., October 1, 1824. His parents, Hugh and Sarah (Howard) Auld, were natives of Ireland, and came to Greene County, Penn., in 1815. His father, who was a farmer, reared a family of six children, of whom Hugh is the youngest. He was reared in Morris Township, and has met with success in his chosen occupation. He is the owner of a farm of 283 acres of well-improved land where he now resides. In 1851 Mr. Auld married Mary J. Auld, and they are the parents of seven children—Sadie R., Will M., Howard H., Mattie J., Mary M., Tom B. and Ida B. Mr. Auld is a Democrat in politics, and in religion a Presbyterian, of which church his wife is also a devoted member.

JASPER BANE, deceased, was born in Amity, Washington County, Penn., October 27, 1827, and died in Greene County in 1866. Mr. Bane was a son of Jacob Bane, the ninth in his family of twelve children. He was reared on the home farm in Washington County, and was a successful farmer through life, owning at the time of his death 111 acres of well-improved land. In 1855 Mr. Bane married Jane, daughter of George Lightner. Mrs. Bane's ancestors were among the early settlers and farmers of Greene County. She is a sister of Henry Lightner, a prominent farmer of Morris Township. Mr. and Mrs. Bane are the parents of five children—Sarah J., wife of Otho Iams; George, who is a farmer by occupation and has charge of the home farm; Mary, wife of D. W. Hopkins; Samuel and Frank. George was born in Morris Township, October 28, 1857, and received his education in the district school. In politics Mr. Bane was a Republican, and in religion a Cumberland Presbyterian, of which church Mrs. Bane is also a zealous member.

CYRUS BRADBURY, farmer and stock-grower, was born in Mercer County, Penn., July 24, 1830. He is a son of John and Jane (Tuttle) Bradbury, natives of New Jersey, and of English descent. In early life his father was a tanner, afterwards a farmer. He came from Washington County to Greene in 1838, and settled on the farm where Cyrus resides. He died at the advanced age of eighty-four years. His wife is eighty-four years of age, and makes her home with Cyrus, the only one of the three children living. He grew to manhood on the farm, receiving his education in the district schools. He has made a success of his farming, and owns 132 acres of well-improved land. In 1861 he married Nancy, daughter of Thomas and Rebecca (Hedge) Moore, who were natives of this county and of English descent. Mr. and Mrs. Bradbury have five children —Mary Ann, Emma B., wife of John Penn; Ella R., wife of George B. Iams; Lizzie J., wife of Thomas A. Welsh, and Dora B. They have also an adopted child—William Washington. Mr. Bradbury is a Democrat in politics. He and wife are members of the Cumberland Presbyterian Church, in which he is one of the trustees.

ENOCH BROOKS, farmer and stock-grower, Swart's, Penn., was born in Morris Township, this county, November 24, 1837, and is a son of Enoch and Mary (Russell) Brooks. His father, who was a farmer, spent his whole life in this county, and died in 1838. His family consisted of seven children, all of whom grew to maturity. Enoch is the youngest, was reared on the farm and attended the common school. He made choice of farming as his occupation, in which he has engaged through life. He has made his own way in the world, and is the owner of a well-improved farm containing 137 acres. He was united in marriage, April 3, 1869, with Elizabeth M. Rush, and they are the parents of seven children—Mary Laura, George R., Anna Bell, Maud L., Perry M., William H. and Robert E. Mr. Brooks is a Democrat, and a member of the I. O. O. F. In 1861 he enlisted in Company D, Eighty-fifth Pennsylvania Volunteer Infantry. He was taken prisoner and sent to Richmond, Va., where he remained for five weeks. He also passed through many of the principal battles and engagements. Mr. and Mrs. Brooks are prominent members of the Baptist Church.

STEPHEN C. CARY, farmer and stock-grower, Swart's, Penn., was born in Morris Township, January 27, 1846. His parents were Abel and Delilah (Mitchell) Cary, natives of this county and of English origin. His ancestors came among the early settlers from New Jersey to Greene County. They were usually farmers, of whom his father was one of the most successful. He died in 1875. Stephen was the ninth in a family of eleven children, six of whom reached maturity. Mr. Cary was reared on a farm, attended the common-schools, and has followed the occupation of his father. He has met with great success in his business, being the owner of a fine farm of 443 acres well stocked and improved. His success in life has been due largely to his own efforts. He was united in marriage April 27, 1872, with Miss Harriet, daughter of Harrison and Elizabeth (Longdon) Conger. Mrs. Cary was born in Washington County, and is of English and Irish descent. Mr. and Mrs. Cary are the parents of six children—William H., Lizzie B., Lawrence G., James W., Fannie D. and Hattie M. In politics Mr. Cary is Republican. His wife is a devoted member of the Cumberland Presbyterian Church.

JOHN M. CONKLIN, farmer and stock-grower, Sycamore, Penn., was born in Washington County, Penn., October 17, 1830, and is a son of Isaac and Lydia (Sayers) Conklin, also natives of Washington County. His father, who was a farmer by occupation, had a family of seven sons and four daughters, all living but one. John was reared on the farm in Washington County, attended the common-schools, and learned the painter's trade. He worked for several years at Claysville, Penn., where he took contracts for painting, and was one of the few who made a financial success of the business. Through his energy, good management and careful investments, he was able, in 1859, to buy a good farm near Beulah Church in Greene County. Ten years later he sold this farm, and in 1872 he again invested in 291 acres of land, where he has since resided. He is a first-class farmer, is the owner of a saw-mill, and is also largely interested in the roller flour-mill at Waynesburg, Penn. Mr. Conklin was united in marriage in Washington County, Penn., in 1855, with Delilah, daughter of Abraham and Elizabeth (Craft) Henkins, natives of Washington County. Mrs. Conklin's father was a farmer by occupation and had a family of seven children. Mr. and Mrs. Conklin have had fourteen children, of these eight are living, viz.: Ida M., wife of James R. Sargent; Lizzie L., Shriver C., Elver D., Charlie T., Annie E., Willie O., Oliver G. and Hollis P. Hollis P. was the oldest son, and met with a very untimely death by falling on a circular saw which cut him almost to pieces. He was one of the promising young men of his neighborhood, and at the time of his death was a consistent member of the Methodist Episcopal Church.

H. DRIER, farmer and stock-grower, Nineveh, Penn.—Among the successful business men of Greene County, we mention the subject of this sketch as one who started out in life in a strange land, with only twenty-four dollars in his pocket, the amount of his earthly possessions when he landed in Pittsburg, in 1865. He was born in Germany February 16, 1844, a son of William and Elizabeth (Barger) Drier. His father, who was a farmer, spent all his life in Germany and reared a family of five children, of whom the subject of our sketch was the third. He received his education in his native country, and also went to school a short time in Allegheny City, Penn., where he learned the carpenter's trade. At the close of his apprenticeship, he had saved sixty-five dollars. Mr. Drier was united in marriage, in 1867, with Sophia, daughter of William Tennemire, and they have a family of five children—William, John, Minnie, Christian and Lizzie. Mr. Drier was a good carpenter, receiving as high as twenty-three dollars for a week's wages. He worked so hard that his health became impaired, and at the suggestion of a physician he went to the country in 1873 and engaged in the huckstering business in Greene County, Penn. The next year he took his family for a visit to his native country. Returning in 1875, he started a creamery at Nineveh, Penn., where he owns a fine farm of 221 acres. Mr. Drier is a Republican. Mr. and Mrs. Drier are devoted members of the Lutheran Church.

JOSEPH DUNN, deceased, who was a farmer and stock-grower, was born in Washington County, Penn., June 2, 1801, and was a son of Samuel and Jemima (McEntyre) Dunn. His mother was a native of Pennsylvania, and his father of New Jersey. They were of English and Irish origin. Joseph was the oldest of a family of six children. He spent the greater part of his active life in Morris Township. In his chosen occupation of farming and stock-growing he met with marked success, being at the time of his death, January 6, 1856, the owner of more than 1,000 acres of land. He was married in Washington County, Penn., October 25, 1827, to Miss Elizabeth, daughter of Richard Montgomery. Her parents were of English and Irish descent. Mrs. Dunn was born in Washington County, June 10, 1807, and now resides with her youngest son in Morris Township. To Mr. and Mrs. Joseph Dunn were born six children, five living— three sons and two daughters, all prosperous and succeeding well in life.

WILLIAM DUNN, of West Union, Penn., is the youngest son of Joseph and Elizabeth (McEntyre) Dunn. He was born in Morris Township, Greene County, Penn., July 4, 1847. His mother, to whom he is greatly attached, resides with him, and although eighty years of age, is still quite bright and active. William was reared on the farm, received a common-school education, and also attended Waynesburg College for some time. He has met with more than average success in his chosen occupation of farming and stock-growing. In 1869 he married Miss Florence, daughter of Jacob Swart. Mr. and Mrs. Dunn are the parents of two children—Dora, wife of John G. Loughman, and Ida. Mr. Dunn is Republican in politics, and one of the influential citizens of his community. Mrs. Dunn is a faithful member of the Methodist Episcopal Church.

JESSE L. HAYS, merchant, Nineveh, Penn., was born at Parkersburgh, West Virginia, October 3, 1857. He is a son of Hon. James W. and Hannah (Minor) Hays, natives of Pennsylvania. His ancestors were among the early settlers of Pennsylvania. His father, who is an editor by profession, served two terms as a member of the State Senate. His family consisted of eight children, of whom Jesse L. is the seventh. Mr. Hays has spent the most of his life in Greene County, and received a good English education. He began clerking in his father's store in early life, and continued in the capacity of a salesman until he engaged in the mercantile trade at Nineveh, Penn., in September, 1882. His long experience as a salesman eminently qualifies him for the business, and he meets with deserving success.

In politics he is a Democrat, and is postmaster at Nineveh.   In 1881 Mr. Hays married Sadie, daughter of Seth Goodwin. Mrs. Hays' father was of German origin, and her mother was English, a descendant from William Penn.   They have one child, Harold G. Hays, born May 30, 1883.

SAMUEL HOPKINS, farmer and carpenter, Swart's, Penn., was born in Greene County, January 10, 1820, and is a son of Daniel and Esther (Johnson) Hopkins. His mother was a native of Washington County, Penn. His father was born in Maryland near Baltimore, and died in 1828. They were of English descent, the first Hopkins having come to this country in the Mayflower and settled at Plymouth, Mass., where Samuel Hopkins' great-grandfather was a Puritan minister. He was also an author of some note, having written several important works on religious subjects. Samuel was the fifth in a family of eight children. He spent his early life on a farm, and received his education from subscription schools. Early in life he learned the carpenter's trade, which, together with farming, he has followed through life. In 1860 he bought his present farm of 150 acres, which is well stocked and improved. In 1845 he married Miss Martha, daughter of David and Lydia (Rogers) Milliken. Mrs. Hopkins' grandfather, John Rogers, laid out the town of Rogersville, and was a prominent citizen of Greene County, where her parents died. They were among the early Presbyterian settlers. Mr. and Mrs. Samuel Hopkins are the parents of three children—Abigail, wife of John Reese; David, a farmer; and Margaret, wife of Dr. Hamilton Borroughs. In politics Mr. Hopkins is a Republican. Following in the footsteps of his grandfathers, who were both soldiers in the Revolutionary war, he enlisted in 1862 in Company A, One Hundred and Sixty-eighth Pennsylvania Volunteer Infantry, and served one year. He and wife are members of the Methodist Episcopal Church, in which he has served as trustee and superintendent of the Sabbath-school.

D. W. HOPKINS, farmer and stock-grower, Swart's, Penn., was born October 31, 1850, on the farm where he now resides in Morris Township. His parents, William and Ellen (Simpson) Hopkins, were natives of this county, and of English and Irish descent. His father was born April 22, 1816, and was the son of Daniel and Esther (Johnson) Hopkins. He died August 12, 1870, being at that time owner of 148 acres of well improved land. His family consisted of five children, three daughters and two sons, four of whom grew to maturity. D. W. was the third in the family, spent his early life on the home farm, and chose farming as his occupation, in which he has engaged very successfully. On February 3, 1880, he married Miss Mary, daughter of Jasper and Jane (Lightner) Bane. Mr. and Mrs. Hopkins have an interesting family of two children—

Nellie Maud and Sarah Lizzie. Their mother is a devoted member of the Methodist Episcopal Church. Mr. Hopkins is a Republican in politics, and one of the enterprising young men of his township.

JOSEPH HUFFMAN, farmer and stock-grower, Nineveh, Penn., was born in Greene County, Penn., July 7, 1838. His parents, John and Nancy (Johns) Huffman, were of English descent. His father was a farmer all his life. Joseph is next to the youngest of a family of eight children, and was reared on the farm in this county, where he attended the common school. He is quite successful as a farmer, and owns a good farm of 150 acres adjoining the village of Nineveh. He sold the lots on which about half of this village now stands. In 1869 Mr. Huffman married Miss Nancy, daughter of John Reese. Mrs. Huffman is also a native of this county. Their family consists of four children—Lizzie, R. E. Lee, Jessie Blanche and John D. Mr. Huffman is a Democrat, and has served as school director in his township. He and wife are zealous members of the Methodist Episcopal Church, in which Mr. Huffman is assistant superintendent of the Sabbath-school.

OTHO IAMS, farmer and stock-grower, Swart's, Penn., was born on Ruff's Creek, this county, September 4, 1846, and is a son of Thomas and Delilah (Huffman) Iams. His grandfather, Otho Iams, came to Greene County from New Jersey in 1790, and settled in Morris Township, and was one of the most prominent and successful farmers of his day. Thomas Iams, his father, died in 1881, leaving to his three sons about 600 acres of valuable land. Otho is the second in a family of seven children. He was reared in Morris Township, where he has been a successful farmer through life. In June, 1881, he was united in marriage with Miss Sarah, daughter of Jasper Bane, and they are the parents of one child—Allen. Mr. Iams is an enthusiastic Democrat, and one of the most enterprising citizens of the community. His wife is a devoted member of the Methodist Episcopal Church.

J. L. IAMS, Swart's, Penn., is a farmer, stock-grower and school teacher. He was born in Morris Township, this county, January 2, 1857, and is a son of Thomas and Delilah (Huffman) Iams. His parents were natives of Greene County, and of English and German ancestry. His father was a prominent and successful farmer and an influential Democrat during his lifetime. His party elected him to several prominent county offices—among others, that of treasurer. He also served a term on the bench as associate judge. Judge Iams and wife were the parents of eight children, five of whom are living. Benjamin H. enlisted in the Eighteenth Pennsylvania Cavalry, under Captain James Hughes, and died in the service of his country. The five living are all residents of this county, except F. P. Iams, Esq., of Pittsburg, Penn. James L. was reared on the farm in Morris

Township, and attended the district school. He also spent some time in Waynesburg College. In 1877 he married Miss Belle S., daughter of Jacob Swart. Mr. Iams is one of the enterprising young men of the county, is an enthusiastic Democrat, and a member of the State Democratic Central Committee.

HENRY LIGHTNER, retired farmer, Nineveh, Penn., was born in Center Township, this county, January 30, 1823, and is the oldest son of George and Sarah (Woods) Lightner. His parents were also natives of Center Township, and among the earliest settlers of the county. His father died in 1867. The family have usually been farmers; some of them, however, have entered the different professions and met with success. Henry's grandfather, Micajah Woods, was an Orderly Sergeant in the Revolutionary war. The subject of our sketch was reared in Center Township until nine years of age. He then came with his parents to Morris Township, where he grew to manhood. He attended the common school and chose farming as a business, in which he has met with marked success. Mr. Lightner's farm consists of 300 acres of well improved land. He was united in marriage in Athens County, Ohio, December 12, 1850, with Eliza J., daughter of Thomas Jefferson and Elizabeth Tewksbury, who were of English descent. Mr. and Mrs. Lightner have a family of nine children—Thomas Jefferson, George M., Samuel, Micajah, William, James, Martha Ellen, Mary Jane and Bertha Ann. Their parents are leading members of the Methodist Episcopal Church.

DANIEL LOUGHMAN, retired farmer and stock-grower, of West Union, Penn., was born June 15, 1813, on the farm where he now resides. His parents, Frederick and Catharine (Hammers) Loughman, came to this county in 1812. They were natives of Maryland, and of German origin. His father was a blacksmith and wagon-maker in early life. He subsequently engaged in farming, and was among the pioneer settlers of Morris Township, where he spent most of his life. He reared a family of thirteen children, of whom Daniel is the twelfth. He was reared on the home farm attending the subscription schools, and has devoted his time principally to agriculture. He owns a well improved farm where he now resides. Mr. Loughman was united in marriage, January 15, 1833, with Rachel, daughter of John and Mary (Red) Stagner, who were of German descent. She was born in Maryland in 1812. Mr. and Mrs. Loughman are the parents of six children—Thaddeus, a farmer; Frederick, a blacksmith; Mary, wife of Oliver McVay; Susan, wife of Warren Conklin; Adaline, wife of S. B. Clutter, and John, (deceased). Mr. Loughman is a Democrat, and he and his wife are prominent members of the West Union Cumberland Presbyterian Church.

WILLIAM LOUGHMAN, West Union, Penn., was born in Morris Township, this county, October 22, 1822, and is a son of David and Christine (Fonner) Loughman. His mother was born in Ireland. His father, who was of German origin and a native of Maryland, spent most of his life as a farmer in Greene County, Penn., where he died in Morris Township. William, the second in a family of seven children, was reared on the home farm, and attended the district schools. He chose farming as an occupation, and when twenty-one years of age he received from his father seventy acres of land which, through industry and a strong determination to succeed, he has increased to 400 acres, well stocked and improved. Mr. Loughman has been twice married: first, in 1846, to Mary J., daughter of William Day, and they were the parents of three children —Lucretia A., Elymus and Irvin. Their mother died in 1852. For his second wife, Mr. Loughman married Elizabeth, daughter of John and Mary (Miller) Longdon, and widow of Harrison Corger. Her parents were natives of Washington County, and of English descent. To Mr. and Mrs. Loughman have been born three children: Hannah C., wife of John Conger; Alice, wife of John Auld, and John G. Mrs. Loughman is a member of the Mount Hermon Baptist Church; and her husband is a Cumberland Presbyterian, in which church he has been an elder for sixteen years, and has also served as superintendent of the Sabbath-school. Mr. Loughman stands high in the community as an enterprising citizen and a sound business man. He never sued or was sued by any one.

DANIEL LOUGHMAN, farmer and stock-grower, Sycamore, Penn., was born in Morris Township, Greene County, Pennsylvania, April 25, 1832. He is a son of Henry and Nancy (Smith) Loughman, also natives of this county, and of Dutch origin. The Loughmans, who are among the prominent citizens of Greene County, have usually been farmers, and were among the early settlers in Morris Township. Mr. Daniel Loughman is the second in a family of ten children, and attended the schools of his township. He makes a success of farming, and is the owner of a good farm of 307 acres where he resides. In 1853 Mr. Loughman married Miss Sarah, daughter of Dennis and Matilda (Huffman) Iams, who were of German origin. Her father was born in Greene County, Penn., and met with great success as a farmer. Mr. and Mrs. Loughman are the parents of ten children—Dennis, George, Belle, Matilda, Dora, Jackson, Ida, Charley, Mattie and Bertha. Their mother is a devoted member of the Baptist Church. In politics Mr. Loughman is a Democrat. He is greatly interested in the educational affairs of his township, and has served as school director for several years.

SILAS M. McCULLOUGH, farmer and stock-grower, Nineveh, Penn., was born in Morris Township, November 9, 1852. He is the only child of John and Caroline (Jennings) McCullough, natives of Greene County, and of Dutch and English descent. They were married in 1852, and his mother died in 1854. His father, who was born October 21, 1832, was a son of Samuel and Elizabeth (Shape) McCullough, who were of Dutch origin. Silas grew to manhood in Morris Township, receiving his education in the district schools. He is a self-made man, and through great industry and economy has been prospered in his farming, which he has made his life work. He owns a good farm of seventy-three acres. In 1877 he married Miss Jennie, daughter of Elymas and Mary (Ross) Pettit, who were of English descent. To Mr. and Mrs. McCullough have been born five children—Clarence A., Grace M., Oscar Lee, Jessie Blanche and Elymas. Mr. and Mrs. McCullough are leading members of the Methodist Episcopal Church, in which he is a trustee and prominent worker.

OLIVER McVAY, a prominent business man of West Union, Penn., was born in Morris Township, Greene County, August 7, 1842. His parents, Silas and Dorcas (Jennings) McVay, were natives of Washington County, Penn., and of Scotch-Irish lineage. His father was a stone-mason by occupation, and later in life he engaged in farming and huckstering for many years. He died in Washington County. His family consisted of twelve children, eleven of whom grew to maturity. Oliver was the fourth in the family, and was reared in Greene and Washington counties, receiving a common-school education. In 1870 he engaged in merchandising, his present business, which he makes a great success. In 1867 he married Mary, daughter of Daniel Loughman. Her mother's maiden name was Rachel Stigner, whose father, Frederick Stigner, was among the earliest settlers of the county. Mr. and Mrs McVay have one child, Silas E., who married Elizabeth, daughter of Elias Conger. They have one child, Pearl. In politics Mr. McVay is a Republican. September 16, 1861, he enlisted in Company D, Eighty-Fifth Pennsylvania Volunteer Infantry, and was discharged for disability in 1862. He is a member of the G. A. R. Post. Mr. and Mrs. McVay are prominent members of the West Union Cumberland Presbyterian Church.

THOMAS PATTERSON, deceased, was born March 17, 1809, in Morris Township, Greene County, where he spent his entire life. His parents, Mark and Nancy (Gregory) Patterson, were natives of Ireland, and among the early settlers of this county. His father, who was a farmer, reared a family of nine children, of whom Thomas was the third. He received his education in the district schools. He spent all his life on a farm, devoting his time chiefly to farming and stock-growing, and at the time of his death, 1876, was the owner of a good farm of 200 acres. In 1831 he married Miss Margaret

Hopkins, and they were the parents of nine children—Daniel, Levi, Mark, John, Esther, Eliza, Catharine, Mary and Margaret. Mr. and Mrs. Patterson were prominent members of the Methodist Episcopal Church. In politics Mr. Patterson was a Republican.

ELYMAS PETTIT, farmer and stock-grower, Nineveh, Penn., was born March 27, 1834. He is a son of Charles and Keziah (Coe) Pettit, natives of Washington County, Penn. Elymas is the fourth in a family of eight children, seven of whom are still living. He was reared on the farm and attended the district school. He made choice of farming as his life-work, and is now the owner of a well improved farm of 157 acres, and a neat, substantial dwelling. In 1856 he married Mary, daughter of Isaac and Sarah (McGlumphy) Ross. Mrs. Pettit is of Irish descent, and is a faithful member of the Baptist Church. Their union has been blessed with three children—Melissa, wife of Henry Breese; Jennie, wife of Silas McCullough, and Charles F., a student at Delaware College in Ohio. In politics Mr. Pettit is a Democrat. In 1862 he enlisted in the first Ringold battalion, and served two years and ten months, being discharged for disability, at Cumberland, Maryland, in 1865.

MATTHIAS PETTIT, farmer, Swart's, Penn., who was born April 23, 1831, is a prominent farmer and stock-grower of Morris Township. He is a son of Charles and Keziah (Coe) Pettit. His father, who was a farmer by occupation, was born July 2, 1801, and died in 1871. He spent most of his life in Greene County, where he reared a family of eight children—five girls and three boys. Matthias is the oldest in the family, and was reared in Morris Township. He has been engaged in agricultural pursuits from his youth, and is the owner of a well improved farm of 125 acres where he now resides. He was married in this county, December 11, 1868, to Miss Ruth, daughter of Nathan Penn. Mrs. Pettit's father was a farmer, of English descent. Her mother's maiden name was Rachel McCullough, who was of Irish descent. Mr. and Mrs. Pettit have a family of four children—Jennie, Mary, Rachel and Richard. In politics Mr. Pettit is a Democrat. He and wife are leading members of the Baptist Church.

THOMAS M. ROSS, ex-county commissioner, Sycamore, Penn., is a prominent farmer and stock-grower of Morris Township. He was born in Washington Township, Greene County, Penn., March 10, 1831, and is a son of Jacob and Abigail (Ross) Ross. Though of the same name, his parents were not related. They were natives of this county, and of English and German origin. His father, who was a farmer, died in 1856. Thomas M. was the sixth in a family of nine children. He was reared on the farm in Richhill Township, where he attended the district schools and made farming his main occupation. He was united in marriage, March

13, 1856, with Sarah Elizabeth, daughter of Benjamin Franklin and Mary (Goodwin) Rickey, who were of English and Dutch origin. Mr. and Mrs. Ross are the parents of eleven children, ten living—Celesta Ann, wife of Benjamin F. Orr; Hiram Franklin, who married Dora, daughter of Daniel Loughman; Catharine I. V., wife of John Church; Philena, wife of Jesse F. Hill; Sadie A., Timothy J., Mary, Emma, Arthur, Stella and Thomas L. A. (deceased). In 1875 Mr. Ross sold his farm and engaged in the business of hucktering until 1881, when he was elected commissioner of Greene County. In 1884 he bought his present farm of 155 acres. He has served three years as director of the poor. He belongs to the Masonic fraternity and the I. O. O. F. Mr. Ross took an active interest in the Granger movement. He is a public-spirited, progressive citizen. He belongs to the Bates' Fork Baptist Church, of which his wife, who died in 1887, was also a devoted member.

REUBEN SANDERS, farmer and stock-grower, West Union, Penn., was born February 17, 1834, on the farm where he now resides. He is a son of Reuben and Fannie F. (Rutan) Sanders. Reuben Sanders, Sr., was an early settler and prominent farmer of Morris Township. His family consisted of thirteen children, ten of whom grew to maturity. The subject of our sketch, who was next to the youngest in the family, was reared on the farm he now owns, and attended the district school. He has made farming his occupazion through life, and is the owner of 182 acres of land well stocked and improved. In 1857 he was united in marriage with Miss Margaret, daughter of Charles and Keziah Pettit. Mrs. Sanders is a sister of Matthias and Elymas Pettit, prominent farmers in this township. Mr. and Mrs. Sanders have one child—Hester Ann, who is the wife of Jonathan Supler. Mrs. Sanders is a faithful member of the Baptist Church.

GEORGE SHAPE.—Among the descendants of the early settlers we mention the name of George Shape, one of the representative farmers and stock-growers of Greene County. He was born in 1842, on the farm where he resides in Morris Township, and is a son of John and Elizabeth (Huffman) Shape, the former a native of Maryland. His grandfather, Peter Shape, came from Maryland to Greene County, Penn., in 1814, and settled on a farm. Here George's father was raised, and spent his life as a farmer. He died in 1858, in his sixty-third year. He reared a family of twelve children, eleven of whom are now living. They are—Peter, Katie, Mary, Julia Ann, Elizabeth, Reasin, George, Eliza J., William, Minerva, Deborah and S. B. Their parents were members of the Cumberland Presbyterian Church. George was the seventh in the family. He has made farming his business, owning at present a fine farm of 135 acres. His brothers are all farmers, except Reasin, who is a first-class carpenter; he also owns a farm where he resides in this township. George is a member of the Cumberland Presbyterian Church at Nineveh, and has served as elder.

JACOB SHOUP, farmer and stock-grower, Swart's, Penn., was born in Fayette County, Penn., May 24, 1825. His parents, John and Margaret (Miller) Shoup, were also natives of Fayette County, and of English and German origin. His father was a millwright and miller by trade and occupation, and followed his chosen business through life. His family consisted of three children. Jacob was the second, and spent the first sixteen years of his life on the home farm in Fayette County. He attended the common schools in Greene County, and chose farming as his occupation, in which he has met with more than average success. Through his own enterprise and industry he has secured a fine farm of 117 acres. In 1860 Mr. Shoup was united in marriage with Miss Catharine, daughter of Frederick and Rebecca (Stewart) Hunnell, natives of this county. Mr. and Mrs. Shoup have four children—William Spencer, Rebecca Ann, wife of Samuel McCullough; George E. and Ulysses Grant. Mr. Shoup is a Republican in politics, and he and Mrs. Shoup belong to the Methodist Episcopal Church.

HUGH SIMPSON, farmer and stock-grower, Swart's, Penn., was born in Morris Township, this county, February 21, 1833, and is a son of John and Mary (Auld) Simpson. His father, a native of this county, of Irish descent, was a mechanic, and died in 1846. Hugh was the oldest of a family of five children, was reared on a farm and received a common-school education. He chose farming as an occupation, and has engaged therein all his life. He is the owner of a well-stocked and improved farm consisting of 162 acres. He was united in marriage, in 1859, with Esther, daughter of Thomas Patterson, and they are the parents of three children—Waitman T., Annie and Maggie. Mr. and Mrs. Simpson are prominent members of the Methodist Episcopal Church, in which he is trustee, and superintendent of the Sabbath-school. In politics Mr. Simpson is a Republican. He has served as school director in his township.

J. W. SIMPSON, farmer and stock-grower, Swart's, Penn., was born in Morris Township, this county, April 23, 1842, and is a son of William and Ruth (Fulton) Simpson. His mother was a native of Washington County, Penn. His father was born on the farm where J. W. resides. This farm first came into the possession of the family through their grandfather, Rev. John Simpson, who was born in Ireland, March 13, 1758. He landed in America August 12, 1791, and came to Greene County in the fall of 1796. He married Miss Rebecca Gregory, who was born in Farmingah, Ireland, August 12, 1767. In 1816 they opened their dwelling as a place for public worship, and the neighbors held meetings there for near forty years.

J. W. Simpson was an only child, was reared on the farm and received a common-school education. He has made a business of farming and has met with success. His farm consists of 197 acres of land well stocked and improved. He was married, September 27, 1866, to America Ann, daughter of Jacob and Permina (Allum) Swart, who were of English origin. To Mr. and Mrs. Simpson have been born seven children—Carrie, Mary, Ruth, Swart, Flora, John and William. Their mother is a zealous member of the Methodist Episcopal Church. In politics Mr Simpson is a Republican. In 1864 he enlisted in Company E, Fourteenth Pennsylvania Cavalry, and was discharged May 30, 1865. He belongs to the Masonic fraternity. He is a member of the Waynesburg Encampment, No. 119, and Waynesburg Lodge, No. 467, I. O. O. F., and also of the G. A. R., Post No. 367, Department of Pennsylvania.

JACOB SWART, farmer and stock-grower, Swart's, Penn., was born in Washington County, Penn., December 25, 1820. His parents, Phillip and Ascnah (Walton) Swart, were also natives of Washington County, and of Dutch and Irish ancestry. Jacob is the second in a family of nine children. He was reared on a farm in Amwell Township, where he received his education in one of the old log school-houses of that day. He chose farming as a business, to which he devoted his entire time until forty years of age. He came to Greene County in 1842, and was united in marriage, May 5, with Paulina, daughter of Charles and Jemima (Barnhart) Allum, who were of English descent. Mr. and Mrs. Swart have twenty-seven grandchildren. They have a family of four sons and five daughters— America A., wife of J. W. Simpson; Amos C., a farmer; Florence B., wife of William Dunn; Virginia I., wife of James Iams, and Senie Jane, Mary E., John N., Henry Clay and Franklin L., deceased. Mr. Swart bought a farm in Washington Township in 1843, and in 1880 he bought his present farm. In 1861 he purchased an interest in a general store, and they continued in business together for two years, when Mr. Swart became sole proprietor. He continued in the mercantile business for fifteen years, and sold his store in 1877. Mr. Swart is a Republican, but is always willing to vote for a good man for office, independent of party or politics. He has been postmaster at Swart's for the past seventeen years. Mr. Swart is a self-made man, his success in life having been due largely to his own enterprise and industry. He is a progressive citizen, ever ready to aid a good enterprise, and was one of those most instrumental in the building of the W. & W. Railroad. He was a member of the building committee and superintendent of the road for two years.

WILLIAM SIMPSON THROCKMORTON, physician and surgeon, Nineveh, Penn., was born March 2, 1838. He is a son of Mofford and Nancy (Simpson) Throckmorton, who were of English and Irish origin.   His mother was born in this county, and his father was a native of New Jersey, and among the early settlers of Greene County, Penn., where he died in 1884.   The Doctor is the ninth in a family of thirteen children, and was reared on the farm in Center Township, where he obtained his early education.   He subsequently attended Allegheny College, but afterwards completed his collegiate studies at Waynesburg College, Penn.   He chose the practice of medicine as his profession, and in 1863 entered Jefferson Medical College at Philadelphia, where he graduated in 1865.   He then began the practice of his profession at Nineveh, in Greene County, where he has been actively engaged ever since, with the exception of the time spent at the lectures.   The Doctor has thoroughly prepared himself for his work, having taken a regular course of lecturers in five of the most noted medical colleges in the United States.   He has an extensive library and keeps his office well supplied with the leading publications in medical science.   He is much attached to his profession, and also takes an active interest in the welfare of his town and community.   He is a leading member of the State Medical Association, and belongs to the Greene County Medical Society, of which he has been president and corresponding secretrry. He was married in 1866, to Miss Caroline M., daughter of Jesse Hill, of Waynesburg, Penn., and they have four children—Jessie, Charley, Willie and Mofford.   Doctor Throckmorton and wife are members of the Methodist Episcopal Church, in which he is trustee, steward, superintendent of the Sabbath-school, and has been an official member for thirty years.   He has been identified with the Masonic and Odd Fellowship fraternities and is forward in every good word and work, a blessing to his generation and community.

PERRY TOWNSHIP.

HON. JOHN BLAIR, the present member of the Legislature from Greene County, Penn., is a farmer and stock-grower by occupation, and was born in Wayne Township, December 25, 1841.   He is the only son of Isaac and Elizabeth (Ross) Blair, the former a native of Greene County, and the latter of Crawford County, Penn., and of Dutch and Irish extraction.   His father, who was a farmer and stone-mason, was born in 1810 and died August 26, 1846.   Mr. Blair was reared on the home farm in this county, and attended the district schools. He has been a successful farmer all his life, and owns a fine farm of 250 acres. In 1861 he was united in marriage, in Monongalia County, W. Va., with Miss Amy, daughter of Jonathan and Charlotte (Bightodah) Brown. Mr. and Mrs. Blair's children are William F., G. W. W., a teacher; Anna, wife of Oliver Lemley; Belle, wife of William Wright; L. L., Olive, C. B. and Ross B. Mr. and Mrs. Blair are members of the Disciple Church. He is a Democrat, and was elected to the House of Representatives in 1886. He had previously held the office of justice of the peace for five years, and was school director for a period of twelve years.

T. W. BOYDSTON, proprietor of the Mount Morris Tannery, was born in West Virginia, November 1, 1844. He is the son of E. L. and Ruhama (Jackson) Boydston, who were of English and Irish origin. They resided in Dunkard Township, this county, where the father died in 1853, leaving a family of six children. Of these the subject of our sketch is the oldest, and was reared in West Virginia, where he received his education in the Military Academy at Morgantown. Early in life he learned the printer's trade, which he followed successfully for some time. He had charge of the printing for the Legislature at Harrisburg, Penn. Since 1877 he has been engaged in his present business at Mount Morris. In 1862 Mr. Boydston enlisted in Company K, Fourteenth West Virginia Infantry, in which he served first as a private, then as Seargeant, and Second Lieutenant. He was united in marriage, in 1877, with Hannah, daughter of James L. Donley. They are the parents of four children—Clara, Sallie, Frederick and Virginia. Mr. and Mrs. Boydston are members of the Methodist Episcopal Church, in which he holds several official positions, and is also greatly interested in the Sabbath-school. He is a Republican, also member of the I. O. O. F., and is Quartermaster of G. A. R. Post, No. 450.

THORNTON E. BOYDSTON, Mount Morris, Penn.—Among the most highly respected citizens of Perry Township is the gentleman whose name heads this sketch. He was born at Mount Morris, October 12, 1833, and is a son of B. and Mary (Wiley) Boydston. His father was also a native of this county, and his mother was born in West Virginia. His father was a farmer all his life, and reared a family of twelve children. The subject of this sketch was next to the youngest in the family, and was reared in his native township. He received his education in the common schools, and engaged in farming as his life work. Mr. Boydston has been successful in his business affairs, and now owns a fine farm of 160 acres. In 1858 he married Susannah, daughter of Joseph R. Donley. Their children are—Emma, wife of L. C. Evans; Sarah A., wife of Lewis Lemley; Mary, Charles B., James and Anna M. Mr. and Mrs. Boydston are consistent members of the Methodist Episcopal Church, in which he serves as trustee. He is a Republican in politics, and has been a member of the school board in his township.

O. J. BROWN, farmer and stock-grower, Mount Morris, Penn., was born in Perry Township, Greene County, Penn., May 21, 1852, and is a son of Reuben and Rebecca (McClure) Brown, also natives of this county. His ancestors were early settlers of Dunkard Township, and of Irish, Welsh and German extraction. His father is a prominent farmer in this county. The subject of our sketch is the youngest in a family of five children. He was reared on the farm and received a good English education. He subsequently attended Jefferson and Waynesburg colleges, and made a special study of surveying and civil engineering. He turned his attention to farming and stock-growing, however, and has a fine little farm of sixty-five acres. In 1884 Mr. Brown married Miss Mary, daughter of Jacob and Fannie (Lemmon) Eakin, and they have one daughter—Hallie May. They are Methodists in religion, and Mr. Brown is superintendent of the Sabbath-school in that church. He is a Democrat in politics, and judge of elections in 1888.

REUBEN BROWN, is a descendant of the early settlers of Greene County, his ancestors having settled near the source of Dunkard Creek in 1801, and removed to Perry Township in 1812. Reuben still owns and resides on the farm where they settled, near Mount Morris, Penn. He was born August 26, 1816, on this farm, where he has spent all his life, except the short time he lived in Monongalia County, W. Va. Here he grew to manhood, receiving his early education in the old log school-house. His father was Reuben Brown, and his mother's maiden name was Rebecca John. They were of Welsh and German origin. His father was born in Loudoun County, Va., was a farmer by occupation, and died in Greene County in 1867, at the advanced age of ninety-seven years. The history of the family shows them to have been farmers and stock-growers, and usually successful in their business affairs. Reuben is one of the prosperous farmers of his township, and owns 200 acres of valuable land. He was married September 20, 1839, to Rebecca McClure, who is a native of Dunkard Township, and the daughter of William and Jane (King) McClure. Her ancestors, who were of Irish extraction, came to Greene County in 1817 and settled in Dunkard Township. Mr. and Mrs. Brown are the parents of five children—James M., who is now engaged in farming and railroading in the West; Susan C., wife of B. Ross; O. J., a farmer in Perry Township; Samantha Jane, who was the wife of L. A. Morris (deceased); and William, who was shot through mistake by a deserter in the late Rebellion. Mr. and Mrs. Brown are active members of the Baptist Church. He takes an active interest in the schools, and has frequently served as school director in his township.

S. A. COWELL, farmer and stock-grower, Mount Morris, Penn., was born in Whiteley Township, Greene County, Penn., October 15, 1864. He is a son of Solomon and Eliza (Mike) Cowell, who were of English extraction. His mother was a native of West Virginia. His father, who was a farmer and stock drover, was born in Greene County, Penn., where he died, leaving a family of fourteen children. Of these the subject of our sketch is the youngest, and was reared in this county, receiving his education in the common schools. He is one of the industrious and enterprising young farmers of his township, and owns a good farm of ninety-eight acres. In 1885 Mr. Cowell was united in marriage with Miss Sarah, daughter of Dennis Fox, a prominent farmer in Perry Township. They have two bright and interesting children—Vincent Earl and Dennis Floyd. Mr. Cowell is a Republican in politics.

D. L. DONLEY, farmer and stock-grower, Mount. Morris, Penn. Among the most prominent members of the large family of Donleys in this county, none are more noted for their liberality and progressive spirit than D. L. Donley, the subject of our sketch. He was born in Perry Township, Greene County, Penn., June 11, 1836, and is the son of J. R. and Sarah (Lemley) Donley. His mother was the daughter of David and Ruhana (Snider) Lemley, and of German and Irish origin. His father is a native of Dunkard Township and is still living at the advanced age of seventy-six years. D. L. Donley's grandparents, James and Susannah (Robinson) Donley, came from Washington County, to Greene County in 1790, and settled on a farm. The subject of our sketch is a nephew of Hon. Patrick Donley, and a cousin of ex-congressman J. B. Donley, of Waynesburg, Penn. He was reared in Perry Township, attended the common schools and early in life was put to work on the farm. He has been successful in his business and is the owner of 500 acres of valuable land. It was through Mr. Donley's influence that the oil field has been opened up in that section, and the largest gas and oil wells are situated on his land near Mount Morris. Mr. Donley was married in West Virginia, August 20, 1861, to Miss Louisa, daughter of Alexander and Sarah (Hague) Evans. Her father was born near Garard's Fort in January, 1806, and is the son of Eleazar and Martha (Vance) Evans. Mrs. Evans is a native of New Jersey and Mr. Evans of Loudoun County, Virginia. He is a retired farmer, owning over 400 acres of land'. Mr. and Mrs. Donley have seven children—Laura, wife of Dr. Owen, of Oak Forest, Penn.; Josephine, wife of D. B. Adams, of Waynesburg, Penn.; Evans, Leanna, Meda, Ellsworth J. and Edward G. Mr. and Mrs. Donley are prominent members of the Methodist Episcopal Church. He takes great interest in educational matters, and has served as school director at Mount Morris.

DENNIS FOX, who is probably as well known as any private citizen of Greene County, is a successful farmer and stock-grower, and was born April 5, 1827, on the farm where he resides. His parents, Henry and Susan (Dulaney) Fox, were descended from the Dutch, and natives of this county. Peter and Mary (Thomas) Fox, his grandparents, came to this county from New Jersey, and settled on the farm which Dennis now owns. Here Peter Fox planted a little willow sprout which he brought with him, and the tree is now twenty-one feet in circumference, by actual measurement. This tree is to remain standing, as Dennis says, a monument to the memory of him who planted it so many years ago. Mr. Fox has a fine farm of nearly 500 acres, well stocked and improved, his barns being among the best in Perry Township. He was united in marriage, January 18, 1848, with Miss Betsey, daughter of David and Elizabeth (McCann) John. She is of Irish and English extraction. Mr. and Mrs. Fox have ten children—Henry, David, Osborn, Kinsey, James, Marion, Susan, wife of Spencer Cowell; Sarah Jane Cowell, and John and Elizabeth, deceased. Mr. Fox is a Republican in politics.

SAMUEL GUTHRIE, a farmer and stock-grower of Perry Township, was born in Greene County, Penn., December 18, 1820, and is a son of Archibald and Elizabeth (Lemley) Guthrie, also natives of Greene County, and of Irish and Dutch origin. His father, who was a farmer and a pioneer settler in Whiteley Township, died in this county in 1845. Samuel is the seventh in a family of ten children and grew to maturity on the home farm, attending the subscription schools. He has successfully followed farming as his chief pursuit, and is the owner of 133 acres of valuable land where he resides near Kirby P. O. Mr. Guthrie's wife was Miss Nancy, daughter of James and Nancy (Stephens) Patterson. Her parents were natives of this county, and of Irish and German descent. Mr. and Mrs. Guthrie's children are—Elizabeth, wife of Alfred Moore, of West Virginia; James P., a farmer; Hannah Martha, wife of Franklin Henderson; and Priscilla, deceased. Mr. Guthrie is a Republican. His wife is a devoted member of the Methodist Episcopal Church.

GEORGE W. GUTHRIE, farmer and stock-grower, Kirby, Penn., was born in Whiteley Township, this county, March 26, 1848. His parents, Solomon and Elizabeth (Fry) Guthrie, are also natives of Greene County, and of English and German origin. His father, for many years a farmer and stock-grower, has now retired from the more active duties of life and resides in Whiteley Township. George is the fifth in a family of six children, and was reared on the farm in Whiteley Township. He is an industrious farmer, paying close attention to his business, and is the owner of a good farm of 123 acres. In 1870 he married Adaline, daughter of John and Hannah (Rose) Cowell, natives of Greene County, and of Dutch extraction. Mr. and Mrs. Guthrie have one daughter—Ida Estella. They are members of the Southern Methodist Church, in which Mr. Guthrie is trustee, and superintendent of the Sabbath-school. He is a Republican, and has served as assessor in his township.

CYRENIUS HAINES, farmer and stock-grower, was born in Greene County, Penn., April 1, 1823. His parents, George and Jane (McCord) Haines, were natives of New York. His mother was of Scotch and Dutch ancestry. His father, who was of English extraction, was a farmer by occupation, and died in 1850 in his seventy-seventh year. Cyrenius is the eighth in a family of eleven children and was reared on the farm in this county, where he attended the common school. Early in life he spent some time as a bookseller but subsequently turned his attention to farming and stock-growing, and is the owner of a farm of 255 acres, well stocked and improved. Mr. Haines has been twice married. His first wife died in 1851, but a few weeks after her marriage. His second wife, whom he married in Virginia in 1852, was Mary Ann, daughter of Burton and Nancy (Sutton) Pride. She is of English origin. Her father was born in 1800 in Virginia. Mr. and Mrs. Haines' children are Francis B., George D., William G., Lewis Spencer, D. D., a farmer; John J. and Melinda A. They have eleven grandchildren— Lewis E., Emerson, John C. and Clarence, children of their oldest son; Franklin, Margaret, Cora Bell and Viola, whose father is George D.; and Ida E., William L., Cyrenius, George and Sarah A., whose father is William G.; Noah L. and D., whose father is Lewis S. Mr. and Mrs. Haines are Methodists in religion. He has been trustee in the church and superintendent of the Sabbath-school.

JACOB HATFIELD, physician and surgeon, Mount Morris, Penn., was born in Monongahela Township, this county, December 19, 1839, and is a son of G. W. and Mary (Richey) Hatfield, who are of English descent and natives of Greene and Fayette counties, respectively. Dr. Hatfield's father is a farmer by occupation. Of his seven children, six are now living, of whom the Doctor is the oldest. He was reared with his parents on the farm in Whiteley Township, where he attended the district schools. At an early age he manifested an inclination for the study of medicine, and went to Columbiana County, Ohio, where he took a regular course. In 1864 he began his professional career at Mount Morris, Penn., where he has since remained in active practice. Dr. Hatfield is very much attached to his profession, and has thoroughly informed himself in its different branches. He has successfully performed several extremely difficult surgical operations. On May 12, 1863, Dr. Hatfield was united in marriage with Caroline, daughter of Henry Morris, of

Whiteley Township. Mrs. Hatfield is of German origin. They have three children—G. W., Maggie N. and Henry Morris. Their oldest son is a physician and is now in practice with his father. He was born and reared in Mount Morris. He first studied medicine with his father, after which he went to Baltimore and attended the College of Physicians and Surgeons, for two years; subsequently took the regular course at the Western Pennsylvania Medical College, at Pittsburgh, Penn., graduating in 1887. Dr. Hatfield and wife are prominent members of the Methodist Episcopal Church, in which he has held various official offices. He is a Republican, and has served on the school board at Mount Morris, Penn.

G. F. HEADLEY, teacher and surveyor, Brock, Penn., was born in Perry Township, Greene County, Penn., June 27, 1853. His parents, Ephraim and Maria (Haines) Headley, were also natives of this county, and of Scotch and English extraction. His father, a prominent farmer in Perry Township, is a son of Jesse and Maria (Cox) Headley. G. F. Headley's grandfather was born in Greene County, Penn. His great-grandfather, Ephraim Headley, was among the pioneer settlers of New Jersey, and one of the first farmers and hunters who came to Greene County, Penn., while it was still inhabited by the Indians. The family have usually been farmers and drovers. The subject of our sketch grew up on the farm, being the second in a family of three children. He attended the High School at Mount Morris, Penn., and also took a college course. For thirteen years Mr. Headley has been successfully engaged as a teacher. He has also given considerable attention to the study of surveying, and devotes a part of his time to that work. He is also a farmer and stock-grower by occupation and owns a good farm where he resides. In 1879 Mr. Headley married Miss S. A., daughter of John Conner, of Perry Township. Mrs. Headley is of German and Irish origin. Their children are Florence B., Julius B., Fred and Gertrude. Mr. Headley is a Republican. He and his wife are members of the Methodist Episcopal Church. In connection with our subject's sketch, we give a brief sketch of his ancestor's advent into Greene County, Penn.: Sometime prior to the American Revolution, the great-great-great-grandfather, Richard Headlee, who was an English sailor, in the the service of Great Britain, concluded to desert the standard of the Stuarts, and seek an asylum in the wilds of North America. After making his escape from the British service, he settled in New Jersey, where he afterwards married. But according to English law, "Once an Englishman always an Englishman," he was not allowed to enjoy the quiet of his new home very long. The British authorities finding out his whereabouts, had him arrested, which was done by a party of twenty British sailors, not however until he had given them an exhibition of his prowess, and felled several of them to the ground in good old British style. He was overpowered, taken back into service and kept seven years from his family. But his long service as a sailor made him familiar with the seaport towns and the American coast, so taking advantage of the situation in the darkness of the night, while near shore, he leaped overboard and swam ashore, and finally united with his family. We know little of his family, except that his son John, who was G. F. Headley's great-great-grandfather, died while in the Patriot army, he being old enough to have a son engaged in the same struggle. Robert Headlee, a nephew of John, was in the expedition sent against the Indians, who committed the Wyoming massacre. Ephraim, G. F. Headley's great-grandfather, lived during the Revolution in New Jersey, not far from Trenton, being within sound of the battle fought at that place. After the war he emigrated to North Carolina, but disliking the country, he removed to Greene County, Penn., where he reared a large family.

W. O. HEADLEE, farmer and teacher, Mount Morris, Penn., was born January 27, 1858, in Perry Township, where he grew to manhood. He was reared on the farm with his parents, receiving a common school education. He also attended the High School at Mount Morris. Mr. Headlee has been for eight years teaching in Perry Township, but engages in farming as his chief pursuit, and owns a well improved farm of 100 acres. In 1880 he was united in marriage with Miss Margaret, daughter of Phineas Headley. Mrs. Headlee is of English origin. They are the parents of four children, viz: Cora, Ray, James Fay and Effie. Mr. Headlee is a Democrat. He and wife are prominent members of the Methodist Episcopal Church. He is a self-made man, is industrious and energetic, and has a great many friends throughout the county.

JOSEPH HEADLEE, farmer and stock-grower, is descended from the early setttlers of Greene County. He was born September 9, 1834, and is a son of Jesse and Maria (Cox) Headlee. His mother was a native of New York. His father who was born in this county, was eminently successful as a farmer and owned 400 acres of land at the time of his death, March 15, 1876. Of his ten children, Joseph is the fourth and was reared on the farm in Perry Township. Mr. Headlee is an energetic, industrious farmer and owns ninety-three acres of well improved land where he resides, near Mount Morris, Penn. He was united in marriage in Greene County, in 1869, with Catherine, daughter of Alexander Henderson. Her mother's maiden name was Catharine Lemley. To Mr. and Mrs. Headlee were born four children, viz: Earnest, Clyde, Mark and M. D. Mr. Headlee has been a member of the Methodist Episcopal Church since 1852. He is a member of the board of trustees, and take great interest in the welfare of his chosen denomination. He was drafted in 1863 and served his regular term in the army. Mr. Headlee is a member of the G. A. R., belonging to the Jesse Taylor Post, No. 450, of Mount Morris, Penn.

J. S. HOY, farmer and stock-grower, born in Whiteley Township, this county, January 18, 1843, is a son of James and Isabella (Kuhn) Hoy, also natives of Greene County, and of German origin. His father died in 1880. He was a farmer and stock-grower, and reared a family of eight children, of whom the subject of this sketch is the third. J. S. was reared in Perry Township, where he has lived since he was one year of age. He received his education in the common schools in this township, and has made farming his life work. Mr. Hoy's farm contains 159 and three quarters acres of well improved land. He was married in this county, January 13, 1869, to Melissa, daughter of Isaac and Anna (Myers) Lemley. Her mother was born in Virginia, and her father in Perry Township, this county. Mr. and Mrs. Hoy have an interesting family of four children; viz., Eliza J., James Isaac, David Arthur, and Cassie Ellen. Mrs. Hoy died in 1884, a faithful member of the Southern Methodist Episcopal Church. Mr. Hoy is a Democrat. He is a genial, agreeable gentleman, and has a wide circle of friends in the county.

MORRIS LEMLEY, farmer, stock-grower and drover, was born in Perry Township, April 2, 1834. His parents, Samuel and Margaret Lemley, were natives of Greene County, and of German extraction. His father, who was a farmer by occupation, moved to Iowa in the latter part of his life, where he died at the age eighty-six. Morris, the fifth in a family of ten children, was reared on the farm and attended the common school. He made his own way in the world, and is the owner of eight hundred acres of land—360 in his home farm. Mr. Lemley's example is worthy of emulation. He first engaged in farming on rented property, and by his patient toil and unfailing industry has succeeded in accumulating a handsome fortune. In 1854 Mr. Lemley married Miss Martha Jane, daughter of Job and Margaret (Simington) Phillips. Their children are: Margaret A., wife of William Headlee; Samuel, a farmer; Emeline, Elizabeth, Josephus, and Spencer who died at the age of twenty-one years. Mr. Lemley is a Democrat. He and his wife are prominent members of the Methodist Episcopal Church.

CLARK LEMLEY, farmer and stock grower, Brock, Penn., was born in Perry Township, November 20, 1849, and is a son of Isaac and Anna (Myers) Lemley. His mother was born in West Virginia. His father is a native of this county and a prominent farmer of Whiteley Township. Clark is the third in a family of six children. He was reared in this county, where he received a common school education. Mr. Lemley has met with success as a farmer and owns 152 acres of good land where he resides. In 1870 he married Miss

45

Rachel, daughter of Eli and Mary (Dulaney) Headlee. Mr. and Mrs. Lemley's children are Haddie L., William L., and Alva G. Mr. and Mrs. Lemley, with their oldest daughter are members of the Methodist Episcopal Church. He is a Democrat in politics.

ASBERRY LEMLEY, farmer and stock-grower, was born June 20, 1823, on the farm where he now resides in Perry Township. He is a son of David and Ruhana (Snider) Lemley, being the oldest of their eight children. His parents spent the most of their lives on a farm in this county, where Asberry was reared and received his education in the common schools. He has made farming his chief pursuit, and is the owner of 300 acres of well improved land. Mr. Lemley was united in marriage, October 12, 1849, in Greene County, Penn., with Miss Rachel, daughter of John and Lydia Headlee. Mrs. Asberry Lemley is of English and German origin. They have eight children; viz., Ruhana, wife of William Howard; Elizabeth, wife of Thomas Patterson; L. L., David, Lydia, Martha, wife of Jonathan Kennedy; and Mary. Mr. Lemley is one of the most industrious and successful business men in his township.

J. W. LONG, deceased, was born in Perry Township, this county, December 3, 1836, and died October 4, 1885. He was a highly respected citizen and one of Greene County's most successful business men, being at the time of his death the owner of over 800 acres of land. Mr. Long was the son of George and Mary (Berge) Long who were natives of Ohio, and of English descent. They spent most of their lives in Greene County, Penn., where his father made farming and stock-growing his chief pursuit. In 1860 the subject of our sketch married Minerva C., daughter of L. G. Vanvoorhis, a prominent farmer of Dunkard Township. To Mr. and Mrs. Long were born six children—F. G., proprietor of the Commercial Hotel at Oakland, Maryland; Frank W., a farmer; Fannie E., John J., Loyd L.and Lawrence George (deceased.) Mr. Long was a Republican in politics. He took an active interest in the schools of his township, and for many years served as school director.

WILLIAM LONG, a farmer and stock-grower, residing near Mount Morris, Penn., was born near Garard's Fort, this county, December 22, 1831. He is a son of Samuel and Adaline (Mestrezat) Long, who were of French and Irish lineage. His father, who was farmer all his life, was twice married, and reared a family of six children, of whom William is the oldest, by the last marriage. He was reared on the farm in Whiteley Township, receiving his early education in the subscription schools. He made farming his chief pursuit, and has met with success, being at the present the owner of 400 acres of good land in this township. In politics Mr. Long is a Democrat, as is also his son, Merritt Leonard Long, who was born in this township, March 7, 1869. His daughter Fannie E., was born

March 30, 1876, in Perry Township. William Long's father died in 1886, and his mother in 1880.

COLEMAN LUELLEN, carriage and wagon manufacturer at Mount Morris, Greene County, Penn., was born in Monongalia County, West Virginia, February 8, 1840. He is a son of William G. and Mary (Norris) Luellen, also natives of West Virginia, and of Welsh and English extraction. Mr. Luellen was reared on the home farm in West Virginia, where he received his education. He worked on the farm until 1861, when he went to Greene County, Penn., to learn the blacksmith trade. He then enlisted under Capt. J. B. Morris, in Company F, Seventh Virginia Volunteer Infantry and served three years and two months. After his return from the war, Mr. Luellen learned the wagon-maker's trade and has successfully engaged in that business at Mount Morris since 1868. He was united in marriage October 5, 1876, with Catharine, daughter of Philip and Rhoda (Dulaney) Hite. Their children are: Carrie L., Benjamin F., James W. and Luretta B. Mr. Luellen is a Republican and a member of the G. A. R. Post, No. 450. He and wife belong to the Methodist Episcopal Church.

SPENCER MORRIS, M. D., Ph. D., of Greene County, Penn., was born at Garard's Fort, Penn., October 26, 1820. He is a son of Jonathan and Sarah (Clymer) Morris, who were of German and English extraction. His mother was a native of Bucks County, Penn. His father was born in Greene County; was a physician and merchant at Garard's Fort, and died July 19, 1848. Dr. Morris is a grandson of the Rev. John Corbly. The Doctor is the third in a family of four children. He was reared in the place of his nativity, and attended the common schools. He subsequently attended Greene Academy at Carmichaels, Penn., afterwards attended college in Virginia. He then began the study of medicine at Cincinnati, Ohio, where he graduated in 1846, and was for some time thereafter in successful practice of his chosen profession in Greene County, Penn. In 1871 he received the degree of Doctor of Medicine from the medical department of the University of Pennsylvania, afterwards the degree of Doctor of Philosophy from the same institution. In 1873 he graduated from the Jefferson Medical College in Philadelphia. For fifteen years he was a popular quiz teacher in that city, having large classes of medical students. In the summer of 1886 he was elected to the chair of lecturer on the symptoms of diseases in the Medico-Chirurgical College of Philadelphia. In 1851 Dr. Morris was united in marriage, in West Virginia, with Belinda A., daughter of John H. Bowlby, and their summer residence is near the Mason and Dixon Line in Perry Township This has been their quiet retreat for several years. Here the Doctor is sought after for his excellent medical advice by patients for miles around.

LEVI MORRIS, son of George and Margaret Morris, was born on the waters of Whiteley Creek, on the 14th day of April, 1783. His mother was the oldest child of Rev. John Corbly, whose second wife and several of their children were massacred by the Indians at Garard's Fort, on the 10th day of May, 1781. Levi Morris was married to Lucretia Stephens in 1809. He bought a farm and went to housekeeping on Dunkard Creek, near the present site of Mount Morris. This farm was all in the woods and the nearest store was at Greensboro, twelve miles distant. There was but little use for a store, however, at that early history of the country, for the clothing worn by both sexes was domestic, or home-made, and coffee was used but once a week—Sunday morning. Mr. Morris, with three of his brothers, volunteered and served in Captain Seeley's cavalry company in the war of 1812. Soon after the war he bought another farm and laid out the town of Mount Morris, which bears his name, and re-sided there until his death. Soon after the war he was appointed justice of the peace, which office he held until near the close of his life. Living near the State of Virginia, a State in which a marriage license was required, and none being required in Pennsylvania, his office was the Gretna Green, to which many of the lads and lassies hied to have their nuptials consummated. Mr. Morris kept the first hotel in Mount Morris, and engaged in milling, farming and stock-raising, always keeping the best blooded stock in the county. He raised a family of eleven children, seven sons and four daughters, all of whom grew to maturity, each raising a family. Margaret married Patrick Donley; Louisa, George Lemley; Hannah, Abner Harrison; Josephus H., Temperance Smith; W. G., Emily Kirby; Jefferson S., Sarah Ingram; Edward F., Elizabeth Smith, and for second wife, Rhetta Roberts; Thomas I., Sarah Way; James B., Keziah Way; Levi A., Samantha Brown; and Lucretia, C. C. Hardin. Levi Morris died an honored and respected citizen on the 20th day of January, 1842, his widow and all their children surviving him. Lucretia Morris, his widow, died April 15, 1885, at the ripe old age of ninety-five years and four months. Her children, grandchildren, and great-grandchildren number over two hundred, and reside in several States. Their son, Major James B. Morris, is perhaps the best known man in the county. He is respected for his liberality and true manliness, both as a soldier and a citizen. He was reared and educated in Mount Morris, and has been employed in farming, milling and stock-growing. He was married in Monongalia County, W. Va., August 26, 1848, to Keziah, daughter of Gideon and Jane (Sturgis) Way, of English extraction. They were natives of Fayette County, Penn., but spent most of their lives in Monongalia County, W. Va. Major Morris and wife have a family of seven children—Mary J., wife of W. F. Lewellen, of West Virginia; Belle M., wife of Jerome Vanvoorhis, of Dunkard Township; Emma L., wife of J. W. Hatfield; George G., a physician at Washington, D. C., and F. K. and S. W., deceased. Their mother is a devoted member of the Baptist Church. Major Morris is a Republican, has been school director at Mount Morris, and was special agent for the U. S. Treasury Department for several years. In 1861 he enlisted in Company F, Seventh West Virginia Volunteer Infantry, and served as Captain until 1862, when he was promoted to the position of Major, in which capacity he served until the expiration of his term, then returned to Mount Morris. The first man killed from Greene County belonged to Captain Morris' Company, and was killed October 26, 1861.

JOSEPH PATTERSON, farmer and stock-grower, Brock, Penn., was born in Whiteley Township, this county, March 29, 1829. He is the oldest son of William and Rhoda (Whitlatch) Patterson, who were natives of Greene County, and of German and Irish ancestry. Like his father, Joseph has been a successful farmer through life. In 1850 he married Elizabeth, daughter of Thomas and Elizabeth Mooney. Mrs. Patterson is of German and English origin. They have eight children, of whom William Franklin is the second. He also is a farmer and stock-grower, and was born in Whiteley Township February 18, 1854. He received a common-school education, and early in life engaged in the mercantile trade at Waynesville for three years. He has since devoted his time to farming and has met with success. He is the owner of 135½ acres of well improved land. Mr. Patterson was united in marriage in Greene County, December 22, 1872, with Elizabeth, daughter of Jacob Whitlatch, and they are the parents of seven children, viz: Rose, David, Enlow, Arthur, Norval, Ada and Harvey. Mr. and Mrs. Patterson are members of the Methodist Episcopal Church, in which he is a trustee. He is a Democrat in politics.

MINOR N. REAMER, dentist, was born in Monongahela Township, Greene County, Penn., February 2, 1846. He is a son of Benjamin and Anna Maria (Minor) Reamer who were of Welsh and German ancestry. His father, a farmer, died in 1866. Minor, the third in a family of four children, was reared in his native township attended the district schools and was subsequently a student in Waynesburg College for one year. Early in life he studied dentistry in Greensboro, where he commenced the practice of his profession in 1871, remaining there three years. He then located at Mount Morris, Penn., where he has since been actively engaged in the practice of dentistry. The Doctor is a Republican. In 1861 he enlisted in Company G., Eighty-Fifth Pennsylvania Volunteer Infantry, and served two years. He is an active member of the G. A. R., belongs to the I. O. O. F. and is officer of the day in Post No. 450, for 1888. In 1871 Dr. Reamer married Miss Fannie, daughter of G. C. Black.

Her mother's maiden name was Rebecca Sowers. They were of German extraction. Doctor and Mrs. Reamer are the parents of three children—Harry B., Nellie E. and Emma D. Their mother is a member of the Methodist Episcopal Church.

Z. T. SHULTZ, farmer and stock grower, Kirby, Penn., was born in Whiteley Township, this county, July 20, 1848, and is a son of Elijah and Ruth A. (Bailey) Shultz, who were of German and English descent. His mother died in 1881. His father, now seventy-four years of age, is a resident of Waynesburg, Penn. The subject of our sketch was reared in Perry Township, where he has engaged in farming most of his life. He received a common-school education, also attended Waynesburg College and subsequently taught for five years. His home farm contains one hundred and twenty-seven acres of well improved land. Mr. Shultz taught in this county, in Iowa, and West Virginia, but has devoted his time wholly to farming since 1872—the year he was married. His wife was Miss Hettie A., daughter of Justus and Mary (Bowen) Cowell, and their children are Minnie M., Harmon R., Elijah F., Gurney W. and Harold L. Mr. and Mrs. Shultz are members of the Methodist Episcopal Church. In politics he is a Republican, and has served as a school director in his township.

A. SNIDER, a retired blacksmith of Mount Morris, Penn., was born in Monongalia County, West Virginia, October 8, 1813. He is a son of Jeremiah and Anna (Rich) Snider who were also natives of West Virginia, and of German lineage. His great-grandfather came from Germany to America and settled in Virginia. Jeremiah Snider was twice married and reared a family of thirteen children. The subject of our sketch was the third child by the second marriage. He was reared on a farm and attended the subscription school in his native township. He was employed as a farm laborer early in life and in 1853 learned the blacksmith's trade with Daniel Bowen, in Waynesburg, Penn. He then engaged in that business at Mount Morris and has met with success. Mr. Snider is the owner of valuable town property and one hundred and sixty acres of land in Perry Township. In 1838 he married Mary Bowers; they have had a family of six children; viz., Lucretia, wife of James Fox; Elmer, a blacksmith, and Lindsey. Jacob Rolla, Mary J. and Eliza, deceased. Mary J. was the wife of Oliver Evans, now deceased. Mr. Snider is a Democrat in politics. He has served as school director and three terms as assessor in his township. He and wife are prominent members of the Methodist Protestant Church.

JESSE SPITZNAGEL, farmer and stock-grower, Brock, Penn., was born in Fayette County, Pennsylvania, February 24, 1838. He is a son of Simon and Jemima (Miller), Spitznagel, who were also natives of Fayette County, and of English and German origin. His father was a successful farmer during his life-time. His family consisted of eleven children, of whom Jesse is the fifth. He was reared on the farm, has been successful in his chosen occupation and owns the farm of one hundred and five acres where he now resides. In 1856 Mr. Spitznagel married Miss Dorotha Whitlatch, who was a native of this county and of German extraction. To Mr. and Mrs. Spitznagel were born five children, viz.—Loziella, wife of Alpheus Wade; Simon E., John, Lewis G. and Lucinda. Mr. Spitznagel is a Republican in politics and belongs to the Methodist Episcopal Church, of which his deceased wife was also a devoted member. Mrs. Spitznagel died March 5, 1887, a faithful wife and kind and loving mother.

SPENCER STEPHENS, farmer and stock-grower, Mount Morris, Penn., was born in Greene Township, this county, September 15, 1839. He is a son of Washington and Joan (Steel) Stephens, being the oldest of their eight children. His parents were of English ancestory. His father was a farmer all his life. Spencer was reared on the farm with his parents, where he attended the district school. He has made farming his main occupation and owns the farm where he resides in Perry Township. In 1865 he was united in marriage in Greene County, with Miss Abigail, daughter of Joseph Conner. Mrs. Stephens is of Irish and English extraction. Their children are Rebecca, Albert, S. C., Leroy, Mary Alice, Stacy and Clara. The family belong to the Baptist Church of which Mr. Stephens is an official member. He is a Republican in politics. He takes an active interest in the education of his children, the oldest two of whom are teachers. . In 1862 Mr. Stephens enlisted in Company A., One Hundred and Fortieth Pennsylvania Volunteer Infantry. He was a non-commissioned officer and served under Gen. Hancock. Mr. Stephens was in the battles of Gettysburg, Chancellorsville and the Wilderness and served until the close of the war.

LEWIS WHITLATCH, farmer and stock-grower, Brock, Penn., was born in Perry Township, Greene County, Penn., January 10, 1855. His parents, Jacob and Catharine (Headlee) Whitlatch, were also natives of this county and of English extraction. His father, who was a farmer through life, died in 1884, a highly respected citizen. His family consisted of eleven children, ten of whom grew to maturity. Lewis is the ninth and was reared on the farm in his native township, where he attended the common school. Mr. Whitlatch has made farming his chief pursuit, and has also engaged to some extent in the mercantile trade. He has made a success of his business and owns a farm of one hundred and seventy acres. In 1884 Mr. Whitlatch married Hannah, daughter of William Conley. She is of English and German origin. They have one child—Goldie Lee. Mr. and Mrs. Whitlatch are members of the Methodist

Episcopal Church. He has been a steward, class-leader and trustee in the church, and held various important positions in the Sabbath-school. In politics he is a Republican.

RICHHILL TOWNSHIP.

F. W. BALDWIN, farmer and stock-grower, Ryerson's Station, Penn., was born in Richhill Township, this county, July 15, 1846, and is a son of S. W. and Nancy A. (Barnett) Baldwin, who were of English, Irish and Dutch lineage. His mother was a native of Greene County. His father, who was born in Washington County, Penn., was a mechanic and farmer by occupation, and died in 1884. The subject of this sketch is the only member of his father's family who grew to maturity. He was raised on the farm with his parents and chose agricultural pursuits as his business through life. He also worked in his father's mill for years until the mill was sold. Mr. Baldwin is the owner of three farms, containing in all 271 acres. He has been very successful in his undertakings. Mr. Baldwin was united in marriage September 14, 1871, with Susan, daughter of George and Elizabeth (Nuss) Woodruff, who are of English and German origin. They have six children, viz.—Eva E., John W., Mary A. L., George M., Ira C. and Michael, who died in his infancy. Mr. and Mrs. Baldwin are members of the Baptist Church, in which he has served as deacon and treasurer.

ELLIS BANE.—Among the prominent farmers and stock-growers who spent a long life in Greene County was Ellis Bane, deceased, who was born in Richhill Township, March 6, 1804, and died in 1882. He was a son of Jesse Bane, a pioneer settler of this county. The history of the family shows them to have been farmers, and usually successful. At the time of his death Mr. Bane was the owner of 400 acres of land. His remains lie in Leazure Cemetery; a handsome monument marks the last resting place. He was twice married. His second wife was Elizabeth Conkey. Three of their children are now living, the oldest being Ellis Bane, who now resides on the home farm, and owns 237 acres of well improved land. He was born in Richhill Township, received a common-school education, has been an industrious, energetic farmer, and successful in his business. Mr. Bane was married in October, 1886, in West Virginia to Lelia, daughter of Joshua and Rebecca (Fitzgerald) Hipsley. Mrs.

Bane is of English and Irish descent. They have one child—Clyde. Mr. Bane is a strict adherent of the Democratic party. His wife is a member of the Presbyterian Church.

A. B. BARNETT, teacher, farmer and stock-grower, was born in Richhill Township, July 11, 1842. He is a son of John and Margaret (Stoughton) Barnett, natives of Greene County, and of Irish and Welsh extraction. His father, who was a farmer, died June 12, 1859. The gentleman whose name heads this sketch is the seventh son and the youngest in a family of eleven children. He was reared on the farm he now owns, and received his education in the district school. He subsequently attended the State Normal School, chose teaching as a profession, and enjoys the well deserved reputation of being one of the foremost educators in the county. He also takes an active interest in the teachers' institutes. Mr. Barnett owns and manages a farm of 151 acres of land well stocked and improved. He was united in marriage February 21, 1873, with Miss Jennie, daughter of Stephen Durbin. Mrs. Barnett is of Irish descent. Their children are—Leni Clare, Neicie and Bessie B. Mr. and Mrs. Barnett are members of the Baptist Church.

JOHN BEBOUT, farmer and stock-grower, was born in Morris Township, Greene County, Penn., January 17, 1845. His parents were Moses and Elizabeth (Smalley) Bebout, natives of Pennsylvania, and of English lineage. His father was a farmer and stock-dealer, and at the time of his death resided in Greene County. He had a family of eight children; of these, seven are living, John Bebout, the subject of our sketch, being the youngest. He received his education in the common school, and from an early age up to the present has been engaged in farming. He owns 337 acres of valuable land where he resides in Richhill Township. Mr. Bebout was married in this county in 1863 to Lizzie, a daughter of Joseph Tilton, a brother of Rev. Charles W. Tilton, a Baptist minister of Jefferson, Penn.; also a brother of Rev. Morgan Tilton, of Rutan, Penn. Mr. and Mrs. Bebout's children are—Charles B., John L., I. Tilton and Willie S. living, and two infant daughters deceased. Mr. Bebout is a Democrat. His wife is a consistent member of the Baptist Church.

I. C. BOOHER, justice of the peace, Ryerson's Station, Penn., is a native of Washington County, Penn., and of Welsh and German ancestry. His father has dealt extensively in horses, and now resides in Richhill Township, Greene County. His family consists of five children, of whom the subject of our sketch is the second. He was reared on the farm and received his education in the common schools, and Greene Academy at Carmichaels, Penn. He remained at home with his parents until he reached his majority, then clerked in a general store for two years. He has, however, devoted his time principally to farming, stock-growing and milling, and for several years owned and operated a valuable mill at Ryerson's Station. The mill was burned down February 19, 1885, resulting in a loss to Mr. Booher of $7,000. He owns the farm where he now resides, containing 130 acres. In 1854 Mr. Booher married Miss Rebecca J., daughter of John Barnett. She was of Irish and Welsh extraction. Their children are—Anderson R., James L., S. E., Jesse L., J. Bentley, Mary M., M. Lattie, Wilmetta and Birdie. Mr. and Mrs. Booher are members of the South Wheeling Baptist Church. He is deacon in the church, and takes an active interest in the Sabbath-school. He is serving on his fourth term as justice of the peace.

JAMES H. BRADDOCK, Harvey's, Penn.—Among the descendants of the early settlers of this county we mention the gentleman whose name heads this sketch. He was born on the farm he now owns, September 18, 1819, and is a son of Francis and Ann (Gray) Braddock. His mother was the daughter of Judge Gray, one of the first associate judges in this part of the State. Mr. Braddock's parents were born in the old fort near Washington, Penn., and were of Irish and English origin. His father died in 1856. Mr. James H. Braddock is the seventh in a family of nine children. He has been a very successful farmer, accumulating quite a good deal of property, the greater part of which he has given to his children. In 1845 Mr. Braddock was united in marriage with Miss Jane, daughter of William and Sarah (Cox) Henderson. Their children are— Adda, wife of Thomas Blair; Frank, a clerk in the War Department at Washington, D. C.; and Sadie, wife of Dr. Teagarden, of West Virginia. Mrs. Braddock died in 1876. In 1883 Mr. Braddock married Miss Belle, daughter of Ephraim McClelland. They are members of the Presbyterian Church, in which Mr. Braddock has been an elder for a period of fifteen years. He also takes an active interest in the Sabbath-school, of which he is now assistant superintendent. In politics he is a Republican.

NEWTON H. BRADDOCK, farmer and stock-grower, was born in Richhill Township, June 1, 1834, and is a son of David and Susan (Crow) Braddock. He is a descendant of the pioneer settlers of this county, a brief history of whom is given in the biographical sketch of F. M. Braddock, also a resident of this township. Newton Braddock is the fourth of a family of nine children. He was reared on the farm in Richhill Township, and attended the district school. He has made farming his occupation and owns 160 acres of valuable land, where he now resides. In 1869 Mr. Braddock married Miss Jane, daughter of Alexander Burns. Their children are—Lizzie N. and David G., Jr. In 1864 Mr. Braddock enlisted in Battery B, First Pennsylvania Light Artillery, and was with the army of the Potomac at Lee's surrender. He taught in the schools of Richhill Township each winter from 1856 till 1873, except the time he spent in the army, and has also served as school director, and was secretary of said board. He is a Republican, and a member of the G. A. R. Post.

F. M. BRADDOCK, farmer and stock-grower, born August 14, 1830, is a son of David G. and Susan (Crow) Braddock, who were of English and Irish and German origin. His father was born in Richhill Township in 1807, and still resides on the old Braddock farm, which has been in the possession of the family for more than a hundred years. His family now living consists of nine children. Francis Braddock, great-grandfather of F. M. Braddock, was one of the pioneer settlers of this county when the western part of it was all a wilderness. He first settled in Richhill Township, he settling on the old Braddock farm which he took from the Government. F. M. Braddock's maternal grandfather, Jacob Crow, was also among the first settlers in this part of the county, and his family of two boys and three girls were murdered by the Indians in Richhill Township. In the Braddock family there are many successful farmers and prominent professional men. As a farmer the subject of our sketch has been very successful, and now owns a 150 acre farm which is in a high state of cultivation. Mr. Braddock was united in marriage November 20, 1862, with Maria J., daughter of Dr. W. B. Porter. Mrs. Braddock was of English and Scotch-Irish ancestry. She died in 1880, leaving a family of three children—Eva L., wife of Charles Buckingham; Sherman F., and Mary, now deceased. In politics Mr. Braddock is a Republican. He has been an able member of the school board in his township.

D. A. BRADDOCK, the fourth son of David G. and Susanna (Crow) Braddock, was born in Richhill Township in May, 1840. He was raised on the farm, attended the common-schools, and has made farming and stock-growing his business, although he has worked at the carpenter's trade to some extent. He owns a good farm of 106 acres near Harvey's, Penn. Mr. Braddock was married in December 1877, near Marysville, Union County, Ohio. His wife's maiden name was Lucella Henderson, daughter of Thomas and Ethel (McGee) Henderson, She was born in West Virginia. Mr. and Mrs. Braddock have one son—J. H. Braddock. Mrs. Braddock is a member of the Presbyterian Church. Mr. Braddock is a Republican in politics. The Braddocks were originally from Loudoun County, Virginia, and were among the first settlers of Greene County, Penn.

ROBERT BRISTOR, deceased.—Among the prominent citizens of Richhill Township, and descendants of the earliest settlers of Greene County, we mention the gentleman whose name heads this sketch. He was born May 31, 1835. His mother's maiden name was Delilah Hixenbaugh. His father was a farmer and surveyor, and one of the most prominent citizens of the county. He was of

German and English ancestry. Robert Bristor, the third in a family of seven children, was reared on a farm in Richhill Township. He was a·successful farmer and stock-grower during his lifetime, being at the time of his death, in 1873, the owner of a farm of 171 acres, where his family now resides. In April, 1856, Mr. Bristor married Eliza, daughter of John and Ann (McNeely) Gillogly, who were of Irish extraction. To Mr. and Mrs. Bristor were born the following named children: John F., J. G., J. H., L. L., W. S., Anna, wife of L. Booher; Lizzie, Robert and William. Mr. Bristor belonged to the Christian Church, of which his widow is also a member. In politics he was a Republican.

ABRAHAM CLUTTER, farmer and stock-grower, was born in Morris Township, Washington County, May 18, 1822. He is a son of William and Sarah (McNay) Clutter, also natives of Washington County, and of German extraction. John Clutter, grandfather of Abraham Clutter, was a soldier in the Revolutionary war, serving under General Washington. The subject of this sketch grew to maturity in his native county, attended the district schools and has made farming his chief occupation. He was married January 12, 1845, to Jane, daughter of James Meek, ex-treasurer of Greene County, and now a resident of Jackson Township. Mr. and Mrs. Clutter are the parents of eleven children, ten of whom are now living, viz.: John, Luella, wife of Thomas Hare; Andrew J., George W., Sadie, wife of William Conkey; Mary J., wife of B. Temple; Rachel, wife of John F. Donley; A. Judson, Frank and Clarabel. Elizabeth is deceased. Mr. Clutter has given his children the advantages of good schools, and they are highly respected in the community. He is a member of the Disciple Church, in which he is a deacon, and takes great interest in the Sabbath-school. In politics he is a Democrat.

WILLIAM CLUTTER, farmer and stock-grower, is a native of Morris Township, Washington County, born March 2, 1828. His parents are Cephas and Laney (Day) Clutter, natives of Pennsylvania, and of German and Irish descent. His father, a farmer of Cen'er Township, is now eighty-five years of age. He reared a family of seven children, five of whom are now living. The subject of this sketch, having been reared on a farm, has made farming his chief pursuit and has met with success in his business, owning a good farm of 132 acres where he resides in Richhill Township. In 1847 Mr. Clutter married Miss May J. Hunnell. They have nine children— Lana, deceased, who was the wife of F. Conger; John M., Jane, wife of S. McVay; Elizabeth, wife of Simon Pettit; Catharine, wife of Thomas Iams; Belle, wife of George Kinney; Ida Ella, and Cephas. Mrs. Clutter died in 1880; she was a member of the Methodist Episcopal Church. In 1881 Mr. Clutter married Mary Shape, of

Morris Township. Mr. Clutter is a Democrat. In 1862 he enlisted in Company A, One Hundred and Sixty-eighth Pennsylvania Volunteer Infantry, and was discharged in 1863, at the expiration of his term of service.

J. M. CONKEY, farmer and stock-grower, was born in Richhill Township, November 9, 1836. His parents, John and Mary (Prong) Conkey, were respectively natives of Virginia and Greene County, Penn., and were of English and Irish and German origin, His father was a plow-maker, and served in the war of 1812. He was also a successful farmer, and accumulated a handsome fortune. He died in 1884. Of his family of nine children, J. M. Conkey is next to the youngest. He was raised on a farm, attended the common-schools and has served three years in the war of 1861; he has been a successful farmer and stock-grower. He owns a well-stocked and improved farm of 137 acres in Richhill Township, and in 1886 purchased the grist-mill at Graysville, which he now operates. In 1866 Mr. Conkey was married to Miss Celestia Moninger, daughter of George and Susan (Biddle) Moninger, who were of English descent. Mr. and Mrs. Conkey's children are Royal, Ada and Jennie. Mr. Conkey is a Democrat. He and his wife are members of the Presbyterian Church.

JAMES HARVEY CONKEY, farmer and stock-grower, born in Richhill Township, August 2, 1840, is a son of John and Mary (Prong) Conkey, who were respectively natives of Pennsylvania and Virginia, and of English, Irish and German origin. His father was a farmer during his lifetime, and died in 1884. His family consisted of seven children, of whom James Harvey is the youngest. He has from his youth been engaged in agricultural pursuits, in which vocation he has met with success and is the owner of 135 acres of well improved land in Richhill Township. In 1867 Mr. Conkey married Anna Eliza Marsh, who is a daughter of Phillip Marsh, and of English descent. Mr. and Mrs. Conkey have seven children—John, Mary, James, Thomas, Emmett, Elsie and Otto. Mr. Conkey is a Democrat. He and wife are members of the Cumberland Presbyterian Church.

HIRAM DAY, retired farmer and stock-grower, was born in Morris Township, this county, December 18, 1814. He is a son of William and Mary (Sutton) Day, who were of English descent. His father, who spent the latter part of his life as a farmer, was a shoemaker in earlier years, and among the first settlers in Morris Township. The subject of this sketch is the fifth in a family of ten children and was raised on the farm, receiving a limited education in the common schools. He came to Richhill Township when he was a young man and opened a farm in the wild woods, where his only possessions were an ax, a maul, iron wedge and a grubbing hoe. He has since accumulated enough to keep himself and family in luxury, and owns 250 acres of well improved land. Mr. Day was first married November 28, 1839, to Miss May E., daughter of Samuel Thompson. Mrs. Day was of German origin; she died March 14, 1863. Their children were Eliza Jane, wife of Warren Burns, and William A. Mr. Day's present wife was the widow of David Dougal. Her maiden name was Dorcas Blair, a daughter of Alexander Blair, who was of Irish descent. Mr. and Mrs. Day have one son, Harvey. Mrs. Day is a member of the Presbyterian Church, Mr. Day is the treasurer of the Sabbath-school. He is a Democrat in politics.

W. S. DRAKE, merchant and dealer in agricultural implements, Jacksonville, Penn., was born in Morgan Township, February 11, 1838. He is a son of Francis and Eliza (Stewart) Drake, who were respectively natives of New Jersey and Washington County, Penn., and of English, Scotch and German origin. His father was a chair maker and painter, and was also skilled in other trades. He died February 20, 1878. The subject of this sketch is the oldest of a family of five children, four of whom are living. He was raised in this county, receiving his education in the common schools of Morgan, Jefferson and Richhill townships. He taught for several years and, in 1860, being desirous of seeing more of the world, he went to Texas, where he again engaged in school teaching until 1862. He then enlisted in the Twenty-ninth Texas Cavalry, was Orderly Sergeant, and served until 1865. While his service was in the Confederate army, yet at heart he was a Union man. In 1865, he, with about one-hundred others, started for the Union lines and were captured and returned, and were in prison when the war closed. After the close of the war Mr. Drake again taught school for a year in Denton County, Texas, and in 1866 returned to Richhill Township, for four years engaging in farming and carpenter work. In 1870 he formed his present partnership with Perry Sowers, dealing in general stock, wool and farming implements. In 1861 Mr. Drake married Miss Julia E., daughter of George C. and Julia E. (Ohlhausen) Parker. Her father was born in Virginia and her mother near Philadelphia, Penn. They were of English and German origin. Mr. and Mrs. Drake have six children—Anna, wife of Silas Jennings; May, John, W. C., George and Emma. Mr. Drake is a Democrat, and a prominent member of the Masonic fraternity.

GEORGE W. FERRELL, a shoemaker by occupation, was born in Center Township, April 16, 1828, and is a son of Peter and Nancy (Huffman) Ferrell who were, respectively, natives of New Jersey and Pennsylvania, and of German extraction. His father was a farmer and his family consisted of ten children, of whom George W. is the eighth. He received a common-school education and early in life learned the shoemaker's trade, which he has made his main occupation. Mr. Ferrell has lived in Jacksonville, Penn., since 1848. He has been twice married—first, in 1850, to Sarah Isabella Pettit, and they were the parents of three children—James M., a merchant at New Freeport, Penn.; W. S., a shoemaker, and Clara I., wife of William John. Mrs. Ferrell died in 1858, and in 1859 Mr. Ferrell married Nancy, daughter of James R. Throckmorton. At the time of their marriage she was the widow of Stephen Durbin. Mr. and Mrs. Durbin were the parents of two children—Jennie, wife of A. B. Barnett, and Mary, wife of W. A. Day. To Mr. and Mrs. Ferrell have been born the following named children—Ida May, deceased, who was the wife of John Henderson; Lizzie O., wife of Perry E. Wright; Effie A. and Harvey D. W. Mr. and Mrs. Ferrell are members of the Cumberland Presbyterian Church, in which he is a trustee. In politics he is a Republican. He is a member and present chaplain of the G. A. R. Post, No. 428. In 1864 Mr. Ferrell enlisted in Company F, Eighty-fifth Pennsylvania Volunteer Infantry and served till the close of the war, being present at Lee's surrender.

H. B. FLETCHER, farmer and stock-grower, was born April 12, 1836, on the farm he now owns, and where he has spent all his life, in Richhill Township. He is a son of William and Nancy (Bane) Fletcher, who were of Irish and English descent. His father was born in Ireland in 1803, came to Philadelphia, Penn., in 1821, and soon after came to Jefferson Township, Greene County, and spent the remainder of his life. He died in 1869. The subject of this sketch is his only child who grew to maturity. He received a common-school education, and has made a success of farming, being at present the owner of 200 acres of valuable land. In 1858 Mr. Fletcher married Mary, daughter of Abraham Rickey, and they have a family of seven children—Edward, J. W., William, Frank, W. C·, Lydia and Clara B. Mr. Fletcher is a Republican. His wife is a member of the Presbyterian Church.

WILLIAM R. FONNER, retired farmer and stock-grower, was born in Morris Township, Greene County, Penn., September 5, 1824. He is a son of Henry and Abigail (Taylor) Fonner, who were of German and English descent. His father was a teacher in early life, in later years a farmer. He came across the mountains and settled in Greene County in 1801, and died in 1851, at the age of seventy-five years. William R. Fonner is the fourth in a family of seven children, six of whom grew to be men and women. He received his education in the schools of the county. In his business as a farmer he has ever exercised good judgment and practiced economy and now owns a fine farm of 200 acres in Richhill Township, where he now enjoys a life of retirement. In July of 1849 Mr. Fonner married

Eliza, daughter of Samuel and Nancy (Flick) Rail, and they had a family of two son, both now deceased, and two daughters—Mary Ann, wife of Daniel Miller, and Hannah J., wife of Miles Meek. In religion Mr. Fonner is a Baptist, in politics a Republican.

A. J. GOODWIN, merchant, Jacksonville, Penn., was born in Washington County, Penn., February 2, 1817, and is a son of John and Sarah (Gardner) Goodwin, natives of Washington County, and of German origin. His father was a weaver and farmer, and reared a family of ten children. The subject of this sketch is the second child, and lived on the farm with his parents until he was fifteen years of age. The family then came to Greene County, and settled on a farm in Center Township. Mr. Goodwin attended school in an old log school-house. He naturally took up his father's occupation, and was engaged therein until he reached his majority. He then began working at the carpenter's trade and stone work, and took contracts for buildings. He was engaged in this business for a period of twelve years or more, and succeeded in gaining a good start in the world. From 1850 to 1874 he devoted his time principally to farming and stock-growing. Since that time he has been in his present business, in the store owned by his son for five years previous to 1874. In 1842 Mr. Goodwin married Miss Eliza, daughter of William and Lydia (Russell) Sargent, and they have four children—Elizabeth, wife of Martin Supler; Lydia, wife of Samuel Grim; J. T., wholesale druggist in Wheeling, W. Va., and William (deceased). Mrs. Goodwin was a member of the Baptist Church until her death in 1871. Mr. Goodwin belongs to the Christian Church, in which he has been superintendent of the Sabbath-school. Mr. Goodwin is (1888) the Prohibition candidate for sheriff of Greene County.

DANIEL GOODWIN, farmer and stock-grower, Wind Ridge, Penn., was born in Washington County, Penn., April 3, 1820, and is a son of John and Sarah (Gardner) Goodwin, natives of Pennsylvania and of German origin. His father was a weaver and farmer, and reared a family of nine children, the subject of our sketch being the oldest. He was reared on the farm on Ten-Mile Creek in Center Township, where he attended the district school. Mr. Goodwin is a very successful farmer, industrious, economical and prudent in his business. He has succeeded in accumulating a handsome fortune. He started in life a poor boy, his first investment in land being the purchase of thirty acres on time when land was very cheap, and when he did not have money enough to pay for five acres at present prices. But through energy and determination to succeed he has been able to add to his possessions, until now he is the owner of 600 acres of valuable land, well stocked and improved. Mr. Goodwin was united in marriage, in 1844, with Miss Julia Ann, daughter of Ezekiel and Catharine (Huffman) Braden, who were of Irish and German origin.

Mr. and Mrs. Goodwin were the parents of five children—Eliza J., wife of Richard Supler; Sarah, wife of D. W. Vanatta; John, Mary A. and Daniel Mack. Mrs. Goodwin died March 5, 1888. Mr. Goodwin is a member of the Baptist Church, in which he has served as deacon for many years. He takes an active interest in the schools of his district, and has served a number of years as school director.

THOMAS L. GRAY, farmer and stock-grower, was born in Marshall County, W. Va., August 19, 1824, and is a son of Matthew and Sarah (Lazear) Gray. They were natives of Pennsylvania, his mother having been born on the farm where the subject of our sketch now resides. His father, who war a farmer all his life, died in 1884. Thomas L. Gray is a member of a family of nine children. He was reared on the farm where he now resides, and has made farming his main occupation, in connection with which he has engaged in the coal business extensively, having opened a valuable bank on his farm about twenty years ago. Mr. Gray is the owner of 600 acres of land, 170 acres being in his home farm in Richhill Township, and 300 acres in Washington County. In 1859 Mr. Gray married Miss Hannah, daughter of James and Hannah Barnhart. Their children are —John W., a farmer; James M., Sarah L., wife of Peter Gibbons; Benjamin Franklin, Margaret, wife of James Braden; Hannah, Jesse L. and Thomas L. Mr. Gray is a member of the Methodist Episcopal Church. In politics he is a Democrat, and has served as clerk and inspector of elections.

ELIAS K. GRIBBEN, farmer and stock-grower, was born in Richhill Township, Greene County, Penn., September 27, 1843, and is a son of James and Nancy (Kerr) Gribben. His mother was a native of Allegheny County, Penn. His father was born in Ireland and came to America at the age of twenty-one, was a farmer all his life, and died in Greene County, Penn., in 1885. His family consisted of eleven children, nine of whom are still living, Elias K. being the third in the family. He has spent his life in farming, and still continues in that business. He is the owner of a fine farm of 140 acres where he resides in Richhill Township. In 1862 he enlisted in Company A, Eighteenth Pennsylvania Cavalry, was in the battles of Hagerstown, Gettysburg, and Brandy Station, Va., was wounded three times, and was discharged in 1864. In 1869 Mr. Gribben married Hester Jane, daughter of Jacob Loar, a prominent citizen of Richhill Township. Mrs. Gribben is of Dutch lineage. Their children are—Jacob L., James Harvey, Olive M. and Charley T. Mr. and Mrs. Gribben are members of the Methodist Protestant Church, in which he is a trustee and superintendent of the Sabbath-school. In politics he is a Democrat, and has served as school director.

46

CAPT. SAMUEL GRIM, farmer and stock-grower, who was born in Richhill Township, March 24, 1837, is a son of Armstrong and Mary Ann (Scott) Grim, natives of this county, and of German and English origin. His father spent his life as a farmer. Of his family of nine children, all grew to be men and women and are now in active life. Capt. Grim is the third in the family, was reared on his father's farm, and received his education in the common schools and Waynesburg College. When the war broke out he gave up his studies and enlisted in Company B, First West Virginia Cavalry, was elected First Lieutenant and served three years. He was afterwards promoted to the position of Captain, and among other engagements he was in the second battle of Bull Run and the battles of Gettysburg and Winchester. After returning from the war, February 25, 1865, he embarked in the mercantile trade, opening a general store at West Finley, Washington County, Penn. After a period of nine years he returned to Richhill Township, settled on a farm, and has since continued in that occupation. He owns the farm where he now resides, which is well stocked and improved and contains 216 acres. Capt. Grim was united in marriage, February 14, 1864, with Lydia J., daughter of A. J. and Eliza (Sargent) Goodwin, natives of Greene County, and of German extraction. Their children are— Francis Sherman, Rosala, wife of James Allison, of Waynesburg, Penn.; Robert Lincoln, Henry Ward Beecher, Edna Blanche, James G. Blaine, Loa Logan and Frances Lydia. In politics Capt. Grim is a Republican. He is Adjutant of the William Smith G. A. R. Post, No. 428.

REV. WILLIAM HANNA, Presbyterian minister, is a native of the Buckeye State, having been born in Trumbull County, Ohio, May 6, 1820. He is a son of Isaac and Martha (Davis) Hanna, who were natives of Pennsylvania, and of Scotch-Irish descent. The subject of this sketch is a descendant of Robert Hanna, the founder of Hannatown, Westmoreland County, Penn. The Hanna family are usually farmers and as a rule have been successful in their business. Rev. Hanna wrote one volume of a history of Greene County, but did not complete the work as it was financially a failure. He has been quite successful in business, and is the owner of a large and well improved farm in Richhill Township, where he resides a part of each year. He also owns two business blocks in Cannonsburg, Penn., and a splendid winter residence at Beck's Mills, Penn., and has considerable personal property. When Mr. Hanna was six years of age his father died. His early life was spent in Fayette County, where he attended the George's Creek Academy. At an early age he became a member of the Presbyterian Church, and was licensed to preach in 1850. His first charge was at Masontown, Fayette County, Penn., where he remained for a period of nine years. He then preached in

Graysville, Richhill Township, Greene County, Penn., six years, and for some time had a charge at West Elizabeth in Allegheny County. He is an earnest temperance man and votes the prohibition ticket. He is a member of the Sons of Temperance. In 1844 Mr. Hanna married Sarah, daughter of Hon. Samuel Nixon, of Fayette County, Penn., who was of Scotch-Irish descent. This union has been blessed with ten children, three of whom are now living, viz: William C., Martha J., and James W. The family are members of the Presbyterian Church.

JAMES HUGHES, farmer and stock-grower, was born near Jefferson, Penn., February 12, 1829. He is the son of James and Margaret (Heller) Hughes, and grandson of Thomas Hughes, founder of Jefferson Borough. His father was a farmer and land speculator, and acted in the capacity of high sheriff of Greene County. He died in 1861. The subject of this sketch is the eighth in a family of ten children. He was reared on a farm near Jefferson, where he acquired his early education. In 1864 he moved from his birthplace to Richhill Township. He owned a general store at Bristoria for twelve years, but has devoted most of his life to farming. He owns over 400 acres of valuable land where he now resides in Richhill Township. Mr. Hughes was united in marriage, October 25, 1854, with Hester, daughter of Valentine Nichols. Her mother's maiden name was Nancy A. Cooper. They were of English origin. Her father was a farmer. He was among the early settlers. Mr. and Mrs. Hughes have four children—Winfield S., whose wife died in 1885, leaving two children—Lulu Z. and Bessie Pearl; Anabel, deceased, who was the wife of J. L. Supler, and mother of one child— Willis W.; George V. and William. Mrs. Hughes is a member of the Cumberland Presbyterian Church. Mr. Hughes is a Republican. He took an active interest in the Granger movement. During the late Rebellion he took an active part in trying to put it down, helping to raise money and men. He also reared his nephew, William G. Milliken, who at the age of seventeen enlisted in Company G, of the Eighteenth Pennsylvania Cavalry. The Hughes, Swans and Vanaters were among the first settlers of Greene County; they settled along the Monono, at or near Jefferson.

WILLIAM JACOBS, ex-treasurer of Greene County, was born in Richhill Township, August 18, 1835. He is a son of Daniel B. and Hannah (Rail) Jacobs, natives of Maryland. His father is a prominent farmer and resides in Franklin Township. William was reared on the farm, attended the common schools and made farming his main occupation until 1884, when he was elected to the office of treasurer of the county. Mr. Jacobs was an efficient officer and made many friends while in that capacity. He was ably assisted by his son, D. W. Jacobs, a steady, industrious young man and a first-class penman. Mr. Jacobs owns a well improved farm in Richhill Township where he resides. He was united in marriage, January 17, 1856, with Hester J., daughter of John Loar, and they have two children—D. W. and Anna B., wife of Robert R. Headley. Mr. and Mrs. Jacobs are members of the Methodist Protestant Church. Mr. Jacobs is a Democrat, aud has served as school director of his township. He is also a prominent member of the I. O. O. F.

S. KNIGHT, undertaker and furniture dealer, Jacksonville, Penn:, was born in Monroe County, Ohio, September 4, 1829. His parents, Stephen and Sarah (Wells) Knight, were natives of Pennsylvania, and of English origin. His father was a farmer by occupation, and died in Ohio. His family consisted of fifteen children, twelve of whom grew to maturity. The subject of our sketch is the ninth in the family. He was reared on his father's farm, received a common school education, and early in life commenced his present business, which he has carried on at Jacksonville, Penn., for nearly half a century. During that time he has been director at twenty-five hundred funerals. Mr. Knight has been twice married—first, December 20, 1849, to Lucy L., daughter of John Conkey, and they were the parents of six children, four living—Anna, J. M., William and Elizabeth. Mrs. Lucy Knight died in 1886. In 1887 Mr. Knight married Charlotte, daughter of Andrew Smith, and sister of the present county treasurer. She is of Scotch descent. His wife is a member of the Church of God, and Mr. Knight is a Cumberland Presbyterian, of which church he is a trustee. He is a Democrat. He has served as school director, and as justice of the peace for ten years. He is a member of the I. O. O. F., belongs to the Encampment, and is one of the best and most highly respected citizens of the county.

JESSE LAZEAR was born in Guernsey County, Ohio, June 25, 1825. He is a son of Francis and Mary (Crow) Lazear, natives of Greene County, Penn., and is among the earliest settlers. His mother was of German origin. His father was of French descent. He died in 1871, at the advanced age of seventy years. Thomas Lazear, grandfather of Jesse Lazear, was apointed magistrate by the Governor, served for years in that capacity. The family have usually been farmers and successful in all their business ventures. Jesse Lazear is the oldest in a family of six children. His parents came to Richhill Township in 1827, where he was raised on the farm and received his education in the common schools. He has made farming and stock-growing his business through life, and has met with success, being at present the owner of a large, well improved farm where he resides near Ryerson's Station, Penn. His residence is a substantial brick building, beautifully located. Mr. Lazear was united in marriage, March 25, 1856, with Miss Alice, daughter of Morford and Nancy (Simpson) Throckmorton, who were of Irish and English extraction.

Mr. and Mrs. Lazear are the parents of the following named children—William, Mary, wife of J. C. McCracken, M.D., Cameron, W. Va.; Fannie, wife of Silas Inghram; and John. In politics Mr. Lazear is a Democrat.

JOHN J. LESLIE, farmer and stock-grower, born in Richhill Township, December 3, 1836, is a son of Samuel and Sarah (Jones) Leslie, who were respectively natives of Ireland and Pennsylvania. His father worked on public-works during his early life, but devoted his time to farming after coming to Greene County in 1834. He settled on a farm in Richhill Township, remaining there until his death in 1869. The gentleman whose name heads this sketch was reared on the farm in his native township, where he attended the district schools. He took up farming as his occupation and has made it a success, owning at present one hundred and fifty-three acres of land, well stocked and improved, where he now resides near Harvey's, Penn. Mr. Leslie was united in marriage, in this county in 1869, with Miss Nancy A., daughter of Spencer Bebout. They were the parents of four children—two now living, Florence and Samuel S. Mrs. Leslie died in 1877. In 1879 Mr. Leslie was again united in marriage, his second wife being Mary G., daughter of Munson Post. They are the parents of one child—Robert P. Mr. Leslie is a member of the Christian Church. In politics he is a Democrat. He takes an active interest in school affairs, and has served on the school board of the township where he now resides.

JACOB LOAR, farmer and stock-grower, was born in Allegany County, Maryland, February 6, 1817. His parents were John and Hester (Stephens) Loar, natives of New Jersey, and of German lineage. His father, who was born in 1794, was a farmer by occupation. He came to Whiteley Township, Greene County, in 1820, and died in 1873 at the advanced age of eighty-four years. His family consisted of fourteen children, eleven of whom grew to maturity. Three of his sons were physicians and two ministers. Jacob, the second in the family, settled in Richhill Township, in 1837, and has been very successful in business. He owns the valuable farm of of two hundred and twenty acres where he now resides. Mr. Loar is prominent and influential in his community, has been a member of the school board and served as the justice of peace for a period fifteen years. He has been three times married—first, in 1836, to Maria Nelson, and they were the parents of nine children, six of whom are now living, viz., John M., a farmer; Nelson, a physician in Bloomington, Illinois; George, a physician in Munroe, Iowa; Margaret Ann, wife of A. K. Allum; Hester Jane, wife of E. J. Gribben and Anna, wife of Oliver Burns. The deceased are James Apoloe, Jacob H. and Catharine who was the wife of B. F. Temple. Mrs. Hoar died in 1864. Mr. Loar's second wife was Sarah Williams widow of Morrison Applegate, who died February 11, 1875. They had one son—William C., a medical student in Indianapolis, Ind., and one daghter, Ora who died April 1888. Mr. Loar was again married, in 1881, to Mary Dinsmore, widow of Benjamin Durbin. She was the mother of six children; viz., Mary, Harvey, Elizabeth, Thomas, William and Bothenia. Mr. Loar is a member of the Methodist Protestant Church, of which he has been steward and trustee. He wife is a Presbyterian.

J. K. LOUGHRIDGE, farmer and stock-grower, was born in Wheeling, W. Va., May 21, 1823, is a son of William and Mary (Kettler) Loughridge. His father was of Scotch origin, born in Coleraine, County Derry, Ireland, came to America during the war of 1812, being six weeks in making the passage. Was married in Phildelphia, Penn., in 1814, where he remained for some time. He afterwards came to Pittsburg and next moved to Wheeling, W. Va., where he engaged in the hotel and livery business, these being the first established in the city. He purchased a portion of the farm on which J. K. Loughridge now resides in 1817. Here he removed his family, in 1827, where he remained until his death, in 1867, being ninety-five years of age. He was one of the first school directors under the free-school system in Richhill Township, Greene County, Penn., and elder of the Unity Presbyterian Church. His mother was of German origin, was born in Philadelphia, Penn., in 1787, where she was married to Briton Sollars. Their eldest child, Levi, was married to Elizabeth Burns and resides in Richhill Township. Their daughter Elizabeth married Alexander Burns and is now deceased. They were both educated at Wheeling, W.Va. Elizabeth was the first female school teacher in Richhill Township, and produced some of the finest specimens of penmanship of the day. After the death of her husband, Mrs. Sollars married Mr. Smith, a painter, in Philadelphia, who lost his life in the war of 1812. She next married William Loughridge, by whom she had nine children, of which seven grew to man and womanhood. Margaret married R. S. Dinsmore, a Presbyterian minister, both are now deceased; Mary taught in the high school at New Castle and afterwards in Ohio, where she married Jesse McBride, a Wesleyan Methodist minister, both are now deceased. William A. married Hannah Grey and is now a carpenter and farmer in Keokuk County, Iowa; Alexander W. married Susan Jennings and is how a stock-merchant in Iowa; Dr. J. H. married Candace Power, was a physician and surgeon in the late war and is now located in Rensellaer, Ind., where he has an extensive practice. Emma, the youngest, married John C. Booher, and is now deceased. John K., the fourth in his father's family, married Harriet Campsey, daughter of James and Isabella (Dougherty) Campsey, Claysville, Penn. The family of Mr. and Mrs. Loughridge, are James H., Willmette, wife of Dr. T. B. Hill; William W., John W., Maud I., David G. C. and Hettie M. Mr. Loughridge took an active interest in the Sabbath-schools at an early day; also took a great interest in the progress of the district schools, acting in the capacity of school director for seven years in succession. His education and the greater portion of his property has been acquired principally by his own efforts, his farms are well situated for farming and grazing, well improved, contains nearly 500 acres and has been his place of residence from early childhood. He is a Democrat in politics. A man of good moral principles and was the first chosen on the jury which found George Clark guilty of the murder of William McCauslain near Carmichael's, Penn.

PHILLIP MARSH, deceased, was one of Richhill Township's representative citizens. He was born in New Jersey in 1811. His parents were Joseph P. and Nancy (Minton) Marsh, natives of New Jersey, and of English lineage. His father was a shoemaker by occupation, which vocation he followed for many years. He had eight children, the subject of this sketch being the fifth. Phillip Marsh was raised in Washington County, Penn., where he had removed with his parents about the year 1824. He came to Greene County and engaged in farming until the time of his death in 1877. He was an elder in tne Cumberland Presbyterian Church and superintendent of the Sabbath-school. In politics he was a Republican. Mr. Marsh was married, November 20, 1835, to Martha, daughter of Ephraim and Martha (Elliott) Post, and they were the parents of the following named children—Ann Eliza, wife of Harvey Conkey; Caroline, widow of Samuel Thompson; Eveline, Lucy, wife of George Jennings; Laura F., wife of Cassius Jennings; Leroy, a farmer; and Ellsworth. Mrs. Marsh is a member of the Cumberland Presbyterian Church.

WILLIAM G. MILLIKEN, merchant, of the firm of Milliken & Supler, Bristoria, Penn., was born on Wheeling Creek, in this county, January 21, 1845. His parents, Joseph and Mary (Hughes) Milliken, were of Irish and English origin. His father, who was a cooper and farmer by occupation, died in this county. Of his family of six children, William is the third, and was reared in Jefferson Township, where hs received his education. In 1862 he enlisted in Company G, Eighteenth Pennsylvania Cavalry, and was a non-commissioned officer. He was taken prisoner at Hanover, Penn. Mr. Milliken participated in the battles of The Wilderness, Spottsylvania, Cold Harbor, Cedar Creek and Winchester, and many others, and was discharged at the close of the war in 1865. He then returned to Richhill Township and engaged in farming until 1881, when he embarked in his present business, in which he has a liberal patronage and meets with success. In 1866 Mr. Milliken married Margaret, daughter of Valentine Nichols. To Mr. and Mrs. Milliken were born five children—Isadora, Mary F., John W., Mettie, and Loyd (deceased). Mrs. Milliken departed this life in 1885. She was a consistent member of the Cumberland Presbyterian Church. Mr. Milliken is a member of the G. A. R. Post, in which he has served as Quartermaster.

JOHN M. MURRAY, physician and surgeon, Jacksonville, Penn., was born in the State of Iowa, April 23, 1846. He is a son of Joseph and Leah (Larimer) Murray, who were natives of Pennsylvania, and of Scotch-Irish descent. His father was a school-teacher in early life, in later years a farmer. His family consisted of nine children, Dr. Murray being the sixth. He was reared in this county and received his literary education in the State Normal School of Erie and Waynesburg College. He studied medicine with Dr. J. T. Iams, then a practicing physician of Richhill Township. Dr. Murray afterwards attended Bellevue Medical College at New York City, where he graduated in 1876. He began the practice of his profession at Wind Ridge, Penn., during the same year, and has met with a liberal and successful patronage. He is an active member of the Greene County Medical Society. In 1879 Dr. Murray married Miss Jennie, daughter of Morrison Applegate. Mrs. Murray was of English descent. She died in 1885, leaving two children —Austin and John C. Mrs. Murray was a member of the Methodist Protestant Church, and Mr. Murray is a member of the Presbyterian.

T. J. McCLEARY, farmer, stock-grower and attorney at law, was born February 20, 1837, in Claysville, Washington, County, Penn., and is the son of William and Susan G. (Wilkinson) McCleary. His father was born near Winchester, Virginia, and his mother was a native of Fayette County, Penn. His grandfather, Thomas McCleary, came from Ireland to America in company with his three brothers. They were all in the army of Washington during the Revolutionary war, Thomas being the only one who lived to the close of the war. After peace was declared he settled near Winchester, Virginia, and engaged in farming, T. J. McCleary's father, who died in Washington County in 1881, had a family of eleven children, of whom the subject of our sketch is the oldest son. He was reared on the farm and received his education in the common schools, the academy and normal school. He taught in Greene and Washington counties a number of terms. He afterwards read law, and has given it his particular attention, although he has lived on the farm the greater part of his life. He owns and deals in Western lands. Mr. McCleary was married in Washington County, August 8, 1860, to Martha J. Rossell, daughter of Rev. Job and Mariah L. (Layton) Rossell, and their children are—W. Clarence, Arthur V., Thomas W., Z. Linn; one daughter, Idesta Ethleen. Mr. and Mrs. McCleary are members of the Baptist Church, and he belongs to the I. O. O. F. and Patrons of Husbandry, or the Grange. He is a Democrat, and accustomed to addressing the public when called upon to do so. The father of Mrs. McCleary, Rev. Job Rossell, is deserving of special mention. He was born July 19, 1813, in Fayette County; was licensed to preach by the Flatwoods Baptist Church. For nearly fifty years he labored in the Master's cause. During all these years to the many people who knew him in Westmoreland, Fayette, Washington and Greene counties, the name of Job Rossell was not uttered without bringing to those who heard it a train of thought by which their better natures were more fully developed, and their love for their fellow man strengthened and broadened. He moved to this township in 1861, locating near Ryerson's Station; was for a number of years pastor of South Wheeling Church. He passed to the other shore on September 21, 1884, there to realize more fully the fruits of his labor here. He is the only man, so far as the writer knows, who gave his whole time to the Baptist Churches and missionary work in this region, in which work he was successful. Many organizations by him were started which are to-day prosperous churches; among which is Fork Ridge, West Virginia. I have told you he was the only man, and yet he was not the only one. During these many years to his good wife was left largely the care of the home and family, and she did her part nobly; her sacrifices were many; for many years she was an invalid, but ever cheerful and bright. She passed to her rest November 30, 1887. During the last years of their lives they were tenderly cared for by Mrs. McCleary and her husband, T. J. and children. Eternity alone can reveal the greatness of these lives, in producing fruit for the Master's kingdom. A handsome bronze monument now marks their last resting place.

B. H. McNAY, farmer and stock-grower, was born in Franklin Township, Greene County, Penn., December 20, 1836. His parents, James and Anna (Dickerson) McNay, were natives of Pennsylvania and among the early settlers of this county. They were of Irish and English extraction. His father was a farmer during his lifetime, and died in this county in his eighty-first year. He reared a family of eleven children, ten of whom grew to maturity. The subject of our sketch is the ninth in the family. He was reared on the farm, obtained a common-school education, and afterwards attended Waynesburg College. He has since been engaged in agricultural pursuits, and owns 240 acres of land where he resides in Richhill Township. Mr. McNay has been twice united in marriage, his first wife being Frances Carson, and they were the parents of three children—J. W., Anna Maud and Leonora M. Mrs. McNay died in 1879. Her husband was afterwards married, in 1882, to Miss Mary, daughter of Thomas Stewart, and they have three children—Mabel

M., H. Earl and Louie.   Mr. McNay is a Republican.   He and wife
are members of the Cumberland Presbyterian Church.

JOHN ORNDOFF, farmer and stock-grower, born in Greene
County April 9, 1839, is a son of William and Salone (Wisecarver)
Orndoff.   His mother was a native of Greene County.   His father,
who was born in Old Virginia, was a farmer all his life, having over
sixty years ago settled in Center Township, where he resided until
his death in 1885.   His family numbered eleven children, of whom
the gentleman whose name heads this sketch is the sixth.   He was
reared on his father's farm, attended common school in Center Township, and has made farming a success.   He is the owner of 435 acres
of valuable land and a fine country residence.   Mr. Orndoff is energetic and industrious, having followed the example of his father who,
when he came to this county, was a poor boy with no earthly possessions but his clothing and a horse and saddle; but by economy
and a determination to succeed, he owned at the time of his death
900 acres of land.   John Orndoff was united in marriage, November
2, 1867, with Minerva, daughter of Matthias Roseberry, and they
are the parents of six children; viz., Oscar F., Amanda S., Alice
M., John B., Jessie L. and Benjamin H.   In politics Mr. Orndoff
is a Republican.   His wife is a member of the Baptist Church.

H. H. PARRY, blacksmith, Bristoria, Penn., was born in Westmoreland County, Penn., February 16, 1845, and is the son of Royal
L., and Elizabeth (Lidea) Parry.   His parents were natives of Wales.
His father was a blacksmith, and followed the trade during his lifetime.   He had a family of thirteen children, five of whom are now
living.   Mr. H. H. Parry was raised on a farm in Richhill and
Washingtown townships.   He received the benefit of a common
school education, and learned his trade early in life.   In 1863 he
enlisted in Company D, Twelfth West Virginia Infantry, and was
in several engagements—among which were the battles of Petersburg, Cedar Creek, Hunter's Raid and Winchester.   At the close of
the war he was discharged by general order.   After his return home he
opened a blacksmith shop, and worked for four years in Aleppo Township, and since that time has been located at Bristoria.   He owns a
small farm, in connection with his shop, also a neat and substantial
residence.   In 1869 Mr. Parry married Miss Mary, daughter of James
McVay, Aleppo Township, one of the prominent farmers and stock-
growers in this county.   Mr. and Mrs. Parry's children are Charles
McVay, M. Jane, Flora B., James M., Harry L. and Mary M.   Mr.
Parry is a Republican, and a member of the G. A. R. Post.

J. E. PATTERSON, physician, was born near Claysville,
Washington County, Penn., March 20, 1848.   His parents were
John and Mahala (Patterson) Patterson, who were of Irish and
German extraction.   His father, who was a farmer all his life, came

to Greene County in 1854, and settled in Center Township on the farm where the subject of this sketch was reared. Dr. Patterson acquired a common school education, after which he attended Waynesburg College and the State Normal School. He began the study of medicine with Dr. Gray, of Jacksonville, Penn., and subsequently attended the Medical College at Cleveland, Ohio. He first engaged in his profession, in 1871, in the vicinity of Graysville this county, where he has since been in active practice, with the exception of a short time spent in Nineveh, Pennsylvania. In 1874 Dr. Patterson married Anna, daughter of Mulford Burroughs, and they are the parents of four children, viz., Charles, John, Alma and Bashie. In politics Dr Patterson is a Democrat.

MASON SCOTT, farmer and stock-grower, was born in Richhill Township, Greene County, Penn., May 3, 1837, and is a son of Capt. John and Charlotte (Mason) Scott, who were of German and Irish descent. His father is a farmer and a resident of Jackson Township, this county. Mr. Mason Scott is the oldest of six children now living. He grew to maturity on his father's farm and received a good common-school education. Early in life he taught school-for a time, but he made farming and stock-raising his chief pursuit. He is the owner of 252 acres of land well stocked and improved, where he resides near Bristoria, Penn. Mr. Scott was united in marriage, December 22, 1866, with Sarah, daughter of James and Jane (Sanders) Lemmon. They were of Dutch and English descent. Mr. and Mrs. Scott's children are Albert, Clara Alice; and Westley, (deceased). Mr. Scott is a Democrat, and an efficient member of the school board of his township.

HIRAM SCOTT, farmer and stock-grower, who was born in Center Township, Greene County, Penn., May 13, 1841, is a son of Elias and Harriet (Kent) Scott, natives of this county, and of Dutch and Irish extraction. His father spent all his life as a farmer, and died in Greene County in 1884. His family consisted of eight children, of whom Hiram Scott is the third. Having been reared on a farm, he has followed farming as his chief pursuit and is the owner of 180 acres in Richhill Township, where he now resides. In 1861 Mr. Scott was united in marriage with Miss Mary, daughter of the late Dennis Iams, who was a wealthy and influential farmer. Mrs. Scott is of German lineage. Their children are Thomas, George B. McClellan, a medical student; Matilda, wife of James Throckmorton; Florence and Charles. Mr. Scott is a Democrat. He and his wife are members of the Baptist Church.

ROBERT SMITH, county treasurer, was born in Washington County, October 29, 1836, and is a son of Andrew and Ellen (Little) Smith, His mother, who was of English extraction, was born in New Jersey. His father was a native of Scotland, where he was a farmer and herdsman.   He died in this county in 1870 at the age of seventy-four years.   His family consisted of twelve children, of whom Robert is the oldest.   He has spent most of his life in Greene County, having received his education in the schools of Richhill Township.   He also attended school for some time in Fayette County. Mr. Smith engaged in farming and stock-growing until he was elected to his present position in 1887.   He was married in this county, May 26, 1859, to Miss Elizabeth, daughter of Thomas and Elizabeth (Caine) Milliken, and they are the parents of the following children, viz., Mary Ellen, who died at the age of fourteen; Arabella, W. D., A. J., T. E., R. M. and J. H. P.   Mr. Smith is actively interested in educational matters.   In 1872 he was elected county commissioner and served two years and ten months in that position.

JAMES L. SMITH.—Among the enterprising young business men of Greene County, few have met with better success than the firm of Smith Bros.   Dealers in general merchandise, Graysville, Penn., successors to J. W. Hays.   James L. Smith. the senior member of the firm, was born in Center Township, this county, March 12, 1856, and is a son of Thomas and Susan (Scott) Smith, natives of Greene County, and of Scotch-Irish extraction.   His father, a successful farmer, now resides in Center Township on a finely improved farm of 300 acres.   The subject of our sketch is the oldest of a family of seven children.   Early in life he learned the blacksmith and wagon maker's trade, in which he engaged for several years.   He was a good mechanic and made a first-class wagon.   Since 1879 Mr. Smith has been in the mercantile business with his brother at Graysville.   He is a Democrat in politics, and is postmaster at Harvey's Penn.   He was married in 1879 to Miss May, daughter of Hon. James W. Hays, ex-member of the Legislature.   They have two children—Jesse F. and Nora.   Mr. and Mrs. Smith are active members of the Baptist Church.

MARTIN SUPLER, farmer and stock-grower, was born in Richhill Township, Greene County, Penn., July 29, 1840, and is a son of William and Lucinda (Cummings) Supler, who were natives of this county, and of English lineage.   His father was a farmer and hotel keeper at Jacksonville, Penn., and died August 20, 1872.   His family consisted of seven children, of whom the subject of our sketch is the second.   He was reared on the farm, attended the common schools and has made farming and stock-growing his occupation all his life, with the exception of the time he spent in the army and a few years during which he engaged in the mercantile trade at Jacksonville.   In 1862 he enlisted in Company C, Eighteenth Pennsylvania Cavalry, and served as Seargeant for his company.   While on picket duty on one occasion he received a gunshot wound which caused him to lose three and one-half inches of bone from his left arm. He was discharged in 1864, having passed through many serious engagements, among which were the battles of Williamsport, South Mountain and Gettysburg. After his return home Mr. Supler engaged in the mercantile business for two years, and has since devoted his time to farming. He owns 135 acres of land with first-class improvements. He was married in this county in September, 1862, to Elizabeth, daughter of A. J. and Eliza (Sargent) Goodwin. They have four children, viz., Jessie L., wife of T. J. Carpenter; Fannie D., A. J. and John B. Mr. Supler is a Democrat, and a member of Smith's Post, No. 428, G. A. R., Jacksonville, Penn.

JOHN M. WRIGHT, born October 12, 1820, is a son of Reasin and Nancy (McGlumphy) Wright, who were of German and Irish and English ancestry. He is the oldest of six children and was raised on his father's farm. When a young man he learned the trade of a millwright. In 1862 he enlisted in Company C, Eighteenth Pennsylvania Volunteer Cavalry, and was discharged at the close of the war, when he returned to Richhill Township, where he still resides. He was married in this county, in 1844, to Hester Ann, daughter of John and Lydia (Boyd) Caseman. Mrs. Wright is of Dutch extraction. Their children are—George W., a farmer; Sarah M., Perry and Elizabeth. In politics Mr. Wright is a Democrat.

G. W. WRIGHT, farmer and stock-grower, born in Richhill Township, February 22, 1849, is a son of John and Hester Ann (Caseman) Wright. He is the oldest of his father's family was raised on the farm and received his education in the common schools. Early in life he learned the carpenter's trade and followed that as a business until 1879, since which time he has both farmed and worked at his trade. Mr. Wright has made his own way in the world. He now owns a well improved farm of 135 acres near Bristoria, Penn. He was married in Vermilion County, Ill., in January, 1871, to Elizabeth J., daughter of Abraham and Mary (Gardner) Kimball, and their children are—Norton, Mary F., Oliver M., Maud D. and Hester L. In religion Mr. Wright is a Methodist, and his wife was a member of the Baptist Church. He is a Democrat and belongs to the I. O. O. F.

P. J. WHITE, merchant, Ryerson's Station, Penn., was born in Aleppo Township, August 4, 1850. His parents, J. M. and Rebecca (Hewitt) White, were natives of Greene County, and of Dutch and English extraction. His father is a farmer and justice of the peace, and now resides on a farm in Aleppo Township. The subject of this sketch is the only member of the father's family now living. He was reared on the farm, attended the select schools and engaged in farming until 1879, when he embarked in the mercantile trade for two years on Hart's Run, in Aleppo Township. He then located at New

Freeport, and carried on a general store until 1883, when he removed to his present location and established the business in which he is meeting with great success. Mr. White was united in marriage in this county in 1872, with Miss Margaret Ann, daughter of W. J. Moore. Mrs. White is of English and Irish lineage. Their children are Mary Rebecca and Hannah E. In politics Mr. White is a Democrat, and was appointed to his present position of postmaster at Ryerson's Station in 1885.

SPRINGHILL TOWNSHIP.

J. R. AYERS, the subject of this sketch, was born in Richhill Township, Greene County, Penn., March 12, 1824, and is a son of Silas and Jane (Rickey) Ayers. His parents were natives of New Jersey, from whence they emigrated to Richhill Township, Greene County, Penn., September, 1807, and are of English origin. His father was a farmer and soldier in the war of 1812, and was engaged in the battles of Lundy's Lane and New Orleans. Of his father's family of eleven children, J. R. is the fourth. He grew to manhood in this county, spent his early life in teaching school, and subsequently chose the occupation of farming and stock-dealing, in which occupation he has been very successful. He owns a fine farm of 200 acres where he resides in Springhill Township. He was married November 9, 1848, to Miss Caroline Dye, who was born in this county November 9, 1829. They are the parents of the following named children: E. L., deceased; R. H., Nanna J., Pennina, Silas and Minor (deceased), Mary M., Ola L., A. D. and J. L. R. H., the second son, who is a farmer, was born in Springhill Township, November 23, 1852. He was reared on the farm, received his education in the district schools. He was married to Miss Avaline White, April 3, 1874. Pennina, widow of E. B. Darling, deceased, was born in Springhill Township, May 20, 1858, and was married March 12, 1874. Mr. and Mrs. Ayers are members of the Baptist Church, in which he is deacon. He is a Republican, and has filled the office of school director and auditor in his township.

JOHN BARGER, retired farmer and stock-grower, who was born in Morris Township, this county, May 25, 1827, is a son of Francis and Sarah (Pettit) Barger. His mother, who is of German and Irish origin, is the daughter of Nathaniel Pettit, an early settler of Morris

Township. His father, whose chief occupation was that of farming, was in early life a shoe-maker and school-teacher. He died in this county April 12, 1854. He was twice married, and the subject of this sketch is the oldest of his four children, aged sixty-one years. Mr. John Barger was a resident of Richhill Township until he was ten years of age, when he moved with his parents to Aleppo, now Springhill Township, and has remained there for over half a century. His education was obtained in the common-schools, and while still a young man he was employed as a farmer for some time. He subsequently established a store in New Freeport, Penn., and carried on a successful business for five years, and in that time he made $10,000. Mr. Barger now owns 400 acres of valuable land, besides good town property. He is a self-made man,—his father, Francis Barger, having been bound out by his father to work for Robert Pelleet, of New York, until he should attain his majority. He,—John Barger—however, managed by industry and economy to get a start in the mercantile trade, with what subsequent success we have already noted. Mr. Barger was united in marriage November 2, 1854, with Emily J., daughter of Noah and Elizabeth (Pettit) Lyon, and their children are—David W., a farmer; James P., a silversmith of New Freeport, Penn.; John W., a teacher, and Homer. Mr. Barger is a Republican, and has been postmaster at New Freeport for a period of twenty years. He and his wife are members of the Christian Church.

JAMES BURDINE, retired farmer and stock-grower, was born in Perry Township, Greene County, Penn., March 7, 1820, and is the son of Levi and Rebecca (Fox) Burdine, who were of Dutch and Irish lineage. His grandfather, Joseph Fox, was a soldier in the Revolutionary war. At the age of five years the subject of our sketch was left an orphan. Most of his early life was spent on the farm in Monongalia County, W. Va., where he attended the common-schools. He was bound out as a farm laborer until eighteen years old, when he came to Whiteley Township, this county. He soon found work on a farm, and received eight dollars per month. On November 22, 1842, Mr. Burdine was united in marriage with Abigail, daughter of Joseph Johnson, of Dunkard Township. Their children are—Dennis, Eliza Jane, Johnson, Mary, wife of J. L. Morford; Harriet A., who was the wife of Lewis Hamilton, and died in 1883; Delila and James Milton. Mr. Burdine's present wife is Fannie, daughter of Rev. John Henderson. They have one child—Orphia. Mrs. Burdine is a member of the Christian Church. Mr. Burdine is a Democrat. He is a self-made man, having begun life as a poor boy, and is now the owner of a fine farm of 118 acres in Springhill Township. He at one time owned over 400 acres. He has paid out over $4,000 of bail money, and has till been able to give his children a good start in life.

W. L. BURGE, farmer and stock-grower, was born in Whiteley Township, Greene County, Penn., August 25, 1827, and is a son of Henry and Rachel (Wildman) Burge. His parents, who were of English and Dutch descent, were natives of this county, and members of the Society of Friends. His father, who died in Virginia in 1866, was a blacksmith, and spent most of his life in that occupation. He was twice married, and his family consisted of fourteen children. The subject of this sketch grew to manhood in Greene County, learned the blacksmith's trade with his father and has followed that as a business for over forty years. In 1861 he went to Virginia and worked at his trade until 1866, when he returned to this county. He has since farmed, and now owns a farm consisting of 118 acres of well-stocked and improved land. In 1850 Mr. Burge married Miss Margaret, daughter of John and Sarah Knight. Mrs. Burge is of English and Dutch ancestry. They have a family of ten children, viz.: Plesa Ann, wife of W. H. Main; Alfred J., William L., Melissa, wife of Albert J. Fordyce; Rachel, wife of John L. Main; Maggie, wife of William H. Dye; Mary M., Ella E., John C. and Rosa E. Mr. and Mrs. Burge are members of the Methodist Episcopal Church, where he has served as class-leader for twenty years, and has also served as steward. Mr. Burge is a Democrat. He takes an active interest in the public schools, and has been for a number of years a member of the I. O. O. F.

THOMAS M. CARPENTER, physician, Deep Valley, Penn., was born in Greene County, January 14, 1843, and is a son of William and Agnes (Derbin) Carpenter. His father, who is a blacksmith by trade, was born in New Jersey, but now resides on a farm in Jackson Township. His mother was a native of Morgantown, W. Va. His grandfather, James Carpenter, was among the earliest farmers of Richhill Township, this county. His father was twice married, and Dr. Carpenter is the oldest child of the first wife. He was reared on his father's farm, obtaining his earliest education in the district school. He studied medicine in the College of Physicians and Surgeons, Baltimore, Md., and is now in active practice as a physician. Dr. Carpenter is a close student, and endeavors to keep himself posted in matters pertaining to his profession. He was united in marriage April 5, 1865, with Miss Margaret J. White, whose parents were of English and Irish origin. Mrs. Carpenter's father, Stephen White, was the first man to build and settle in Deep Valley. Dr. and Mrs. Carpenter are the parents of the following named children: Emma, William, Virginia, James, Stephen, Sarah (deceased), Harriet and Jordan. Winfield Burdine, the youngest child was adopted by Mr. and Mrs. Carpenter when only nine days old. The Doctor is a Democrat, and a member of the Greene County Medical Society. He and wife belong to the Methodist Protestant Church.

P. C. DINSMORE, M. D., Deep Valley, Penn., was born in Richhill Township, Greene County, Penn., January 9, 1854. He is a son of Thomas and Elizabeth (Dickey) Dinsmore, natives of Greene and Washington counties, respectively. They are of Irish and English ancestry. Dr. Dinsmore's father is a farmer and stock dealer now residing on a farm in Washington County. The Doctor is the oldest in a family of six children, and was reared in his native township. He attended the graded schools of Washington County, and commenced the study of medicine with Dr. Silas McCracken, of Claysville, Penn. He practiced for a year in West Virginia, was a student in the Cleveland Medical College one year, and subsequently attended Baltimore Medical College, where he graduated with the honors of his class in 1887, and ex-graduate of Medico Chirurgical Faculty, Philadelphia. The token of honor bestowed on Dr. Dinsmore on this occasion was a gold medal, which he still retains as a souvenir. Dr. Dinsmore has been very successful in his profession, to which he is greatly attached. He was united in marriage August 10, 1881, with Miss Mary B., daughter of George and Harriet Hunt, and they have two children—Thomas A. and George H. In politics Dr. Dinsmore is a Democrat.

JAMES M. FERRELL, Merchant, New Freeport, Penn.— Among the most prominent business men in this part of Greene Greene County we mention the gentleman whose name heads this sketch. He was born at Jacksonville, Penn., April 13, 1851, and is a son of George W. and Sarah (Pettit) Ferrell. His ancestors were among the early German settlers of the county. His father was a shoe-maker all his life, and was in business in Jacksonville for over forty years. His father was twice married, having three children by the first marriage and eight by the second. Mr. James M. Ferrell attended the common schools and Jacksonville Academy at Jacksonville, Penn. Early in life he taught school for a period of nearly three years. In 1873 he engaged in the mercantile trade at Jacksonville, and in 1876 he was appointed salesman for the Singer Sewing Machine Company, for which he acted as general agent for three years, with Harrisonburg, Va., as headquarters, where he and his family lived during the time. In 1882 Mr. Ferrell located at New Freeport, where he established a general store. He is eminently qualified for his business. His affable manner and obliging disposition, coupled with a determination not to be excelled or undersold, have drawn to his store many of the affluent and influential citizens of Springhill Township and surrounding country. He owns a commodious store building, which enables him to carry an extensive stock. Mr. Ferrell was married October 26, 1876, to Miss Frances Henrietta, daughter of Hon. James W. Hays, of Waynesburg, Penn. Mrs. Ferrell was born in Washington, D. C. Their children are—

47

Russell Hays, Jessie Virginia and James Wilson. They are members of the Cumberland Presbyterian Church. Mr. Ferrell is a Republican, and for a time was postmaster at Jacksonville. He is a member of the I. O. O. F. and the Encampment, and in 1875–'76 was representative to the Grand Lodge at Philadelphia, Penn.

F. H. GRIFFITH, a farmer and stock-dealer, residing in Springhill Township, Greene County, is the oldest son of Samuel and Lydia (Blake) Griffith. He was born in Marshall County, W. Va., October 13, 1858, but has spent most of his life in Greene County, Penn., where he came with his parents at a very early age. He attended the schools of Springhill Township, and while still a young man he began farming as his chief pursuit. He has met with more than average success, and has a valuable farm of 150 acres. In 1881 Mr. Griffith was united in marriage with Miss Joanna, daughter of Edward Dowlin, of West Virginia. Mrs. Griffith is of English ancestry. They have two children—Shannon A. and Caddie A. Mr. and Mrs. Griffith are members of the Church of God. He is superintendent of the Sabbath-school, and his political views are Republican.

SAMUEL GRIFFITH, farmer and stock-grower, who was born in Maryland, August 1, 1835, is a son of Daniel and Mary (Strickler) Griffith, who were, respectively, natives of West Virginia and Maryland, and of English origin. His father, who was a farmer and stock-grower, died in this county in 1848. The subject of this sketch is the second in a family of nine children. He was reared on the home farm and attended the district school. Early in life he made choice of farming as his occupation, and has met with great success. He started in life as a poor boy, working for twenty-five cents per day, and has succeeded in accumulating a handsome fortune. His farm, which lies in West Virginia and Greene County, Penn., consists of 257 acres of well improved land, and he has a neat and substantial residence in Springhill Township, where he has lived for twenty-six years. In 1857 Mr. Griffith was united in marriage with Miss Lydia J., daughter of Nathan and Susannah (Richardson) Blake, and they have a family of nine children, viz.—F. H., Susan Mary, wife of John Earnest; Sarah E., J. J., Thomas J., Clarabel, Margaret, Bruce and Martha. Mr. Griffith is a Republican. He and wife are members of the Disciples Church.

LEWIS W. HAMILTON, farmer and stock-grower, was born in Whiteley Township, Greene County, Penn., September 19, 1848, and is a son of William and Margaret (Maple) Hamilton. His mother was a native of this county, and died October 29, 1869, and his father was born in Greene County, Penn., where he spent most of his life. He was a farmer by occupation, and died April 3, 1879. He reared a family of fifteen children, of whom Lewis W. is the youngest. He was reared on the farm, receiving a common-school education. He has made farming his chief pursuit, and has followed it very successfully. On March 10, 1872, Mr. Hamilton married Miss Harriet A., daughter of James Burdine, of Springhill Township. Mrs. Hamilton died in 1883. Their children are— George W., Mary Ellen, Thomas J., Eliza Jane and James W. (deceased). On October 20, 1884, he was again united in marriage, his present wife being Maria M., daughter of John C. Church, of Isabella County, Mich. They have one child—Calva E. Mr. Hamilton is a Democrat; his wife is a member of the Methodist Episcopal Church.

ENOCH HAMILTON, farmer and stock-grower, was born in Whiteley Township, this county, September 20, 1844, and is a son of William and Margaret (Mapel) Hamilton. His parents were of English and German origin, and were natives of this county. His father, who was a farmer and stock-grower, died in 1879. He was reared in Springhill Township, where he attended the common schools. Here he has spent much of his life as a farmer, and has met with marked success. He owns 118 acres of well improved land where he lives near New Freeport, Penn. Mr. Hamilton was united in marriage in 1871 with Elizabeth, daughter of John and Mary (Philson) Tustin. Her parents were of German and English descent. Mr. and Mrs. Hamilton are the parents of the following named children: Delilah Ann, John W., William C., Elizabeth E., Fannie H., Cora L., Festus C. and Lewis W. In politics Mr. Hamilton is a Democrat.

W. P. HOSKINSON, farmer and stock-grower, who was born in this county, December 28, 1838, is a son of George and Sophia (Adams) Hoskinson. His parents were natives of Waynesburg, Penn.,and his ancestors, who were of English extraction, were among the pioneer settlers of Greene County. Mr. Hoskinson's great-grandfather, Adams, was killed by the Indians. His grandfather, Robert Adams, built one of the first brick houses in Waynesburg—the house now occupied by Henry C. Sayers, Esq. Mr. Hoskinson's father was a saddler by trade, and among the prominent citizens of the county, in which he served as associate judge, and also as register and recorder. He died in Waynesburg, July 24, 1884. He was twice married, and by the first marriage there were eight children, of whom the subject of this sketch is the third. W. P. Hopkinson was reared in Waynesburg, where he received his early education. Most of his early life was spent as clerk in a store, and he was given the management of his father's business. In 1860 he bought a half interest in the store, and bought his father's interest in 1861 and carried on a successful business for a period of twenty years. He has since devoted his time to farming and owns 200 acres of valuable land near New Freeport. Mr. Hoskinson was married June 21, 1860, to Rebecca, daughter of Phillip and Matilda (Garrison) Shough. Her father is a prominent farmer of Gilmore Township, having at one time owned over seven hundred acres of land. Mr. and Mrs. Hoskinson are the parents of four children—Phillip D., a clerk and salesman; George W., a farmer; Mary S. and Robert L., who is a student at Waynesburg College. Squire Hoskinson is an active members of the Baptist Church, in which he is a trustee and deacon. He belongs to the I. O. O. F. and the Masonic fraternity.

JOSEPHUS ISIMINGER.—The history of the Isiminger family commences in Greene County with Abraham Isiminger, who came from New Jersey to this county and was among the pioneer German set-tlers. His descendants have been usually farmers. The subject of this sketch, Josephus Isiminger, was born in this county November 3, 1839, and is a son of Andrew and Sarah (Kughn) Isiminger, who were of German and English extraction. His father was a farmer and reared his son to that occupation. Josephus Isiminger, is the sixth in a family of twelve children; attended the district school in Whiteley Township. He owns a good farm where he resides, and has also spent some time at the carpenter's trade, in connection with his agricultural pursuits. In 1861 Mr. Isiminger married Miss Maria Lemley, and they had five children—Nicholas, Eliza J., Eliza-beth R., John and William. Mrs. Isiminger died in 1873. She was a member of the Baptist Church. Mr. Isiminger's second wife was Miss A. M. Dollison, to whom he was married in 1879. They have two children—Elias and Eva. Mrs Isiminger is not a member of the Baptist Church, but she is of Baptist faith.

JACOB ISIMINGER, farmer and stock-grower, was born in Greene County, Penn., February 17, 1830. He is a son of Andrew and Sarah (Kughn) Isiminger, who were also natives of this county, and of German extraction. His father's family consisted of five sons and four daughters, all of whom grew to maturity. Jacob Isiminger was the oldest and was reared in Whiteley Township, on the farm where his father now resides. He attended the common schools and chose farming as an occupation. He is the owner of 100 acres of fine land where he resides, near Deep Valley Postoffice, in Spring-hill Township. Mr. Isiminger was united in marriage, June 1, 1859, with Hannah, daughter of William and Elizabeth (Hinerman) Miller, and they are the parents of four children, viz: McClelland, Stanton, Henry and Willie. Mr. and Mrs. Isiminger are members of the Baptist Church, and Mr. Isiminger has been superintendent of the Sabbath-school for years. He is a Democrat in politics.

JOHN H. MILLER, M. D., Deep Valley, Penn., was born in Springhill Township, Greene County, October 6, 1858, and is a son of Hiel and Mary (Warrick) Miller. His parents were also natives of this county, and of Irish and English lineage. His father who was a farmer all his life died in 1864. Mr. Miller was then in his sixth year and was the eldest of four children. He received his education in the district schools, and at the age of fifteen obtained a certificate and taught his first school. He was for sometime thereafter engaged in teaching the country schools of the county. He then worked for a time in the glass works at Martin's Ferry, Ohio, in which place he was appointed policeman by the town council. He had previous to this time begun the study of medicine, but was obliged to abandon it for the lack of funds. In 1885 he entered the College of Physicians and Surgeons, at Baltimore, Maryland, and in 1886 he became a student in the Western Pennsylvania Medical College, graduating with high honors. He was a diligent and successful student, and was elected president of his class. Dr. Miller returned to Greene County, where his genial manner and professional skill soon won for him a good practice. He has had unusual success in surgery. He was married in Deep Valley to Miss Charlotte, daughter of Joseph and Elizabeth (Geary) Nuss. Her parents were of German origin. Dr. and Mrs. Miller have four children, three now living—Leon, Furman and Floyd. The Doctor and wife are members of the Methodist Episcopal Church. He is a Democrat, and a member of the Greene County Medical Society.

JOHN MILLER, farmer and stock-grower, was born in Springhill Township, Greene County, Penn., June 20, 1845, and is a son of Jacob and Sarah (McConnell) Miller, who were of Irish and German origin. His father was a farmer and stock-grower, and died in this county in 1881. Of his family of eleven children, John Miller is the ninth. He was reared on the farm, attending school in the old log school house of the district. Since his marriage in 1870, he has devoted much of his leisure time to study, and has acquired his education without assistance. He is is now able to read and write and keep his accounts correctly. Mr. Miller owns the farm where he resides, consisting of 123 acres of well improved land. Mr. Miller's wife was Miss Caroline Reeves. She is a daughter of Phineas and Matilda Reeves, and of Irish origin. Her ancestors were among the pioneers of Greene County. In politics Mr. Miller is a Democrat.

J. L. MORFORD, farmer and stock-grower, was born in Springhill Township, this county, November 23, 1847, and is a son of Isaac and Elizabeth (Brown) Morford. His parents were of Irish and German ancestry, and were natives of Greene County. Mr. Morford's ancestors were among the pioneer settlers of the county. His grandfather, James Morford, was a pioneer farmer. Isaac Morford, his father, who spent his life in this county, was killed at Burton, West Virginia, November, 1864, where he was shot by a man who opposed him in a political discussion. His family consisted of six children, of whom the subject of this sketch is the youngest. He was reared on his father's farm, receiving his education in the common schools. He chose farming as his occupation through life and has been very successful, owning at present a fine farm of 122½ acres near New Freeport, Penn. In 1866 Mr. Morford married Miss Mary, daughter of James Burdine. They are the parents of seven children, viz: James B., Mary Ann Eliza., Valma L., Elizabeth A., Samuel M., Lewis Q. and Delilah Harriet. In politics Mr. Morford is a Democrat.

JOHN McNEELY, farmer and stock-grower, New Freeport, Penn., was born in this county March 8, 1842. He is a son of John and Elizabeth (Coen) McNeely, natives of Greene County, and of English extraction. His father was a farmer. His family numbered eleven children, of whom John is the fifth. He spent his early manhood on the farm, receiving his education in the common schools. He has made farming his life work, and his home farm contains 278 acres of valuable land. In 1861 Mr. McNeely was united in marriage with Mary, daughter of Michael and Sarah (Taylor) Roupe. Mrs. McNeely is of Dutch origin. Their children are—Jacob, a farmer; Rachel, wife of Himus Null; Nancy, wife of William Roupe; John, Elizabeth and Robert, Mr. McNeely is a Democrat. His wife is a member of the Baptist Church.

J. H. RINEHART, M. D., New Freeport, Penn., was born in Franklin Township, Greene County, Penn., January 28, 1859. He is a son of William H. and Ruth Ann (Bowen) Rinehart, residents of Springhill Township. Dr. Rinehart is the third in a family of eight children. He attended the common-school and was later a student of Waynesburg College. He studied medicine with Dr. P. C. Dinsmore, of Deep Valley, Penn., and also attended the Starling Medical College at Columbus, Ohio, where he graduated in 1887. He then entered the practice of his chosen profession at New Freeport, Penn., his present location. In 1888 he formed a partnership with Dr. I. N. Owen, an old and experienced physician who has been in active practice in Greene County for many years. At the early age of seventeen the Doctor began teaching school, spending some time in that employment both in this county and in West Virginia. He began the study of medicine at the same time and also paid considerable attention to the study of surveying and civil engineering. He has been through life a diligent student and gives promise of a successful career.

W. H. RINEHART, farmer and stock-dealer, son of Jacob and Abigail (Huss) Rinehart, was born January 6, 1827. His parents were natives of Greene County, and of German descent. The Rinehart's were among the earliest settlers of the county. Several members of the family were killed by the Indians, and others were taken captive when children growing up among the savages. They were almost without exception farmers, but some few a member of the family were professional men. Mr. Rinehart's father, who was a farmer and stock-dealer, died in 1874. The subject of this sketch is the oldest of a family of seven children. He was reared on the farm, receiving his education in the district school in Franklin Township. He has made farming and stock-dealing his occupation and now owns the farm where he resides in Springhill Township. In 1852 Mr. Rinehart was married to Miss Ruth Ann, daughter of Corbly and Joanna (Garrison) Bowen, who were of German, English and French origin. Mrs. Rinehart's paternal grandmother was a member of the Corbly family who were murdered by the Indians near Garard's Fort, this county. Mr. and Mrs. Rinehart are the parents of the following children—M. E., a resident of Deep Valley, Penn.; J. H., a practicing physician; Joanna, wife of Scott Lippencott; Arabell, wife of J. C. F. Milligan; S. Cora and Maude B. The family are members of the Methodist Episcopal Church.

JAMES STILES, merchant and justice of the peace, Deep Valley, Penn., was born in Monongalia County, West Virginia, January 4, 1841, and is a son of Thomas and Frances (Cross) Stiles. His father, who was a farmer, died in West Virginia in 1852. The subject of this sketch, the youngest of seven children, was reared in his native county, where he received a common-school education. After his father's death he was apprenticed as a bound boy until twenty-one years of age. In 1869 he entered the employ of Hon. H. S. White, as a salesman, and formed a partnership with him the same year. This partnership was dissolved in 1871, and Mr. Stiles located at Deep Valley, where he established a general store. In 1883, in company with J. K. Null, he erected the mill at Deep Valley, and later he dissolved partnership with Mr. Null. Squire Stiles has met with success in business and is an honorable, high-minded gentleman. In politics he is a Republican. In 1869 he was united in marriage with Jennie, daughter of Rev. D. Charnock, of Wheeling, W. Va. They were the parents of one child, James, deceased. Mrs. Jennie Stiles died in 1871. In 1873 Mr. Stiles married Emma J., daughter of George Wright, they are the parents of seven children—Ora Belle, Lucy H., Minnie P., James G., Nellie A., Christie and Goldie. Mrs. Stiles is a member of the Methodist Episcopal Church. In 1875 Mr. Stiles was elected justice of the peace, which office he has since held continuously. In 1864 he enlisted in Company N, Sixth West Virginia Infantry, and served until the close of the war. He is an active member of the G. A. R. Post, No. 550, and is now Adjutant.

THOMAS STROPE, farmer and stock-grower, Deep Valley, Penn., was born November 22, 1823, and is a son of Thomas and Sarah (Elems) Strope. His parents were of English descent. His father, who was a farmer during his lifetime, died in 1848. Mr. Thomas Thrope is the fourth in his father's family and the eldest who grew to maturity. His opportunities for an education were very limited. He is a self-made man and now owns 290 acres of well improved land. When he was a small boy he worked by the month and then worked on a farm as a tenant. He also learned the tanner's trade, at which he was employed until twenty-four years of age. Mr. Strope's first wife was Eliza Mitchell, who lived twenty-five years after their marriage. They had one child, George W. Mrs. Sarah Jane Strope, the present wife, was the daughter Jacob Miller, a prominent farmer of Springhill Township. Mr. and Mrs. Strope are the parents of two children—Park L. and Purman D. Mr. Strope is a Republican. He is a member of the Masonic Fraternity and the Patrons of Husbandry. He and wife are members of the Church of God.

W. T. WHITE, farmer and stock-grower, Deep Valley, Penn., was born in Monongalia County, West Virginia, April 30, 1842. He is a son of Michael and Mary A. (Russell) White, who were also natives of West Virginia, and of German extraction. Mr. White's father was a farmer through life, and died in Monongalia County, W. Va., in 1868. Of his family of four children, W. T. White is the second. He was reared on the home farm and received his education in the common-schools. Having chosen farming as his occupation, Mr. White came to Greene County, Penn., in 1872, and settled on a farm in Springhill Township where he now resides. His farm consisting of 185 acres, is well stocked and improved. In 1868 he was married to Miss Harriet, daughter of William and Elizabeth (Odenbaugh) Kent. Mrs. White is of English descent. They have four children—Luella, a school teacher; Guy W., Nettie E. and Charles F. Mrs. White died March 13, 1888. The family are members of the Methodist Episcopal Church, in which Mr. White takes an active interest. He is also greatly interested in school affairs and has been one of the most efficient members of the school board in his township. In 1861 he enlisted in the Sixth West Virginia Volunteer Infantry in Company N., where he served until the close of the war, being a non-commissioned officer.

JOSEPH WHITLATCH, farmer and stock-grower, was born in Whiteley Township, this county, November 22, 1821, and is a son of Joseph and Barbara (Hostetler) Whitlatch. His mother was born in Fayette County, and his father in Greene, and they were of English and Dutch extraction. His father was a farmer and distiller by occupation. His grandfather, Thomas Whitlatch, who was an energetic and industrious farmer through life, was born in England and emigrated to America, coming to Greene County among the earliest settlers. The subject of this sketch, who is the sixth in a family of ten children, resided in Whiteley Township until he was twenty-four years of age. He has followed his father's occupation and has been very successful, being now the owner of 220 acres of well-improved land. Mr. Whitlatch was united in marriage, December 11, 1845, with Miss Jane, daughter of Thomas Owen, who came from Wales. They are the parents of thirteen children—Elizabeth, wife of George Plantz; Benson, who died July 5, 1888, aged thirty-eight years; Barbara J., wife of George Murphy; Sarah Ann, wife of John Springer; Susan Caroline, wife of William Patterson; Mary Ellen, wife of John Nicholas; John W., Peter O., Belle, wife of James Brewer; Viola, William, Isaac N., and David (deceased), who was their oldest child, died April 12, 1880, aged thirty-three years. Mr. Whitlatch is a member of the Baptist Church, in which he has been a deacon for twenty-three years, and also superintendent of the Sabbath-school. The other members of the family are members of the Church of God. Mr. Whitlatch is a Republican, and has been school director in his township. He went into the army as a private in 1864, and served until the close of the war.

WILLIAM WILDMAN, farmer and stock-grower, was born in Gilmore Township, Greene County, Penn., October 31, 1847, and is a son of Joseph and Frances (Cumpston) Wildman. His parents were born in Dunkard Township, and were of English descent. His father spent his life as a farmer. His family consisted of nine children, of whom William is the seventh. He was reared on the home farm, receiving his education in the common schools. Since early life he has made farming his chief pursuit, and has met with unusual success. Mr. Wildman has made his own way in the world, and is now the owner of 175 acres of well-improved land. In 1868 he married Miss Ruth, daughter of Alexander Compston. Mrs. Wildman is of German origin. Their children are—Anna C., wife of Jacob Tustin; Fannie, Eliza Ellen, Harriet, Charles W., and Rebecca (deceased). Mrs. Wildman is a member of the Methodist Episcopal Church. In politics Mr. Wildman is a Democrat.

WASHINGTON TOWNSHIP.

SILAS BARNES, retired farmer, P. O. Ruff's Creek, was born on the farm where he now resides in Washington Township, Greene

County, Penn., August 22, 1810. His parents were Jacob and Phœbe (Crayn) Barnes, who were natives of Pennsylvania. They were the parents of nine children, of whom six are living. The subject sf our sketch is the second of these children, and was united in marriage, in 1832, with Catharine Johns. She was born in Washington Township, this county, in 1816, a daughter of Jacob and Elizabeth (Smith) Johns, who were pioneers of Greene County. Mr. and Mrs. Barnes are the parents of three children—Maria, Elizabeth and John. Mr. Barnes was reared on a farm and has been engaged in farming through life. He owns 300 acres of land. He served as sheriff of the county by appointment, was elected treasurrr in 1847, and in 1878 was elected associate judge and served one term. Mrs. Barnes died in November, 1886.

JAMES BOYD, farmer (deceased), was born in Greene County, Penn., September 10, 1813. His parents, Richard and Mary (Pitney) Boyd, were natives of Maryland, but settled in Greene County, Penn., and remained until their death. James Boyd was united in marriage, April 14, 1839, with Martha Decamp, who was born in Washington County, November 2, 1816. She was a daughter of Runion and Hannah (Winget) Decamp, who departed this life in Iowa. To Mr. and Mrs. Boyd were born eight children, six of whom are living— Permelia, Minerva, wife of George W. Johnson; James, Martha J., Mary S., wife of B. R. Bell, and Hannah J., wife of James C. Bell; the deceased being Elizabeth E., who was the wife of Samuel J. Graham, and Emeline. Mr. Boyd was a farmer, and at the time of his death owned 176 acres of land where his widow and family reside, at Hope P. O., Greene County. He was a consistent member of the Baptist Church, of which Mrs. Boyd is also a member. Mr. Boyd's death occurred August 2, 1885, and he was much mourned, not only by his own family and immediate friends, but as a good citizen throughout the township and county.

ROBERT BRISTOR, farmer, P. O. Hackney Penn., was born in Washington Township, Greene County, August 11, 1818, a son of James and Catharine (Sibert) Bristor, the former a native of Pennsylvania and the latter of Virginia. They settled and remained in Greene County until their death. Robert Bristor was united in marriage, June 15, 1841, with Margaret Oliver, who was born in Washington Township, November 18, 1821. Her parents were Samuel and Elizabeth (Holingsworth) Oliver, the one a native of New Jersey and the other of Pennsylvania. They also settled in Greene County and remained until their death. Mr. and Mrs. Robert Bristor have ten children—Mary J., widow of Shadrach Mitchell; James N., Melinda, wife of Samuel Kelley; Caroline, wife of Joseph Smith; Timothy J., Hannah M., wife of Joseph Martin; Rachel E., Oliver D., John W., and George W. (deceased). Mr.

Bristor has always lived on a farm, and has devoted himself to stock-raising and the care of his land of which he owns 200 acres where, with his family, he now resides. He and his wife are consistent members of the Bethlehem Baptist Church..

SYLVESTER CARY, farmer, deceased, was born in Washington Township, Greene County, Penn., May 6, 1819. His father and mother were Daniel and Mary Cary (nee Cooper), who were natives of Washington County, where they were married, then settled in Greene County, remaining till their death. Sylvester Cary was twice married, his first wife being Miss Hannah Cooper, born August 14, 1820, a daughter of Zebulon Cooper. By this marriage Mr. Cary was the father of nine children, only one of whom—Elmas W.—is now living. Mrs. Cary died in 1858. Her husband then married, March 10, 1859, Sarah J. Cooper; she was the widow of Nathaniel Cooper, and was born March 29, 1833. Her father and mother were John and Martha Cooper (nee Atkinson), who were natives of Pennsylvania, and after marriage residents of Washington County until death. By his second marriage Mr. Cary was the father of five children—Laura B., wife of Oscar Day; Thomas S., Alice S., wife of John M. Simpson, John C.; and Hannah M., deceased. Mrs. Cary by her first marriage is the mother of one child—Flora S., wife of John Andrew. Sylvester Cary, deceased, was one of the substantial citizens of Washington Township, In connection with the farming he made quite a success of stock-dealing during his life, and at his death was the possessor of a fine farm containing about 600 acres. He belonged to the Methodist Protestant Church, of which his widow is also a member. Mr. Cary's death occurred January 3, 1886, and it proved a great loss not only to his family but also throughout the community in which he lived.

JAMES W. CLOSSER, farmer, grain and stock-dealer, Waynesburg, Penn.—Among the stirring and prosperous business men of Greene County, we take pleasure in mentioning the name that heads this biographical sketch. He was born in Amwell Township, Washington County, October 15, 1852, and is a son of Andrew J. and Sarah (Totton) Clösser, who were natives of Pennsylvania, married and settled in Bethlehem Township, Washington County, where they remained through life. On September 24, 1882, James W. Closser married Miss Elazan Garner, who was born in Washington Township, April 4, 1858, and is a member of the Baptist Church. Her parents were Matthew and Sarah (Huffman)Garner, the latter of whom is deceased. Mr. and Mrs. Closser's family consists of three children—Daniel, Hallie J. and James I. Although reared on a farm, Mr. Closser has been engaged in various pursuits since starting out in life for himself. He is at present dealing in grain, stock and agricultural implements, besides managing his farms which consist of about 600 acres, owned in partnership with his brother Henry.

JESSE CRAIG, deceased, was born in Virginia, October 20, 1799; and following in the footsteps of the early pioneers, while still a boy, came to Pennsylvania and settled in Greene County, on March 12, 1829, he married Miss Hannah Evans, who was born in Washington County, April 27, 1803, a daughter of David and Elizabeth Evans, both deceased. By this marriage Mr. Craig was the father of one child, David, who married Nancy Matthews. Mr. Craig lost his wife by death, January 27, 1831; but realizing that it was not good for man to be alone, on April 22, 1832, he was married to Miss Sophrona Cary, who was born on the farm where she and family reside, March 5, 1815, a daughter of Abel and Eunice Cary (*nee* Woodruff). Her parents were natives of New Jersey, and early in life settled in Greene County, Penn., remaining until their death. By the last marriage Mr. Craig was the father of thirteen children, of whom nine survive him—Cephas, married Eunice Bigler; Daniel, married Malinda Bane; Sarah, wife of Abel Turner; Abel, married Sarah J. Rejester; Eunice, wife of John G. Barr; Hannah, Eleanor, wife of Silas Hoover; Margaret, wife of George Stilwell, and Sophrona, wife of William Taylor. Thomas (married Leah Horn), Mary, Elizabeth and Jesse, being deceased. Mr. Craig was a successful farmer, and stock-raiser through life, owning at the time of his death a farm of 150 acres. He was a member of the Baptist Church, of which his widow is also a member. He filled in his lifetime the office of justice of the peace of Washington Township. He departed this life, April 26, 1882; and by his death the township lost a good citizen and his family a kind husband and father.

ENOCH DURBIN, retired farmer, Swart's Station, Penn., was born in Richhill Township, Greene County, July 24, 1820, a son of Stephen and Mary Durbin (*nee* McDonell), the former a native of Maryland. After marriage they resided in Richhill Township until their death. Enoch Durbin was united in marriage the first time in 1845, with Mary M. Stagner, born in Morris Township in 1819, a daughter of John and Mary Stagner. By this marriage Mr. Durbin is the father of four children—Peter H., George W., Eliza J., wife of Thomas Iams; and John (deceased). Mrs. Durbin died May 27, 1866. Four years after her death, December 7, 1870, Mr. Durbin took for a second wife Eliza Hopkins, born January 27, 1818, on what was known as the old Hopkins farm, where she and family still reside. Her parents were Daniel and Esther Hopkins (*nee* Johnson). The former was born in eastern Pennsylvania, November 27, 1782, and his wife in Washington County, November 8, 1787. They were married November 15, 1811, and settled in Maryland, then lived in Washington County, Penn., one year and moved to Greene County in 1816, remaining until their death. Mr. Hopkins died October 10,

1828, and his widow October 5, 1866. They were the parents of eight children, of whom six are living—Margaret, Levi, Eliza, the wife of subject of this sketch, Samuel, Abigail, the wife of Rev. J. T. Riley, and Aranna. The deceased are William S. and John J. Enoch Durbin has been a farmer all through life, and he, wife and sister-in-law are all members of the Methodist Episcopal Church.

G. W. DURBIN, farmer, Sycamore, Penn., was born in Morris Township, Greene County, December 20, 1849, a son of Enoch and Mary Durbin (*nee* Stagner). His father and mother were natives of Richhill and Morris townships respectively. They remained in this county after their marriage, Mrs. Durbin departing this life in 1866. Sometime after her death Mr. Durbin contracted a second marriage with Miss Eliza Hopkins, and now resides in Washington Township. George W. Durbin chose as his life partner, September 11, 1875, Miss Jennie L. Fonner, who was born in Morris Township, November 4, 1854, a daughter of James and Eliza Fonner (*nee* Taylor). Her parents were natives of Greene County, where they were married and lived until Mr. Fonner's death, March 16, 1883. His widow is still living. To Mr. and Mrs. Durbin have been born five children—James R., Lizzie B., Albert F., Charlie B. and Maggie E. Mr. Durbin is a farmer by occupation and has made that his life work. He is the possessor of a 100-acre farm on which he and family reside. Both he and wife are consistent members of the Bates' Fork Baptist Church; and he is a leading director of the school board, taking great interest in the educational affairs of the township.

JOHN EDGAR, farmer, Castile, Penn., is one of the substantial farmers and stock-dealers of Washington Township, Greene County, where he was born May 2, 1845. His parents were Isaac and Margaret Edgar, the former a native of New Jersey, and the latter of Washington County, Pennsylvania. After marriage they settled in Greene County and remained until 1868, then lived in Washington County till 1874—the year of Mrs. Edgar's death. Her husband died in 1875. John Edgar was united in the holy bonds of matrimony February 9, 1869, with Mary A. Keys, born in Washington County, September 24, 1850. Her parents, Daniel and Ruth (Bane) Keys, are natives of Washington County where they still reside. Mr. and Mrs. John Edgar are the parents of nine children—Daniel A., Ida R., Maggie M., Lucy L., William K., John, Anna M., Minnie and Clarence. Mr. Edgar has been engaged in farming and stock-dealing all his life. He owns 228 acres of land in one tract, on which he and his family reside. They are consistent members of the Baptist Church, in which he has served as deacon for three years. He has also been a member of the school board of his township.

STEPHEN FULTON, farmer, Castile, Penn., was born in West Bethlehem Township, Washington County, August 16, 1818, a son of Stephen and Jerusha Fulton (*nee* Cary). His mother was a native of Greene and his father of Washington County, where they settled after their marriage and remained through life, Mr. Fulton's death occurring in 1847 and his widow in 1858. September 16, 1847, Stephen Fulton wedded Miss Mary Greenlee, who was born in Washington County, December 26, 1822. She is a daughter of Samuel and Nancy Greenlee (*nee* Gantz), the one a native of Maryland and the other of Fayette County, Penn. After marriage they resided in Washington County until the death of Mrs. Gantz in 1863. Her husband died in 1876. Stephen Fulton and wife are the parents of eight children, five of whom are living—Emma, wife of Zephaniah Johnson; Samuel G., Henry H., Eliza, wife of Amos Shirk, and Albert G.; Nancy, Margaret and Ruth, are deceased. Mr. Fulton has always lived in the country and engaged in farming throughout his life, which has been one of usefulness and activity, and he has acquired for himself and family a farm of 120 acres, where he now lives. They are both members of the Mount Zion Baptist Church.

SPENCER B. GARNER, farmer, P. O. Waynesburg, was born in Greene County, Penn., March 10, 1851. His father, Matthew—son of Samuel and Catharine (Miller) Garner—was born in Washington Township, August 9, 1820; and September 29, 1844, wedded Sarah, daughter of Amos Masters. She was a native of Greene County, and died August 5, 1851. After her death Matthew married Sarah, daughter of John Huffman, December 24, 1854. She was also a native of Washington Township, and died August 23, 1871. Her husband then married, October 3 1872, Miss Maria Keigley, his present wife, a native of the same township and a daughter of George and Anna Keigley, both deceased. Spencer B., the subject of this sketch, was united in marriage, September 16, 1875, with Ella Huss, who was born in Greene County, Penn., August 7, 1854, a daughter of William H. and Maria Huss (*nee* Keys), the former a native of Greene and the latter of Washington County. Mr. Huss is deceased and his widow is now living with her daughter, Mrs. S. B. Garner. To Mr. and Mrs. S. B. Garner have been born two children—Weatha and Isa G. Mr. Garner has been a farmer, stock-dealer and miller through life, and owns 184 acres of land in Washington Township. He and wife are members of the Bates' Fork Baptist Church.

T. J. HUFFMAN, farmer and stock-dealer, Ruff's Creek, Penn., was born in Washington Township, December 17, 1849. His parents, George and Susannah (Stagner) Huffman, are natives of Greene County, where they reside at present. Mr. Huffman, the subject of this sketch, was united in marriage, May 25, 1871, with Eliza M. Mattox, who was born in Morris Township, this county, October 12, 1852, a daughter of John and Clarissa Mattox (*nee* Rial). Her mother was a native of New Jersey and her father of Greene County,

Penn., where they settled after marriage and remained till the death of Mr. Mattox; his widow survives him. Mr. and Mrs. Huffman are the parents of four children, one living—George E., born May 24, 1880; and Lonny, Ida and an infant, deceased. Mr. Huffman is a member of the Baptist and his wife of the Cumberland Presbyterian Church. Mr. Huffman was raised on the farm where he now resides with his family and parents, and in connection with his farming, has dealt in all kinds of stock, making the raising of fast horses a specialty; of these the principal ones are "Slow-Go," and two that Vanderbilt bought. Mr. Huffman has always been known as one of the most successful and enterprising farmers of his township·

G. W. HUFFMAN, farmer and stock dealer, P. O. Ruff's Creek, was born in Washington Township, Greene County, Penn., January 17, 1845. He is a son of George and Susannah (Stagner) Huffman, who are natives of Greene County, where they were married and have resided all their lives. Mr. Huffman was united in marriage, September 20, 1866, with Phœbe J. Baldwin, who was born in Washington County, March 27, 1846. Her parents, Amos and Sarah (Lindley) Baldwin, were natives of Washington County, but moved to Iowa where they both died. Mr. and Mrs. Huffman are the parents of two interesting daughters—Cora B. and Sadie A. Mr. Huffman was brought up on a farm, and in connection with his farming interests has made the raising of fine stock a specialty. He owns 380 acres of land where he and family live, and a fifth interest in 700 acres in Kansas. The whole family are consistent and leading members in the Bethlehem Baptist Church.

ANDREW HUGHES, retired farmer, Ruff's Creek, Penn., is one of the old pioneers of Greene County, having been born in Washington Township, November 1, 1810, a son of Nathan and Nancy (Sharon) Hughes. Mrs. Hughes was a native of England, and her husband was born in Greene County, Penn., where they resided from the time of their marriage until their death. Andrew Hughes was united in marriage, September 25, 1834, with Hannah Crayne, born in Washington Township, April 4, 1815, a daughter of Daniel and Hannah (Clawson) Crayne, the one a native of Greene County, Penn., and the other of New Jersey. After marriage they made their home in Mr. Hughes' native county until their death. Mr. Andrew Hughes and wife are the parents of two children—Asa and Samuel. Mr. Hughes was raised on a farm and has been a tiller of the soil all his life. He owns the 200-acre farm where he now lives with his family. He and wife are members of the Bethlehem Baptist Church, in which they have ever been regarded as among the most prominent and faithful workers.

ZEPHANIAH JOHNSON, retired farmer, Castile, Penn.—The subject of this sketch is one of the substantial pioneer farmers of

Greene County, having been born in Morgan Township, December 21, 1812. His parents were Zenas and Phœbe (Wolf) Johnson, who were natives of New Jersey, and after marriage moved to Greene County, Penn., and spent the remainder of their lives. March 6, 1837, Zephaniah Johnson took unto himself a wife in the person of Miss Rachael Ulery, born in Greene County, February 24, 1819. Her parents were Stephen and Jane (Crayn) Ulery, who were natives of Washington County, Penn., but moved to Knox County, Ohio, remaining until their death. By this marriage Mr. Johnson is the father of the following children—Phœbe J., wife of Isaac Keys; Stephen, Zenos, Daniel and Sarah. Mrs. Johnson departed this life July 21, 1853. After her death Mr. Johnson was united in marriage, in 1857, with Mrs. Mary Horn (*nee* Moore), a daughter of Joseph and Mary Moore, both deceased. By the last marriage Mr. Johnson is the father of one daughter—Ellen. Her mother departed this life May 21, 1872. Mr. Johnson has always lived on a farm, to which, in connection with stock-raising, he has given his care and attention through life. His farm consists of 234 acres. He is named among the prominent citizens of his township, and is a leading member in the Mount Zion Baptist Church.

GEORGE W. JOHNSON, farmer, P. O. Ten-Mile, was born in Morgan Township, Greene County, Penn., May 21, 1818. His parents were Zenas and Phœbe (Wolf) Johnson, who were natives of New Jersey, where they were married, then moved to Greene County, Penn., remaining till Mrs. Johnson's death, which occurred in 1819. Her husband then married Sarah Crayn. Both died in Greene County. The subject of our notice was united in marriage, November 4, 1841, with Eunice Smith, born in Amwell Township, Washington County, April 16, 1821. She is the daughter of Peter and Priscilla (Cooper) Smith, the former a native of Germany, and the latter of Washington County, Penn., where they were married, and after settling for a short time in Greene County, returned and died there. Mr. G. W. Johnson and wife are the parents of five children —Smith, I. B., Phœbe J., wife of Othaniel Rhoads; Zephaniah and George A. Having been reared on a farm, Mr. Johnson has been a tiller of the soil all his life, and owns the farm of 170 acres where he now lives with his family. He has served as a member of the school board of his township, and both he and wife are members of the Baptist Church.

ZENAS JOHNSON, farmer, P. O. Ruff's Creek, born in Greene County, Penn., April 12, 1827, is a son of Zenas and Sarah Johnson, the former a native of New Jersey, and the latter of Greene County, Penn., who after marriage settled and remained in this county until their death. Our subject was united in marriage, October 28, 1862, with Sarah J. Watson, born in Washington County, Penn., October

HISTORY OF GREENE COUNTY.

28, 1839, who is still living and is a consistent member of the Methodist Episcopal Church. Her parents were John and Mary A. (Almost) Watson, the former a native of Ireland, and the latter of Greene County, Penn., who settled in Washington County after marriage, where they remained until their death. To Mr. and Mrs. Johnson have been born eight children—George B., Daniel D., Silas C., Sadie, Emma, Maggie, Jennie and Cora. Having been raised on a farm, Mr. Johnson has made farming his business through life, and through industry and economy has secured for himself one of the best farms in Washington Township, consisting of 257 acres.

D. W. JOHNS, farmer, P. O. Ruff's Creek, is a descendant of one of the Pioneer families of Greene County, Penn. He was born in Washington Township, May 21, 1838, a son of Jacob and Elizabeth Johns (*nee* Ross), who are natives of Greene County, the former of Washington Township and the latter of Morgan. They have resided in Washington Township ever since they were married. The subject of this sketch was united in marriage, February 24, 1870, with Rachael Meek, who was born in Washington Township, November 17, 1842, a daughter of John and Elizabeth Meek (*nee* Boyd), who were natives of Greene County, where they remained until their death, Mr. and Mrs. Johns have two children—Thomas S., born June 5. 1871; and John F., born February 8, 1873. Mr. Johns was raised on a farm and has been engaged in farming and dealing in stock all his life. He owns 345 acres of land where he and family live. He and wife are members of the Bethlehm Baptist Church.

JACOB JOHNS, a retired farmer of Ruff's Creek, Penn., is one one of the pioneers of Washington Township, Greene County. He was born on the farm where he and family reside, December 3, 1806, and is a son of Jacob and Elizabeth (Smith) Johns, the former a native of Delaware and the latter of Washington County, Penn., who settled in Greene County after marriage and remained until their death. Jacob Johns was united in marriage March 27, 1834, with Elizabeth Ross, born in Morgan Township, Greene County, May 29, 1816. Her parents, John and Phœbe (Eaton) Ross, were natives of Greene County and residents therein until their death. Mr. and Mrs. Johns are the parents of eight children, four of whom are living and married, as follows: J. R., to Mary J. Huffman; D. W., to Rachael Meek; Abner, to Elizabeth Meek; and Jacob, Jr., first to Lourinza R. McClelland, then to Josephine V. Hickman. The deceased are— Phœbe, Timothy, Thomas, and Elizabeth, who was the wife of Jacob Hoge. Mr. Johns has been engaged in farming all his life and owns about 500 acres of land in Greene County. He held the office of justice of the peace of Washington Township for ten years, and filled the positions of assessor, auditor, inspector and tax collector of his township.

48

GEORGE KEIGLEY, farmer, Waynesburg, Penn., was born in Washington Township, Greene County, April 8, 1831, a son of George and Anna Keigley (*nee* McCaslin). They were natives of Pennsylvania, where they were married and remained in Greene County until their death. Both departed this life where the subject of this notice now resides. March 21, 1869, George Keigley married Similda J. Rose, who was born in Guernsey County, Ohio, March 27, 1845, a daughter of Thomas and Elizabeth Rose (*nee* Haines). They were natives of Pennsylvania but lived in Ohio until about 1850, when they returned to Fayette County, Penn., where Mrs. Rose died in 1852. Mr. Rose married again and moved to Greene County, Penn., then to Fulton County, Penn., where he died November 10, 1887. To Mr. and Mrs. Keigley have been born eight children— Laura V., Homer L., Mary M., Jessie I., Sadie E., Louie, Anna P. and Thomas H. Mr. Keigley is a saddle and harness-maker by trade, which he followed about fifteen years, after which he engaged in the service of his country in Company F, Pennsylvania Cavalry, and served nine months. He and his wife are faithful members of the Baptist Church.

JOHN M. MARTIN, farmer and stock-dealer, P. O. Ten Mile, was born in Morgan Township, Greene County, August 12, 1823. His parents were Thomas and Mary (Bradbury) Martin, natives of New Jersey. They were married in Washington County, Penn., and made their home in Greene County, where Mr. Martin died. Mrs. Martin died in Missouri. After her husband's death, she lived with her children, who were—John M., the eldest and the subject of this sketch; Thomas and David C. John M. was united in marriage January 18, 1848, with Miss Martha Moore, born in Washington County, Penn., in 1819. Her parents were Joseph and Mary (Shackleton) Moore, both deceased. By this union Mr. Martin is the father of four children—Joseph T., Martha A. and James J., living; and Mary E., deceased. Mrs. Martin departed this life in 1880. February 8, 1881, Mr. Martin was again united in marriage with Isabella (Barr) Montgomery. She was born in Washington County, and is a daughter of Samuel and Sarah Barr, the former deceased. By his last marriage Mr. Martin is the father of two sons—Charles A. and Ira H. He was raised on a farm and made farming his business through life, having also delt somewhat in stock. He owns about 200 acres of land in Greene County, and is one of the industrious and substantial citizens of Washington Township.

L. W. MEEK, farmer, P. O. Swart's, was born on the farm where he and his family reside in Washington Township, December 26, 1858. He is a son of Cary and Jane Meek (*nee* Milliken), who were natives of Greene County, Pennsylvania, where they were married, settled and remained until their death. He died in

October, 1873, and his widow in November of the same year. They were the parents of four children—L. W., A. W., Josie and Lillie. L. W. Meek was united in marriage with Sena Buchanan, born in Waynesburg, March 18, 1859, a daughter of David and Cassie Buchanan (nee Swart), the former a native of Greene and the latter of Washington County, Penn. They reside in Morris Township, Greene County. Mr. and Mrs. Meek are the parents of two children—Cassie J. and David B. Mr. Meek was raised on a farm and has given considerable attention to stock-dealing in connection with the care of his farm which consists of 140 acres. He has also taken much interest in the educational affairs of his township and has served as a members of the school board. His wife is a member of the Cumberland Presbyterian Church.

CEPHAS MEEK, farmer, Ruff's Creek, Penn., is a descendant of one of the pioneer families of Greene County. He was born in Washington Township, January 24, 1832, a son of John and Elizabeth (Boyd) Meek, who were natives of Greene County, where they were married, settled and remained until their death. She died December 24, 1869, and her husband February 3, 1878. They were the parents of eleven children, eight of whom are living. Cephas Meek was united in marriage April 2, 1868, with Phœbe J. Conklin. She was born in Washington County, Penn., December 2, 1838, a daughter of William and Catharine (Ross) Conklin, natives of Washington and Greene counties respectively. They were married in Greene and settled in Washington County. He departed this life June 25, 1880; his widow is still living. Mr. and Mrs. Meek are the parents of one child, William R., born January 11, 1869. Mr. Meek has been engaged in farming all his life and owns a farm of 145 acres. He was a member of the school board of his township for six years, and also served as judge and inspector of elections. Mrs. Meek is a member in the Cumberland Presbyterian Church.

ASA MITCHELL, a retired farmer of Ruff's Creek, Penn., was born in Washington Township, Greene County, October 6, 1811. He is a son of Shadrach and Margaret (Rinehart) Mitchell, the former a native of Maryland and the latter of Greene County, Penn., where they were married and remained until their death. January 25, 1835, Asa Mitchell married Miss Rachel Johns, born in Washington Township, December 1, 1815. She is a daughter of Jacob and Elizabeth (Smith) Johns who, after marriage, settled and remained in Greene County until their death. To Mr. and Mrs. Asa Mitchell have been born eight children, of whom four are living—Jacob J., John, Maria and Catharine, who is the wife of George V. Shirk; and Shadrach, Thomas, Delilah and Mary J. (deceased). Mr. Mitchell was raised on a farm and has been engaged in farming all his life. He owns 227 acres of land where he now lives with his family and he is one of the most substantial and highly respected citizens of Washington Township.

M. M. McCLELLAND, retired farmer, Ruff's Creek, Penn., was born on the farm where he and his family reside in Washington Township, Greene County, December 22, 1824, a son of John and Nancy McClelland (nee Montgomery). His father was a native of Pennsylvania and his mother of Harford County, Md. They were married in Greene County, Penn. Mr. McClelland departed this life in 1840, and his widow May 5, 1862. The subject of our sketch was united in marriage February 27, 1848, with Elizabeth Mettler, born in Columbia County, Penn., May 6, 1826, a daughter of Daniel and Waty Mettler, (nee Baker). They were natives of Pennsylvania, married there, and in 1831 moved to Knox County, Ohio; from there they moved to Williams County, in 1860, and in 1866 went to Iowa, where he died December 13, 1884. His widow survives him, making her home with her children. Mr. and Mrs. McClelland have ten children, of whom five are living—Sarah F., wife of J. D. Iams; Cary, Elmira, wife of Stephen Cox; Emma J. and Ettie. The deceased are Melvin T., Waty A., Marinda, Mary and Lourinza. She was married October 30, 1878, to Jacob Johns, and died September 7, 1879. Mr. McClelland was raised on a farm and has been engaged in farming almost all his life. He owns 345 acres of land, constituting one of the finest farms in Washington Township. He was elected to the office of county auditor in 1856 and served the term of three years. In 1868 he was elected county commissioner, and served three years. He is now serving a second term as justice of the peace of Washington Township, having at different times successfully filled almost all the township offices. He has also been a member of the Masonic order for twenty years. His wife is a faithful member of the Bethlehem Baptist Church.

JOHN PETTIT, farmer, Swart's was born in Washington Township, Greene County, Penn., January 22, 1831, a son of Isaac and Cynthia Pettit (nee Hathaway), who were natives of Greene County and residents there until their death. In 1860 Mr. Pettitt was united in marriage with Rachel Pettit, who was born in Morris Township January 2, 1840, a daughter of Charlie and Keziah Pettit, natives of Greene County and residents there until their death. To Mr. and Mrs. John Pettit have been born seven children—Eliza, wife of G. H. Loughman, who is the mother of two children—Olie M. and Stanley J; Isaac, Mary A., wife of George Fry; Kizzie, Charlie, Frank and Nora. Mr. Pettitt was raised on a farm and has been engaged in farming all his life. He owns 325 acres of land, all in Washington Township. He and wife are consistent members of the Baptist Church.

JOSEPH H. PETTIT, farmer, Swart's, Penn., was born in Washington Township, Greene County, May 6, 1837, a son of Isaac and Cynthia Pettit (*nee* Hathaway), who were natives of Greene County, where they remained until their death. She departed this life in 1873, and her husband in 1881. December 13, 1862, Joseph H. Pettit was united in marriage with Elizabeth Hedge, born in Greene County, February 2, 1846. She is a daughter of Aaron and Eva Hedge (*nee* Fonner), natives of the same county, both deceased. The latter departed this life April, 1888. Mr. and Mrs. Pettit are the parents of eight children, six of whom are living—Laura, Jessie, Cynthia, Martha, George and Bert; and Eva and Mary, deceased. Having been reared on a farm, Mr. Pettit has made farming his occupation through life, and owns 148 acres of land where and his family live. Mrs. Pettit is one of the faithful members of the Baptist Church.

JOHN ROSS, retired farmer, Dunn's Station, Penn.—The subject of this biographical sketch is one of the pioneer citizens of Washington Township, Greene County, born on his present farm, November 3, 1820. He was the oldest child of Thomas Ross, a native of this county, who died in 1832. His mother's maiden name was Hannah Denney, a native of Jefferson Township, who after marriage resided in Washington Township until her death in 1847. They were the parents of seven children, of whom three are living. John Ross married Miss Maria Loughman, October 7, 1847. She was born September 20, 1825, in Morris Township, of which her parents, David and Christina (Fonner) Loughman, were also natives and residents therein until their death. Mr. and Mrs. John Ross have eight children—Hannah B., wife of John Kendall; David, Mary J., Lydia, wife of John W. Kelley; Timothy, Christina A., Maria I. and William, (deceased). Mr. Ross was born and raised on the farm on which he now resides, and like his ancestors, has made farming and stock-raising his business through life. His home farm consists of 237 acres of excellent land. He has most acceptably filled the offices of auditor and assessor of his township, and served as member of the school board for fourteen years. He and his wife are among the most prominent members of the Baptist Church.

THOMAS ROSS, farmer and stock-dealer, P. O. Ruff's Creek, was born in Washington County, Penn., October 8, 1833. He is the son of Benjamin and Hannah Ross (*nee* Johns,) both natives of Washington Township, Greene County, where they were married and where they returned after a few years spent in Washington County, and remained until their death, which occurred in the house where the subject of this sketch and his family now reside—his father having departed this life in 1863, and his mother in 1868. Six of their twelve children still survive them. Thomas Ross was united in marriage May 11, 1870, with Helen M. Lindley, born in Washington County, January 10, 1844, a daughter of Zebulon and Julia Lindley (*nee* Parkinson), natives of the same county, and residents therein during their whole life, with the exception of a short time spent in Ohio immediately subsequent to their marriage. They were the parents of three children, all now living. Mrs. Lindley died in 1873 and her husband in 1887. To Mr. and Mrs. Ross have been born two daughters—Estella J., born May 26, 1872; and Clara H., born February, 23, 1871, died September 29, 1878. Mr. Ross was reared on a farm. In 1859, at the age of twenty-six, he went to California and engaged in the mining business. Returning to his native county in 1863, after an absence of four years, he has since devoted himself to stock-dealing and the care of his farm of 290 acres in Washington Township. He and his family are members of the Baptist Church, and for the consistency of their Christian character are highly respected throughout the community.

BENJAMIN SHIRK, retired farmer, Ruff's Creek, Penn., born in Lancaster County, Penn., July 23, 1815, is a son of Michael and Barbara (Alobough) Shirk, also natives of Lancaster County. They were married and lived there until about 1830, when they moved to Coshocton County, Ohio, and remained until Mrs. Shirk's death. Mr. Shirk again married and moved to Illinois, where he died. On September 5, 1839, Benjamin Shirk first married Margaret Martin, born in Washington Township, Greene County, June 13, 1818, a daughter of Amos and Ruth Martin, both deceased. To Mr. and Mrs. Shirk were born seven children, five of whom are living—Michael M., Daniel, George V., Joel and Amos; and John and Benjamin F., deceased. Mrs. Shirk died February 20, 1859. In 1860 Mr. Shirk married Elizabeth (Turner) Ullom. She was born in Greene County, February 6, 1827, a daughter of Za and Elizabeth Turner, who departed this life in Greene County. By his last marriage Mr. Shirk is the father of three children—Charles, Maggie and Benjamin F. Mr. Shirk has been a tiller of the soil all his life, and at one time owned 700 acres of land. He has given this all to his children, except the farm of 325 acres where he and his family reside. He and his wife are consistent members of the Baptist Church, of which his deceased wife was also a member. Mr. Shirk has been a member of the school board, and judge of the election at different times. He is one of Greene County's oldest and best known citizens, having lived in Washington Township for fifty years.

J. H. SMITH, farmer, P. O. Sycamore, was born in Washington Township, Greene County, Penn., January 17, 1841. His parents, Jacob and Nancy Smith (nee Hill), were natives of Greene County, where they have always resided. His death occurred in 1887, and her death May 2, 1888. Mr. J. H. Smith was united in marriage June 6, 1861, with Martha Armstrong, who was born in Washington County, Pennsylvania, September 24, 1842. Mrs. Smith is a daughter of James and Elizabeth Armstrong (nee Richie), the former a native of New York, the latter of Ohio, who after marriage settled in Washington County, Pennsylvania, and from there moved to Marshall County, West Virginia where she died in 1853. After her death he married again and moved to Richhill Township, this county, and died in 1881. The widow is still living. To Mr. and Mrs. Smith have been born five children: Anna, wife of G. M. Fordyce; Mary L., Maria B., Ida M. and Jacob H. Mr. Smith has been engaged in farming through his life, and owns 112 acres of land where he and family reside. He and wife are consistent members of the Baptist Church.

JOHN WALKER, farmer, Ruff's Creek Penn., was born in Center Township, Greene County, January 6, 1818. His parents were Joseph and Rebecca (Higinbotham) Walker, the former a native of New Jersey and the latter of Fayette County, Pennsylvania. They were married in Greene County where they remained for several years, when they moved first to St. Clairsville, Ohio, then to Moundsville, West Virginia. From that point Mr. Walker commenced running on the Ohio River. About this time he disappeared very mysteriously, and his family never knew what became of him. His widow, with her family, moved to Centre Township, Greene County, and married George Williams. They lived first in Washington, County Penn., then moved to Wellsburgh, West Virginia. Mr. Williams died in Ohio County, West Virginia. His widow then moved to Washington County, Penn., then to Greene County where she was first married, and made her home with her son until her death. The subject of this sketch was united in marriage, November 7, 1839, with Rachael Supler. She was born in Richhill Township, Greene County, September 12, 1820, a daughter of John and Mary (Sargent) Supler, natives of Pennsylvania. They were married and settled in Richhill Township, where they remained until their death, To Mr. and Mrs. Walker have been born twelve children: John L., Minerva, George S., William W., David L., Rebecca, Nancy, Jackson V., and Fannie M., living; and Joseph L., Samuel H. and Mary M. deceased. Mr. Walker is a farmer and owns about 367 acres of land where he and family reside in Washington Township, Greene County Pennsylvania.

WAYNE TOWNSHIP.

GEORGE W. BELL, P. O. Hoover's Run, one of the oldest residents of Greene County, Penn, was born in Virginia, September 30, 1809. His parents were Jason and Sarah (Noll) Bell, natives of Virginia, where they married and settled, afterwards removing to Washington County, Penn., then to Greene County, where his father died in 1873 and his mother in 1840. George W. was the seventh of their nine children, and was joined in the holy bonds of wedlock, February, 8, 1844, with Clementine, daughter of William and Sarah Tygart (*nee* Eagon). Mr. Tygart was a native of Virginia, and his wife of Greene County, Penn., where they spent their married life He departed this life in Guernsey County, Ohio, in the year 1846, and his wife in April, 1857. Mr. Bell and wife are the parents of nine children: Sarah J., Felix, Julia A., wife of David Stoneking; Maria, wife of J. Harvey Stewart; Mary, wife of Eli Pethtell; Josephine, wife of William Cole; Susan R; William H. and Eliza abeth M. deceased. Mr. Bell has always lived on a farm, and his life has been characterized by great industry and economy, as a result of which he owns a fine farm of 500 acres in Greene County, also 100 in West Virginia, and 7,000 at interest. He has served as justice of the peace for ten years; has been a member of the school board, and was at one time assessor of Jackson Township.

HON. MATTHIAS BRANT, Spragg's, Penn., is one the most successful farmers and stock-raisers of Greene County, and owns 300 acres of land. He was born in Wayne Township, December 29, 1828, a son of Christopher and Susan Brant (*nee* Meighen). His father was a native of Maryland, and his mother of Greene County, Pennsylvania, where they were married and lived until 1863, when Mrs. Brant died. Mr. Brant then moved to Fillmore County, Minnesota, where he died in November, 1857. They were the parents of thirteen children, of whom Matthias was the oldest, and was united in marriage, June 28, 1868, with Mary Shaw, who was a native of Greene County, where she remained through life. By this marriage Mr. Brant is the father of six children, of whom four are living— Susan M., Gertrude M., William H. and Fanny; Emma being deceased. Mrs. Brant departed this life in August, 1880. Mr. Brant married for his second wife, October 25, 1883, Elizabeth, daughter of John and Mary (Varlow) Fitzgerald, natives of County Carey, Ireland, where they were married. They soon after emigrated to America, settling in West Virginia where they now reside. Mr.

Brant taught school for sixteen years, beginning when sixteen years of age. He was elected member of the State Legislature in 1878 and re-elected in 1880. He has been a member of the school board for about thirteen years. In politics he is a Democrat. He and his wife are honored members of the Catholic Church at Waynesburg.

KENDALL J. BRANT, Spragg's Penn., was born in Gilmore Township, September 23, 1839, a son of Christopher and Susannah Brant (*nee* Meighen). The father was a native of Maryland, and the mother of Greene County, Penn., where they were married and resided until Mrs. Brant's death, which occurred in May, 1863. Her husband died in November, 1857, in Fillmore County, Minnesota. They were the parents of thirteen children, of whom Kendall J. was the twelfth. He was twice married, his first wife being Minerva, daughter of John and Margaret (Hamilton) Spragg, who are natives and residents of this county. Mr. and Mrs. Brant were married December 16, 1860, and were the parents of two children—Margaret C., wife of William E. Spragg, and Matthias L. Mrs. Brant departed this life February 15, 1865. Mr. Brant was afterwards united in marriage, December 17, 1871, with Maria, daughter of James and Eliza (Rush) Stewart, natives of Greene County, living in Franklin Township. By this marriage Mr. and Mrs. Brant have seven children—Susannah G., Lida A., Priscilla, Lydia, Minerva, James D. and William E. Mr. Brant was reared on a farm and is now one of the most successful farmers in this township. He has also been much interested in the raising of fine, stock in which he has dealt quite extensively. His farm consists of about 200 acres.

RICHARD T. CALVERT, Blacksville, West Virginia, was born in Wayne Township, Greene County, Penn., April 16, 1836. He is a son of John and Eleanor Calvert (*nee* Thralls). His father was born in Mapletown. After marriage they lived in this county until his mother's death which occurred in 1857. His father then married Margaret, daughter of James Marshall. She died February 9, 1888; her husband is still living. Richard Calvert's wife was Sarah J. Conklin, born in this county December 1, 1832. They were married October 19, 1859. Mrs. Calvert's parents were Josiah and Cassandra (Brown) Conklin, deceased. Mr. and Mrs. Calvert have five children, three living—Cassie A., Thomas and John; Martha E. and an infant being deceased. Mr. Calvert is a farmer, and by industry and good management has made a good home for himself and family where he now lives, on a 228 acre farm in Wayne Township.

JOHN F. COEN, merchant and postmaster, Dent, Penn., born in Wayne Township, Greene County, March 8, 1844, was the only son of Francis and Barbara (Cumberledge) Coen, natives of Pennsylvania, who were married in Greene County and resided there until Mr. Coen's death in December, 1843. His widow was afterwards married to Isaac Stiles and now lives in West Virginia. John F. Coen's wife was Miss Mary Kent, born in Greene County, February 18, 1841, and married May 1, 1866. She is a daughter of William and Elizabeth (Odenbaugh) Kent. Her mother is deceased. Mr. and Mrs. Coen have no family of their own but have adopted two sons, William H. and Benjamin T. Mr. Coen was raised on the farm which he now owns consisting of ninety acres. When eighteen years of age he went into the army, enlisting in Company A, One-hundred and Fortieth Pennsylvania Volunteers, and remained three years, during which time he was in a number of hotly contested battles. He has filled the offices of assessor and auditor of his township; has been engaged in merchandising since 1880. He and wife are members of the Methodist Episcopal Church.

EPHRAIM COLE, farmer, Hoover's Run, Penn., was born June 11, 1842. His parents, Jeremiah and Delilah (Filson) Cole, were natives of Maryland, they were married in Greene County, Pennsylvania, where he died March 14, 1870, and she February 6, 1871. Jeremiah's first wife was Christener Crotinger, a native of Maryland, but died in Greene County, Penn. Ephraim was the youngest of eight children, and was united in marriage July 12, 1862, with Missouri, daughter of Adam and Sabia Geho (nee Garrison). Mr. Geho was a native of Ohio and his wife of Maryland. They were married in Washington County, Penn., then moved to Greene County in 1889, where they resided until Mr. Geho's death, May, 1871. Mrs. Geho is still living. Mr. and Mrs. Cole have seven children—Benjamin T., Simon T., James C., Albert M., Everett P., Mary E. and William G. Mr. Cole's farm contains 105 acres. He has served as school director two terms. He and wife are member of the Patrons of Husbandry Lodge at Kughntown; and the whole family except the two youngest children are consistent members of the Bethel Baptist Church.

JAMES L. COLE, farmer, Hoover's Run, Penn., was born March 30, 1840. He is a son of Jeremiah and Delilah (Filson) Cole, who were natives of Maryland. Subsequently they removed to Greene County, Pennsylvania, where Mr. Cole, Sr., departed this life March 14, 1870 and his wife February 6, 1871. They were the parents of eight children, James L. was the seventh and was united in marriage November 26, 1865, with Maria, daughter of Adam and Sabia (Garrison) Geho. Mr. Geho was a native of Ohio; they were married in Washington County, Pennsylvania, settling in Greene County in 1839. The former departed this life May, 1871; his widow is still living. Mr. and Mrs. Cole have three children—Sarah C. and Elizabeth J., both born May 26, 1867, and Edward L., born November 13, 1870. Mr. Cole devotes all his time to stock-raising and the care of his farm containing 102 acres. He has served as inspector of elections of Wayne Township; he and his wife are members of the Patrons of Husbandry Lodge at Kughntown.

HENRY COLE, deceased, was one of the most prosperous farmers of Greene County, owning at the time of his death a fine farm of 858 acres. He was born April 25, 1819 and died March 15, 1882. His parents were John and Mary Cole (*nee* Crotinger), who were natives of Maryland, came to Greene County, Penn., early in life, where they made their home until Mr. Cole's death in May, 1862. His wife died in November, 1868. Henry was the second of their nine children and April 2, 1840, married Elizabeth, daughter of George and Ellen King (*nee* Stewart). Mrs. Cole's parents were native of Pennsylvania and residents in this county until their death. Her mother departed this life January 24, 1843, and her father in 1863. Mr. and Mrs. Cole were the parents of nine children—Mary A., wife of Hiram White; Sarah, wife of William D. Phillips; George W., Frances E., wife of Abram Tustin; John L., James H., Josephus; and Jacob and Peter, (deceased). Mrs. Cole is still living and resides on the old homestead in Wayne Township.

HENRY CONKLIN, Brock, Penn., born in Greene County, November 17, 1834, is a son of Josiah and Cassandra Conklin (*nee* Brown), who were also natives of this county, where they were married and remained through life. His father died in September, 1856, and his mother August 13, 1884. Of their ten children, eight are now living. Henry is the third child and was united in marriage November 22, 1857, with Eleanor Hoy, born in this county January 16, 1839. She is a daughter of James and Isabella (Kuhn) Hoy, also natives of Greene County. Mr. Hoy died November 8, 1878; his widow is still living. Mr. and Mrs. Conklin are the parents of eleven children—James H., Sarah E., wife of Richard Stewart; Sanford M., Israel, Ruie, William A., Lissie J., Clara B., Emma L., Lewis H.; and John S., (deceased). Mr. Conklin is one of the most substantial farmers and stock-dealers of Wayne Township, and owns 400 acres of land. He has served as school director in his township. He and wife belong to the Methodist Episcopal Church.

A. J. CUMBERLEDGE, P. O. Dent, was born in Monongalia County, W. Va., August 24, 1838. His parents were George and Elizabeth (Lantz) Cumberledge, the one a native of Maryland and the other of Greene County, Penn., where they were married, then moved to Monongalia County, W. Va., and remained until their death. His father died November 17, 1881, and his mother October 23, 1884. They were the parents of sixteen children, nine living, and were united in marriage August 14, 1818, by James Dye, Esq. A. J. Cumberledge was united in marriage August 14, 1856, with Martha J. Grim, born in Greene County, September 30, 1841, a daughter of Christian and Dorcas E. Grim (*nee* Carpenter), both deceased; the latter died May 28, 1888. Mr. and Mrs. Cumberledge have six children—Harriet, wife of William L. Harker; George, Samuel L., Dorcas E., Martie; and Emma (deceased). Mr. Cumberledge is a shoe-maker by trade, but has engaged in farming all his life. His present farm comprises 140 acres. He enlisted in the service of his country in Company N, Sixth Virginia Volunteers, remaining in the war three years and two months. He belongs to the Masonic order, and his wife is a member of the Methodist Episcopal Church.

JOHN FREELAND, Pine Bank, Penn., was born in Monongahela Township, Greene County, May 15, 1814. His parents were George and Nancy (Fitch) Freeland, also natives of this county, where they were married and remained until Mrs. Freeland's death, December 23, 1863. Her husband died May 16, 1873. Of their four children, two are living—Sarah, and John, the subject of this sketch, who was united in marriage September 20, 1840, with Minerva Cleavenger, born in Greene County in 1823. She is a daughter of Edward and Mary (Kline) Cleavenger (deceased). To Mr. and Mrs. John Freeland were born nine children, six now living, viz.—George, who married Eliza E. Jolley; Cyrus F., who married Nancy E. Owen; Mary A., wife of W. J. Bell; David L., who married Sarah J. Kiger; Elizabeth J., wife of W. Lowther; and Martha A. The deceased are Edward A., Charles A. and William L. Mrs. Freeland died January 26, 1877, a faithful member of the Methodist Episcopal Church. Mr. Freeland afterwards, May 16, 1879, married Agnes Wright, born in Greene County, February 28, 1838. Her parents were John F. and Agnes (Vance) Wright, also natives of this county and residents therein until their death. Her mother died in 1874 and her father. in 1880. Mr. Freeland was raised in Mapletown. He began teaching school when twenty-one years of age, and taught until 1876. He has since given all his time to the management of his farm, which consists of 122 acres. Mr. Freeland is a member of the Methodist Episcopal and his wife of the Baptist Church.

SAM. H. HEADLEY, merchant at Pine Bank is a descendant of the Headleys, who emigrated from the north of England in 1689 and settled in East Jersey. Francis Headley, his great-grandfather, was born in 1731, and who remained in Essex County, N. J., until after the close of the war of the Revolution, and in 1790 traded his farm in New Jersey for 1,400 acres in Randolph County, Va. (now West Virginia). He had one brother, Joseph Headley, who settled on North Ten Mile, Washington County, Penn. Francis Headley died in Randolph County, Va., in 1805. He had several children. Samuel Headley, his grandfather, was born in the year

1765, and was married to Abigail Trace in the year 1788; he and his wife moved from Essex County, N. J., in 1790 with his father, Francis. Samuel Headley (his grandfather), had a family of eight children. An older claim or title was established for the land in Randolph County, Va., so all was lost and the family moved to other parts. Samuel Headley moved to Jefferson Township, Greene County, where John Headley, his father, was born in the year 1809. He learned the blacksmith trade with John Young during the years 1828 and 1829, and in 1833 commenced business in Washington Township. He was married to Eliza Hoffman during that year, and in 1843 moved to Tom's Run in Gilmore Township, where he is now living. His first wife died in 1875, and in the same year he was married to the widow Silveous, who died in 1888. He had a family of eight children by his first wife, Sam. H. Headley being the third child. He was born in Washington Township in 1838. In 1856 he left home to attend school, working nights and mornings for his board, and for several years he taught school during the winter and attended school during the summer. In 1868 he commenced the mercantile business with T. J. Hoffman as a partner, and in 1872 set up for himself at Pine Bank. He was married to C. J. Fletcher, of Blacksville, W. Va., in the year 1870. They have one child—Robert B. Headley, who was born in 1871. Sam. H. Headley and son religiously are Friends.

WILLIAM H. JOHNSON, farmer, P. O. Blacksville, W. Va., was born in Wayne Township, Greene County, Penn., November 4, 1840, a son of William and Nancy Johnson (*nee* Lantz). Mrs. Johnson was born in Monongalia County, W. Va., and her husband was a native of Greene County, Penn., where they lived until his death, November 16, 1857. Mrs. Johnson was afterwards united in marriage with Henry Stephens, who died June 8, 1877; the widow is still living. William H. Johnson's wife was Sarah A. McDougal, born in Wayne Township, October 24, 1843, and married January 30, 1862. She is a daughter of Alexander and Sallie (Franks) Mc Dougal, the former deceased. Mr. and Mrs. Johnson have three children, viz.—Nancy A., wife of John McPhillips; Minerva J., wife of Josephus Thomas; and John W. Mr. Johnson is one of the enterprising farmers of Wayne Townhip, where he owns 115 acres of land. He filled the office of justice of the peace in his township two terms, has served as school director six terms, and held the position of assessor and inspector of elections. He and his wife are members of the Southern Methodist Church.

J. S. KENT, farmer, Dent, Penn., was born in Centre Township, Greene County, January 31, 1835. His parents, William and Elizabeth (Odenbaugh) Kent, were natives of this county and residents therein until Mrs. Kent's death, May 4, 1868. Her husband afterwards married Jane White, widow of Rev. Michael White, of West Virginia; they live in Wayne Township. William Kent is the father of eleven children, seven boys and four girls, of whom nine are living. In 1858 J. S. Kent was united in marriage with Rebecca Morris, born in West Virginia in 1837, a daughter of James and Sarah Morris, the former deceased. By this marriage Mr. Kent is the father of one child—William J. Mrs. Kent departed this life September 25, 1860. Mr. Kent was a second time united in marriage, August 20, 1861, with Catharine Eddy, born in Wayne Township, January 5, 1830, a daughter of John and Sophia Eddy (*nee* Steel). Mr. and Mrs. Kent have a family of three boys and three girls, five living—Elizabeth, wife of Jesse Coen; Minerva, wife of Thomas Hoy; John R., Hiram W. and Michael I.; and Nancy J. (deceased). Mr. Kent is one of the most enterprising citizens of Wayne Township, and owns 237 acres of land where he now lives with his family. His wife is a member of the Methodist Episcopal Church.

JAMES KNIGHT, Oak Forest, Penn., one of the enterprising young farmers of Wayne Township, was born January 27, 1848, and is a son of David and Mary Knight (*nee* Fry), who are natives of Greene County, Penn., where they were married and now reside in Centre Township. They are the parents of nine children, seven of whom are living. James Knight's wife was Elizabeth S., daughter of Jacob and Frances (Tustin) Cole, natives of Greene County and now residents of Waynesburg. Mr. and Mrs. Knight were married August 29, 1868. Their children are—John H., Frances A., William M. and Mary C. As noticed in the beginning of this sketch, Mr. Knight is a farmer by occupation, and has also given much attention to the raising of fine stock. His farm contains 156 acres.

WILLIAM LANTZ, Dent, Penn., was born April 27, 1835, on the farm where he and family reside in Wayne Township. His parents, Jacob and Delilah (Coen) Lantz, were natives of Greene County and residents therein through life. His father died in 1858 and his mother in 1866. They were the parents of five children, three living. William is the youngest, and was united in marriage May 22, 1856, with Minerva, daughter of William and Elizabeth (Odenbaugh) Kent, the latter deceased. Mrs. Lantz was born in this county November 24, 1837, and is a consistent member of the Methodist Episcopal Church. Mr. William Lantz and wife are the parents of seven children—Mary, wife of William Wiley; William, who married Belle Phillips; Ulysses and Emma; Harriet, Delilah, and an infant (deceased). Mr. Lantz has been eminently successful as a farmer and stock-dealer, and owns 480 acres of good land in Greene County.

GEORGE W. MOORE, Spragg's, Penn., was born in Whiteley Township, Greene County, January 3, 1834. His parents, James and Matilda (Franks) Moore, were also natives of this county, where after marriage they settled and remained all their lives. After Matilda's death, Mr. Moore married Elizabeth (Brown) Provence, who is still living. Mr. Moore is deceased. He was the father of eleven children, six living. George W. is the third child, and was united in marriage, July 26, 1859, with Louisa R. Phillips, born in Cumberland Township, September 26, 1840, a daughter of Job and Margaret (Simington) Phillips, natives of Greene County, where they remained until Mrs. Phillips' death, after which he married Mary Mason. To Mr. and Mrs. Moore have been born seven children— James E., Thomas L., Job, Peter C., Elizabeth L., Lafy E. and Matilda M. Mr. Moore's occupation is that of farming and stock-dealing, and he owns 275 acres of land in Wayne Township. He and wife are among the most prominent members of the Methodist Episcopal Church.

HON. JESSE PHILLIPS, Spragg's, Penn., born in Whiteley Township, February 10, 1824, is a son of Richard and Abigail (Starkey) Phillips. His parents were natives of Greene County, where they spent their whole life. His father died in the year 1877, and his mother in 1879. They were the parents of eleven children, of whom our subject is the second, and was united in marriage, December 22, 1845, with Mary, daughter of David and Nancy (Gorden) Spragg. They were also natives of this county, where they remained till Mr. Spragg's death in 1877. His wife died in 1886. By this marriage Mr. Phillips is the father of twelve children—William D., Richard, Caleb, Levi, Adam F., Thomas E., Jesse L., Deborah F., James L., John W.; and Otho and Nancy E. (deceased). Their mother departed this life in 1871. She was a faithful member of the Methodist Episcopal Church. Mr. Phillips' second wife was Deborah, daughter of David and Nancy (Gorden) Spragg, now deceased. By this marriage Mr. and Mrs. Phillips have three children—George Daniel, and Clemmie (deceased). Although raised on a farm and devoting much of his time to agricultural interests and stock-raising, Mr. Phillips has also been actively engaged in political affairs. He is a Democrat, and in 1881 was elected associate judge, having polled nearly as many votes as his three competitors. In April, 1888, he sat on the jury which found George Clark guilty of murder in the first degree, for the killing of William McCausland. This was the first verdict of murder in the first degree ever found by a jury in Greene County. Mr. Phillips has a fine farm of 500 acres, and he and wife are members of the Patrons of Husbandry Lodge of Kughntown. The whole family are members of the Methodist Episcopal Church.

WILLIAM D. PHILLIPS, Hoover's Run, Penn., is one of the most successful of the younger farmers of Greene County. He was born in Wayne Township, December 22, 1846, a son of Jesse and Mary (Spragg) Phillips, natives of Greene County, where Mr. Phillips still resides. Mrs. Phillips died in the year 1871. William D. is the oldest of twelve children, and was united in marriage, August 4, 1866, with Sarah, daughter of Henry and Elizabeth (King) Cole, also natives of Greene County, where Mrs. Phillips' mother still resides. Her father departed this life March 15, 1882. Mr. and Mrs. Phillips have eight children—Mary E., Justice, Henry C., James P., Adam P., Frances A., Walter S. and Sarah E. The subject of our sketch was reared on a farm and is greatly interested in all matters pertaining to agriculture and stock-raising. He owns 200 acres of land in Wayne Township. He and wife are members of the Patrons of Husbandry Lodge of Kughntown, and are also communicants in the Methodist Episcopal Church of that place.

JOHN Mc. PHILLIPS, P. O. Spragg's, is one of the substantial young farmers and stock-dealers of Wayne Township, where he was born August 26, 1862. He is a son of Armstrong and Eleanor (Spragg) Phillips, also natives of Wayne Township, and residents therein all their lives. His father died August 13, 1870, aged thirty years and four months; and his mother died December 25, 1870, aged thirty-three years, seven months and twenty days. John Mc. is their only child. He was united in marriage, December 17, 1882, with Nancy A. Johnson, a daughter of William H. and Sarah A. (McDougal) Johnson, whose sketch appears in this history. Mr. and Mrs. Phillips have two children—William A., born February 7, 1884, and Ora A., born November 10, 1887. Mr. Phillips owns 219 acres of good land where he resides with his family. In religion Mr. and Mrs. Phillips are members of the Methodist Protestant Church.

DAVID SPRAGG (deceased) was born May 2, 1806, in Wayne Township, Greene County, Penn., on the farm now owned by the heirs of Otho Spragg. He was a son of Caleb and Deborah (McClure) Spragg, who were married November 6, 1798. The former was born September 22, 1778, and died April 20, 1854. The latter was born August 1, 1780, and departed this life September 22, 1860. They emigrated from Trenton, N. J., to what is now Wayne Township, Greene County, Penn., where they reared a family of twelve children, six sons and six daughters. Eleven of these grew to be men and women, one daughter dying in infancy. The oldest daughter, Amy, was born April, 1800, and was united in marriage with Joseph Wells. They were the parents of a large family. John was born June 30, 1801, and was married to Margaret Hamilton in 1820. To this union was born eleven children. He departed this life February, 1888. Sarah was born December 30, 1802. She remained single through life, and died in 1865. Uriah was born October 7, 1804, and was married to Susannah McLaughlin in 1820. He was the father of seven children, and departed this life in 1875. William was born February 28, 1808, and married Nancy Maple in 1833. They were the parents of four children. He died in 1872. Jeremiah was born September 26, 1809, and was married in 1832 to Sarah Shriver. This union was blessed with three children. He died March 3, 1878. Otho was born October 5, 1811, and was united in marriage in 1833 with Lydia Shul. They were the parents of two children. He departed this life March, 1882. Elizabeth was born July 4, 1814, and was married to Simon Strosnider in 1833. She was the mother of eight children, and departed this life February, 1884. Rebecca was born May 17, 1817, and was married to W. J. Casgray, December 15, 1842. To them were born seven children. She died May 6, 1881. Deborah was born November 9, 1820, and was united in marriage, in 1848, with Thomas Hoge. She was the mother of one child, and departed this life in 1849. David (deceased), who is the subject of this sketch, was the fifth in the family, and was united in marriage, at the age of twenty-one, with Nancy A. Gordon, who was born November 3, 1806, and died March, 1886. She was a daughter of William Gordon, and was reared in Whiteley Township, Greene County, Penn. Her parents, with all their children except herself, moved to Perry County, Ohio, in 1836. To Mr. David Spragg and wife were born five children. The oldest, Mary, was born in 1827, and was married to Hon. Jesse Phillips in 1845. She was the mother of twelve children, and departed this life September 29, 1872. Caleb A. was born December 18, 1829, and is one of Greene County's most substantial citizens. He was united in marriage, November 6, 1851, with Sarah Johnson, a daughter of William and Nancy (Lantz) Johnson. The former is deceased, and the latter is living. By this marriage Mr. Caleb A. Spragg is the father of five children—Sylvenus L., a prominent physician of Pittsburgh, Penn.; Francis M. and David G., of Harrison County, Mo.; William E., proprietor of the marble works at Waynesburg, and Clara N., wife of Corbly K. Spragg. Mrs. Spragg departed this life December 21, 1882. After her death Mr. Spragg was again united in marriage, April 6, 1884, with Matilda Porter, a daughter of John and Hannah (Rinehart) Porter. This union has been blessed with one child—Porter M. In connection with the raising of stock and the management of his farm of 125 acres, upon which he has bestowed much care and attention, Mr. Spragg has filled various offices in his township, and served as a member of the school board two terms. William, the second son of David and Nancy Spragg, was born November 14, 1832, and was married to Sarah A. Brock, October, 1859. They were the parents of six children. He departed this life October 10, 1872. Adam, the third son, was united in marriage with Lydia Pettit, December 3, 1858. To this union was born four children. He died September 10, 1872. Debbie, the youngest daughter, was born May 14, 1839, and was married to Joel Strawn in 1858. They were the parents of six children. Mr. Strawn died in 1871. David, our subject, died February 7, 1877, on the farm known as the Spragg homestead, in Wayne Township. He was from his early youth engaged in land speculations and farming. He obtained but a limited education, but being a great philanthropist he proved a blesings to the community in which he lived. At the age of thirty-five he became a member of the Methodist Protestant Church. He possessed good social qualities. His wife was of a kind disposition, and their home was one of the most attractive in the neighborhood. He and his wife lived a long and happy life together, and were known to every one in that neighborhood as "Uncle Dave" and "Aunt Nancy Spragg."

HENRY M. SPRAGG, postmaster, Spragg's, Penn., is one of the most successful farmers of Greene County, and owns about 300 acres of land. He was born August 8, 1837, a son of Jeremiah and Sarah Spragg (*nee* Shriver), who were natives of this county, where they were married and resided until his father's death, March 10, 1878; his mother is still living. Henry M., the youngest of their three children, was united in marriage, March 19, 1862, with Eliza, daughter of John and Kezia Kent (*nee* Shields), natives and residents of this county. Mr. and Mrs. Spragg are the parents of five children—McClelland, Lazear, Simon T., Laura S. and Harriet E. Mr. Spragg has served his township as constable, assessor and school director; and is a member of the Independent Order of Odd Fellows Lodge, of Blacksville, West Virginia.

ISRAEL STEWART, deceased, was born in Greene County, Penn., May 17, 1830, a son of James and Mary Stewart (*nee* Blair), (deceased). Mr. Stewart was united in marriage, March 24, 1853, with Rebecca Phillips, born in Wayne Township, December 18, 1827, a daughter of Richard and Abigail (Starkey) Phillips, natives of Greene County, and now deceased. Mr. and Mrs. Stewart were the parents of ten children—Thomas L., Richard, James, Elizabeth M., wife of Kenney Strosnider; Jesse H., Spencer M., Mary J., wife of Thomas Calvert, Abigail F. and Sarah P.; and George W., (deceased). Mr. Stewart was a stone-mason by trade, but in later years devoted his time to farming, and owned 300 acres of land near Blacksville, West Virginia. He was a deacon in the Baptist Church, of which his widow and family are also members. He died October 29, 1887.

ABRAHAM, TUSTIN, farmer, P. O. Hoover's Run, Penn., was born in Wayne Township in 1848, a son of John and Mary (Bumgarner) Tustin, natives of Greene County, where his father died in the year 1882, and his mother in 1850. They were the parents of five children, of whom Abraham is the third. On September 2, 1862, he chose for his life companion Miss Frances E., daughter of Henry and Elizabeth (King) Cole, who were natives and residents of this county, where Mr. Cole died March 15, 1882; Mrs. Cole is still living. Mr. and Mrs. Tustin's children are—John L., Elizabeth M., Jacob H., Sarah C., Lucy J., Margaret E. and Osa E.; Fanny M. and Rachel A. being deceased. Mr. Tustin was reared on a farm, and although comparatively a young man, he has been greatly prospered in his farming and stock dealing, and owns 191 acres of land in Wayne Township. He and wife and two of their children are members of the Patrons of Husbandry Lodge of Kughntown, and belong to the Oak Shade Methodist Episcopal Church.

REASIN WHITE, farmer, Oak Forest, Penn., was born in Franklin Township, January 13, 1833. His father is the Rev. David White, founder of what is known as "White's Church," near Waynesburg. He is now over ninety years of age and still quite active in mind and body. His mother's maiden name was Leah Strosnider; both were natives of Greene County. Mrs. White departed this life in 1867. On June 3, 1854, Mr. Reasin White married Miss Elizabeth, daughter of Daniel and Jemima Rogers (*nee* Pettit), also natives of this county, where they were married and first settled. They afterwards removed to Ohio, where Mr. Rogers died in 1883. Mrs. Rogers departed this life January 21, 1886, in Wayne Township, Greene County, Penn. Mr. and Mrs. White have five children, two of whom are living—Judge D. and Samuel K. The deceased are: Mary E., David W. and Israel. Mr. White is one of the most industrious and highly respected farmers in his community, and owns 200 acres of excellent land. He and family are faithful members of the Pursley Baptist Church.

JOHN I. WORLEY, farmer and stock-dealer, Blacksville, West Virginia, is a descendant of one of the first settlers of Wayne Township, Greene County, Penn. He was born December 1, 1823, on the farm where he and family reside in Wayne Township. His father, David Worley, was born in Wayne Township, May 8, 1775, on the farm now owned by John I. His mother, Margaret Cather, was a native of Franklin Township, born May 20, 1780. They were married December 30, 1799. Three of their ten childern are living, viz.: William C., of West Virginia; Dr. Asberry, of Fayette County, Ohio, and John I. Their father died September 10, 1851, and the mother December 5, 1853. Mr. John I. Worley was twice married, his first wife being Miss Maria Gordon, with whom he shared his fortunes, December 21, 1843. Mrs. Worley was born in Franklin Township, January 6, 1824, a daughter of Bazil and Sarah (Shriver)

Gordon (deceased). By this marriage Mr. Worley is the father of seven children—Sarah, wife of R. W. Dougan; William G., David R., Jesse L., Alpheus B. and Lizzie, wife of Rev. James E. Mercer; and Maggie, (deceased). Their mother departed this life February 7, 1877, a consistent member of the Methodist Protestant Church. On June 17, 1879, Mr. Worley chose for his second wife Mrs. Delilah Higgins, born in Whiteley Township September 15, 1830, a daughter of Mark and Susan Gordon (deceased). Mr. Worley was brought up on a farm and has always followed his present occupation. He owns 600 acres of land in Greene County. He has served as justice of the peace in Wayne Township, an office which his father held for forty years. He has held almost all the important offices of his township, having ever been one of its most highly respected citizens. He and Mrs. Worley are consistent members of the Methodist Episcopal Church.

ROBERT ZIMMERMAN, farmer, Spragg's, Penn., was born in Greene County, December 19, 1819. His parents, Henry and Elizabeth (Mitchell) Zimmerman, were natives of Maryland, where they were married, then moved to Greene County, Penn., near Waynesburg, and remained until their death. Robert and his brother Henry are their only children living. On December 17, 1840, Robert married Mary Flick, a native of Greene County and daughter of Daniel Flick. To Mr. and Mrs. Zimmerman were born six children, four living—Elizabeth, wife of Lot Rose; Susan, wife of Solomon Lemley; Eliza, wife of Hudson Kiger; and Henry, who married Caroline Headley. The deceased are Daniel and William. Mrs. Zimmerman died August 5, 1852. February 1, 1855, Mr. Zimmerman married Catharine, daughter of John Cree, also a native of this county. By this second marriage he is the father of one child— Ruth, wife of Bowen Stephens. Mrs. Catharine Zimmerman died September 2, 1860. Robert Zimmerman afterwards married Dorcas Rinehart, January 5, 1862. She was born in Franklin Township, November 8, 1819, a daughter of John T. and Susannah Rinehart. Mr. Zimmerman owns 204 acres of land where he and family reside in Wayne Township.

WHITELEY TOWNSHIP.

A. M. BAILEY, retired farmer, Kirby, Penn., is one of the pioneers of Whiteley Township, where he was born on his present farm April 30, 1814. His father, Joab Bailey, was a native of Chester County, Penn., and when only twelve years of age came with his parents to Greene County, where he married Miss Jane Mundell, a native of Greene Township, this county. They lived on Muddy Creek a few years and then purchased the farm on Pleasant Hill in Whiteley Township, now owned by Abner M., and remained on that farm until their death. They were the parents of nine children, of whom only three are living, viz.: Abner M. and two sisters, Jaen and Eliza A. Mr. A. M. Bailey was united in marriage the first time, in 1838, with Elizabeth South, born in Dunkard Township in 1816, a daughter of Enoch and Ruth South (*nee* Gregg). By this marriage he is the father of six children, four living—Benjamin, Presley, Ruth, wife of William Patterson, and Jane, wife of Jasper Morris; and Ellis and Joab E. (deceased). Mrs. Bailey died in 1849. In 1855 Mr. Bailey took unto himself a helpmate in the person of Mrs. Mary Cowell, who was born in Dunkard Township, this county, in 1824, a daughter of Thomas and Rachael Bowen (*nee* Fordyce). By this union Mr. Bailey is the father of four children, two living, viz.: Abner J. and Elvador; and Elizabeth and Susan A., (deceased). Mrs. Mary Bailey died in 1874. In 1877 Mr. Bailey was united in the holy bonds of matrimony with Miss Margaret Taylor, who was born in Washington Township in 1825, a daughter of Thomas and Angeline Taylor (*nee* McCaslin). Mrs. Margaret Bailey departed this life in 1885. Then Mr. Bailey was married the fourth time, November 24, 1885, to Mrs. Ruth A. Hoover, born in Jefferson Township, December 10, 1840, a daughter of Thomas and Elizabeth Wickersham (*nee* Randolph). During the early years of his life Mr. Bailey was actively engaged in farming and stock-dealing, from which he has secured enough of this world's goods to keep him in comfortable circumstances the remainder of his days. In 1867 he was elected to the office of county treasurer and served one term very creditably. He and his wife are members of the Methodist Protestant Church.

DAVID BARE, Kirby, Penn., is one of the pioneers of Whiteley Township, Greene County, where he was born September 29, 1818, a son of David and Susannah (Rittenour) Bare. His father was a

HISTORY OF GREENE COUNTY.

native of Bedford County, Penn., and his mother of Washington County, Maryland, where they were married and remained till 1810, at which time they moved to Fayette County, Pennsylvania. In 1812 he enlisted in the service of his country, and the same year his wife moved with the family to Greene County. She departed this life in 1845; her husband died in 1862. They had a family of fourteen children, nine of whom are living. Mr. David Bare was united in marriage May 13, 1840, with Lucinda Hickman, who was born in Greene County in 1822, a daughter of Abraham and Mary (Nelson) Hickman. By this marriage Mr. Bare is the father of six children —Martin B., Eliza, wife of John M. Bradford; Mary A., wife of Andrew Pitcock, and John; the deceased are James and Emily. Mrs. Bare died in 1853. Then in 1860 Mr. Bare married Rebecca Lemley, born in Whiteley Township, November 5, 1822, a daughter of Ezekiel and Sarah (Bowers) Lemley. By this marriage Mr. and Mrs. Bare have four children—Benjamin F., living; and Sophrona, Emma and an infant, (deceased). Mr. Bare is a blacksmith by trade, which he followed about forty-eight years; since that time he has been engaged in farming, and owns eighty acres of land in Whiteley Township. He filled the office of assessor of his township. In religion he and his wife are Methodists.

HENRY BOWERS, farmer, Lone Star, Penn., was born in Virginia, January 1, 1826. He is a son of Solomon and Peggy Cowers (*nee* Bradford), who were natives of Whiteley Township, Greene County, Penn., where they were married, then moved to Virginia and remained until their death. They had twelve children, eight of whom are now living. Henry is the oldest son and was united in marriage October 21, 1847, with Catharine Barockman, born in Virginia, July 27, 1824. She is a daughter of John and Barbara Barockman (*nee* Franks), natives of Pennsylvania, who after marriage moved to Virginia and remained until their death. Mr. and Mrs. Henry Bowers are the parents of seven children, four dead—Lucinda, Elizabeth, Clark and Marion; and three living— Morgan, Sarah E. and Josephus, who married Josephine Fuller, and is the father of two children—Charlie E. and Lizzie M. Mr. Bowers is a farmer, as we learn from the heading of this sketch, and is the owner of a fine farm of 170 acres. He and his family are members of the Methodist Protestant Church, in which he has been one of the trustees for about ten years.

M. C. BRANT, P. O. Kirby, is one of the leading business men of Newton, Pennsylvania. He was born in Cameron, West Virginia, September 29, 1858, a son of Eli and Sarah Brant (*nee* Spragg), natives of Wayne Township, Greene County, where they lived until about 1856, at which time they moved to Cameron, W. Va., and remained till 1859, then returned to Wayne Township. When the war commenced, Mr. Brant enlisted in behalf of his country's cause, and while in service contracted the disease of diphtheria from which he died. After his death his widow was united in marriage with Abraham Gump, whose sketch appears in this work. M. C. Brant was united in marriage February 14, 1885, with Edna Thompson, born in Center Township, Greene County, August 22, 1859. Her parents, Elijah and Sarah Thompson (*nee* Hoge), were natives of Center Township, and residents there until Mr. Thompson's death which occurred in 1861. Sometime afterwards his widow was united in marriage with Lisbon Staggers, whose sketch also appears in this book. Mr. M. C. Brant and wife are the parents of one child, Jay F., born February 22, 1886. Mr. Brant was raised on a farm, and acquired a good common-school education. In 1884 he opened a general store in Newton, where he has a large and liberal patronage. His wife is a consistent member of the Baptist Church.

DAVID L. COWELL, farmer, Kirby, Penn., was born in Dunkard Township, Greene County, November 5, 1829, a son of Daniel and Susannah Cowell (*nee* Bowers). The former was also a native of Dunkard, and the latter of Whiteley Township, where they were married. They then settled in Dunkard Township and remained until their death. They were the parents of twelve children, only four of whom are living. September 15, 1864, David L. Cowell married Miss Harriet Long. She was born in Whiteley Township October 15, 1843, and is a consistent member of the Methodist Episcopal Church. Her parents, Samuel and Adeline Long, were natives Greene County and residents therein until their death, which occurred in Perry Township. Of the five children born to Mr. and Mrs. Cowell, three are living—William L., Ellsworth and Amanda. Throughout his life Mr. Cowell has been engaged in stock-dealing and farming, in which he has been eminently successful, owing at present a fine farm of 400 acres of land in Whiteley Township.

JOHN M. COWELL, Lone Star, Penn., is a descendant of one of the pioneer families of Greene County. He was born in Whiteley Township, January 1, 1851, on the farm where he and his family now live. His parents were Solomon and Eliza Cowell (*nee* Michael). The former was born in Greene County and the latter in West Virginia where they were married, settled in Whiteley Township on the farm now owned by John M., and remained until Mr. Cowell's death which took place in 1879. Mrs. Cowell is still living in Newton. They were the parents of thirteen children, five living. September 23, 1873, John M. Cowell married Mary J. Norton, born in Butler County, Penn, December 29, 1855. Her parents were Martin K. and Rebecca Norton, also natives of Butler County, who now live in the State of Iowa. To Mr. Cowell and wife have been born seven children—Minnie L., Wesley A., William S., Charles N., John E., Sadie R. and Cleveland. Mr. Cowell's farm consists of 246 acres, and on it can be found fine horses, cattle and sheep, the raising of which has formed an important part of his business. He is a public spirited citizen, and has held the office of school director in his district. Mrs. Cowell is a consistent member of the Methodist Episcopal Church.

JOHN A. CUMMINS, Waynesburg, Penn., is one of the most industrious farmers of Whiteley Township, where he was born September 14, 1840. His parents, William and Catharine Cummins, are natives of Greene County and reside in Whiteley Township. They have a family of ten children, of whom nine are living. September 14, 1878, John A. Cummins married Miss Hannah Rush, a native of Franklin Township. To them have been born four children—William A., Lona O., Catharine E., and John B. Having been raised on a farm, Mr. Cummins has made a business of farming and stockdealing all through his life, and as a result of his faithful and persistent labors is now in possession of an excellent farm of about 230 acres in Whiteley Township, where he and family live. His wife is among the most consistent and prominent members of the Methodits Protestant Church.

JOHN FOX, Kirby, Penn., one of the substantial citizens of Whiteley Township, Greene County, was born in Perry Township, April 25, 1830. His parents were Henry and Susannah (Delany) Fox, who were natives of Greene County, where they were married and remained till death. He departed this life October 29, 1882, and she December 25, 1875. They were the parents of ten children, of whom six are living. Mr. John Fox was united in marriage December 13, 1849, with Dorothy Hains, who was born in Whiteley Township October 15, 1830, a daughter of John and Jane Hains (*nee* John), who were natives of Greene County, lived in Whiteley Township until 1857, then moved to West Virginia where Mr. Hains died in 1887. His widow is still living. They had a family of eleven children— Eli, Christopher C., Matilda, wife of Winfield S. Vandruff; Jane, wife of John L. Walters; Taylor, Daily, Luther, Maggie, wife of George Patterson; William and Nancy; and Walter, (deceased). Mr. Fox is quite a genius in his way, and successful in almost every undertaking. His principal business is farming, and he owns 475 acres of land in Greene County. He filled the office of justice of the peace of his township for five years; and at different times has held the positions of auditor, constable, assessor, trustee and member of the school board. He and his wife belong to the Methodist Episcopal Church.

JOHN S. FULLER, farmer and stock-dealer, P. O. Lone Star, was born in Whiteley Township, Greene County, Penn., April 24, 1833. His parents are Daniel and Nancy (Whitlatch) Fuller, the one born in Fayette and the other in Greene County, where they were married in Whiteley Township and remained through life. He departed this life April 22, 1874, and she December 14, 1876. They were the parents of eight children, all but one living. Subject's grandparents were natives of Ireland. The grandfather was born in the city of Dublin, and the grandmother in the county of Tyrone. They were married after emigrating to America. Mr. John S. Fuller was united in marriage August 13, 1852, with Emily Phillips, born in Greene County September 28, 1837. She is a daughter of Elmer and Elizabeth Phillips (nee Vandruff), natives of this county, the latter deceased. Mr. Fuller and wife are the parents of seven children, five living—Nancy, wife of Henry Zimmerman; Josephine, wife of Josephus Bowers; Smith, Bowman and Ida M.; Elizabeth and Daniel L. being deceased. Mr. Fuller owns 700 acres of land where he and his family reside, and has taken considerable interest in the raising of fine stock, being the first to bring a herd of thorough-bred short-horned cattle into Whiteley Township, in 1883. He was a member of the school board two terms; served as assessor three terms and as assistant assessor for many years. Both he and his wife are members of the Methodist Protestant Church.

ABRAHAM GUMP, farmer and stock-dealer, is a descendant of one of the pioneer families of Greene County, Penn. He was born in Whiteley Township, December 15, 1832, a son of John and Dorcas Gump (nee Whitlatch). His father was a native of Virginia, and his mother of New Jersey. They were married in Whiteley Township, Greene County, Penn., residing there until their death; she departed this life in 1840 and her husband in 1863. They were the parents of thirteen children, of whom only two are living, viz.: Cassandra, now the widow of Jacob Lemley, and Abraham, the subject of our notice, who was united in marriage the first time March 4, 1852, with Maria Adamson. She was born in Waynesburg, a daughter of Cyrus and Elizabeth Adamson, now deceased. By this union Mr. Gump is the father of two children, one living—John C; and Samantha A., deceased. In the spring of 1857, Mr. Gump and family moved to Warren County, Illinois, and about two months later Mrs. Gump met with a sad accident resulting in her death. While alone in the house with her little family, in passing too near the grate her clothes took fire and were burned off before any assistance could reach her and she died in about sixteen hours from the effect of the burns. This occurred May 16, 1857. Mr. Gump afterwards returned with his family to Whiteley Township, Penn., and was united in marriage

June 16, 1867, with Sarah Brant, (*nee* Spragg). She has two children—Otho and Matthias. Her parents, Otho and Lida (Shull) Spragg, were natives of Greene County, and residents of Wayne Township until Mrs. Sragg's death March 23, 1874. Her husband died April 12, 1882. By his last marriage Mr. Gump is the father of three children—George M., Corbly and Debbie. Mr. Gump has been a farmer and stock-dealer all his life, and he and his wife own about 650 acres of land in Greene County. They are consistent members of the Methodist Episcopal Church, and his deceased wife also.

SOLOMON GUTHRIE, a retired farmer of Kirby, Penn., was born in the house where he and his family reside in Whiteley Township, Greene County, April 7, 1816. He is a son of Archibald and Elizabeth (Lemley) Guthrie, who were natives of Pennsylvania. They were married in Greene County, afterwards settling in Whiteley Township, where Mrs. Guthrie died. After her death, Archibald married Mary Scott, who is still living. He died August 23, 1845. He was the father of twelve children, of whom eight are living. Solomon Guthrie was united in marriage January 31, 1839, with Elizabeth Fry, born in Centre Township, November 20, 1818. Mrs. Guthrie's parents were George and Elizabeth Fry (*nee* Beckingbaugh), who were natives of Greene County. To Mr. and Mrs. Guthrie have been born ten children, of whom seven are living—Susan, wife of Robinson John; Elizabeth S., wife of Benona John; George W., Lucinda, wife of Abraham Shull; Solomon E., Jessie L. and William F.; Job, Maria and Archibald B. being deceased. Mr. Guthrie has been engaged in farming all his life, and owns 120 acres of land where he and his family reside. He and Mrs. Guthrie are consistent members of the Methodist Church.

G. W. HATFIELD, farmer, P. O. Lone Star, was born in Whiteley Township, Greene County, Penn., July 30, 1816. His parents were Jacob and Rebecca (Mundle) Hatfield, the former a native of New Jersey and the latter of Greene County, Penn., where they were married and remained through life. In 1839, G. W. Hatfield married Miss Mary Richie, born in Fayette County, Penn., in 1806, daughter of James Richie. Mr. and Mrs. Hatfield have seven children, six living—Jacob, James, Hiram, William, Elizabeth, wife of Lindsey Stephens and Madison, and Frank, (deceased). Mr. Hatfield has always lived on a farm, and has been one of the most enterprising and successful farmers and stock-dealers in the county, where he owns 900 acres of land. He served his district on the school board for about twelve years. Mr. and Mrs. Hatfield are exemplary members of the Methodist Protestant Church.

CHRISTOPHER JOHN, deceased, was born May 26, 1820, on the farm where the family reside in Whiteley Township. His father and mother were James and Margaret (Robinson) John, natives of eastern Pennsylvania. They were married in Greene County and settled on the farm now owned by the heirs of Christopher John, (deceased), and remained until their death. His father died January 16, 1874, and his mother July 20, 1852. They were the parents of eleven children, five now living. Christopher John was united in marriage in 1839 with Nancy Fox, born in Greene County, March 23, 1823, a daughter of Henry and Susannah (Delany) Fox, natives of Greene County, now deceased. Mr. and Mrs. John's family consists of eleven children, seven living—Barbara, wife of David Lockhart; Sarah J., widow of George Connor; Margaret, wife of R. Fox; Kinsey, Reasin, Elizabeth, wife of I. N. Kiger; and Sidonia, wife of William Vandruff. Henry, Susannah, Franklin and William, are deceased. Notwithstanding the fact that Mr. John, like the rest of the early settlers, received but a limited education, he was quite a successful farmer through life, and owned 550 acres of good land in Greene County at the time of his death, which occurred August 11, 1888.

DR. G. W. MOSS, deceased, was born in Washington County, Penn., May 5, 1836. His parents were Jennings J. and Ellen (Winnet) Moss. After marriage they resided in Washington County until 1844, at which time they moved to Richhill Township, Greene County, for a few years, then returned to Washington County, and remained until their seven children grew to maturity. They again retraced their steps to Greene County, and remained until their death. Only four of their children survive them. Dr. Moss was the third, and acquired his education in the common schools of Greene and Washington counties. He graduated in the Jefferson Medical College at Philadelphia in 1870, and afterwards took a course of lectures at Bellevue, N. Y. He began the practice of medicine at Jefferson, Penn., and in 1856 located at Newtown, where he was actively engaged in the profession until his death, January 16, 1888. The Doctor was united in marriage February 15, 1863, with Sarah J. Hudson, who was born in Newton, Penn., November 17, 1846. Mrs. Moss is a daughter of John and Sarah J. (Morris) Hudson, the former a native of West Moreland and the latter of Greene County, where they were married. They settled in Newtown, where Mr Hudson departed this life in August, 1884. His widow still resides at Newtown. They were the parents of nine children, of whom five are living. Dr. and Mrs. Moss were the parents of one daughter— Ethel H., born March 4, 1882. The Doctor was a member of the I. O. O. F., was a Knight Templar in the Masonic order, and belonged to the Methodist Episcopal Church, of which his widow is also a faithful and devoted member.

HENRY MORRIS, farmer, Fordyce, Penn., was born in Jefferson Township, Greene County, February 25, 1824. His parents, Peter and Elizabeth (Renner) Morris, are natives of this county, where they were married and remained until Mrs. Morris' death. Her husband is still living and resides in Whiteley Township. They were the parents of seven children, of whom three are living. Henry is the oldest child, and was united in marriage May 31, 1846, with Eliza Morris, who was born in Franklin Township, December 7, 1828. She is a daughter of John and Jemima (Pipes) Morris, now deceased. Mr. Henry Morris and wife have seven children—Caroline, wife of Dr. Jacob Hatfield; Lindsey, John, George W., Andrew J. and Milton R; Franklin being deceased. Mr. Morris is one of the progressive business men of his township, in which he has been engaged in farming and stock dealing all his life. He owns a fine farm of 370 acres. He served one term as director of the poor. His wife is a consistent member of the Methodist Church.

ELIJAH MORRIS, farmer, Fordyce, Penn., was born in Jefferson Township, Greene County, January 7, 1809, a son of Henry and Edie (Hickman) Morris. They were natives of this county, where they were married and lived a number of years, then moved to Noble County, Ohio, where they died. Their son, Elijah, was united in marriage October 10, 1830, with Nancy Morris, a native of Ohio and daughter of Isaac and Mary Morris. By this marriage Mr. Morris is the father of ten children, seven are living—Peter, Mary, wife of John Morris; David, Abner, Richard, Simon and Sarah J., wife of Eli Stoops; and Andrew J., Elizabeth and Selah (deceased). Mrs. Morris died in 1850, and in 1864 Mr. Morris married Nancy Ketcham (nee Mofford), a native of Greene County and daughter of William and Susan Mofford. By this second marriage Mr. Morris has one child—Emma E., wife of Johnson Stickels. Mrs. Morris died December 23, 1867. Mr. Morris is a farmer, and owns 152 acres of land in Whiteley Township, where he and family reside.

RUFUS PATTERSON, Kirby, Penn., is one of the substantial young farmers of Whiteley Township, where he was born August 11, 1861. His father, William Patterson, a native of the same township, was united in marriage the first time with Rhoda Whitlatch, born in Perry Township, this county. By this marriage Mr. William Patterson was the father of fourteen children, of whom ten are living. His wife departed this life in 1852, and November 6, 1856, Mr. Patterson was again united in marriage with Sophia Kuhn, the mother of Rufus, the subject of this sketch. She was born in Whiteley Township, October 29, 1815, a daughter of Abraham and Eleanor Kuhn (nee Mooney), the one a native of Germany and the other of Ireland, who after marriage settled in Greene County, Penn., remaining until their death. By his last marriage Mr. William Patterson is the father of two children, of whom only Rufus is living. Mr. Patterson died May 13, 1887. March 2, 1887, Rufus married Emma Connor, who was born in Perry Township, this county, February 12, 1861, a daughter of Simon and Nancy Connor (*nee* Herrington), who resides in Whiteley Township. Like his father, Mr. Patterson was raised on a farm, and makes farming the business of his life. He owns 160 acres of land (the old Patterson home), where he and family reside.

ARTHUR SHRIVER, farmer, Kirby, Pennsylvania. Among the younger class of farmers and stock-dealers of Whiteley Township, we mention the name that heads this sketch. He was born in Whiteley, April 26, 1845, his parents being Jacob and Elizabeth (Inghram) Shriver, who were pioneers of Greene County where they were married, July 5, 1831, and remained through life. He departed this life February 1, 1885, and she February 22, 1855. They were the parents of ten children, nine living. The subject of our sketch is the youngest son. 1873, on October 2, he married Miss Ella Hickman, who was born in Whiteley, January 7, 1848. She is a daughter of Gilmon and Phœbe (Cloves) Hickman, natives of Greene County and residents of Whiteley Township. To Mr. and Mrs. Shriver have been born three children, two living, Minnie M. and Lizzie P. Mr. Shriver was reared on a farm and has been a successful farmer and stock-dealer through life, owning at present 200 hundred acres of excellent land where he lives with his family. Mr. Shriver is a member of the Methodist Episcopal Church.

A. J. SMITH, farmer, Kirby, Penn., born in Washington Township, December 14, 1833, is one of the pioneers of Greene County. His parents were Dennis and Sarah Smith, who were natives of this county and residents therein till death. His father died in Missouri. In 1855, A. J. Smith married Miss Phœbe J. Estle, born in Jefferson Township in 1828, a daughter of Matthias and Mary Estle (*nee* Stewart) who were natives of this county, both now deceased. Mr. and Mrs. Smith's family consists of six children, of whom four are living: Leroy W., Mary A., wife of Frank Johnson; Sarah M. and Elizabeth E.; Abraham and Matthias being deceased. Mr. Smith was reared on a farm and, following in the footsteps of many of his ancestors, he has made the tilling of the soil the pursuit of his life. He owns ninety-seven acres of good land where he resides with his family. Mr. and Mrs. Smith are faithful members of the Methodist Protestant Church.

LISBON STAGGERS, retired farmer and stock-dealer, Kirby, Penn., was born in Franklin Township, Greene County, December 17, 1820, a son of John and Catharine Staggers (*nee* Maple). His parents were natives of Franklin Township and residents there until their death. His mother died in 1851, and his father, December 16, 1882. They were the parents of fifteen children, of whom seven are living. Lisbon, the subject of this sketch, is the fifth, and was first united in marriage, December 16, 1843, with Eliza J. Mooney, born in Franklin Township November 20, 1820, a daughter of Thomas and Cassandra Mooney (*nee* Inghram), now deceased. To Mr. and Mrs. Staggers were born nine children, four living—Cassandra, wife of Albert Rice; Arthur, Catherine M., wife of Sebastian Bowlby and James M. The deceased are Thomas J., William F, John, Martha E. and Harvey. Their mother died May 31, 1864. After her death, Mr. Staggers was again united in marriage, September 16, 1866, with Sarah Thompson (*nee* Hoge), who was a native of Centre Township, this county. She was born July 14, 1835, a daughter of Joseph and Mary Hoge (*nee* Cowen) the latter deceased. By the last marriage Mr. Staggers is the father of six children, five living—Hamon, Alice, Ida, Lisbon C., and Elva; and Selah, (deceased.) Mr. Staggers was reared on a farm and has made the care and management of his farm his life work. He owns 300 acres of good land where he and his family now live. Both he and his wife are communicants of the Baptist Church.

LINDSEY STEPHENS, Kirby, Penn, was born in Greene Township, June 23, 1836, a son of Barzilla and Margaret (Lantz) Stephens, who were natives of Greene County, where they were married and have since resided. Mr. Barzilla Stephens departed this life, April 24, 1884; his widow survives him and resides with her children, of whom three are living. Lindsey is the second of their five children, and was united in marriage, September 26, 1861, with Margaret Fordyce, born in Whiteley Township, December 30, 1843, a daughter of Benson and Maria (Nicholas) Fordyce, the latter deceased. By this marriage Mr. Stephens is the father of one daughter, Amanda. On October 27, 1863, Mrs. Stephens died, leaving to her daughter the example of her christian character and consistent life, On February 23, 1865, Mr. Stephens married Elizabeth J. Hatfield. who was born in Whiteley Township, September 4, 1846, a daughter of George W. and Mary (Richie) Hatfield, residents of the same township. Mr. and Mrs. Stephens have a family of seven children, of whom four are living—Nora, John, James and Harry; the deceased being Lafayette, Ida and Salina. Mr. Stephens has always lived on a farm and has been an industrious farmer and stock-dealer all his life. He and his wife own 975 acres of land in Whiteley Township. He has been a member of the Masonic Order for about thirty years; and he and wife are members of the Methodist Episcopal Church.

SIMON R. STROSNIDER, farmer, Waynesburg, Penn., was born in Whitcley Township, Greene County, March 9, 1834, a son of Peter and Charlotte Strosnider (*nee* Gordon). His father was born in Whiteley and his mother in Franklin Township. They were married and lived in Greene County until 1850, after which time they moved to Perry County, Ohio, where they died. They had a family of eight children, of whom seven are living. Simon R., their son, was united in marriage, October 12, 1862, with Sarah A. Inghram, who was born in Waynesburg, January 11, 1843. Her parents were Arthur and Susannah Inghram (*nee* Eagon), natives of Greene County, both now deceased. To Mr. and Mrs. Strosnider have been born four daughters, Dolly, Lillie A., Laura V. and Lucy O. Mr. Strosnider was reared on a farm and has carried on the business of farming quite successfully all his life, at present owning 120 acres of land constituting his home farm. He filled the office of auditor of his township with credit to himself and his constituents. Dolly, the oldest of the four daughters was born August 26, 1864, united with the congregation at Mount Pleasant Church, March 13, 1881, she departed this life at the home of her parents, February 4, 1888, she was loved and respected by all who knew her.

A. M. TEMPLE, farmer, Fordyce, Penn., is a pioneer of Whiteley Township, Greene County. He was born October 11, 1825, a son of John and Elizabeth Temple (*nee* Douglass), the former of Greene and the latter of Fayette County, Penn., where they were married. They lived at Garard's Fort, Greene County, until 1831, when they moved to the farm where the subject of this sketch now resides. Mr. John Temple died three weeks later; his widow survived him until 1873. They had a family of four children, three living. Mr. A. M. Temple was united in marriage, in July, 1846, with Lucy Greene, born in Franklin Township, September 13, 1829, a daughter of Morris and Sarah (Grooms) Greene. By this marriage Mr. Temple is the father of three children—Benjamin, living, and Elizabeth and Rebecca, deceased. Mrs. Temple died, June 17, 1881, having been a faithful member of the Methodist Episcopal Church. April 20, 1882, Mr. Temple married Mrs. Anna M. Burwell, who was born in Jefferson Township, June 13, 1832, a daughter of Jacob and Nancy Waychoff, the former a native of New Jersey and the latter of Greene County, Penn. Mr. Temple is a cooper by trade, which he followed about twenty-five years. He has since engaged in farming and stock raising, and owns a good farm of 300 acres. He has filled the offices of director of the poor and jury commissioner. He is a member of the Methodist Episcopal and his wife of the Baptist Church.

JAMES R. ZIMMERMAN, farmer, P. O. Delight, was born in Franklin Township, Greene County, Penn., September 15, 1840. His parents were William and Eliza A. Zimmerman (*nee* Seals), natives of the same township, where they were married, settled and remained until their death.   He departed this life, January 21, 1852, and she, in October of the same year.   They were the parents of seven children, of whom six are living, viz: William H., James R., Caroline, wife of Robert McGlumphy; Enos, Anna E, wife of Perry Cummins, and Vanamburg; Maria, deceased.   Like his ancestors, the subject of our sketch was raised on a farm, and has always been engaged in farming and stock-dealing.   Through industry and good management he has succeeded in getting a good farm, consisting of 225 acres, where he resides.

CPSIA information can be obtained at www.ICGtesting.com
Printed in the USA
LVOW10s0749110913

351843LV00011B/219/P